BLACK AF HISTORY

BLACK AF HISTORY

THE UN-WHITEWASHED STORY OF AMERICA

MICHAEL HARRIOT

DEYST.

An Imprint of WILLIAM MORROW

For Karen

DEYST.

HarperCollins books may be purchased for educational, business, or sales promotional use. For information, please email the Special Markets Department at SPsales@harpercollins.com.

FIRST EDITION

DESIGNED BY RENATA DE OLIVEIRA
ILLUSTRATIONS © 2023 BY JIBOLA FAGBAMIYE

Library of Congress Cataloging-in-Publication Data has been applied for.

ISBN 978-0-358-43916-5

23 24 25 26 27 LBC 6 5 4 3 2

INTRODUCTION   1

1   EARTH, WIND, AND AMERICA   11

2   THE CHURCH FIGHT THAT STARTED SLAVERY   27

3   THE WORLD, RECENTERED   56

4   SURVIVAL AND RESISTANCE: THE BLACK AMERICAN REVOLUTION   78

5   DRAPETOMANIACS: GET FREE OR DIE TRYING   104

6   THE NEGRO, SPIRITUAL   130

7   THE BLACK EMANCIPATION PROCLAMATION: A POEM   157

8   CONSTRUCTION   188

9   SOMETHING ELSE   209

10   WHITES GONE WILD: UNCLE ROB EXPLAINS "SEPARATE BUT EQUAL"   233

11   SO DEVILISH A FIRE: THE BLACK WOMEN WHO STARTED
THE CIVIL RIGHTS MOVEMENT   259

12   THE RACE WAR III: THE CONSPIRACY THEORY THAT WAS TRUE   287

13   THUG LIFE: THE OTHER CIVIL RIGHTS MOVEMENT   309

14   THE GREAT WHITE HEIST   334

15   THE RACE OF POLITICS: UNCLE ROB EXPLAINS
THE TWO-PARTY SYSTEM   354

16   HOMEWORK   375

ACKNOWLEDGMENTS   385   ·   WORKS NOT CITED: BLACK AF HISTORY HACKS   386
·   ENDNOTES   390   ·   INDEX   416

INTRODUCTION

I remember when I discovered America.

It happened around 8 p.m. on November 4, 1980—the night Ronald Reagan was elected president. I was on my knees, crying, sending desperate pleas to my Lord and Savior Jesus when I was interrupted by my grandmother summoning me. Perhaps she had discovered my sisters' candy stash. Maybe she needed me to fix the vertical hold on the floor-model television. Or, as any child who grew up in a Black home could tell you, maybe she just needed a cold glass of water.[*] When she saw the tears streaming down my face, she asked what was wrong. I confessed to one of the cardinal sins of my household: I was listening to grown folks talking.

I told her that I couldn't understand how she was so calm when our worst fears had been realized. I knew that we were going to have to hightail it to Canada now, and told her she should join me in prayer as I asked Jesus to protect and guide us as we drove to our new home across the border. Between sobs, I asked her if we were waiting for daybreak to leave. An evening getaway seemed safer to me, even though my mom had terrible night vision. From the look on her face, it was clear that she had no idea what I was talking about.

I spilled the beans about how I overheard her tell my mother a few weeks ago, "If Reagan is elected, he'll send Black people back in the cotton fields."

That sent my young mind spinning. I didn't know how to pick cotton! Would I have to give up my dream of playing point guard for

---

[*] *In Black households, children are mostly fetchers of icewater, mail, and inkpens.*

the Los Angeles Lakers and my future side hustle as a tambourine player in Earth, Wind & Fire to get a cotton-picking degree in picking cotton? Plus, I could read, and you know what happens to slaves who could read! I told her not to worry about me, though: I had already packed a bag with my favorite Underoos, some corduroy pants, and a few sweatshirts. According to the 1979 edition of the *World Book Encyclopedia*, Canadian winters could be quite brutal.

After my grandmother and mother finished explaining sarcasm between guffaws, I felt relieved, albeit a little embarrassed. I still wasn't quite sure if they were trying to make me feel better about our impending enslavement, but I took their word that I didn't have to learn the secret language embedded in negro spirituals. Just in case, I gave them a hand-drawn map of what I thought was the best escape route. If all else failed, we could simply "follow the drinking gourd," which of course was the code name for the Big Dipper. I volunteered to show them how to find the Big Dipper in the night sky, because you never knew if the fugitive slave catchers had an APB out on our canary yellow station wagon. While they had no interest in learning about Underground Railroad–based astronomy, my grandmother did have one question.

"Mikey, where did you learn all this stuff from, boy?" she asked.

Now I was confused. I couldn't tell if she was impressed or perturbed. She had always told me that there are no stupid questions, but she was coming dangerously close to proving her adage wrong.

"Where do you think I learned it?" I replied. "The middle room."

* * *

In 1952, James and Marvell Harriot built a house for their eight children in Hartsville, South Carolina, a scant twenty-two miles from the forced labor camp where James S. Bradley enslaved 253 human beings, including Marvell's great-great-grandfather Ervin. The Harriot house had four bedrooms, one bathroom, a dining room, and a living room you could enter only if you were entertaining company, had obtained written and verbal permission, or if somebody who had the Holy Ghost died. But the best room was in the center of the house, a den-style family room that would eventually become known as the "middle room." Five generations of the Harriot family would play, pray, laugh, sing, dance, and learn about the world from the middle room's vantage point. Long before I was born, my grandfather lined the entire middle room with sturdy oak shelves, and over the years, to this very day, everyone in the Harriot clan has deposited their books there. It rivals almost any independent bookstore and some libraries, with stacks and stacks of books on topics from science fiction to history. It also contained a state-of-the-art television set, turntable, and hi-fi eight-track tape player that mostly played James Cleveland albums, episodes of *Trapper John, M.D.*, and election results. The burnt umber carpet was where I learned how to play Uno, Spades, and Acey-Deucy (the remedial version of backgammon). The middle room was also a stage for family talent shows, a courtroom, and—most importantly—the homeroom, study hall, and resource center for all four pupils enrolled in the Dorothy Harriot Elementary School for Dorothy Harriot's Children.

When I was a child, my mother chose to homeschool my sisters and me. As an adult, she informed me that my early homeschooled education was an experiment due to her belief that "a Black child cannot fully realize their humanity in the presence of whiteness." Although she drilled us on mathematics, grammar, and the Bible, our schooling was primarily self-directed, courtesy of the middle room. I read anything and everything, which led to many awkward incidents, like the strange side-eye I received at church after I read *The Autobiography of Malcolm X* at nine years old and began ending every sentence with "if it is Allah's will." When I was twelve, after reading the science-fiction novel *The Soul of the Robot*, I stumbled across W. E. B. Du Bois's *The Souls of Black Folk*. That couldn't be much different, right?

I was scarcely two pages in when I read this:

After the Egyptian and Indian, the Greek and Roman, the Teuton and Mongolian, the Negro is a sort of seventh son, born with a veil, and gifted with second-sight in this American world,—a world which yields him no self-consciousness, but only lets him see himself through the revelation of the other world. It is a peculiar sensation, this double-

consciousness, this sense of always looking at one's self through the eyes of others, of measuring one's soul by the tape of a world that looks on in amused contempt and pity. One feels his two-ness,—an American, a Negro; two souls, two thoughts, two unreconciled strivings; two warring ideals in one dark body, whose dogged strength alone keeps it from being torn asunder. The history of the American Negro is the history of this strife,—this longing to attain self-conscious manhood, to merge his double self into a better and truer self. In this merging he wishes neither of the older selves to be lost.[1]

Reading this, my brain fired off a dozen questions. Where was this alternative universe that had reduced Blackness to an afterthought? And through whose eyes did Du Bois see himself? I would later discover *The Mis-Education of the Negro*, in which Carter G. Woodson explains that in the American education system, the entirety of Black people's existence "is studied only as a problem or dismissed as of little consequence."[2] Du Bois eloquently echoed this sentiment, asking, "Between me and the other world there is ever an unasked question: unasked by some through feelings of delicacy; by others through the difficulty of rightly framing it. All, nevertheless, flutter round it. How does it feel to be a problem?"

I eventually realized that my middle room education was the inverse of Woodson's miseducated negro. My mother had reverse-engineered a curriculum founded on the words and works of great thinkers like Dorothy B. Porter, Arturo Schomburg, Zora Neale Hurston, and John Edward Bruce, all of whom, in one way or another, are manifestations of Du Bois's mission to manufacture a new measuring tape. I am but a bastard child born with the privilege of wandering into an already constructed house that Du Bois built.

The history I discovered in the middle room wasn't just an alternative version of American history; it was the story of an *entirely different place*, wholly incompatible with the whitewashed mythology enshrined in our collective memory. I have never known that place because that America, in reality, does not exist.

That story of America is a fantastical, overwrought, and fictive tale. It is a fantasy where Christopher Columbus discovered a land that he never set foot in. It is the story of the Pilgrims on the *Mayflower* building a new nation. It is George Washington's cherry tree and Abraham Lincoln's log cabin. It is the story of slaves who spontaneously teleported themselves here with nothing but strong backs and a brainful of negro spirituals. It is Betsy Ross's sewing kit and Paul Revere's horse and Thomas Jefferson's pen and Benjamin Franklin's eyeglasses and George Washington's teeth and liberty and justice for all. And it is a history predicated on lies.

History can never be objective or unbiased because, no matter how hard the storytellers may try, the perception of reality prejudices all stories. The academic field of history is dominated by white men handicapped by the inability to see whiteness's impact on America's biography. The best historians try to approximate the truth by unbending the collection of funhouse mirrors through which the past has been viewed, but it isn't simply a counterfeit version of history, it is a fable that erases the reflection of an entire people to ensure that the mythology of the heroes lives happily ever after.

Because of the middle room, I was not burdened with unbending the funhouse mirror of America's past. For me, the writings of Du Bois, Woodson, and the other Black chroniclers of yesteryear were not counternarratives to a blanched, whitewashed version of a *somewhat true* story. For me, the America that existed in the middle room is the real America. In my education, we are the sun and everything in the history of this nation's existence is simply rotating around the Blackness illuminating our universe.

When we are dead, and all the things that ever were have turned to dust, we will *not* be history; we will be things that once were. A few of us, however, will have lived a life so notable that a white man might deem it worthy of bending his opposable thumb to register our existence into posterity. The best we can hope for is to become a part of *white history* because American history *is white history*.

Except for this one.

This history is Black AF.

HISTORY, UNWHITENED

Something was wrong with me.

I was always "in a daze." I couldn't sit still. Long before I was eventually diagnosed with the most acute form of attention deficit/hyperactivity disorder, I was just "hyper."

Although we now understand that ADHD is a common mental neurodevelopment issue that affects millions of children, I was diagnosed as "bad." My mother tried to combat my hyperactivity with diet, forbidding my sisters and me from eating anything that contained Red Dye No. 5 or sugar (except on Fridays, when I could choose between a roll of Life Savers or a pack of Chiclets). In fifth grade, I spent months in the Harriot household's version of juvenile house arrest when I was caught tracing my mother's name on an interim report that described me as "smart but have trouble following directions." The third deacon-in-command at church nicknamed me the "absent-minded professor."

And then there were the coats.

Coats were the bane of my childhood existence. I always lost them. I left them on church pews, in cars, and *especially* at school. And because coats are the most expensive part of a kid's wardrobe, I have received more dressing-downs from my mom about coats than anything except my propensity to forget to pull the garbage can to the curb on trash day. If there is a heaven for jackets, it is almost certainly filled with the misplaced winterwear purchased by Dorothy Harriot. I *always*, always lost my coat.

So, in fifth grade, when I begged my mother to buy me a "goosedown"—a feather-filled ski jacket with removable sleeves that had become the latest fashion, of course she gave me a lecture about how I'd have to suffer frostbite and hypothermia for the next two winters if I lost that puffy coat. The day my mother bought that goosedown from the Army Navy store was the second-happiest day of my sartorial life, exceeded only by the parachute pants and *Ghostbusters* tee I received for my birthday a few years later.

One day, I was walking home from elementary school, which required me to walk past the hangout spot where all the thugs cut school to smoke cigarettes and look at "nekkid magazines." I was in one of my trademark dazes when the scent of menthol-laced smoke alerted me to the fact that I was being followed. By the time I tried to run, it was too late. This crew surrounded me and demanded I give up the goosedown. I thought of my mother's wrath. I thought of all the long-lost jackets from the past, from the bootleg Members Only to the Sears Toughskin with corduroy sleeves. I thought of my mother's frostbite warning and the days in middle room solitary confinement in my future.

I refused.

They beat it off me.

I struggled so hard that, while they got the body of the jacket, they couldn't get the sleeves. But what good are warm arms when you're walking home with the rest of your body fighting off cold? Of course, I kept it a secret. I wasn't embarrassed about the mugging as much as I was afraid of my mother's wrath when she realized that I no longer had the item on which she had spent an entire $56. I knew she wouldn't buy the mugging story. I had to get it back before she found out. So instead of telling her that I had been robbed, I told my two older cousins, Fred and Squeak, along with my best friend, James Bond.* They were already in junior high. They probably knew the culprits. A few days later, as I shivered home from school, avoiding the Newport shortcut, they yelled out to me to come over.

They had found it!

There, wearing my sleeveless goosedown was my next-door neighbor, Freaky-D. Freaky-D wasn't big, but he was fearless. At thirteen, he was already smoking marijuana and drinking Colt 45. Apparently, he had been casing my goosedown for months. Surrounded by my investigative squad, Freaky-D swore that he had owned the coat for over a year. His friends, whom I recognized as the muggers, backed him up. They corroborated his story, insisting that he had had the coat for over a year. After a few minutes of interrogation, Double-O, Fred, and Squeak bought his story and let him go. As they walked away, Freaky-D let me know it wasn't over.

---

* *We called him "Double-O Seven," which was eventually shortened to "Double-O."*

"I'mma remember this, Mikey," he yelled. "Freaky-D don't steal!"

The next morning, I was called into the principal's office. Sitting there was my mother, along with Freaky-D and the vice principal of the Hartsville Junior High School. With tears in his eyes, Freaky-D recounted how I had masterminded the plot to convince my friends to steal his jacket. As illogical and preposterous as it sounded to me, to the jury in the principal's office, Freaky-D's testimony was perfectly plausible.

I vehemently objected to Freaky-D's lie, explaining that there was no evidence for this wholly untrue story. He was the *real jacket thief.* Unbeknownst to me, Freaky-D had proof, which was why my mother was summoned to the school. Staring a hole into my soul, she reached into my bookbag and pulled out the evidence that confirmed the true history of the goosedown jacket . . . the sleeves of which matched perfectly.

* * *

What you are about to read is a true story. The names have not been changed to protect the guilty.

In most history books, America is colonized by European "settlers." In chronicling this nation's past, historians recognize that the English, Dutch, Spanish, and French colonists are human beings with different backstories, cultures, and motivations. We know the political incentives, economic concerns, and social mores that explain away the theft, violence, and genocide they committed against the savage silhouettes that we are too unbothered to name. The people and cultures whose blood water the stolen landscapes are usually dehumanized by simply remaining anonymous. The stolen Africans are not Akan or Nyamwezi; they are just "slaves." The various indigenous nations who were extinguished are never Oceti Sakowin or even Iroquois; they are just "Indians" or, at most, "Native Americans." Yet, somehow, the states and colonies that replace them have borders, legislatures, and distinguishable features.

Black AF History does not upset this timeless tradition of American scholarship. It uses the same scholarly conventions to which we have become accustomed. To make sure the reader isn't disoriented by a new historical standard, this book recognizes that the English, Dutch, Spanish, and French land thieves are just "white people." While it may sometimes seem abrasive, confrontational, and even dismissive, this book recognizes that the only difference between a burglar and a "settler" is who writes the police reports. In fact, the only difference between the Black AF version of history and the way America's story is customarily recounted is that whiteness is not the center of the universe around which everything else revolves.

While this book does not seek to deify whiteness, it also does not obfuscate the flaws of Black heroes. In this history, Martin Luther King Jr. is a human being who is sometimes afraid. Booker T. Washington and W. E. B. Du Bois are rivals, but their ultimate goal is the same—to get free. In this book, enslaved Africans are not victims, they are warriors from the Ashanti Kingdom and the founding fathers of the Gullah culture and the creators of America's first democracy.

And while this book is not the complete history of Black people in America, it acknowledges that too much has been stolen for that to ever exist. In this book, there is no America. In this book, the country we know as the United States is just a parcel of land that was stolen and repurposed as a settler state using European logic and the laws of white supremacy. This book is a story about a strong-arm robbery. It is about family and friends trying to recover what was stolen. It is the testimony, and the verdict that a jury of our peers has never heard.

I can do that in *my history*. Freaky-D taught me that.

Years later, I asked Freaky-D about that jacket. He acknowledged that he knew it was stolen when he bought it from the thieves. According to Freaky-D, the guys strung him along about the sleeves for days, promising that they would eventually be delivered. He claims he didn't know the coat was mine until Fred, Double-O, and Squeak confronted him about it, which is when he came up with the plan to get the sleeves. And because all history is infused with the historian's values, in Freaky-D's version of history, receiving stolen property doesn't make him a thief.

Like Freaky-D, America don't steal.

This is the Black AF history of America.

This book is the sleeves.

1

EARTH, WIND, AND AMERICA

I have an uncle named James.

For most of my life I had no idea his name was James. To me, he was "Uncle Junior." James Harriot Jr. was alternately a salesman of marijuana, a Black Panther, a Vietnam veteran, and a trusted deacon in his church. He knew things. A *lot of things*. Like how to use a bandsaw, or bait a hook with a live worm. He was infinitely more complex than that, but to me at age ten, that was the essence of my uncle Junior.

One sweltering summer day, I was visiting his house, which sat on a pond with actual peacocks running around in the yard, playing outside with my cousin. We asked Uncle Junior for some water, and he made us stand on the porch and drink it, ensuring that we were not committing the ultimate sin of Black households—running "in and out that door." When he collected the drinking glasses, I remember looking through the screen door, watching him put a record on the turntable. I can never forget the music that came out.

He said their names were Earth, Wind & Fire.

I want to say that Earth, Wind & Fire is the greatest band in history, but there might be white people reading this book, and I wouldn't want to cause any Beatles fans to have a conniption. I honestly don't know what a conniption is, but my uncle Junior said it a lot. All I know is that it is a medical emergency that is nearly as dangerous as a hissy fit, which is the deadliest kind of fit. But this is not the time for that. This is the time for understanding that Earth, Wind & Fire is basically Jesus-less gospel music. I'm willing to bet you aren't aware of just how many Earth, Wind & Fire songs you know, because they are as ubiquitous as church hymns. And to top it off, they had the three elements of all Great Black Music:

1. **THEY WORE JUMPSUITS.** All great music acts must wear jumpsuits. It is a mandate passed down from the Godfather of Soul's backing band, the J.B.'s. Since then, if you want to be great, there must be a point in your career where you must dress like a NASCAR crew that fell in a vat of sequins and rhinestones. Many people wonder why André 3000 dressed so weird, but I saw Outkast in concert last summer and Dre dressed exclusively in jumpsuits, and I realized: Y'all won't let him be great.

2. **FALSETTO.** Prince. Eddie Kendricks. Michael Jackson. Philip Bailey. All great Black singers must have an extra octave that is reserved for the Holy Ghost and heartbreak.

3. **A HORN SECTION.** I don't care what kind of music you are playing—the fact is, *everything sounds better with a horn section.* Everything. Everyone since the beginning of time knows it. Ask Joshua how he brought down the walls of Jericho. Ask a soldier what instrument he wants played at his funeral. Ask Jesus what sound will signal his return.

Uncle Junior *loved* Earth, Wind & Fire, which, of course, meant that I became obsessed with Earth, Wind & Fire. And, according to him, the only proper way to listen to "The Elements" was on vinyl. Of course, he owned compact discs and cassettes, and even had an eight-track tape player. But for my eldest uncle, Earth, Wind & Fire albums should only be played in their purest form, from beginning to end. Luckily, my favorite EWF tune was the second song on the first side of their album *That's the Way of the World.*

Have you ever heard *That's the Way of the World*? If you are Black, the answer is yes. If you have ever been to a cookout, the answer is yes.

If you have an aunt who owns a leather miniskirt or a leopard-print blouse, the answer is yes. If you have ever smelled incense burning in a room with a ceiling fan, the answer is yes. To this day, every time I hear it, I remember what joy sounds like. What love tastes like. What home feels like. All of a sudden, I'm a kid again, standing on my uncle's porch, listening to my aunts tell stories through the screen door while my uncle Junior explained the way of the world.

Perhaps the only thing Uncle Junior loved more than the group he called "The Elements" was correcting people's stories. Whenever my family members gathered, the children would usually sit on the floor while the adults entertained each other with stories that stretched back generations. And without a doubt, every time somebody got "creative" with their version of a "vent," Junior was there to make sure the truth was told. When my mother recounted the tale of the time Uncle Junior brought home a skittish black cat and hid it in the bathroom closet so my grandparents wouldn't know about it, and how that cat went on to leap out in the middle of the night and nearly claw her to death, Uncle Junior reminded her that the cat was *technically* more of a midnight gray, and in reality, it barely scratched her. When my aunt Marvell delighted us with the story of how my grandfather saved an entire family from a blazing house fire, he would interrupt to point out that it was mostly smoke and very few flames. He would eventually take over the story and tell it with less hyperbole, yet still, he would somehow make his version the more interesting one. He was a living, breathing fact-checker; a human footnote with impeccable storytelling technique. It was his passion.

Uncle Junior wasn't necessarily a killjoy, either; he was just some-one who was as concerned about the fidelity of the family stories as he was about imparting the history of the sound of God's house band. Knowing this, I would sometimes use this particular idiosyncrasy to endear myself to him. If Uncle Junior wasn't at a family gathering, I would call him up afterward and regurgitate the stories back to him while he made his corrections. I trusted his version would be the de-finitive version *and more interesting.* But truthfully, I didn't really care about the family epics as much as I just enjoyed hearing him attempt to rectify the misrepresented facts. Not only was it hilarious to me, but it gave me a chance to have one-on-one time with my uncle. This on-going habit didn't just strengthen my storytelling muscle and inform me about my family, it also taught me not to trust *anyone's* version of history unless I corroborated it with an independent source, which, ironically enough, is the same method I used to learn the story of America.

* * *

The true origin story of America is intriguing enough without embellishment, a tale that includes cannibalism, cross-country adventures, and the type of brazen incompetency that almost doomed this experiment in thievery. But of course, to save face and maximize profits, the story was revised until we ended up with the swashbuckling blockbuster that we now know, filled with idealistic, barrel-chested white saviors who immaculately conceived of a brand-new kind of democracy with nothing but a few muskets and an abundance of Caucasity. Sprinkle in a few Pilgrims, a handful of savage "Indians," and, for diversity's sake, a few Black characters who learn the value of hard work through four hundred years of free labor, and you've got yourself a hit!

The account of America's creation you probably learned starred a group of Englishmen we now call the "Jamestown settlers."[*] In the safe-for-work, fairytale edition of the history of America, the English were a mighty empire who forged a new nation out of clay and ingenuity.[†] But had my uncle Junior lived back then, he would've been like, "Those guys? Mighty? Nahhhh." During their time, these so-called adventurers had garnered an international reputation for being unsuited for manual labor, let alone planning a new society. "Do not obtain your slaves from Britain," wrote Roman consul Cicero. "Because they are so stupid and so utterly incapable of being taught that they are not fit to form part of the household of Athens."[1] This incompetency would create the need for a transnational human trafficking

---

[*] *It was all the Protestants in England could afford because the Catholic Church had nearly cornered the booming real estate market in the New World.*
[†] *Let's forget the enslaving part, for now.*

infrastructure as well as a reasonably believable cover story to justify the intergenerational dehumanization and theft committed by these so-called enlightened ones.

By the late sixteenth century, England and Spain were beefing over which version of Christianity was best when James I ascended to the throne of England in 1603. James, a Protestant, was intent on thwarting Catholic-aligned Spain's global domination by getting in on the rapidly growing colonizing industry. In 1534, the English Parliament declared that the country had "no superior under God" other than the British king Henry VIII, who had split with the Catholic Church so he could marry his sidepiece.[2] So, while the Catholic Church had served as an early investor for Spain, Portugal, and the other white empires, Britain didn't have access to the church's seed money. Without the colonizer's version of *Shark Tank*, the arrogant members of the British elite did not fret. The other countries may have had a head start, but the English were not burdened by faith or religion. They were free to colonize in the name of a superior higher power: Cash Money.* When Queen Elizabeth I granted charters to colonize the North American territories "unclaimed by Christians," the first four attempts failed. To be fair, the only reason they failed was because of disease, lack of food, lack of navigation skills, and the inability to convince the natives of English superiority. No one knows what happened to the fourth attempt, aptly named the Lost Colony of Roanoke. But the English kept trying. They truly believed they were going to find the Garden of Eden, with trees dripping diamonds and streams filled with gold. There was no way they could leave all those untold riches to the people who lived on the land. They had to have it.

It would be easy to upend the story of America's founding by turning these colonizers into villains. However, the men who hopped on the *Susan Constant, Discovery*, and *Godspeed*—the three ships chartered by King James's joint-stock Virginia Company of London—were too incompetent to be characterized as evil. Although they had never mined, farmed, or built anything in their home country, these clowns were still confident that they could sail across the ocean and

---

* *Not the record company; they wouldn't take over until 1999–2000.*

conquer an entire continent, sight unseen. Of all the conquering cultures in the world, the English were perhaps the *least* qualified colonizers. But, to their credit, they were gifted in the area of cockiness, if nothing else.*

Aside from securing the rights to Virginia's gold, silver, and copper mines, the First Charter of Virginia charged the colonizers with "propagating of Christian Religion to such People, as yet live in Darkness and miserable Ignorance of the true Knowledge and Worship of God," and to "bring the Infidels and Savages, living in those parts, to human Civility."[3] In other words, they were going to rob these people of their land, culture, and history. But in exchange for an entire civilization, the Brits would introduce the natives to white church music *and* hats with buckles! Seems like a fair trade-off, no?

On April 26, 1607, the 104 English barbarians arrived at the gates of Tsenacommacah, a territory in modern-day eastern Virginia occupied by thirty-one individually governed tribes. Because they lacked basic geographical fluency and had an enormous amount of hubris, the whites considered the entire east coast of North America, from Canada to Florida, to be Virginia, and declared it their own, ignoring the fact that there was an entire functioning civilization here, with a government that wouldn't go down without a fight. This area was ruled by King Wahunsenacah, whom the whites called "Powhatan," which was actually a term used to describe Wahunsenacah's collective community.† As soon as he received word that some pale people were near the shore, Wahunsenacah dispatched a welcoming committee to greet them with twenty or thirty arrows, as he had done with all the previous boatloads of "suspicious"-looking people lurking around his neighborhood. After a brief melee, Wahunsenacah's boys retreated and decided to wait to make their move.

From the moment Wahunsenacah and his crew first encountered these pale-faced philistines, the natives could tell there was going to be trouble. First of all, this group was going to struggle with food: the mid-Atlantic region was going through the worst drought that had

---

* *There was nothing else.*
† *For future reference, we will not erase the history and culture of people by using the white version of indigenous people's names. Plus, white people are actually terrible at naming things.*

been experienced in seven hundred years, not to mention that their arrival in late April meant it was too late to start planting any crops anyway. Additionally, the spot chosen by the Jamestown colonizers was the worst real estate in the area. Although the brackish water surrounding the settlement on three sides offered protection, by June, they realized that American mosquitos hit different. They also didn't seem to know how hygiene works, because, for some reason, they figured they could relieve their bowels in the same place they gathered their drinking water.

Perhaps the Virginia Company's biggest mistake was *who they sent* to conquer the new land. Unlike Portugal and Spain, who had a head start in the white-people-discovering-things trend, England was relatively new to the colonizing game. Portugal and Spain had a class of explorers and soldiers whose full-time job was conquering. Instead of sending uncouth conquistadors,* the British sent wealthy Protestant aristocrats to stake out the area, led by Captain Christopher Newport and whose ranks included Captain John Smith, a celebrated English mercenary who had been wounded in battle, captured, and sold as a slave. As part of the British expedition, Smith was arrested for treason and imprisoned until the ships landed at Virginia and the crew unsealed the orders naming him as the leader of the colony, despite his having no experience at farming, governing a colony, or leading people. Things were off to a wonderful start.

Even the few laborers among the group were not accustomed to living off the land, which set the venture capitalists turned pioneers up for disaster. In his diary, Smith lamented that there were few bars, beer houses, or restaurants in the newly stolen land, forcing the adventurers to survive on boiled water and a pint of wheat and barley per day. Most of their grain supply had been stored on the ship for twenty-six weeks, providing a great albeit unorthodox source of protein—the worms that had infested the food stores. In another bout of hubris, when Captain Newport dropped them off and told them he'd be right back with supplies, the group seemed to forget how long that journey took, and didn't even bother to *try* and plant crops. The hapless British

---

* *Literally, "conquerors."*

aristocrats sat clueless in a new land, withering away in the Virginia winter, while the Powhatan nation luxuriated nearby in their heated homes.*

While Newport was on his journey back, Smith was out "discovering" stuff that had already been discovered, when one day he found himself surrounded by two hundred Powhatan men. Thinking quickly, Smith attempted to use his native guide as a human shield, which didn't go over well with the guys with the arrows. Smith was "shot in his thigh a little,"[4] captured, and taken to Wahunsenacah.† Paramount Chief Wahunsenacah arrived at the interrogation session in style, wearing pearl necklaces, a fur coat of raccoon, an entourage of advisors, and "young women, each a great chain of white beads over their shoulders, their heads painted in red, and with such a grave and majestical countenance as drove me into admiration to see such state in a naked savage."[5] Wahunsenacah served Smith a heavy brunch and decided to let him go. As long as the white men kept their distance, the chief of chiefs believed the two groups could coexist in peace, which was a strange concept for the Europeans. The natives had to be up to something, they figured, a theory advanced by Smith, who insisted that the natives were going to eat him until he outsmarted the king of the savages and convinced Wahunsenacah to let him go.

But Wahunsenacah could see that the inept immigrants were struggling and took pity on them. While he didn't know if their faces were so pale because of malaria, dysentery, or that poop-drinking thing (the answer was "all of the above"), he decided to help the settlers out by sending over some food until Newport came back from grocery shopping in England.

Back in England, everyone was excited because Newport‡ had returned with bags of gold discovered by the Jamestonians. The investors figured that this whole colonizing thing was a great plan. Not only did the investors donate supplies, but 120 more laborers and set-

---

* *The Powhatans had actually figured out central heating.*
† *Smith claims he was "kidnapped," but he probably just didn't understand the natives when they read him his rights.*
‡ *If you're wondering if he's somehow connected to the cigarettes, the answer is yes.*

tlers joined Newport for his return to Virginia. They were not exactly received by a party when they landed back on the shores. By the time Newport returned with provisions, craftsmen, and crew on January 2, 1608, sixty-six of the original settlers had succumbed to starvation, sickness, or Powhatan arrowheads. Thankfully, Newport wasn't around when the Brits back home realized that the settlers' supposed "gold" was actually iron pyrite—literally, fool's gold.

After they received the first shipment of supplies, the colonists went to work. Apparently they hadn't learned a single thing about saving their rations, and, like any intelligent, civilized society, they once again *ate all their provisions* and returned to the meager-living time they had just survived. (You know how it is when people who live in bad neighborhoods start receiving government handouts!) To avoid starvation, Newport and the colonists came up with the whitest plan ever created: they were going to go back to Wahunsenacah, the emperor of the not-hungry Powhatan people, and bestow on him the honor of becoming an English vassal. After all, who in their right mind would turn down the privilege of becoming an honorary white man?* There was only one problem with this genius idea: Wahunsenacah did not kneel *for anyone.*

You don't become the president of Tsenacommacah by kneeling. In fact, Wahunsenacah lived by two rules:[6]

1. "He who keeps his head higher than others ranks higher," and
2. "He who puts other people in a vulnerable position, without altering his own stance, ranks higher."

The whites didn't know what they had coming for them.

After crowning Wahunsenacah, the settlers demanded more food from their new fellow countryman. When the colonists informed the chief that he was now a subject of King James I, not only did the Powhatan end their welfare program, but Wahunsenacah's warriors surrounded the Jamestown settlement and warned the beggars not to

---

* *Wahunsenacah, that's who.*

leave their lily-white gated community unless they had some arrow-proof vests. Unable to hunt, fish, or gather food without being attacked, the settlers were back to square one.

Word got back to England that the settlement was flailing worse than Kenny G in an HBCU halftime show. Not only weren't they finding any gold, but when they ventured out into the countryside and climbed the highest hills in the area, they *still* couldn't see the Pacific Ocean. (Yes, they seriously thought they could find a path to Asia a few miles from their settlement.) King James was so determined to save his investment that he issued a new charter for the Virginia Company along with a fleet of nine ships, loaded with supplies and five hundred colonists. It was the largest fleet ever amassed in the history of the country . . . until they were separated in a hurricane, and yellow fever and the "London Plague" broke out aboard two ships. Then two more were lost at sea. By the time the British re-up arrived in Virginia, the supplies were essentially gone, but there were *more people to feed*.

Smith and the Jamestown governors had to instill a campaign of law and order to keep the desperate colonists from turning the English outer suburbs into a ghetto. In October 1609, Smith was asleep on a sack of gunpowder when it accidentally caught on fire, burning a ten-inch patch of skin in his groin area.[*] Fortunately, he was on a boat and jumped in the water, where he almost drowned. After his transport to England was delayed for weeks, John Smith left Virginia as an utter failure, with nothing to show for his work but a journal, a few stories, and charbroiled genitals. After Smith's unfortunate weenie roast, Wahunsenacah summoned Smith's replacement, John Ratcliffe, and twenty-five of Virginia's most important whites to a big dinner with the promise of more Powhatan government handouts. At the banquet, Ratcliffe discovered that the food baskets were empty and that he had walked straight into a trap. That night, Ratcliffe was kidnapped, skinned alive, and burned at the stake. It was all part of Wahunsenacah's plan to rid his land of

---

[*] *Don't act like you don't take afternoon naps on boats of combustible material. I'm just waking up from my dynamite siesta right now.*

the pesky whites once and for all by doing what he should have done all along—let them starve.

With its shoddy leadership in shambles, Jamestown was doomed. As the third winter came upon the settlement, the newcomers were at an all-time low, forced to eat leather belts, their pets, and, eventually— each other. Yes, that's right: researchers have found evidence that the few remaining Jamestonians survived the period known as the "starving time" by murdering pregnant women and eating their own children.[7] The heralded "first Americans" were cannibals.

In May 1610, 142 survivors of King James's ill-fated fleet arrived in a ship they managed to build in Bermuda. One of the passengers, John Rolfe, had lost his wife, daughter, and all of his belongings in the Bermuda shipwreck. By the time he reached Virginia, all he had was a few tobacco seeds that he had collected in Bermuda. He had heard about the new trend of "drinking" smoke that was becoming popular in Europe and decided to plant those West Indian tobacco seeds. As it turned out, Virginia soil was perfect for tobacco cultivation.

When Rolfe and company landed, Wahunsenacah was still trippin'. The number one chief rocka had almost successfully starved out the white invaders and still commanded a large native force. When the Bermuda ship arrived, in fact, only sixty of the hundreds of English colonizers were left. But one extremely savage colonist, Deputy Governor Samuel Argall, had a plan. Argall was the embodiment of pure evil, known for attacking French and Dutch settlements and claiming them for the king. When Argall failed at capturing a settlement, he would just resort to Plan B and set fire to it, as he did with a Jesuit colony and a French settlement in present-day Maine. Argall first tried to force Wahunsenacah into submission by burning native villages to the ground. When that didn't work, he discovered that Wahunsenacah's weakness was his daughter, Matoaka. (The white folk called her "Pocahontas," because . . . as we had established, they were terrible at names.)

In April 1613, Argall kidnapped Matoaka by luring her onto his ship. He offered to exchange her for English prisoners who had ventured outside the camp. When Wahunsenacah agreed, Argall reneged on the deal and demanded more provisions. Wahunsenacah agreed again, but Argall would never release his daughter; instead, she converted to Christianity and was married off to Rolfe. It turns out, the white conversion plan worked on the second try. Wahunsenacah told his warriors to chill out and gave Rolfe thousands of acres as a wedding dowry. In 1614, Rolfe exported a few barrels of his first tobacco crop and the English *loved it*. It was the first positive news from the Virginia Company since the fake gold incident in 1608.

With its success evident, the question became who would farm this new cash crop. The few settlers that remained were not quite the agricultural type, considering they could barely keep themselves alive. To solve the problem, Argall took John and Matoaka to England for an investor relations trip in 1616. However, the trip was cut short when Matoaka died suddenly of an unknown illness. Her tribesmen believed she was poisoned, while some historians think it was a respiratory illness or dysentery.* Whatever the cause, Argall brought the newly widowed Rolfe back to Virginia without a solid plan.

Meanwhile, back in Virginia, the Chickahominy natives, who weren't under Wahunsenacah's confederacy, helped feed the lazy British settlers, who *still hadn't planted enough food* to feed themselves. When Wahunsenacah died in April 1618, the natives decided to stop offering government assistance to the settlers. Ending this welfare-to-work program would doom the unskilled English encroachers. They desperately needed help. The only thing that could possibly save the English colony would be an influx of immigrants who knew what they were doing.

Once again, Jamestown was on the precipice of failure. The English investors were demanding their money, but King James didn't have it. Rolfe had land, but it was essentially worthless because he couldn't farm it. After a summer heat wave, colonists were preparing for a second "starving time" because investors were refusing to send more supplies until they got paid. In July 1619, the Virginia Company held its first legislative assembly. During the meetings, the assembly decided that if the company was going to survive, the colonists should probably grow enough food to feed themselves. Instead of using 75

---

* *My own research indicates it was the lack of seasoning.*

percent of the land to grow tobacco while depending on the native welfare system, America's first white legislative body limited tobacco production to 25 percent of a plantation's output and decided to give away plots of land to investors. While this plan seems reasonable on its head, the truth was these fools *still* didn't know how to farm, and hadn't even attempted, so to pretend they'd suddenly understand that and be able to provide for themselves was truly outlandish. There's a word for doing something over and over again and expecting different results:

American.

This America experiment was pretty much over. With no food, no gold, and rumors swirling around their homeland about their people-eating habit, where would they even find a skilled, hardwork-

ing people who knew how to build a country from scratch? Certainly not England. You heard what Cicero said!

Then James Rolfe's homeboy showed up with some cargo that would save the bumbling British colonists from extinction.

On October 12 or 13, 1616, Spanish captain Manuel Méndez de Acuña left Spain with a letter authorizing the private ship to transport kidnapped Africans from Africa to Vera Cruz, Mexico. Although the *San Juan Bautista* was only licensed to carry 200 enslaved people, Acuña left Luanda, Angola, with at least 350 stolen Africans. By the time the 115-ton vessel reached Jamaica, approximately 143 had died. Like most slave traders, Acuña had planned it this way; human traffickers routinely packed their vessels to maximize profit. In Jamaica, he sold 24 young children and headed for Vera Cruz, where he declared he was carrying 123 humans as cargo. Sixty were missing.

Shortly before the *San Juan Bautista* arrived in Mexico, twenty-five Englishmen on a small boat had attacked it in July 1619. After stealing sixty of Acuña's stolen cargo, they had split them between the 160-ton *White Lion* and the 100-ton *Treasurer*. The thievish Brits decided to head for the Virginia Colony, where they had no chance of being arrested or attacked. When the *White Lion* landed at Point Comfort in "about the latter end of August," Virginia governor Sir George Yeardley, along with the colony's supply officer, Abraham Peirsey, negotiated a dirt-cheap price for the ship's cargo—"20. and odd negroes" in exchange for food and the "best and easyest rates they could."[8]

And with that, the Jamestown project was saved. *This* is what made the land worth something. The enslaved labor was worth more than tales of gold and diamond trees. Now that they had a cash crop, abundant land, and people who knew what to do with it, the abject failure of an experiment had transformed into an unprecedented success. But why Virginia, of all places? Why would a smuggler bypass more successful outposts to go to a failing colony? How did they know they would be welcomed? In the rare case this story is told, it is cast as a tale of happenstance and coincidence, but of course, it is actually one of deception, trickery, and greed.

When John Rolfe took his newly stolen wife to England for that investor relations trip, he traveled to England and returned to the colonies on a ship captained by the vicious Samuel Argall. As soon as they returned, Argall was summoned back to England to answer charges of cruelty against the colonists and for running an international crime ring. To get back to England, Argall had to catch a different ride, as his ship was being captained by Argall's homeboy, a notorious pirate named Daniel Elfrith, who had essentially made a career out of stealing on the high seas. Elfrith had borrowed the *Treasurer* from Argall and hit the jackpot by stealing the stolen Africans from the *San Juan Bautista*.

Four days after the arrival of the *White Lion*, Elfrith sold "two or three negroes" in Virginia.[9] He probably could have sold more, but he had to leave in a hurry, as Virginia's new governor, George Yeardley, recognized the ship as a well-known pirate vessel and ordered him to leave. Yeardley couldn't resist purchasing a few low-priced human beings before giving him the boot, though. He just knew that it had to be quick; he didn't want his name sullied for dealing with pirates. Virginia didn't need that kind of trouble.

Less than a year later, in March 1620, the Virginia Colony's first census recorded seventeen women and fifteen men who were "not Christians in the Service of the English." One of them would show up in later documents as "Angela" or "Angelo, a negro woman." Angela arrived in America as a passenger of Daniel Elfrith's thieving, enslaving, kidnapping, village-burning, self-contained criminal enterprise, the *Treasurer*. It was the ship Argall used to kidnap Matoaka and burn native settlements up and down the coast. It was a stealer of souls that was fueled by greed and theft. And it is as American a thing that ever existed.

Here, in the folds and creases of the tale of pilfered people, is where America truly lies. That other mythical history that is shared in schools is as real to me as is Atlantis or Oz. It is a gargantuanly tall tale, refined from years of incessant yarn-spinning that has been sugarcoated and stuffed down throats. But in the middle room world built by Du Bois and his progeny, we ask the real question to America:

How does it feel to be a stealer of men?

Or is that the way of the world?

THREE LITTLE QUESTIONS

1. **What is the difference between a "settler" and an "invader"?**
   a. The number of guns you bring to the invasion.
   b. It depends on who's telling the story.
   c. Invaders become settlers after they vanquish the people they invaded.
   d. Two different spellings.

2. **Who were the first Americans?**
   a. The people who were living in the place when the name "America" was invented.
   b. The people who came up with the name "America" but had never been there.
   c. The people who had united their states in the place called "America."
   d. White people.

3. **Rank these savages from least civilized to most civilized:**
   a. People who fought to prevent invaders from stealing their land.
   b. Human traffickers.
   c. People who stole from human traffickers.
   d. People who bought stolen property from human traffickers.
   e. Cannibals.

ACTIVITY

GREETINGS FROM YOUR FUTURE COLONIZER

As Director of Corporate Communications for the Virginia Company of London, you are tasked with writing a one-page letter introducing the British colonists to Wahunsenacah. As truthfully as possible, explain the motives, plans, and intentions of your company in a way that is least likely to result in the Powhatan putting an arrow through your chest.

2

THE CHURCH FIGHT THAT STARTED SLAVERY

There are entire books about the history of European religion, social caste systems, and how Europeans turned the African continent into a factory for raw human material. But to understand the origins of America's constitutionally enshrined human trafficking system that legally reduced people to chattel, we must go back to the inception of the transatlantic African trade that formed the foundation of America's color-based social hierarchy.

It started at church.

The Church.

After a little-known woodworker named Jesus died, Christianity began trending in Europe. Long before the conservative Christian movement co-opted the idea of using Christianity for the purpose of expanding a political base, the Roman Empire thought it might be a good idea to combine church and state for the sake of politics and world domination. The "Holy" Roman Empire eventually fell, but the idea of using God's infallible human intercessor—the pope—as a political leader continued, making the Catholic Church the most powerful institution in Europe. The Vatican had its own army, settled disputes between countries, and even negotiated treaties. In 1054, "the church" split into two factions (the Eastern Orthodox Church and the Catholic Church), each controlling different parts of the European continent.

As it relates to our story, all you need to know is this: Since 711, North African and Arab Muslims known as Moors controlled different parts of Al-Andalus, or the Iberian Peninsula, which was home to the countries we now know as Spain and Portugal. To get control of their respective homelands, Spanish and Portuguese nobles assured the pope that the Latin Church would see an increase in tithes and offerings if the church supported the *Reconquista*—the four-hundred-year-old struggle to rule the Iberian Peninsula. The papacy jumped at the chance to expand its territory and gain some revenue. So in 1123, Pope Callixtus proclaimed that the *Reconquista* was part of the Crusades—a series of religious wars to control the Holy Land and make non-Christians disappear.[1] During this constant conflict between the Christian and Islamic kingdoms, Africans, Eastern Europeans, and Asians were all subject to varying forms of servitude. Although slavery existed during this time, it was never exclusively race-based, nor was it as widespread and entrenched as it would become in the Americas.

By the time Spain and Portugal reconquered their homelands in the early 1400s, centuries of warfare had left both countries in dire financial straits. Meanwhile, other European countries had emerged from the Dark Ages, finished their Crusades, and revitalized their economies. If Portugal or Spain had any chance of existing alongside their European counterparts, they both needed new sources of income—and the best way to do that seemed to be through gaining control of the peninsula. This land grab spawned an intense rivalry the likes of which wouldn't be experienced again until the dawn of the Prince vs. Michael Jackson debate.

After John of Aviz and his sons took control of Portugal from the Moors, he was crowned king. But he still had to figure out how to curry favor with the pastor by putting a little extra in the offering plate. Because Portugal was essentially a new country, they didn't have a great credit score and their options were limited. Luckily, King John's son Henrique was obsessed with two things: boats and Africa.[2]

In 1415, when he was just twenty-one years old, Henrique had distinguished himself in battle when he helped capture the North African city of Ceuta, which was slowly becoming an important trading outpost for Portugal. After the siege, Henrique heard stories that Africa was rich in gold, treasure, and unsophisticated Africans. Hank wasn't even thinking about the slave trade at the time; he had a simpler idea. Instead of expanding their territory through warfare, what if they found new, unexplored territories and just took the resources and the land from the African savages? Seemed easy enough, but there was one problem:

Monsters.

During the Middle Ages, the bravest white adventurers would embark on voyages for the sake of honor, glory, and—obviously— money. Back then, items that weren't locally available were highly coveted, especially pelts, precious metals, and spices.* In the event that these seasoned salt-seeking seafarers didn't return home, most people assumed the fearless travelers must have run into some kind of undefeatable beast, a story bolstered by the fact that every time European sailors tried to explore the West African coast, they never made it farther south than North Africa's Sahara Desert coast. It *had to be* monsters. What else but a saber-toothed leviathan could defeat these gallant pathfinders in rickety ships?

Undeterred, Henrique sailed off to figure out where the Africans trading in the North African province of Ceuta were getting all this gold. But time and time again, he failed miserably on his mission to make it there. How was Portugal going to satisfy Europe's most vital institution—the Catholic Church—if he didn't have a pot of gold? If he didn't figure something out quick, the church might just let his neighbors in Spain take over. Then Henrique got another bright idea: cultural appropriation.

For centuries, African Coptic sailors had been sailing in smaller boats, called lateens, with triangular sails instead of the big ships with old-school square sails used by the Europeans. Henrique asked one of his African servants captured during the *Reconquista* how to build these ships and avoid sea beasts. After the servant laughed for about

---

* *I know you're expecting a seasoning joke here, but we're better than that.*

forty-five minutes at his captor's belief that a gang of oceanic gremlins was out there taking down ships, he informed them that the sea thugs weren't killing white people; it was the wind! Using this new knowledge, Henrique assembled a few local cartographers to draw new maps. Instead of charting the land and the seas, Henrique's boys drew charts of the ocean currents and cornered the exploring market by mastering the "trade winds." By the time Henrique was put in charge of the Portuguese version of the Knights Templar and appointed Grand Master of the Military Order of Christ on May 25, 1420, he had taught a generation of Portuguese sailors how to maneuver ocean currents in these new lateen-rigged caravels, earning a name that would last forever: Prince Henry "the Navigator."

In 1441, Henry sent two knights—Nuno Tristão and Antão Gonçalves—off in their late-model Portuguese ships to explore Africa and see what they could find. While filling his boat with seal pelts, Gonçalves ran across a naked African and his Berber female servant, the first native Africans Gonçalves had encountered in his twenty years of exploration. So, of course, he kidnapped them. When Gonçalves met up with Tristão's boat, the two decided to see if Tristão's African servant—who just happened to be with them— could interpret the unclothed Black prisoner's language and tell them where the gold was. The captured African basically told his kidnappers that he wouldn't be driving a camel if he knew where to find gold. He pointed the knights toward a nearby fishing camp, and the sailors took ten Africans this time, including the chief, figuring *one of them* had to know where to find some gold. The next day, the brilliant but bloodthirsty white knights used the naked captives to lure the African "savages" into the open. Gonçalves and Tristão were shocked to find themselves ambushed by 150 Africans who opened a can of African whoop-ass on the Portuguese warriors. Tristão ran back to his ship and kept sailing south to search for gold, but Gonçalves was shook. He decided to head back to Portugal with his seal skins and the ten captives.

By the time Tristão returned to Portugal, Gonçalves had already sold the seal skins and was prepared to split the profits from the expedition with Tristão. Tristão was astonished at his share of the take, wondering who his partner had bamboozled into paying such an exorbitant amount for a shipload of monk seals. The bulk of the money hadn't come from the seals, Gonçalves explained. Most of the duo's profits came from the human cargo.

In 1442, when Henry sent Gonçalves on another expedition, Gonçalves brought the African chief along, figuring he could ransom the chief back to the Africans. Sure enough, in exchange for the African abductee, Gonçalves received a big stash of ostrich eggs (don't ask), a small amount of gold dust, and an ox-hide shield. Finally, an African negotiator brought out a hundred men, women, and children in a parade and allowed Gonçalves to choose any ten in exchange for the chief. The next year, Tristão returned, but this time, instead of ransoming or kidnapping his human cargo, he bartered for fourteen of the village's captives and resold them in Portugal. In 1444, the Portuguese discovered it was easier to barter for their human cargo than capture them. And with that started an entire new economy: one of stealing human souls. Nuno Tristão and Antão Gonçalves can go down in history as the first Europeans to purchase Africans from Black slave traders and resell them in Europe.

When Henry heard about the sale, he was no longer interested in the ostrich eggs, the seal pelts, or the spices; he wanted to know more about this people-trading thing. But Henry hadn't cleared this practice with the church and didn't know what the pope would think. Sure, they had "enslaved" Moors, Jews, and non-Christians during the Crusades, but that was a military thing—not a pure cash grab.

When explaining his rationale to the church, Prince Henry would argue that, technically, he wasn't an "enslaver" because true Christians would never do that. Instead, he allowed Portuguese "missionaries" to "save" Africans by converting them to Christianity. The argument worked. By 1446, more than thirty Portuguese ships had filed applications with Prince Henry for people-stealing licenses. In 1455, Pope Nicholas V granted Henry a monopoly on the African human market—as long as they baptized their cargo.[3]

Henry had finally found gold in Africa.

Portugal's only problem was that it was a hassle to sail to Africa, snatch up some humans, travel back past Portugal, and try to sell the stolen Africans in Western Europe. Plus, there wasn't really a big demand for African labor in Europe because the market was flooded with Moorish indentured servants and the remnants of feudalism. But with the age of empire-building came the need for labor. Explorers could "discover" land and soldiers could conquer kingdoms, but if Henry could commodify the labor necessary to build and maintain these empires, he would control a commodity more precious than any mineral or spice. So, a year after Gonçalves brought the Africans back to Portugal, Henry set up the Casa da Guiné. This state-run commercial entity would essentially become the prince's version of Amazon, a one-stop shop for goods imported from Africa, *especially Africans*. For the next fifty years, the Casa da Guiné would import around a thousand Africans per year to sell to willing slavemakers around the world.[4]

Portugal continued to rule the seas for years after Henry the Navigator's death, sparking a less-than-friendly rivalry with its Spanish neighbors and earning the undivided attention of all of Europe. Businessmen and ambitious explorers from around the world found themselves in Portugal trying to make a living on Portuguese ships that benefited from his charting of the oceans. Because of this exploration and colonization, the Portuguese Empire eventually stretched from Europe to Japan, covering South America, Africa, and the Caribbean. Despite the African continent offering every natural resource in the world, because Portugal led the way in human trafficking, African bodies became the key to European expansion in the New World. And perhaps no one is more responsible for the four-hundred-year competitive empire-building race than Henry the Navigator, whose advancement in exploration and charting the world's sailing routes made Portugal the first modern European empire.

. . . Okay, maybe there was one guy.

While Portugal was filling up the church's coffers in the lucrative spice trade and the African resources-raiding market, Spain struggled financially. It tried to emulate Portugal's success on the seas, but Portugal always seemed to beat it to the rich African ports. The two countries had even gone to war for a while, a war that ended with Portugal pulling a brilliant move.

On September 4, 1479, after the two countries had fought for five years over which royal family should run the Iberian Peninsula and own the African coast, Portugal had to admit that Spain had won and ceded their rule on part of the peninsula to Queen Isabella and her husband, Ferdinand. In exchange, the defeated Portuguese rulers asked the Spanish for just one thing: Portugal only wanted exclusive ownership of everything they discovered on the high seas. Spain could have the rest.

The Spanish quickly signed the deal and laughed all the way to the bank, as Portugal hung its head, stifling its own chuckles. Isabella, Spain's new queen, felt empowered and protected by the *Aeterni regis*, the church-ratified deal that made Spain's royalty the "eternal ruler" of the peninsula, except for the relatively small sliver of Portuguese land. She didn't care about those tiny boat-driving Portuguese idiots. They were probably going to get devoured by monsters anyway. And all Portugal managed to get in return for this deal was *everything else in the world*.

According to the treaty that was ratified by the church, Portugal now owned the entirety of the Great Sea Ocean (the Atlantic Ocean) and everything in it, all the way to India. All of Africa now belonged to Portugal (as long as they could get past the sea dragons). This also meant that Portugal owned all of . . . well, in 1479, nothing else existed in the Atlantic Ocean besides Europe and Africa. Of course, there was that weird guy who kept coming around talking about sailing west to India.

That guy was crazy.

This strange guy wasn't wealthy, smart, or talented, but he had started working on Portuguese ships at the age of ten—even though he was Italian—and had absorbed everything the Portuguese seafarers taught him. He considered himself to be Portuguese at heart because he was obsessed with Henry the Navigator (who was already dead), and eventually married a noblewoman from Portugal (noblewomen love sailors—ask Popeye). The guy had been telling anyone who would listen that he could find a path to India by sailing west, *away from Africa*, which was unheard of.

The nascent navigator drew up a few rudimentary maps, charted a course, and applied to King John II of Portugal's court for a sponsorship to explore three times. But Johnny Jr. repeatedly told the passionate ocean pioneer that his maps were wrong. King Henry VII of England also said no. Desperate, the obsessed sailor headed to Spain, where he ran into a fellow Italian who had just moved to Spain to work as a banker. The banker was a smooth-talking geography nerd. He told the sailor that his maps were wrong, but as the banker and the sailor became friends, they discovered that they had the same obsessions. Eventually, the banker revealed that he wasn't just a banker; he was in Spain working for one of the wealthiest families in Europe, the de' Medicis.

The banker made a deal: if the sailor could get someone to buy ships for the voyage, the banker would get his bosses to finance everything else. But where would the explorer get ships? Luckily, there was one person willing to bet on a strange sailor off the word of a geography nerd: Spain's new queen, Isabella.

Isabella was still steaming over the fact that her rivals now owned an entire ocean and everything in it. She doubted that the weird sailor guy could sail west to India, but it would solve all of Spain's problems if he could. Portugal had just discovered a long path to India by sailing around Africa, which meant the Spanish crown's days were numbered if Portugal controlled Africa *and* India. Isabella desperately needed a way to even the playing field, and the only thing that could do that was more territory. It was a long shot, but even if the guy didn't find a western passage to India, what was the worst that could happen? (Besides the underwater Godzillas, that is.) So Isabella wrote a check for a factory-refurbished ship and two pre-owned caravels and made it out to the sailor: one Christopher Columbus.

On August 3, 1492, Columbus set sail for India. He first spotted land in the modern-day Bahamas and explored Cuba before wrecking one of his ships on the coast of modern-day Haiti. During his initial voyage, Columbus noted that the "Indians" were so primitive that he "could conquer the whole of them with fifty men" and rule the land as he pleased.[5] (You might want to stick a pin in that.) Columbus knew that Isabella *hated* slavery, but since her army had already captured much of the Iberian Peninsula, she had soldiers to spare. These conquistadors would have no problem dominating these island people, Columbus figured.

When Columbus returned, he pulled into a rest stop in Portugal and discovered that he had just happened to park his boat right next to King Johnny Jr.'s vessel. (Incredibly, the previous sentence is not a joke.) Knowing that everything in the Atlantic Ocean belonged to Portugal, the sailor intentionally kept the news of his discovery from the king. By the time the information wafted through the Iberian Peninsula, Junior had already filed a claim arguing that the newly discovered land belonged to Portugal. His skilled cartographers had charted a course to this place *that no one had ever seen.* And as it turns out, their maps were accurate.

Both sides went to the new pope to settle the dispute. Junior argued that this place they called the "West Indies" was not actually *in India*, and since papal decrees were essentially the word of God since the islands were in the Atlantic Ocean, the land legally belonged to Portugal. On the other hand, Isabella argued that God's representatives didn't even know about the islands when those treaties were made, therefore the Columbus territories belonged to Spain.

To settle the controversy between his churchgoers, on May 4, 1493, Pope Alexander VI drew an arbitrary line on a map. He declared that everything west of the line, including the islands discovered by Columbus, belonged to Spain. Since Portugal already owned Africa, the papacy decided that east of the line still belonged to Portugal. The only problem with this deal was that *there wasn't anything east of the imaginary line besides Africa.* A year later, the Treaty of Tordesillas officially sealed the decision. Isabella had essentially used Portugal's old tricks to win ownership of the West Indies.

Spain quickly dispatched its army of conquistadors to ravage the Caribbean islands of gold, spices, and natural resources, which helped them gain favor with the church. However, Portugal only had a small population and a meager land army with which it could colonize its expanding empire. But of course, it "owned" Africa, and Henry the Navigator had created a literal corporate infrastructure for buying and selling Africans.

Although Columbus's friend had lost a lot of money on his investment in the voyage, he recognized that Columbus had made a contribution. But he wasn't convinced Columbus should get all the credit. After all, it was mostly the banker's idea! Theoretically, *he* should be as famous as Columbus! But how could he convince the public?

So the banker went to Portugal's new ruler, King Manuel I. Like his great-uncle Henry the Navigator, Manuel the Fortunate was all about exploration and expansion. Manuel, however, wasn't worried about Spain's exploration of the West Indies. He was content to let Spain have a few islands in the middle of nowhere because, in 1498, Portuguese explorers had finally found a sea passage to India. On the way back, the Portuguese Armada had even found an island *east* of the pope's infamous line.

Still, Mannie was impressed by the banker's knowledge of geography, especially when the banker detailed his previous expeditions to the West Indies. The banker showed Manuel charts and maps of places that no one had ever seen. The slick-tongued financier even wrote two books detailing his travels that became extremely popular in Europe. Enchanted by the tales, Manuel convinced the banker to quit banking and join a Portuguese expedition as the Armada's official cosmographer. There was only one problem: the banker was lying.

He *was a banker*! It's not like he studied atlases he bought from gas stations or downloaded from Google Maps. Accurate maps were treasured back then, and this smooth-talking banker bamboozled Mannie into believing he had charted the known world, even though he didn't even know how to pilot a ship! Half of the expeditions he told King Manuel about were totally made up! Still, Manuel fell for it, and put the banker in charge of the Portuguese Armada's next trip.

During their journey, the crew slowly realized that their cosmographer didn't know anything about cosmographing and had barely been on a ship in his life. For instance, when the explorers discovered a river on January 1, 1502, the banker didn't even know he was in charge of naming things, so he just called it the "January River," or Rio de Janeiro. As for the new land, later merchants looked around and recognized a tree growing in abundance—the brazilwood—and began referring to the new island by its most abundant export, the "land of the Brazil."

It stuck.

By the time the expedition returned to Portugal, the banker's ruse was up. The crew realized that he didn't know anything about navigating. In fact, the banker was so terrible at his job that more experienced navigators had to explain that they hadn't been island hopping—they were exploring one giant landmass.

The banker still couldn't let Columbus one-up him. So he ran back to Spain and started spreading the rumor that Portugal had found a new continent all because of him. He even produced a letter that most historians now believe was a hoax, which gave him credit for everything on the official Portuguese map, including the new continent and its banal name—the "New World."

After Christopher Columbus died in 1506, the banker began spreading the idea that he had taught Columbus everything he knew about exploring, and the public started to buy it. In 1507, someone took all the geographic information from Henry the Navigator, Portuguese explorers, and the late Christopher Columbus and combined it into one atlas, the *Introduction to Cosmography*. The book was meant to accompany a mass-produced wall map and globes. It had no new information and held no historical significance except for the fact that it published that fake letter from the banker and the authors suggested a new name for the New World: "I see no reason why anyone could properly disapprove of a name derived from that of Amerigo, the discoverer, a man of sagacious genius. A suitable form would be Amerige, meaning Land of Amerigo, or America."[6]

Three decades later, Gerardus Mercator's influential map would name the North and South Continents after the charlatan Amerigo Vespucci. Even though he had done nothing, Vespucci's name would be entrenched in history, making his namesake the perfect one for a country built on deception and lies.

By the early 1500s, the crown had profited dramatically from Columbus's exploration. In 1503, Isabella created the Casa de Contratación—a trading corporation that was essentially the Spanish version of the Casa da Guiné. Isabella put Vespucci in charge of its maps, pilot training, and ship licensing in 1508. Spain was mining copper and gold and farming sugar in their new colonies in Hispaniola, Cuba, Puerto Rico, and throughout the Caribbean. The conquistadors forced the indigenous islanders into servitude and killed those who didn't submit. But in 1512, Catholic priests convinced King Ferdinand to pass a set of regulations that officially forbade enslaving colonial natives. The Laws of Burgos originated from Catholic friars who disliked the inhumane treatment. The priests wrote damning letters and pleading sermons suggesting that the Spanish should convert the new Indians to Christianity instead of abusing them.

The priests' protests didn't matter. The indigenous people were dying anyway. The natives had no natural immunity to European illnesses, so entire Caribbean populations died from diseases. Hispaniola's native Taíno population went from half a million to two hundred in less than fifty years because they were literally allergic to white people. It took forty years for 90 percent of Cuba's population to disappear. Puerto Rico took thirty years.[7]

But those priests were not altogether altruistic in their protests. This was not about human rights. They fully understood that building an entirely new society required human subjugation. Nearly all of them agreed that there was a better way to go about colonizing the New World: African slaves.

Desperate, the Spanish colonizers took the priests' advice and brought African slaves to the New World. But because Portugal still owned the African human being market, the first Africans in the Spanish colonies were actually bought from Portuguese traders, enslaved on the Iberian Peninsula, and then hauled as cargo to the New World. The Spanish believed that these Africans would be immune to European diseases and "sturdier."

Meanwhile, Portugal was making a fortune from harvesting the brazilwood trees and growing sugar in Brazil. Then Portugal discovered an actual gold mine in Brazil. South America turned out to be a profitable investment, but how was Portugal's small population supposed to colonize *two* continents and extract the resources of an entire "New World"?

The answer brings us back to Nuno Tristão and Antão Gonçalves.

Remember when Tristão and Gonçalves purchased that first batch of humans? When the African negotiator paraded out the prisoners, those 150 captives included Europeans, Jews, Berbers, and some Africans. As a devout Christian, Gonçalves knew the church wouldn't appreciate him bringing Muslims back to Portugal after ousting the Moors from the peninsula. The Europeans already likely had their own religion, as did the Jews. But Gonçalves figured that the darker Africans would be less likely to flee captivity, would work harder, and be easier to convert to Christianity. One simple-minded decision would later be reinforced by Henry the Navigator's rules, Catholic decrees, the Casa da Guiné's rudimentary version of corporate regulations, and stereotypes that would last until this very day. Gonçalves scanned the diverse parade of prisoners and asked himself which ones would make the best slaves.

Then he chose the Black ones.

THREE LITTLE QUESTIONS

1. **Christopher Columbus did not:**
   a. Discover America.
   b. Consider himself to be an Italian.
   c. Know what he was doing.
   d. All of the above.

2. **Who is responsible for slavery?**
   a. Henry the Navigator.
   b. Nuno Tristão and Antão Gonçalves.
   c. White people.
   d. Every society had slavery. Plus, the Africans sold slaves, too. Why must you make everything about race?

3. **The new discoveries were called the "New World" because:**
   a. It was new to white people.
   b. The people in the "Old World" weren't good at naming things.
   c. The "world" only consists of places white people conquered.
   d. It wasn't.

KEY TERMS

AFRICAN: People from the continent of Africa except for Egypt, Morocco, and any place that taught, conquered, or civilized a European country. Unlike their white counterparts, Africans are not separated into distinct cultural, geographical, or political groups unless they are from Egypt, Morocco, or a place that taught, conquered, or civilized.

CHRISTIAN: A follower of the European version of the teachings of Jesus Christ.

EUROPE: The part of the Eurasian landmass that was designated as a continent to recognize the corner of the world where white people live. Asia's taint.

MOORS: Originally used to describe Africans who conquered parts of the Iberian Peninsula, later to mean anyone with dark skin, worshippers of Islam, or any group of Africans that was smarter than white people.

WHITE PEOPLE: An arbitrary, non-scientific, phenotypical classification for people of European descent created by people of European descent. People who don't use washcloths.

BEFORE "BEFORE": THE FIRST AFRICAN AMERICANS

lthough we have already recounted the tale of the *White Lion*, the *Treasurer*, and Christopher Columbus, you should know that the origin story of African people in America does not begin in 1619, nor does it begin with slaves.

In fact, the people who were kidnapped, loaded onto ships, transported across the ocean, and forced into a lifetime of human bondage were not slaves—they were doctors, priests, children, wives, and warriors who were coerced into this racialized forced labor system through violence or the threat of violence. That they survived this legal, state-sanctioned act of collective terrorism is a testament to their unextinguishable strength. But they didn't just survive. With the jagged fragments of their homeland stowed away inside their unerasable memories, they crafted a new world that not only sustained them but also transformed this pilfered property into a place that even the white men would call "home."

Just as it may seem obtuse to pigeonhole Greeks, English, Spanish, and Germans into a homogeneous gob of indistinguishable "white people," it does a disservice to lump the different societies, kingdoms, and people together from a continent three times as big as Europe and just simply refer to them as "slaves."* The Mandinka people from the West African Mali kingdom were not the same as the Kongo people, although both had civilizations and empires that made Europe's empires look like ghettos.

Since the beginning of time, the condition we broadly refer to as slavery has existed in so many different iterations that it is almost unfair to sweep all the different variations of human bondage under the umbrella of one language's inadequate definition. Is a prisoner of war the same as a domestic servant? Does an unpaid worker serving a period of indentured servitude fall synonymous with a woman forced to enter an arranged marriage? Is criminal incarceration indistinguishable from mandatory military conscription? These are just a few historical examples of people who have been broadly defined as "slaves."

But unlike in Europe or elsewhere in the world, color-based slavery was regulated as a part of America's founding document. Slaves from antiquity were still seen as human, and their enslavement was not solely based on skin color. Slavery existed in Africa before white people showed up, but human beings were not commodified or chattel. In pre-colonial Africa, enslaved people had legal rights, their status was not passed down to their children, and they did not serve as a major labor force. In fact, most of the previous iterations of human bondage around the world offered a path to freedom. To be fair, it is much easier to refer to America's unique institution as "slavery" than it is to call it the "perpetual, race-based, constitutional, human trafficking enterprise that legally reduces human beings to chattel through the means of violence or the threat thereof." That's quite a mouthful. But at its heart, that's what it is.

And what is America?

Is it a plot of dirt littered with the discarded bones of those who stood in the way of manifest destiny, or is it a constitution?

---

* *Plus, Europe is not a continent; it is a dingleberry of the Asian landmass. Just look at a map.*

Is it an assemblage of huddled masses yearning to breathe free, or is it merely a series of borders on a map? Was this idyllic dreamland of opportunity always here, beckoning the conquering swords of history to unearth its existence? Was it manifested from destiny out of thin air and gradually expanded across this continent like a virus?

These are not rhetorical questions. To understand the history of Black people in this country, we must first come to a consensus on how we define "this country." Because if what we refer to as "Black history" includes the jigsaw puzzle currently known as "the United States of America," then the twenty-something enslaved Africans who arrived in Virginia in 1619 were more than a century late to the cookout.

Almost one hundred years before 104 white "adventurers" from the Virginia Company of London landed on a Virginia beachhead on May 14, 1607, Africans had already ventured to America, slaughtered natives, and built plantations. In the words of the immortal historian Ray J: "We hit it first."

Juan Garrido was the first documented African American.

Much of what we know about Garrido comes from his *probanza*, or résumé, which states that while he was from West Africa born and raised, exploring is where he spent most of his days. Born around 1487, Garrido moved to Portugal before eventually landing in Spain, converting to Christianity, and changing his name to what translates as "Handsome John" (because, *of course*).[1] Some researchers speculate that he was a formerly enslaved Kongolese man whom someone eventually freed. In contrast, historian Ricardo Alegría[2] believes Garrido was the son of an African king who sent him to Portugal as an emissary. In any case, in 1503, at fifteen years old, Garrido joined explorer Juan Ponce de León's expedition to the New World, landing on Hispaniola. From there, Garrido and Ponce de León enslaved and killed Taíno around the Caribbean, searching for the Fountain of Wealth.[*][3]

---

[*] *That Fountain of Youth thing was a myth created years after Ponce died.*

In 1508, Garrido was one of about fifty soldiers, conquistadors, and enslaved men whom Ponce de León (whose name translates roughly as "Ponce the León") selected to go on a gold-stealing quest on the island of Borikén. However, the natives there weren't down with having their wealth hijacked by newcomers who weren't from their hood. Tired of the constant raping, pillaging, and enslavement, the indigenous Carib and Taíno people joined forces and went to war against the armed robbers. But by then, the traveling bandits had given the Caribbean island a nickname that inspired an influx of Spanish thieves to come searching for treasure: Puerto Rico. How could any adventurer/larcenist resist the temptation of a "port of riches"?

On April 3, 1513, Garrido, Ponce de León, and their squad of strong-arm gangstas, still searching for a place to rob, stepped onto the shore of a new land. As they arrived on the coast, they decided to name the location in honor of the Easter season. Because "Land of Now & Later–Colored Linen Suits" was too hard to translate into Spanish, Ponce decided to name the land after *La Pascua Florida*—the Feast of Flowers. They only stayed for five days, but their discovery still arguably makes Garrido a two-time Black founding father. Ponce decided to head back to Spain and was eventually rewarded with the rights to govern La Florida and steal all its riches, on one condition: he had to read a proclamation to the natives that they were now the subjects of King Carlos I.[4]

Look, I know this sounds stupid, but in the 1500s, very few process servers had ships with alternators strong enough to cross the Atlantic, so this is how white people *claimed* stuff—they literally just yelled out that they "claimed this land," and that was it. So when Ponce showed up later without his handsome Black friend, the natives weren't as friendly as Ponce assumed they'd be. But Ponce kept trying. In 1521, Massa P pulled up in South Florida with horses, supplies, and two hundred men, intent on conquering the land. During his previous tries, Ponce had met a member of the indigenous Calusa people who promised him that their prospective subjects would meet the conquerors with open arms.

When Ponce and his crew arrived at present-day Charlotte Harbor, the Calusa were anxiously waiting to meet their new neighbors. Ponce had barely made it through his speech welcoming the Calusa to Spanish rule when one of the Calusa warriors' housewarming gifts—an arrow dipped in the sap of one of the most poisonous trees in the known world—pierced his thigh.* Ponce's whole staff, crew, and record label hightailed it back to Cuba, and the thuggish conquistador who brought slavery, colonialism, genocide, and death to New World natives died from the wound. In the first case of whitesplaining, Spain would blame Ponce de León's death on the "very savage and belligerous"[5] Calusa Indians, who were "not accustomed to a peaceful existence."

While Ponce de León was initiating his five-century plan to gentrify Miami Beach, Garrido had hooked up with a new white friend, conquistador Hernándo Cortés, and joined the Spanish conquest of Mexico. After participating in the genocide of more than one hundred thousand Aztec warriors,[6] Garrido settled in Mexico, married, had children, and eventually became the first human being to grow wheat in the Americas.† Unfortunately, everyone knows corn tortillas are superior to whole-wheat ones, so Garrido's flour plantation didn't make him a wealthy man. That's when his conquistador homeboy Cortés tempted him with one last heist.

According to Cortés, there was another island, west of Mexico, filled with gold, pearls, and treasure that was ruled by a tribe of Black Amazon warrior women.[7] Garrido figured it was an in-and-out job; he and his not-so-good-looking white friend could easily defeat a group of bedazzled Keishas. So Garrido borrowed a few bucks for the expedition and hit the seas with his Cortés, only to find a barren wasteland that had very few Black

---

* *I'm not laughing! That's the way I cough.*
† *That we know of. Colonization kinda messed up the indigenous people's records.*

warrior women sporting gold herringbone necklaces. Garrido returned to Mexico broke and disappointed, and Cortés later named the newly discovered peninsula after the mythical Black pagan warrior queen Calafia. Calafia didn't exist, but it's worth noting that a Black man was on the mythical island of California nearly a century before the *Mayflower* left England.

In 1538, dead broke, with three kids to raise in Mexico, Garrido submitted his claim for a pension to the king of Spain, summarizing his credentials:

> *I, Juan Garrido, Black resident of [Mexico City], appear before Your Mercy and state that I am in need of making a probanza to the perpetuity of the King, a report on how I served Your Majesty in the conquest and pacification of this New Spain, from the time when the Marqués del Valle [Cortés] entered it; and in his company I was present at all the invasions and conquests and pacifications which were carried out, always with the said Marqués, all of which I did at my own expense without being given either salary or allotment of natives or anything else. As I am married and a resident of this city, where I have always lived; and also as I went with the Marqués del Valle to discover the islands which are in that part of the southern sea [the Pacific] where there was much hunger and privation; and also as I went to discover and pacify the islands of San Juan de Buriquén de Puerto Rico; and also as I went on the pacification and conquest of the island of Cuba with the adelantado Diego Velázquez; in all these ways for thirty years have I served and continue to serve Your Majesty—for these reasons stated above do I petition Your Mercy. And also because I was the first to have the inspiration to sow wheat here in New Spain and to see if it took; I did this and experimented at my own expense.[8]*

By the time Garrido died in 1550, other Africans, free and enslaved, had already made their mark on this new world.

In 1521, a few months after Ponce de León died from thigh poisoning, conquistadors landed on the present-day South Carolina coastline. The Spanish crew completed a preliminary survey, but, to prove that they had "discovered" new territory, they kidnapped sixty natives and brought them back to Hispaniola. Excited about the prospects of bling, Spanish bureaucrat Lucas Vásquez de Ayllón wrote to Spain and assured the crown that he wasn't as stupid as Ponce. He even took one of his captives back to Spain to testify that there was no danger at all in South Carolina. After exploring the coastline once more in 1525, Ayllón eventually returned to the shores of South Carolina on August 9, 1526. With him, he brought more than six hundred passengers who were ready to fulfill his new colonizing contract with Spain. Along with hopeful residents, supplies, and even livestock, Ayllón brought dozens of African slaves.

One reason Ayllón isn't known as one of the great explorers of his time is that he was *terrible* at exploring. He crashed a ship and lost most of his supplies on the first day. Then, in November,[9] the angry indigenous people joined the enslaved Africans and organized America's first slave revolt, setting fire to buildings in the settlement. Ayllón and his ragtag band of colonizers hopped back on their ships and jetted back to where the good, sane white people were, leaving everything behind. Of the six hundred who arrived with Ayllón, only 150 made it back to safety.

No one knows what happened to the enslaved Africans who revolted at San Miguel de Gualdape. Only a few returned with Ayllón, and most historians assume they assimilated with the Native Americans. Several tribes in North and South Carolina, including the Lumbee, trace their heritage back to a mixture of indigenous people, whites, and African Americans. What we do know for sure is that both African and Native American populations had one thing in common: *resistance*.

Juan Garrido was not the only free Black man on the North American continent. Another legendary African would prove to be more of an explorer than any of the handsome, rebellious Black Americans who came before him. And while Garrido was never a permanent resident of Florida, Puerto Rico, or California, Mustafa Azemmouri, who went by the street name Esteban, became a legend in places that wouldn't be called

"America" for at least two centuries. Not only did he explore more of the North American continent than Lewis or Clark, but he did it before most of the Jamestown settlers were even born.[10]

A couple of months after Ayllón's attempt failed, explorer Pánfilo de Narváez departed Spain with about 600 people who intended to establish a settlement in La Florida, a merry band of land bandits that included 450 troops and slaves, along with wives, indentured servants, and navigators. Nearly 100 of Narváez's men deserted the mission when they heard about Ayllón's disastrous experiment during a rest stop in Hispaniola. Sixty more prospective colonizers died in a hurricane along the way. By the time Narváez landed near present-day St. Petersburg, he only had about 400 men.[11]

On April 13, 1528, after making his formal declaration, Narváez ran into a group of coastal natives. Communicating through sign language, Narváez explained that he was looking for gold.

"Oh, then you're looking for the Apalachee," they told him. "They have plenty gold."

Álvar Núñez Cabeza de Vaca, whose account[12] of his adventures with Esteban forms most of the historical record, noticed that everything Narváez told the indigenous tribe that he was looking for was followed by the revelation from the natives that the Apalachee had whatever he needed in droves. Narváez was convinced—he was going to rob the Apalachee. That's also when the Carolina gentrifiers made a crucial mistake identifiable to anyone who has ever watched a horror movie or the documentary series about the crime scene investigation team led by Scooby-Doo: they "split up."

Esteban knew that splitting up is the most ill-advised move in all of history. It would later cause the Revolutionary War, the Civil War, and the destruction of the Five Heartbeats.* And if you notice, this book does not contain a single chapter about Harriet Tubman telling passengers on the Underground

---

* *I still stand by the fact J.T. could actually sing better than Eddie King Jr.*

Railroad, "You go this way; I'll go that way." A dedicated student of history will learn that splitting up ranks somewhere between "let's take their land" and "maybe I should put this shoe polish on my face for the Halloween party" in the top five whitest moves of all time. But because another member of the expedition enslaved him, Esteban stayed quiet, planning ahead.

Cabeza de Vaca, on the other hand, tried to tell his boss that this was a bad idea, but on May 1, Narváez split his crew into two contingents. One hundred sailed along the coast to find a suitable spot to set up shop, while three hundred of his fighters marched through the unclaimed continent to separate the Apalachee from their gold. Along the way, they enslaved members of the tribes they encountered, stole their food, and plundered the Indian villages.

The expeditionaries finally entered Apalachen territory on June 25, immediately taking the women as hostages and enslaving the few men who were around. Narváez settled down in his new territory and forced the female natives to make food for his men. Before looking for gold, the new warlord made everyone else leave the village (so the conquerors would have fewer mouths to feed), and then took care of his most pressing task—declaring that the land now belonged to Spain.

As soon as he began reciting his Castilian declaration of claimsmanship, the Apalachee warriors rained down arrows that easily pierced the Europeans' "good armor."[13] The Spanish were under attack. For three weeks, the so-called savages had the Christian warriors under siege, forcing them into desperation and starvation.* Although wild game surrounded the village, the Spanish soldiers were so afraid that they couldn't even hunt. Meanwhile, Esteban was just chilling. He had no allegiance to the Spanish and was used to being hungry and terrified. So after a month of arrow-dodging, when the Spanish decided to make a break for it, Esteban grabbed his duffel bag and headed out too.

---

* *Wahunsenacah would have been so proud.*

As the conquistadors sprinted for the coast, the disgruntled natives chased them, killing every white man they saw. Not only did the Spanish get their mollies whopped, but they also had to trudge through the Florida swamp hungry, goldless, and enduring a "shower of arrows." Cabeza de Vaca and Narvaèz eventually decided to retrace their steps in hopes that the Aute, one of the tribes they had enslaved on the way to the Apalachee, would let bygones be bygones and offer shelter to the Spanish. But when they arrived at the Aute village, the Indians had burned their encampment to the ground and vanished.

As it turned out, there was communication between tribes up and down the coast, warning of the fleeing conquerors. And all these tribes knew that if anyone could get rid of the white bandits, the Apalachee could. And the Apalachee *did*. They chased the Spanish to the Gulf of Mexico, surrounded them, and waited while the Spanish hid along the coast with dwindling provisions, no ships, and a few horses. Desperate, the Spanish decided to eat the horses, melt every piece of metal they owned, chop down some trees, and make rafts, in hopes of escaping to anywhere. On September 22, Esteban's Spanish slavemasters pushed five thirty-three-foot-long boats into the sea.[14] Two of the surviving rafts landed in Texas, and for four years, Esteban watched his white enslaving army die off while he thrived. By 1532, only four of the original six hundred were still alive: Esteban, Cabeza de Vaca, and two other white boys.

For the next two years, the four men traveled throughout Texas and Mexico, and reached as far as New Mexico and Arizona. Ironically, Esteban proved his worth to his former enslavers by *helping them escape* after Texas natives repeatedly enslaved the colonizers during their thirty-five-hundred-mile overland trek through present-day Texas to New Spain (or Mexico). As an Arabic-speaking African who traveled with Spanish-speaking Christians, Esteban displayed a remarkable propensity for language and communication. He was able to learn sign language and interact with tribes throughout the Southwest and Mexico. For saving his Spanish travelers' lives numerous times, when they reached Mexico City, the Spanish rewarded Esteban with the whitest gift ever: he was reenslaved.

When Esteban and his compadres arrived in Mexico City, they were greeted by Antonio de Mendoza y Pacheco, a viceroy and close friend of King Carlos I of Spain. Entranced by Esteban's stories, Mendoza demanded that the African be sold to him, and almost certainly introduced Esteban to his two famous conquistador buddies—Hernán Cortés and Juan Garrido.

Although there is no written account of Esteban meeting the only free Black man in New Spain, when Cortés heard of Esteban's travels, he begged the king's permission to go gold hunting in the western part of the continent. Carlos, however, had a better idea. After receiving letters from Viceroy Mendoza gushing about "Esteban el negro,"[15] he chose Esteban to lead an unarmed contingent of indigenous Mexicans to explore the territory north of Mexico City. Esteban, without the help of a single white man, led a hundred Mexican Indians across the Sierra Madre, a feat that had been unsuccessfully attempted by every notable Spanish explorer on the continent. Along the way, Esteban seemed able to befriend every group of natives he encountered, even those who were initially hostile.

Esteban supposedly met his death during this journey in 1539 at the hands of the Zuni, a tribe near the border of Arizona and New Mexico. Some non-European scholars, however, believe he may have convinced the Zuni into helping him fake his death so he could finally be a free man.[16]

Regardless of what happened, Esteban would eventually be erased from American history. However, Native American tribes still share stories of the mysterious black-skinned man who discovered more of America than Christopher Columbus, Ponce de León, and Leif Erikson combined. In fact, the elders who passed down the oral tradition of Pueblo Indians in New Mexico have a distinct way to describe their first encounter with European colonizers:

"The first white man our people saw was a black man."[17]

THREE LITTLE QUESTIONS

1. **The first African Americans:**
   a. Discovered America.
   b. Should be considered founding fathers.
   c. Were not colonizers.
   d. Cannot be called "African Americans" if America did not exist.

2. **What should the indigenous people of North America be called?**
   a. "Indians."
   b. "Pre-Americans."
   c. What's North America? Do you mean Turtle Island?
   d. Whatever they want to be called.

3. **Who were the first "settlers" in America?**
   a. Technically, it's the indigenous people.
   b. The people Ayllón left behind.
   c. The colonizers who named themselves "settlers."
   d. All of the above.

ACTIVITY

COLONIZER OR NAH?

On the following list of people, place a C beside the names of those who should be considered colonizers:

1. Esteban.
2. Juan Garrido.
3. The Ayllón expedition.
4. Pánfilo de Narváez.
5. Ponce de León.
6. Conquistadors.
7. Discoverers.
8. Someone who comes to your house and refuses to leave.
9. Enslaved Africans who are brought to a land against their will.
10. Squatters.
11. A king who never set foot on your land.
12. A king who never set foot on your land but sends someone to conquer you.

13. A person who comes to a land and respects the laws and traditions of the people who are there.

14. An outsider who decides to live on unoccupied territory.

15. An indigenous nomad who decides to live on unoccupied territory.

16. A person who wants to "civilize" people who are already civilized.

17. People from another country who come to steal land.

18. People from another country who didn't steal land but enjoy the benefits of stolen land.

19. People from another country who fund land theft operations.

20. America.

THE REAL WAKANDA

In 1324, Musa I, the tenth *mansa*, or king, of the West African empire of Mali, began a four-thousand-mile pilgrimage to Mecca. Before his hajj, the African and the Muslim worlds had heard little about the emperor who united many parts of modern-day Mauritania and Mali (Melle), and Europeans had no clue who he was. But after his trip, Mansa Musa literally put the kingdom of Mali on the map, and to this very day, historians universally consider him the wealthiest human being in all of human history.

Born around 1280 as Kanga Musa, a name that refers to his mother, Kankou Hamidou, Musa was born into the matriarchal Mandinka society. Although his father was not a royal, Musa was appointed a "deputy" to the empire and assumed the throne in 1312 when the previous king took a pilgrimage to Mecca and did not return.

While Europe was slowly emerging from the poverty, war, disease, and the Great Famine that killed one in every ten Europeans between 1315 and 1316, Musa was building universities, mosques, and city centers throughout the empire of Mali. Instead of conquering land through war, he expanded his empire through annexation as he used his control of gold and salt to connect disparate city-states into one empire. It is said that by the end of his life, it would have taken an entire year to go from one end of the Mali Empire to the other.

Because of this, Mansa earned more titles than LeBron James. He was called Emir of Melle, Lord of the Mines of Wangara, Conqueror of Ghanata, Lion of Mali. The only titles he never earned were Best Rapper Alive, Mother of Dragons, and the Hardest-Working Man in Show Business. At its height, scholars say, the kingdom had four hundred densely populated cities in the Niger Delta. The University of Sankore in Timbuktu, Mali, still stands where he built it after conquering the area.

Most accounts say that he took sixty thousand men on his hajj with him and balled out along the way, much to white people's dismay. Never one to be stingy with his money, Musa is reported to have handed out gold bars to poor people along his travel route. Almost every version of his hajj tells the same story: King Musa handed out so much gold to the poor, it actually *collapsed the entire gold market in the Middle East*! So what did he do to fix this?

In perhaps the greatest money move ever made, the king borrowed all the gold his crew could carry from Cairo. Of course he didn't need it, but the scarcity of the precious metal settled the market. Then, like the baller he was, he simply repaid the Egyptian moneylenders back, plus interest. I'm sure he also included a note that said, "My bad. I'm not used to hanging out with broke people."

When he returned to Mali, Musa brought back some of Spain's and Egypt's most prized architects and builders, creating an even wealthier kingdom. Historians say that by the time he returned from Mecca, he controlled most of the gold and salt in the Mediterranean. Coincidentally, this is when the kingdom of Mali began showing up on European maps. How and when Mansa Musa died is a topic of fierce debate, but in our extensive research, we could not determine whether Mansa Musa released his tax returns.

3

THE WORLD, RECENTERED

There are so many "worlds."

Centuries after pharaohs, emperors, czars, sultans, khans, caliphs, and kings all took turns ruling the disparate, sometimes simultaneously existing regimes that historians then and now refer to as the "world-ruling empires," a brand-new dynasty emerged, in South Carolina. Just as Rome, Egypt, Athens, or Carthage are considered by ancient historians as "world capitals," for Black Americans, South Carolina stands as the capital of the known world. Understanding the history and legacy of Africans in America, and America itself, cannot begin with the tea-tossing frat boys of Boston or even the self-righteous constitution-writers of the North. America's fortune, fame, and even its independence began in South Carolina.

In many ways, the Palmetto State served as the template for America's pseudo-democracy—a system in which labor and intelligence was stolen from West Africa and enforced via the enslavement and exploitation of their peoples. South Carolina's white settlers benefited from the evolution of human bondage in Virginia. If you recall, where we last left off, the Jamestown colony was on the verge of collapse because the bumbling bluebloods didn't know how to farm, hunt, build, or survive, and were starving to death despite having land galore. While the Brits were loving the tobacco coming their way, the colonies still weren't exactly making a profit, to the point that the Virginia Company couldn't even pay its investors. They needed people with the know-how and muscle to do things, but the rumors about disease, arrows to the leg, and colonizers literally having each other for dinner didn't help generate enthusiasm among working-class Englanders to try out the new land. Even the poorest citizens had no desire to cross the ocean for a chance at starving to death.

To solve this personnel problem, the Virginia Company came up with a novel solution. On November 18, 1618, the company passed the Orders and Constitutions, which included a provision that would rescue the failed experiment. Instead of enticing workers with money, the Virginia Company's "Great Charter of privileges, orders, and laws" offered free land grants to anyone who provided funds for poor people to move to the colonies.[1] An affluent landowner would receive the rights to fifty acres for each "head" they brought over, garnering as much as two hundred acres for a family of four. After a period of indentured servitude, the poor immigrants could hope to purchase land on credit from the wealthy landowners, move to unreserved land and claim "squatter's rights," or sell their skills to the highest bidder.[*]

Of course, this system was flawed. The colonizing class are perhaps the most skilled loophole finders of all time, and what these Virginians lacked in farming and survival skills, they more than made up for with their propensity for exploitation. In 1638, George Menefie came up with a bright idea for how to scam his way into free land without losing his labor force after the indentured servants served their obligatory time of peonage. Menefie, a merchant, farmer, and member of the governor's council, was able to receive a patent for 3,000 acres, 1,150 of which he claimed for "the Negroes I brought out of England with me."[2] A year later, when Menefie earned another 3,000 acres for importing sixty more Africans, everyone jumped on the buy-one-slave-get-fifty-acres-free bandwagon. Then, in 1662, Virginia's legislature officially sealed the fate of its negro servants:

---

[*] *The standard seven-year period of indentured servitude was based on the biblical principle called the Lord's release, found in Deuteronomy 15. It's actually where Equifax got the idea from.*

*WHEREAS some doubts have arrisen whether children got by any
Englishman upon a negro woman should be slave or ffree, Be it
therefore enacted and declared by this present grand assembly, that all
children borne in this country shalbe held bond or free only according
to the condition of the mother, And that if any christian shall committ
ffornication with a negro man or woman, hee or shee soe offending shall
pay double the ffines imposed by the former act.[3]*

Unlike the poor English, Irish, and native indentured servants,
the African imports *and their children* were now considered property.
The Black headright scheme exploded after this. In the twenty-five
years after the colonial legislature made slavery intergenerational
and perpetual, 125 land patents were approved, resulting in 1,649
Africans being shipped to Virginia.[4] Jamestown's labor shortage was
finally over, and a new system of big-government handouts emerged.
After all, what is capitalism if not a chance for capitalists to capitalize?

By creating a legally binding, race-based, intergenerational, per-
petually oppressed class of human beings, Virginia revealed that all
that nonsense in the colony's first charter about God, liberty, and the
"true religion" was a farce. Slavery was an *American* idea, not a product of the time. No law was passed in England that legalized slavery.
France's *Code noir* was similar, but it would come two decades after
Virginia's declaration. From its inception, America was always a pyr-
amid scheme where the wealthy benefited from the labor of the poor.
And truly, there is only one term that befits Virginia's codified system
of racial peonage: white supremacy. South Carolina would not just
take note—they would up the ante by creating their own version of
racial hierarchy that built on all the "advances" Virginia made with
headrights and human chattel.

In 1663, a year after slavery officially became a Virginia birth-
right and over a hundred years after Lucas Vásquez de Ayllón made
his bumbling attempt to gentrify South Carolina, King Charles
granted eight "Lord Proprietors" the rights to establish the British
colony of Carolina and essentially rule the land as makeshift mon-
archs. One of the first acts of business was to enlist British political
philosopher John Locke to coauthor the Fundamental Constitutions

of Carolina. (Coincidentally, Locke—who is known as the "Father of Liberalism," and whose philosophy on the fundamental rights of "life, liberty, and property" inspired a little document called the Declaration of Independence—was a major investor in the Royal African Company, the white-owned business that trafficked more enslaved Africans to America than any other entity.)[*] Locke enumerated the laws and rules for Carolina's organizing document, including a clause that would come to forever be known as Article 110, which stated, "Every freeman of Carolina shall have absolute power and authority over his negro slaves, of what opinion or religion soever."[5] Carolina's white supremacy was baked into the social structure as one of the colony's founding principles, and slavery proliferated.

The proprietors of the Carolina territory faced a plight similar to the situation recently overcome by Jamestown's venture capitalists. Not only did South Carolina's new residents have to deal with a hostile indigenous population, but the indentured English farmers had never seen a climate and soil like this. When South Carolina's early white residents saw what Virginia's elite class did with a few pieces of human property and access to headrights, they checked the stock price for slaves and said, "Hold my ale." The Carolina colony would build an empire of slavery.

In 1672, Morris Matthews was granted several hundred acres overlooking the Ashley River, a few miles outside of England's first pre-planned city in the American colonies, Charles Towne at Albemarle Point. Four years later, Matthews gave up and sold the property to Thomas and Ann Drayton, a wealthy English couple who owned several forced labor citrus camps in Barbados. To expand their agricultural empire, the Draytons claimed headrights based on their stolen Africans still living on their Caribbean properties. Instead of transporting all their Bajan captives to Carolina, though, they decided to supplement their enslaved stock by abducting a few prisoners from Africa's Windward Coast. The Draytons' business plan was impeccable—they now had amassed all the free labor they needed to build their bootleg version of Tropicana.

---

[*] *"Coincidentally" means "of course," right?*

The Draytons' plantation, Magnolia, was located at the conflu-ence of the Ashley River, the Stono River, and the Atlantic Ocean, which made it perfectly accessible to the rest of the world. However, the brackish water made growing tobacco, vegetables, or most food staples nearly impossible on a large scale, and the phosphorus-rich Lowcountry soil didn't allow for the citrus farming the Draytons had mastered in Barbados. When the Draytons tried to jump on the silk-worm bandwagon, that failed too. As white colonists in Carolina suc-cumbed to an outbreak of malaria and yellow fever,[6] in a tale as old as America, the Draytons began running out of time, money, and food.[*] Curiously, the Draytons noticed, their enslaved servants didn't seem a bit worried. When they investigated, the privileged not-actual-planters discovered that the Africans had been growing their own food, including a crop that the Draytons had never seen produced by any English laborer or white Barbadian bondsman. The Africans were growing rice.

Rice growing is a difficult venture. Planting, growing, and har-vesting the staple requires the engineering of levees, dams, and dikes. Aside from the west coast of Africa, the only regions in the world that produced rice on a large scale were in Asia and a few in Italy.[7] In a humid climate like Carolina, it is a backbreaking prospect that fosters disease, dehydration, and exhaustion. But even in these conditions, the Draytons' stolen human class were able to persevere, saving the family from starvation—and the entire Carolina economic system from collapse—with the introduction of America's first edible cash crop.

The Draytons were not engineers, nor were they farmers, but they had money, "absolute power and authority" over their "negro slaves," and a sense of just how valuable it would be to grow this crop on a massive scale. So they proceeded to raid Sierra Leone and the West African "Rice Coast" to pilfer the people who would provide the knowledge and the manpower to continue growing the grain that would become a South Carolina staple. Their genius plan had a few

---

[*] *There were very few grocery delivery services in the area.*

flaws, however. The slave thieves figured they could just throw a net over a few Africans, and they would all magically have advanced horticulture degrees in rice growing that would directly translate to the Carolina colony.* Naturally, these "enlightened" men did not take into account that Africa—a continent larger than the United States, Brazil, Italy, and China combined—was rich with biodiversity and thereby necessitated different methods of cultivation.

In Africa, there were *rice cultures*—each with its own distinct botanical adaptation according to the topography, geography, and soil. In the rain-fed upland regions of present-day Sierra Leone and Liberia, women dropped grains into shallow holes made by a special hoe, then covered the seeds with the heels of their feet. In the Senegambian swamps, growers planted rice in pottery and transferred them to the swamps after the seedlings grew roots. South of the Gambia River, near Guinea, African agriculturalists constructed "an elaborate network of embankments, dikes, canals, and sluice gates that serves to bar the entry of marine water while retaining rainfall for field saturation and rice cultivation."[8] And in America, the embezzled empirebuilders from different languages, cultures, and countries were forced to adapt their ways of knowing to create an entirely new Africanbased rice-growing system that the wealthiest, most "enlightened" white men in the world couldn't figure out for themselves.

Since the beginning of this people-stealing project, the slave system relied mostly on Black males who had the muscle to perform laborious tasks, and so, like in most slave societies, men greatly outnumbered women in the colonies. In Virginia's Surry County, for instance, there were 145 men for every 100 women in the 1670s.[9] But in the South Carolina colonies, the male-to-female ratio would eventually reach a one-to-one ratio after plantation owners realized that African women were the ones who possessed the engineering and agricultural knowledge necessary to grow what would become known as "Carolina Gold."

In the early 1700s, Indian agent Thomas Nairne observed that

---

* *Shhh . . . Don't tell them.*

African women were not only capable of most rice-growing tasks, but they seemed to know better than the men around them.*[10] After a few calculations, Nairne hypothesized that his large forced labor camp could increase his production by 50 percent if he put the women in the field alongside the men. Nairne was right. In most West African rice societies, men rarely did any farming aside from the occasional heavy lifting. Nairne would never be able to test out his hypothesis (he was tortured and killed by Yemassee natives for thinking he could "negotiate" a settlement after stealing their land). Still, by 1710, enslavers knew to demand the same price for African women as they did for African men.[11] And thus came the influx of women into the area. On Governor Robert Allston's Georgetown, South Carolina, plantation, the women did most of the farming, while the men cut and hauled wood or performed other tasks.[12] The women were also responsible for milling, dehusking, and winnowing the rice into an edible product. To achieve this, they combined West African technology with the resources available in South Carolina. They built the tools and engineered complex machinery. Instead of using palm leaves to separate rice from its hull, they used Carolina sweetgrass to weave baskets for tossing the rice into the air. They milled the rice with their handmade mortar and pestles and built the tools to turn the land.

Every time these rice plantation owners imported more Africans, their empire expanded. As historian Peter Wood notes in *Black Majority*, "With respect to rice cultivation, particular know-how, rather than lack of it, was one factor which made black labor attractive to the English colonists."[13] Some, like the Draytons, enslaved hundreds, and saw their profits soar as a result. By the time the first shots of the American Revolution were fired, Magnolia Plantation had ballooned to 1,872 acres, an area twice the size of present-day Harlem, with hundreds of head of livestock that roamed vast acres of "cowpens." When Nairne was calculating the exact worth of putting his enslaved females to work, he also remarked that "South Carolina abounds with cattle, to a Degree much beyond any other English Colony . . . People

---

* *Indian agents were men who were authorized to negotiate and communicate with natives on behalf of the white government.*

have 1000 head but for a man to have 200 is very common."[14] And just as the naturally gifted female horticulturalist "field gals" were adept at growing and harvesting rice, South Carolinians discovered that slaves from the plains of Ghana and Gambia were skilled at herding cattle. Unlike the white "buckaroos"[*][15] and poor "crackers" who used whips, the Black cattlemen used salt, fire, and dogs to corral the livestock when the plantation owners needed to find them again (usually around tax time), making the "cow boys" as valuable as the "field gals."[16]

And as a result of their ingenuity, hard work, and savvy? These men and women died.

Life on a rice plantation was so fraught with disease and death that planters generally didn't expect their human capital to live past nineteen. One Charleston owner remarked that he "would as soon stand fifty feet from the best Kentucky rifleman and be shot at by the hour, as to spend my night on a plantation in summer."[17] The low life expectancy, combined with an infant mortality rate that was ten times the rate for white infants, had one bright spot. On rice plantations, the high risk of catching malaria, yellow fever, or other contagious diseases meant the white people didn't bother their enslaved as much as they did on other types of plantations. Unlike those in many other slave societies, South Carolina's enslaved worked on the "task system."[18] Enslaved people were responsible for their own food, clothing, and even their medical care. Each captive had a required amount of work they had to complete, and once they were done, they were released from their enslavers' oversight to work in their own gardens, sew their own clothes, or make their own money. Charleston even had an elaborate "tag" system that allowed enslaved people to sell goods and food at the market.

From this white-man-free vacuum emerged a new culture and language that was a hybrid of those of the Africans from the Caribbean colonies and the Baga, the Fula, the Kissi, the Kpelle, the Limba, the Mandinka, the Mende, and the Wolof of West Africa. They balanced the memories of their motherland on the bridges of their noses and hid

---

* *From* buckrah, *the Gullah word for "white man," which is from* bakara, *the Ibo word for "white man."*

them on the tips of their tongues. Their collective souls merged and became the Gullah-Geechee, a cultural force that no white person would ever have power and authority over.

> *And if'n de wood God neh de cornstock Jesus mek'em tink dat, dey flam.*
> *Look yea, bubba. Dem boi know we go to de goat-smellin. Ain no churn.*
> *I been grōn. So, gwin nie. Dah bukrah mek me box dem in da teets, wit*
> *dey stingy bookey. I jook 'im tuh ya got tuh tote'em. Feh ye get out de*
> *do' tell titi nem cumbayah fuh a bog. Ayn lük in huh nie ye nana face in*
> *bout lemm yeahs. Dayne finna badmout me with dey mout all box-up.* [*]

That's the Geechee language. During their spare time, the transplanted Africans created a whole new language by combining West African dialects, Caribbean patois, and white people's English. Geechee lingers in the way I speak to my sister and mother when they call from Monck's Corner, South Carolina. It renews itself every time I cook a chicken bog[†] (which is different from "some perlo"[‡]) the way my uncle Junior taught me. ("One knuckle uh wadda, wait fuh de wadda to staht bussin, mash a top on it, low it down tuh ya get a lee-lil fie. After ten minutes, outcha fie but *do not take the top off* till ye mek ye plate. *Bimm.*") And even if you're not from the South, you speak it and you don't even know it. When you bring your own "tote" bag to the farmer's market, you're using a derivation of the Kikongo word *tota*, or "pick up." Thinking about checking out a movie? If you buy a box of Goobers, you're using a Kimbundu word for peanut, *nguba*.

This was where it all began: from the work of women who knew how to build, engineer, plant, and harvest. It's the food and the cul-

---

[*] *"Furthermore, if their wooden God or their cornstalk Jesus allows them to believe in such tomfoolery, they're crazy. Pay attention, brother: Those people are aware that we would kick their asses. I'm not a child. In fact, I've been an adult for an interminable amount of time, so perhaps you shouldn't even enunciate such fantasies. Those white people may force me to punch him in the mouth, with their flat posteriors. I'd punch him so hard you'd have to carry him home. But, before you leave, please tell your sister to stop by in the immediate future and enjoy some rice perlo. Because I haven't seen her in nearly eleven years, I don't want her to curse me out and have a frown on her face."*

[†] *It's "a chicken bog," not "some chicken bog." A bog is a whole thing, like a pie or a ninny.*

[‡] *Which is kinda like a bog, but not as boggy. Also, I had to look up how to spell "perlo" because, although I have eaten it my entire life, I literally have never seen it in writing until fifteen minutes ago. I would have gone with "perloe."*

ture of my known world. It's coded into the culture and language of America. And Black people created it from scratch.

By 1776, South Carolina was the number one exporter of rice to England, the number one supplier of salted meat to the Caribbean, and had the highest per capita income in the British colonies.[19] And the colony that had intended to recruit white people to grow citrus was now majority Black. In the five years before the American Revolution, South Carolina had imported more enslaved Africans than all the other ports in all the other American colonies combined.[20] Over the life of America's legalized transatlantic human trafficking system, 40 percent of this country's human imports passed through Charleston Harbor, earning the South Carolina city the title of the "slave capital of the New World."[21]

As they lived in these relatively insulated worlds they had created, their Creole became a tool of survival and resistance, allowing the enslaved to communicate with their fellow captives in stealth, right in front of their ignorant masters. As a result, rebellion also became contagious in the culture of South Carolina's enslaved. On May 6, 1720, "the negroes in South Carolina" murdered plantation supervisor Benjamin Cattle along with an unnamed white woman.[22] An armed rebellion occurred again in August 1730 when enslaved Africans armed themselves one Sunday morning and "conspired to destroy all the whites."[23] Three more took place on the South Carolina rice coast in 1739, the most famous of which occurred not far from where the Draytons' son John had just purchased the first of more than a hundred properties with the intergenerational wealth built from African labor. South Carolina's 1712 slave codes were based on the slave code of Barbados, which protected the enslaved from "the Cruelties and Insolences of themselves or other ill-tempered People or Owners."[24] But something was about to change.

Somebody finnah box dem bukrah fess loose!

THREE LITTLE QUESTIONS

1. **Jamestown is considered the first American settlement because:**

   a. It was the first English settlement in North America and history books are written in English.

   b. Someone told me that.

   c. Indigenous natives, Spanish settlers in Florida, and Black people don't count.

   d. The poor white welfare recipients deserve *something*.

2. **Black history begins:**

   a. When humanity begins.

   b. When Juan Garrido arrived in Florida.

   c. When the first enslaved Africans arrived in 1619.

   d. Every year on February 1.

3. **American history begins:**

   a. With Greek and Roman mythology.

   b. When Christopher Columbus *didn't* arrive in America.

   c. When the Jamestown colony started receiving welfare.

   d. 1776.

NAME THE RACE

Assign the race of Asian, Black, Hispanic, Native American, white, or "Other" to the following people.

1. A person whose ancestors were from France, except for one great-great-grandfather, who was from Africa.

2. A person whose ancestors were from Africa, except for one great-great-grandfather, who was from France.

3. A person who emigrated from Ireland before Irish people were considered white.

4. A Spanish-speaking indigenous native of Texas when it belonged to Mexico.

5. An English-speaking indigenous native of New Mexico.

6. A person whose ancestors are from Spain.

7. A person who comes from Mexico whose ancestors are from Spain.

8. The indigenous Taíno of the Dominican Republic side of the island of Hispaniola who speak Spanish.

9. The indigenous Taíno of the Haitian side of the island of Hispaniola who speak French.

10. A Spanish-speaking descendant of Africans enslaved in the Dominican Republic.

11. Jesus.

12. A person from Egypt.

13. A person from Hawaii.

14. An indigenous person from the Spanish-controlled Philippines.

15. A Portuguese-speaking Brazilian whose ancestors were African.

16. A Spanish-speaking descendant of indigenous Incas and Juan Garrido who emigrates from Mexico.

17. A descendant of the indigenous people on the California peninsula when it belonged to Mexico.

18. A descendant of the Inuit people of Alaska.

19. An Italian settler whose ancestors are from the North African port in Tunisia that was considered part of Italy.

20. A person whose heritage you don't know.

ANA NZINGA
The King of Queens

Historical revisionists and people who jog in place at stoplights often dismiss the impact of white supremacy and slavery by smugly reminding others that Africans enslaved their fellow Africans. While this is a simplistic summary of how colonialism works, the "20. and odd" enslaved Africans who arrived on the *White Lion* in 1619 were probably from the Ndongo Kingdom in present-day Angola.[1] Five years later, Ana Nzinga's actions would disrupt the business of the original slave traders.

After the death of her father, King Kiluanji of Ndongo, Nzinga's brother had her sterilized and ordered her son to be killed so she would not become queen. Nzinga fled to nearby Matamba, but when her brother realized he couldn't defeat the Portuguese on his own, he begged Nzinga to negotiate a treaty.

She agreed, and when she arrived to meet the Portuguese governor, they used a common tactic to belittle her: offering her a floor mat while the European leaders looked down on her from their chairs. Unfazed, Nzinga ordered a member of her court to get on all fours and sat on his back, placing herself at their level to negotiate the treaty. Although the treaty didn't end the trade of enslaved human beings altogether, it required the removal of Portuguese forts that facilitated the slave trade.

Of course, being the colonizers that they were, the Portuguese reneged on the agreement and continued to take "slaves and precious items" from the Ndongo. After her brother died, Nzinga had her brother's son, the heir to the throne, killed. And when her rival, Hari, teamed up with the Portuguese enslavers and declared that a woman could never control the kingdom, Nzinga fled to Matamba. She slowly increased the size of her army, kidnapped their queen and the queen's daughter, and eventually returned to Ndongo to take her throne. By 1648, Nzinga was the ruler of the Ndongo and the Matamba.

She called herself the king.[2]

Researchers say Nzinga defied gender norms by deciding to "become a man." Not only did she dress in traditional male attire, but she also required her stable of husbands to dress as women.

When the Portuguese declared war, she personally led her troops into battle and was by all accounts a fearless warrior and exceptional tactician. Using guerrilla warfare and implementing the war strategy of the Imbangala, Nzinga fought the Portuguese to a standstill for thirty years, all the while expanding her empire. In doing so, she also declared that any African enslaved by Europeans would be free in her kingdom.

When she defeated a neighboring army, she would integrate the conquered troops and force the leaders to teach her armies all their tactics, essentially creating an unstoppable force. After conquering a new land, Nzinga only had one rule for her subjects:

No slave trading.

Of course, this wasn't just an act of benevolence. As Nzinga's empire grew, she also depleted the Portuguese supply of human chattel, which crippled their slave economy while diminishing their army.

On November 24, 1657, the Portuguese gave up.[3]

They gave Nzinga the rights to all the land and agreed to a peace treaty. She spent the rest of her life resettling slaves, establishing trade, and reestablishing her kingdom. Nzinga lived until the age of eighty-one. After her death, Portugal eventually reinstated its claim. Eight years later, Ndongo became part of the Portuguese Empire, but the descendants of the "Mother of Angola" would resist colonialism forever.

THE UNENSLAVING OF JEMMY

A t daybreak on Sunday, September 9, 1739, twenty or so Africans gathered at the Stono River, about twenty miles from Charleston. At least nineteen were Angolan, and their acknowledged leader was a man named Jemmy. Despite being thousands of miles from the West African region where he was born, Jemmy had a warped familiarity with the environment: the climate, soil, and topography of South Carolina were similar to his homeland, as were the people. At the time, only fifteen thousand of the state's forty-five thousand citizens were white, so even in America, Jemmy was surrounded by Black faces.[1] His status as a warrior, a fearless leader, and a fellow African convinced his co-conspirators that they could overcome all the wrath and retribution that all the white gods could summon. They held the power.

Before his capture, Jemmy could not have fathomed such an inhumane institution as the enslavement system that lay beyond the horizon of the African coast. Even though there was slavery in Africa, America's version was intergenerational, unending, and, by definition, reduced humans to a form of animate chattel. Although he was now a bondservant who was likely literate in at least three languages, including English, Portuguese, and his native tongue, some historians believe Jemmy probably served as

a Kongol or Angolan warrior who was captured and sold during
an incursion with a neighboring kingdom. He was likely trained
in combat, strategy, and the tactics of war. Jemmy was a leader.
He was a man. He was a human being. Above all, Jemmy was
not a slave.

Plus, Jemmy knew things. Jemmy knew that a recent
malaria outbreak had decimated Charleston. His linguistic
flexibility allowed him to communicate without fear of the
uneducated white men who knew nothing of rice or cattle. This
ability to speak Portuguese meant he probably understood the
Spanish agents sneaking through plantations, spreading rumors
that enslaved people would be free if they could make it to the
free Black community of Fort Mose in Spanish Florida. Jemmy
the Rebel knew that the healthy white Charlestonians would
be in church on Sunday for the annual Feast of the Nativity of
Mary. He knew that South Carolina had just passed a law that
required every free white man to carry a firearm. He also knew
the law wouldn't go into effect for two more weeks. He knew a
just God would eventually give him freedom. He knew the white
men never would.

But Jemmy could not wait for God or white men. He didn't
just want to be free himself. Jemmy wanted *everyone to be free*. And
Jemmy had a plan.

Jemmy's crew met before daybreak on September 9, 1739,
and knew exactly where they were going. After crossing the
Stono Bridge, they broke into a hardware store and armory that
sold guns and munitions. They executed the two shopkeepers,
decapitated them, confiscated the firearms, and kept things
moving. The group proceeded to the plantation owned by the
Godfrey family, killing the owner and his two children. When
they arrived at Wallace's Tavern before dawn, they didn't
murder the innkeeper, because, according to Jemmy's co-
conspirators, Wallace was "a good man and kind to his slaves."[2]

He would be the only white man spared.

By daybreak, the makeshift army had traveled only three
miles of the 150 to Fort Mose, and yet the group had doubled

in size. Some of their newly emancipated cohorts had joined voluntarily, while others were conscripted into teaming up with the rebels to keep the news from spreading. By eleven o'clock, somewhere between sixty and one hundred Africans were on the prowl, flying a banner, playing drums, dancing, and chanting, "Liberty." People who were lucky enough to escape the group's wrath reported that the rebels were drunk, unaware that war dancing was a form of communication in the West African military tradition that had survived by embedding itself in the Gullah-Geechee culture.

By late afternoon, after traveling ten miles, the troops paused in an open field before crossing the Edisto River, likely calculating that word of their previous handiwork would cause other enslaved Africans to join their ranks during the night. They weren't worried about being caught. They had killed every white man who laid eyes on them, except for one who spotted them just before noon. They had chased him, but he was on horseback and escaped. Unfortunately, the "one guy" who got away was William Bull, the lieutenant governor of South Carolina.

When an impromptu white militia summoned by Bull found the self-freed slaves, a battle broke out.[*] Twenty whites were killed, and at least thirty of the Black militia died, while others were captured, imprisoned, and interrogated. The murdered insurgents were decapitated and their heads affixed to posts entering the city—a practice that would become an American tradition.

The incident inspired fear across South Carolina. For months, wives and daughters of slaveowners were moved out of the state. The state assembly raised a special patrol along the Stono River and offered rewards to natives if they captured escaped Africans, but their efforts were largely unsuccessful. One of the initial twenty leaders remained at large for at least twenty years.

The Stono Rebellion changed the face of slavery in the slave capital of the world and, by proxy, in America as a whole.

---

[*] *Not break-dancing.*

As a result of it, whites temporarily paused the slave trade for a decade, blaming the violence on the fact that these rebels were born in Africa. In its wake, white entrepreneurs formed a new industry by creating American-born slaves. Masters encouraged reproduction among the slaves they already owned, while slave traders traveled the country buying human beings from estate sales, auctions, and indebted enslavers. When the transatlantic slave trade eventually reopened, they avoided the Congo-Angola region because, the geniuses concluded, it wasn't the brutal idea of perpetual, intergenerational human bondage that had caused Jemmy and his friends to lash out. Apparently, it was geography.

Perhaps the most significant legacy of Jemmy's war were the draconian measures the legislature put forth to replace South Carolina's 1696 slave code. The post-Stono legislation forbade slaves from growing their own food, earning money, learning to write, or gathering in groups of three or more. It prohibited Black males from traveling together in groups of seven or more without the presence of a white man. It also gave owners the right to kill any enslaved person who was rebellious, and went as far as to regulate which colors and fabrics an enslaved Black person could wear. It was a legal code of complete and total oppression. Because white people were the minority, South Carolina's white population used cruelty as a tool to suppress their worst fears.

Nearly every state's laws governing the enslaved were based, in part, on the Negro Act of 1740, proving that the uniquely American version of human subjugation was never just a thoughtless experiment. It was ingrained in the fabric of America. It was intentional: a color-coded, never-ending, legally protected, constitutionally enshrined system of human trafficking that extorted labor, intellectual property, and talent in the most brutal way imaginable. It was born out of fear and white supremacy. And yet with all the enlightened philosophies, whips, and muskets this country could muster . . .

It still could not make a slave.

HOW WHITE PEOPLE WERE INVENTED

n his essay "The Souls of White Folk," W. E. B. Du Bois said:

The discovery of personal whiteness among the world's peoples is a very modern thing—a nineteenth and twentieth century matter, indeed. The ancient world would have laughed at such a distinction. The Middle Age regarded skin color with mild curiosity; and even up into the eighteenth century we were hammering our national manikins into one, great, Universal Man, with fine frenzy which ignored color and race even more than birth. Today we have changed all that, and the world in a sudden, emotional conversion has discovered that it is white and by that token, wonderful![1]

For most of human history, the term "race" didn't exist. It emerged in the late sixteenth century to describe a type of thing, including a "race of wine," or a "race of saints." Before then, every culture on the planet had their own stratification. Europeans considered Asians to be "white." Even when Enlightenment-era philosophers began categorizing species, they subdivided humans by geographic regions . . . Until white people needed slaves. That's when, according to professor Gregory Jay, "Whiteness . . . emerged as what we now call a 'pan-ethnic' category, as a way of merging a variety of European ethnic populations into a single 'race.'"[2]

Just as Carl Linnaeus provided the standard for the classification of plants in *Systema Naturae*, François Bernier developed the first comprehensive classification of humans. In a 1684 French journal article, Bernier used an old term to describe his theory on human taxonomy. The article was titled "Nouvelle division de la terre, par les différentes espèces ou races d'hommes qui l'habitant," which translates to "A New Division of Earth by the Different Species or Races Who Inhabit It." In 1775, Friedrich Blumenbach's *On the Natural Varieties of Mankind* created five different divisions of humanity, with "Caucasians" at the top.

But even then, whiteness wasn't clearly defined. The first iteration of white supremacy was more about everyone else. In 1705, Virginia banned criminals and "any negro, mulatto or Indian" from holding office.[3] Now that you have the backstory, it is easy to see the lineage. Personally, James Madison "thought it wrong to admit in the Constitution the idea that there could be property in men."[4] But in *Federalist* No. 54, he debates the very value of Black life and concludes:

> *The federal Constitution, therefore, decides with great propriety on the case of our slaves, when it views them in the mixed character of persons and of property. This is in fact their true character . . . It is the character bestowed on them by the laws under which they live; and it will not be denied, that these are the proper criterion; because it is only under the pretext that the laws have transformed the negroes into subjects of property.*

White supremacy soon became one of the foundational principles of America. For instance, have you ever wondered why each item in the Bill of Rights is an *amendment* instead of a part of the Constitution? It's because Madison didn't think the Constitution needed one since, according to Locke and the rest of the Enlightenment faves, the important rights were universal and God-given. But Virginia refused to ratify the Constitution without one. Patrick Henry, one of the largest human traffickers in Virginia, had already helped craft his state's Declaration of Rights, worried that the new federal army could arm Black soldiers or—even worse—free their slaves!

"In this state there are two hundred and thirty-six thousand blacks, and there are many in several other states," said Henry during Virginia's ratification debate. "May they not think that these call for the abolition of slavery? May they not pronounce all slaves free, and will they not be warranted by that power?"[5]

Madison borrowed, conceded, and quelled fears of Black retaliation by adapting George Mason's writings in the Virginia constitution to form the Second Amendment to the U.S. Constitution: "A well-regulated Militia, being necessary to the security of a free State, the right of the people to keep and bear Arms, shall not be infringed."

A year after ratification, the 1790 Naturalization Act further cemented the supremacy of whiteness by limiting American citizenship to any "free white person . . . of good character." And if you think the concept was limited to Southern states or slaves, nope. This adoption of white supremacy was found up and down the coast. In 1821, New York changed its constitution to take away the right to vote from free Black citizens. Delegate Samuel Young justified the change with Enlightenment race theory, explaining, "The minds of the blacks are not competent to vote."[6] Delegate Peter Livingston asked if Black people "have intelligence to discern, or purity of principle to exercise, with safety, that important right."[7] Even the Supreme Court agreed. In the 1857 *Dred Scott v. Sandford* case, the court ruled that Black people "are not included, and were not intended to be included, under the word 'citizens' in the Constitution," adding:

> They were at that time considered as a subordinate and inferior class of beings who had been subjugated by the dominant race, and, whether emancipated or not, yet remained subject to their authority, and had no rights or privileges . . . They had for more than a century before been regarded as beings of an inferior order, and altogether unfit to associate with the white race either in social or political relations, and so far inferior that they had no rights which the white man was bound to respect.[8]

Notice, the Supreme Court said this about *all Black people*—not just slaves. White supremacy is a foundational principle of America.

This line of thinking was further extended in 1924, when the Racial Integrity Act of Virginia defined a white person as a person "who has no trace whatsoever of any blood other than Caucasian," forever establishing the "one drop" rule. Still, it was almost impossible to accurately define whiteness. At one time, the Irish weren't considered white. Or Jews. Or Italians. They were only accepted into the club when they proved they could join in the oppression of people who were not like them. At one time, Hispanic people were not white. Now there are "white Hispanics" and "non-white Hispanics."

It's a beautiful magic trick.

Even Du Bois thought so. As he explained, "But what on earth is whiteness that one should so desire it? Then always, somehow, some way, silently but clearly, I am given to understand that whiteness is the ownership of the earth forever and ever, Amen!"

This is where I disagree with Du Bois. Whiteness is not a social construct, nor is it as eternal or as confident as it seems. Whiteness is fleeting. It is a ghost; a shadow of an imaginary thing. It is the result of an insecurity that not only justifies man's inhumanity to man, it reinforces the subconscious doubt in one's own inferiority. Superiority does not require subjugation. A superior human being has no need.

But what on earth is whiteness?

Whiteness is fear.

4

SURVIVAL AND RESISTANCE

THE BLACK AMERICAN REVOLUTION

This is the story of survival, a great escape, and how one young boy summoned the courage to fight tyranny against a racist chicken.

Though you may scoff at the notion of a racist chicken, you were not there when a neighbor's rooster terrorized my cousins Reggie and Metia for two years. I don't know if that craven cock woke up and waited at the end of that dirt road all morning, or if he used the alarm clock embedded in the soul of all roosters, but every day, when the Kershaw County, South Carolina, school bus dropped them off at their bus stop, that chicken would be waiting for them, head bobbing, chest poked out, ready to chase them home. And trust me, he had perfect attendance . . . until Eric started going to school.

Eric was the youngest of my aunt Marvell's children and had heard the frightening accounts of the foul fowl long before he entered kindergarten.* Because he wasn't as fleet of foot as his older siblings, he concocted a plan for his first day of school. He brought some crackers, hoping to appease the farm foe with the free saltines. And it worked! The chicken stopped chasing them. It waited at the top of the road for its afternoon snack, and then would blithely let them amble home.

---

* *My grandmother Marvell's oldest daughter was also named Marvell. Yes, I have an "Aunt Junior."*

Eric had saved his sister and brother from the prospect of a vicious eye-pecking. But of course, his plan was not foolproof. Unaware of Eric's barnyard pacification plan, my aunt Marvell kept her normal cracker-purchasing regimen. So when Eric woke up one bright and sunny morning to discover that the family was out of ransom Ritz, he didn't know what to do.

He didn't tell Metia or Reggie, because he figured that his brother Reggie, a five-time champion in the underground elementary school knuckle-fighting circuit, would pluck him in the back of the head or, even worse, on the tip of the earlobe. And he knew Metia would yell at him and call him names. She would yell at him and call him names regardless, but he couldn't imagine the names she would summon if he didn't keep that racist rooster off their tail. On the way home from school that day, Eric was eerily quiet. He had no course of action. He couldn't tell anyone. As the bus pulled up to their stop, he could see that cock-a-doodle bully waiting and watching. It was dinnertime. As Eric walked down the stairs and the bird inched closer, Metia noticed something was wrong and began to panic. "Get the crackers, Eric!" she yelled. "Get the crackers!"

Reggie knew what was up. There was no time for plucking around, so he hopped off the bus and ran like the devil. But Metia, wearing plastic jellies and a jean skirt, knew there was no hope of escaping this birdwrath. She began to pray. She pleaded with the chicken, whose beady eyes signaled fury, hate, and hunger (or maybe that's how chickens looked every day). She begged her brother to get the crackers. *Please get the crackers.* But on this day, there would be no crackers.

But, as with all oppressed people, there will come a breaking point, when push meets shove. This was that day for Eric. He could not run like Reggie. He would not hope for divine intervention like Metia. Instead, Eric decided to fight. That courageous kindergartner cousin of mine stood toe-to-claw with that dastardly piece of poultry, pulled off the belt from around his waist, and swung it with the fury of a thousand Marvells. From that day forward, Eric would need no crackers. He had freed his family from barnyard brutality forever.

In a cracker-related incident nine decades earlier, ten days before Kwanzaa in 1773, a secret organization called the Sons of Liberty staged a riot against a new parliamentary law that was messing around with their source of tea.* When the British government heard about the disturbance, they sent soldiers to quell the discord. Then came the Intolerable Acts—laws that weren't *slavery*-level intolerable, but were about matters as inconvenient as high-priced tea or taxation without representation.† A few months later, after more riots, looting, and gang violence,‡ the British decided to send a few goons to instill law and order. The American Revolution had begun. Muskets, fighting, you know the spiel. The plot climaxed when the white men banded together and wrote a declaration to the white man who was oppressing them, before more musket-related fighting ensued.

Whether it was the French and Indian War, the unthinkable prospect of natives living on their own land, or whining about a lack of liberty while their slaves battled South Carolina mosquitos, yellow fever, and ornery mistresses on air-conditioning-less South Carolina rice plantations, white people were always grabbing their muskets to go fight about something. But this time, while the white people were off fighting, the Black American population saw an opportunity where none previously existed: they now had a chance to *get free*.

To understand the story of the War of Independence from the perspective of an African in America, one must first realize that prior to this era, the idea of American patriotism was all but nonexistent, because *there was no America*. Remember, there was a South Carolina, a Virginia, and other British colonies, but each had its own unique laws and social structures. The only thing that bound these respective groups of white people together for this war was their increasing discontent with their privileged overlords overseas. Such was the case for Black people in this land far from any homelands: oppressed and disenfranchised, they had no allegiance to either set of white people in this quarrel. Just like my belt-wielding cousin's relationship with oppressively aggressive chickens, enslaved people just wanted to be left alone. The causes of the conflict were inconsequential; the freedoms the whites were fighting for had little bearing on their day-to-day. But

---

* *As you can see, crackers are very important in American history.*
† *Back then, White America was very adamant about low taxes. It was a simpler time.*
‡ *To be fair, nonviolent protest hadn't been invented yet.*

it was a springboard for a very particular type of rebellion. Their every action during the Revolution can be summed up in two distinct motives: survival and resistance.

When it is taught in schools, the American Revolution is described as having been born out of the white man's indignation about how he was being governed. And sure, all that stuff about tea and taxes definitely riled up the colonists. But while that was all going down, a rumor was spreading through the colonies that *really* provoked their anger: allegedly, England was going to outlaw the practice of owning human beings.

The rumor had some backing to it. Some years prior, in 1771, James Somerset, an enslaved African, had escaped from a Massachusetts customs officer while they were traveling in England. Somerset was recaptured by his master, Charles Stewart, who tried to sell Somerset to a Jamaican plantation. Instead of complying, Somerset resisted and filed a case arguing that slavery was not legally enforced by British law, which made him a British citizen like everyone else. In 1772, the Court of King's Bench ruled on the case of *Somerset v. Stewart* that slavery wasn't *illegal*, but it wasn't enforceable by law. Since Stewart couldn't produce a contract, the court could not say that "the cause set forth by this return is allowed or approved of by the laws of this kingdom." Therefore Somerset "the black must be discharged."[1] Upon hearing the news, at least a dozen enslaved Africans in Massachusetts petitioned British courts for their freedom, while dozens others just absconded, taking the chance while the legality was being debated. In Augusta, Virginia, slaveowner Gabriel Jones advertised for his missing captive Bacchus, whom Jones surmised would "attempt to get on Board some Vessel bound for Great Britain, from the knowledge he has of the late Determination of *Somerset's Case*."[2] The rumors of British abolition fueled the snowballing sentiment across the colonies that London would "cheat an honest American of his slave,"[3] though in actuality, the case had little effect beyond Massachusetts.

Early in the British-American conflict, some enslaved Black men, like Peter Salem, who was emancipated to serve in the Framingham, Massachusetts, militia, fought for the white men to obtain his freedom. Others, like William Lee, who was the "favorite slave" of

George Washington, were involuntarily enlisted by their owners. But these men were part of individual state militias, each with their own set of rules. When it came time for the Continental Congress to create a national army, Southern gentlemen couldn't bear the thought of fighting alongside the men they considered less than human.

On July 10, 1775, seven days after George Washington became commander in chief of the new Continental Army formed from the disparate militias, he instructed his adjutant general to ban Blacks from fighting, as it would be seen as an embarrassment. That month, General Horatio Gates wrote the Continental Army's recruiters, "You are not to enlist any deserter from the ministerial army, nor any stroller, Negro, or vagabond, or person suspected of being an enemy of the liberty of America."[4] By November, all the Black soldiers who served in state militias were kicked out, so that a new all-white army would be fighting for America by the time the white people signed their Declaration of Independence in 1776.

The British, however, saw America's enslaved population as a tactical advantage. Not only could conscripting them prevent the Brits from having to import soldiers from across the ocean, but the economic impact of this maneuver could function as an embargo on the agrarian class. After receiving an arse-whipping by the American militia in ungentlemanlike guerrilla warfare at Lexington and Concord in April 1775, the Brits realized that they would need a few more thugs on their team. So three days after the April brouhaha in Massachusetts, Virginia's royal governor, John Murray, 4th Earl of Dunmore, declared martial law and seized the local militia's armory in Williamsburg, declaring that it belonged to the Royal Crown.*

You know how Virginians are about their guns, so once someone had their hands on the firearms, they figured that the governor's next step would be to confiscate their human property. Murray, a slave-owner himself, had no such actual intentions, but an angry white mob ran him out of the Governor's Palace regardless. In retaliation, on November 7, 1775, Governor Murray of Virginia, struck a blow: "all *indented servants, Negroes,* or others (appertaining to rebels)" would be

---

* *Not the Crown Royal. It was not in a purple velvet bag.*

declared "*free*, that are able and willing to bear arms, they *joining his Majesty's troops*, as soon as may be, for the more speedily reducing this Colony to a *proper sense* of their duty, to his Majesty's crown and dignity."[5]

Lord Dunmore knew that the idea of armed slaves[*] exacting revenge on their masters would scare the bejeezus out of the wig-wearing colonists. In an even more bubblegut inspiring move, the governor formed the eponymous Lord Dunmore's Ethiopian Regiment, a British military unit composed of African freedom fighters. Perhaps the Ethiopian Regiment's uniforms, featuring sashes inscribed with the words "Liberty to Slaves," most aptly described the self-freed warriors' revolutionary position.

The formerly enslaved Colonel Titus Cornelius was typical of the Ethiopian Regiment's legendary troops. Shortly after his twenty-first birthday, Colonel "Tye" tied up a few pieces of clothes with a string and vamoosed from John Corlie's New Jersey property to Virginia the day after a local newspaper published Dunmore's proclamation. Upon arriving, he enlisted in Dunmore's all-Black regiment, capturing the captain of the Monmouth militia during one of his first times on the battlefield. Major General William Franklin (the acknowledged illegitimate son of Benjamin Franklin)[†] noticed Tye's skills as a soldier and promoted him to the leader of the Black Brigade, a group of elite guerrilla fighters stationed in New Jersey. Under Tye's direction, the integrated group burned down the houses of Patriots, stole cattle, and freed slaves from white Patriots. Tye was particular about his targets, who were mostly slaveowners and military leaders,[6] and he was strategic: freeing the enslaved not only gave him a network of allies and spies, but it also enlarged his crew with soldiers who were familiar with the terrain. The Quakers in the New Jersey countryside were terrified of this "regiment of negroes who are fitted for and inclined towards barbarities, are lacking in human feeling and are familiar with every corner of the country."[7] Of course, Black men using guerrilla tactics for the sake of their freedom was *totally* different

---

[*] *The number of enslaved Africans who reached Lord Dunmore varies from three hundred to five thousand because some just ran away.*

[†] *Yes, Ben Franklin was a deadbeat dad.*

from the so-called Patriots' use of guerrilla tactics for the sake of white men's freedom. Apparently warfare was far more barbaric than the American system of slavery. But who's counting?

George Washington was counting. The prowess of the Ethiopian Regiment and Black Loyalists made General Washington and other colonial leaders rethink their "no negroes" rule. By January 1777, the white Patriots had begun to send their enslaved men to fight in their stead in local militia skirmishes, and Surgeon General Benjamin Rush privately wrote Patrick Henry suggesting that Washington should be replaced as commander in chief for his intransigence. After losing twenty of his own enslaved to the British, Washington finally relented and permitted free Blacks to serve in the Continental Army, later allowing each colony to handle its own recruiting.

In January 1778, still desperate for manpower, the Continental Congress suggested that states should consider allowing the enslaved to serve in the Patriot army, a prospect that was "received with great resentment as a very dangerous and impolitic step" in South Carolina in particular.[8] Considering the history of revolt in the state, arming Black people was the last thing they needed. In Northern states, many of the states integrated their already-existing forces, though some were majority Black, like Rhode Island's First Regiment, which is considered the first Black American military unit. The Rhode Island legislature guaranteed freedom for all enslaved men who fought in the Revolution, a move soon followed by other states, including Virginia, the ground zero for American-style slavery.

England then set its eye on quelling the rebellious colonies by capturing one of the wealthiest, most important cities in all of America: Charleston. With its harbor, the rice export, the trade economy, and the colonies' dependence on its food supply, Chucktown was an economic powerhouse—and the Brits knew that losing it would deliver a devastating blow to the colonists.

The first British invasion attempt came in June 1776. When the British attacked Charleston, so many white men emerged from the colony's backwoods to protect the headquarters of American slavery that the redcoats were forced to retreat. The English soldiers and their Northern Loyalists were unaccustomed to the Lowcountry heat, but they would not give up. After another skirmish, the British had an idea. On June 30, 1779, British General Henry Clinton, stationed at Philipsburgh, proclaimed:

> *Whereas the enemy have adopted a practice of enrolling NEGROES among their Troops, I do hereby give notice That all NEGROES taken in arms, or upon any military Duty, shall be purchased for the public service at a stated Price; the money to be paid to the Captors.*
>
> *But I do most strictly forbid any Person to sell or claim Right over any NEGROE, the property of a Rebel, who may take Refuge with any part of this Army: And I do promise to every NEGROE who shall desert the Rebel Standard, full security to follow within these Lines, any Occupation which he shall think proper.*[9]

Because Charleston was the "slave capital of the New World," nearly twenty-five thousand Black people unenslaved themselves, most of whom joined the British forces. In Charleston, many became part of Clinton's infamous all-Black military unit, the Black Pioneers.[10] The Black soldiers were acclimated to the heat and ready to fight. Some of them were integrated into other units, such as Colonel Stephen Blucke, who succeeded Colonel Tye as the leader of the Black Brigade.

In the South, most of the slave defectors joined the side that offered them the chance for self-preservation, which just happened to be the guys in the red coats. Take Boston King, for instance. King was born in the Palmetto State to a literate enslaved woman from Africa in 1760. When the British took control of Charleston in 1780, King was working as a carpenter and a cowboy twenty-eight miles outside the city. He went to visit his parents in Charleston one day and another servant stole his horse and stayed away two days. King had already suffered a cruel beating after someone wrongly accused him of stealing nails, so he knew what would happen if he returned to his place of service after being missing for two days. Instead, he offered his services to the English.

Soon after he enlisted, King caught smallpox and the English left him for dead. Luckily, the American troops were so afraid of smallpox that he was able to recover and rejoin the British Army. During a tour of Charleston, the Brits left him behind again while he was visiting another formerly enslaved smallpox survivor. Captured by a Loyalist deserter, King feigned interest in being reenslaved until he was able to plot his escape—but not before he burned down the turncoat's plantation and stole fifty horses. His bravery earned him a post as the personal servant of a British officer, who then became captain, then a commanding officer. When his English superior officer dispatched King on a secret mission on horseback to deliver a message to other Loyalists, King rejected the offer for a horse and traveled by foot. Had he been caught, he would have been re-reenslaved. Instead, he delivered the secret message, was rewarded three shillings for successfully completing the mission, and joined the crew of a British naval vessel that was eventually captured *again*.

While he was imprisoned at a detainment facility on the shore of a New Jersey river and threatened with re-re-reenslavement, King escaped into the river at low tide and walked to New York. By 1783, the United States had won in the championship round of the American Revolution playoffs and Southern slaveowners were convening in New York to find their escaped property. During his incarceration, however, King wrote a letter that convinced a British officer to allow him on a ship that was transplanting Black Loyalists to Nova Scotia in Canada as payment for their military service.[11] King made it safely and eventually began preaching to a congregation in Halifax until he accepted England's offer to help formerly enslaved Africans of Nova Scotia start a settlement in Freetown, Sierra Leone. King would spend the rest of his life preaching throughout West Africa and England.

King was one of an estimated one hundred thousand Africans who temporarily or permanently escaped enslavement during the Revolutionary War—as many as escaped on the Underground Railroad during its entire history of existence.[12] Twenty-five thousand escapees were from South Carolina alone. This mass self-emancipation worked specifically *because* the slaves who freed themselves were not loyal to a team. As early Black historian George W. Williams wrote in 1883, when people spoke of Black patriotism in the American Revolution, "Negroes were rated as chattel property by both armies and both governments during the entire war. This is the cold fact of history, and it is not pleasing to contemplate. The Negro occupied the anomalous position of an American slave and an American soldier. He was a soldier in the hour of danger, but a chattel in time of peace."[13]

These African warriors were as useful to the cause of American liberty as slaves were to the cause of American wealth. Just as they had become tools of the white man, so had they become the white man's fighting forces. While they sought the opportunity for freedom, they were hoodwinked into hitching their stars to patriotism or loyalty, as Du Bois noted in *The Gift of Black Folk*:

> *He used his own judgment and he fought because he believed that by fighting for America he would gain the respect of the land and personal and spiritual freedom. His problem as a soldier was always peculiar: no matter for what America fought and no matter for what her enemies fought, the American Negro always fought for his own freedom and for the self-respect of his race. Whatever the cause of war, therefore, his cause was peculiarly just. He appears, therefore, in American wars always with double motive,—the desire to oppose the so-called enemy of his country along with his fellow white citizens, and before that, the motive of deserving well of those citizens and securing justice for his folk.[14]*

From the arrival of the *White Lion* and the *Treasurer* to the second that you are reading these words, these two congruent themes of survival and resistance describe the existence of being Black in what is now America. The goal was never to become American, but to live, and live freely. To become and remain whole human beings. "The history of the American Negro is this strife," wrote Du Bois. "This longing to attain self-conscious manhood, to merge his double self into a better and true self."[15] At the dawn of the battle for American independence, Black people in the colonies had a glimpse of liberty, and they looked to extend that moment for eternity.

FEAR OF A BLACK NATION

When comparing them side by side, the story of the American Revolution ain't got nothing on the Haitian Revolution. For Black people, Haiti represents the most beautiful story of strength, resistance, and freedom that has ever been told. It is the story of a people who thrust off the chains of bondage and took their liberty from the hands of their oppressors.

For others, Haiti is a tragedy. But when discussing anything having to do with the country of Haiti, we should never forget that every bit of struggle in Haiti is related to the legacy of slavery, capitalism, and American hypocrisy. Whenever the country is enveloped in unrest or described as a "s**thole" country, it is important for us to remember that Haiti currently and has historically suffered from a worldwide collusion between America and European countries intent on making the tropical paradise fail. To blame Haiti's problems on white people is not a harebrained hypothesis. Yes, Haiti is poor. Yes, there is widespread government corruption in the country. But there is also one other unignorable fact: America did this.

We know Christopher Columbus was a lightweight scammer who never set foot on the North American continent—he landed on what is now Haiti, which was later renamed Hispaniola by eventual Spanish colonizers. In *A Pest in the Land: New World Epidemics in a Global Perspective*, Suzanne Alton writes that most historians estimate the population of the island of Hispaniola was around half a million to one million people when Columbus's fleet arrived. Columbus immediately took possession of the island, began redirecting the native Taíno people's food and resources to the Europeans, and enslaved the natives, eventually killing the population with disease and brutality in what is described as "surely the greatest tragedy in the history of the human species."[1]

Twenty-five years after Columbus set foot in the place we now call Haiti, less than fourteen thousand Taíno were alive.[2] So the Spanish began importing African labor, believing them to be more sturdy workers. By the time the French took control of one-third of the island and established the colony of French Saint-Domingue (or Santo Domingo), there were zero natives, twenty-five thousand Europeans, twenty-two thousand free coloreds, and seven hundred thousand African slaves, according to the French census.[3] By 1789, Saint-Domingue had become the most profitable outpost of the French Empire, producing 60 percent of the world's coffee and 40 percent of the sugar imported by Britain and France, two of the biggest colonial empires on the planet.

Around the world, the concept of revolution had gone viral. North of the island, the germ had caused a rebellion that created a brand-new country called the United States of America. A revolution was happening in France, too. Thomas Paine, one of America's Enlightenment thinkers, was publishing articles defending political revolutions called *The Rights of Man*, asserting that freedom was a universal right that all human beings deserved. That spirit of rebellion, revolution, and the offering of "deez hands" was about to show itself in Haiti.

On August 14, 1791, a tropical storm was bearing down on the island when a group of enslaved Africans met in the Bwa Kayiman (Alligator Forest) to hold a secret ceremony. Historical accounts would later call this meeting a "voudou ceremony" and refer to the attendees as "slaves." Had these freedom-seeking Africans been white, we would call them "founding fathers" who were planning a revolution.

Enslaved voudou priest Dutty Boukman, a large, warrior-like man who was either kidnapped from Senegambia or born in Jamaica, led the meeting, alongside priestess Cecile Fatiman, an actual princess whose father was likely a Corsican prince. In the driving rain, with the thunder as her drum, Fatiman danced under the lantern of the lightning, holding a long, sharp knife above her head while the others lay facedown in the mud, repeating her words. Fatiman used her knife to slit open the neck of a stout black pig and offered a sip of the warm porcine lifeblood to everyone present[4] while Dutty gave his version of the Declaration of Independence:

> *The Good Lord who created the sun which gives us light from above, who rouses the sea and makes the thunder roar—listen well, all of you—this god, hidden in the clouds, watches us. He sees all that the white man does. The god of the white man calls him to commit crimes; our god asks for good deeds. But this god who is so good orders revenge! He will direct our hands; he will aid us. Throw away the image of the god of the whites who thirsts for our tears and listen to the voice of liberty which speaks in the hearts of all of us.[5]*

The meeting adjourned, and the representatives of enslaved Africans returned to their plantations to tell the others about the event they had been planning for months. A week later, eighteen hundred slave concentration camps would be burned to the ground, and more than a thousand plantation owners would suffer the same fate as that unfortunate hog. The rebels in Haiti were not concerned with taxation, representation, or tea. They were fighting for the universal freedom that all men desire: liberty, straight up.

While most historians agree that the stormy exercise in democracy was the genesis of the Haitian Revolution, it was also the largest slave rebellion in the history of the *world*.

Contrary to most assumptions, the enslaved revolutionaries did not consider their rebellion against slavery as a rebellion against France: no, they were fighting for Black people. The racial hierarchy in Haiti was more complex than just skin color, and it involved four separate classes:

GRANDS BLANCS: The white planter class was the wealthiest of Haiti's enslavers and usually owned multiple slaves and large plantations.

PETITS BLANCS: They were just as white as the planters, but not as rich. Many were shopkeepers, artisans, teachers, and small business owners. Because these categories were not officially defined, it is impossible to accurately estimate the *petit blanc* population, but Haiti's combined white population numbered about forty thousand.

FREE PEOPLE OF COLOR: These were about thirty thousand people of mixed race in Haiti, many of whom were children of white Frenchmen and enslaved women. French enslavers often emancipated their mixed-race children. Many were wealthy and were often more pro-slavery than the *petits blancs.*

SLAVES: Numbering about seven hundred thousand, enslaved Africans outnumbered everyone else on the island.

For months, a rumor filtered through the slave quarters that the king of France had issued a decree of emancipation that was suppressed by the colony's governor and the white ruling class, or the *grands blancs.*[*] That rumor might have been spread by Haiti's free people of color, who actually *had* been granted citizenship by the French Revolutionary Government in May 1791, only to have white colonizers refuse to comply. Therefore, free Blacks and mulattos who joined the revolt considered themselves royalists—soldiers fighting in the name of the king of France. By combining their struggle for

---

[*] *Literally, the "big whites."*

full equality with the fight for the abolition of slavery, the free people of color had turned the Haitian Revolution into a "Black thing."

In just two weeks, the rebels took a third of Saint-Domingue while the whites tried to organize their own army. That September, the slavery squad struck back, killing fifteen thousand Black fighters. Meanwhile, in France, the National Assembly realized that this group of angry free and enslaved Black warriors might actually gain control of the wealthiest colony in the Caribbean. To prevent the Black takeover, they finally granted full citizenship rights to free people of color and sent six thousand French soldiers to quell those pesky negroes. After gaining citizenship, free people of color were split into two factions. As the children, consorts, and family members of the white ruling class, many free people of color owned slaves and joined the *grands blancs* in their war to protect slavery. Others fought alongside the rebels to dismantle the system.

The revolt was not led by a single organized military leader but a collective of similarly minded freedom-seekers. François-Dominique Bréda—one of those free Black men whose citizenship had been denied—joined the rebellion in its early stages. He initially worked as a battlefield doctor, until the other rebel leaders noticed he was a master strategist and tactician. Bréda tried to negotiate a peace treaty with the white planters, offering to free their captured countrymen in exchange for modest reforms—an extra day of rest and an end to using the whip. Even though he was an educated man and willing to negotiate in good faith, the whites refused to meet with him. According to French custom, honest negotiations could only occur between equals. Therefore, dealing with a free Black man was tantamount to an admission of equality.

Before that snub, Bréda's main goal had been to end the war and become a French citizen. He was not necessarily concerned with eradicating the practice of slavery and considered himself a soldier for the king. However, in 1792, others began to notice a change in the military leader's language. He had started using words like "freedom," "equality," and "emancipation." By 1793, Bréda was fighting for revenge.

Soon, the largest colonial powers on the planet were easing their way into the fight for the profitable island. Napoleon was starting wars all over Europe, so Britain employed a defensive tactic that would later become a foundational principle of all hip-hop battles: "If we're beefing, then nothing is off-limits!"[*] Not-So-Great Britain had just gotten their butts kicked by the rebels in America eight years prior, and so they saw a takeover of Haiti as a way to make up for those losses. Plus, they were concerned about British property. If the Saint-Domingue revolt was successful, the slaves in Britain's nearby Jamaican colony might start getting ideas. So England sent six hundred soldiers from Jamaica, promising to help restore white supremacy if the *grands blancs* allied with England.

Spain, which controlled the city of Santo Domingo[†] in the Spanish colony next door, also wanted in on the Haitian riches and offered to ally with Bréda's forces. On August 29, 1793, disparate camps of Black warriors gathered at Spanish-controlled Camp Turel, where Bréda formally announced his rank and his new name:

> *Perhaps my name has made itself known to you. I have undertaken vengeance. I want Liberty and Equality to reign in Saint-Domingue. I am working to make that happen. Unite yourselves to us, brothers, and fight with us for the same cause.*
>
> *Your very humble and obedient servant,*
> *Toussaint Louverture[6]*

The French panicked. They had heard about this military genius who could speak Creole and French, quote Greek

---

[*] *"Thou shalt Ether"—Nas 3:16.*

[†] *The Spanish-held city of Santo Domingo is a totally different place from the French colony of Saint-Domingue. I'm trying to schedule a meeting with white people about coming up with names.*

philosophers, recite passages from the great Italian thinkers, and command an army with a mixture of guerrilla and European war tactics. The British had just captured France's principal naval base on the island, and now the Spanish were teaming up with the Black Alexander the Great? On the very same day as Louverture's Turel speech, the French bureaucrats in Haiti made an announcement of their own:

Slavery was abolished in Saint-Domingue.

Louverture still thought of himself as a French citizen and wanted his fellow soldiers to be free. But he also knew that a lowly commissioner didn't have the authority to end enslavement, suspecting it was just a tactic to keep him from allying with Spain. And what about the British? Would he have to beat them, too? Spain was intent on gaining control of the entire island and had already offered Louverture a knighthood and a salary to fight with their army. Scholars still argue whether Louverture was playing the Spanish against the French for mutual destruction, or if he was vacillating between the teams who gave him the best chance for true emancipation. In any case, Louverture turned on Spain. Toussaint was now fighting against the British, for France.

On April 29, 1794, Black soldiers killed 150 Spanish soldiers at a garrison and left a note threatening to kill all white men unless they returned to their country. Stunned, the Spanish generals accused Louverture of treason, but he wrote to them explaining that he was sick in bed when that attack happened, denying involvement. When the suspicious Spanish commander summoned Louverture to a meeting, Toussaint showed up with a posse that was slightly smaller than Beyoncé's backup dance team—150 men—asking, "What's up? I heard you had my name in your mouth?" The Spanish leader—who was essentially Louverture's commanding officer—invited Louverture to dinner a few days later, but Louverture never showed up. From then on, to make sure Louverture's loyal fighters didn't attack Spain's soldiers, the Spanish commander essentially held Louverture's wife and children hostage every time Toussaint went out to fight.

Spain had no idea why Louverture would switch sides. By now, France didn't even have a substantial number of troops on the island. He claimed it was because France had technically abolished slavery, that it was because of liberty and freedom and all that jazz, but a May 1794 letter would later reveal a different motive.

A few months earlier, Toussaint discovered that two other Black generals, both of whom had also allied with Spain, had been secretly rounding up enslaved women and children to sell to the Spanish forces. When he confronted his Spanish superior, the Spanish commander ordered Louverture to do the same, but Louverture refused. That was the moment he decided he couldn't fight with Spain. As long as the French maintained their pledge to abolition, Toussaint would fight on behalf of the French king.

In a few short months, it became clear to Spain that the Black resistance would not quit. Realizing this, the Spanish commanders packed up their things and took the first ship back home. After the Spanish withdrawal, Louverture could turn his attention toward Great Britain. The brilliant commander made light work of the world's greatest navy. On May 10, 1792, the British met with Louverture and agreed to a truce, leaving only a few soldiers in northern Saint-Domingue.

Haiti's Black freedmen posed an existential threat to slavery in the Caribbean. When Toussaint heard that the new governor of Jamaica was fearing a similar situation on his island, he sent him a letter explaining that Jamaica wasn't too far from Saint-Domingue—and he could *easily* be over there in a few days if those colonists wanted to catch some hands, too.

Jamaica's white governor responded by withdrawing all remaining British troops from Haiti, even in the areas Louverture agreed that they could keep. All told, Britain's war in Haiti cost the British Empire. Jamaica's governor was so deathly afraid of Toussaint's influence that the British Army wouldn't even allow the "Black Shot"—Black Jamaican soldiers who fought for Britain in Haiti—to "come back to Jamaica."*

In 1801, Louverture issued a constitution for the island, named himself governor-for-life, and declared independence. But while Louverture had managed to kick out the Spanish and the British, the war wasn't over—the French were still in. Napoleon Bonaparte, often ranked as one of history's greatest military leaders by people who never heard of Hannibal Barca, decided he was the only one who could seize Sainte-Domingue back from Louverture and the Black freedom fighters, and he sent his brother-in-law, Charles Leclerc, to restore French rule, along with General Donatien-Marie-Joseph de Vimeur, the viscount of Rochambeau. Rochambeau's father was a great French military strategist who had helped the United States defeat the British a few years earlier. The viscount was a great military leader in his own right, but the great Napoleon knew that Rochambeau possessed another quality that would make him valuable to Leclerc: Rochambeau hated Black people.

Leclerc and Rochambeau were stunned at the discipline and fortitude of Louverture's well-trained troops. However, in 1802, after the defection of his two top generals, who were promised positions in the French Army in exchange for their loyalty, Toussaint Louverture surrendered to the French under the condition that his soldiers would become part of the French Army and that slavery would not be reinstated. He planned to retire at his plantation, but the French had another plan. French general Jean Baptiste Brunet tricked Louverture into meeting with him, shipped him to France, and locked him in prison in the French countryside, where Louverture eventually starved to death.

---

* *Thus answering the question Inner Circle would pose two centuries later: If the Black Jamaican soldiers were indeed "bad boys," Louverture discovered, "whatcha gonna do when they come for you?"*

They joined Toussaint Louverture.

In case you're wondering, of course, the French reimposed slavery. After Louverture's capture, Leclerc died, leaving Rochambeau in charge to release his white supremacist fury on the island. And his fury knew no bounds. He decapitated any Black people not wearing a French uniform, including women and children. The "Roach" imported fifteen thousand attack dogs from Jamaica that had been trained to kill anyone who was not white. He bound and gagged captives in sacks and drowned them. Perhaps Rochambeau's most ruthless tactic was the "fumigational-sulfurous baths."[7] He marched the prisoners of war onto French ships, where he burned stockpiles of sulfur. The resulting sulfur dioxide eventually suffocated the prisoners.

The racist French general had invented the gas chamber.

But the rebels did not quit. After Louverture's capture and the other Black generals' defection to the French side, the freedom fighters resorted to guerrilla tactics. They wore the French Army down, causing them to hire Polish mercenaries as reinforcements. Sickened by the inhumanity of what Rochambeau had ordered the soldiers to do, one of Toussaint's former commanders, Jean-Jacques Dessalines, decided to abandon his position in France's army and lead the rebels. When Dessalines marched into Port-au-Prince in his French uniform, whites cheered his arrival. Dessalines waited for the applause to die down and told them that he remembered what it felt like to live as a slave. As the whites gathered around, Dessalines announced his plans to restore peace to the island:

He was going to kill all the white people.

The formerly enslaved soldier proceeded to capture and hang a hundred white people in Port-au-Prince. When Rochambeau realized that he might have to face an army that was now using white people's tactics, he advised the white people of Saint-Domingue to follow his own plan and leave. And with that—Haitians had freed themselves. The lesson would send shock waves around the world. With nothing but a knife, a pig, and relentless fortitude, Haiti's enslaved people had defeated the greatest white empires in Europe of that time.*

On January 1, 1804, Dessalines's Declaration of Independence announced that Saint-Domingue was now the first independent Black state in the Western Hemisphere. General Jean-Jacques Dessalines ordered the freedmen to destroy any Frenchman who remained on the island, announcing, "We have rendered to these true cannibals, war for war, crime for crime, outrage for outrage."[8]

The citizens of the newly freed country would forever remember the history of their brutal oppression at the hands of Europeans. Dessalines and the new citizens tossed the Spanish and French names, renaming the country in the language of the now extinct Taíno people: the island would be called Ay-ti or Haiti, meaning "the land of the mountains." Since that day, a white man has never ruled the place we now call Haiti.

Today, Haiti's legacy is often tarnished, known more for its tragedies than its rich legacy. But the reason for its impoverishment today is that America and France instituted what is possibly the most racist economic foreign policy that ever existed, and upheld it for over two centuries. They did this while other European powers watched quietly. Understanding what two of the most powerful countries in the world did to Haiti requires a suspension of disbelief, because it is so absurd that it sounds like fiction.

Two decades after Haiti gained its independence in 1804, France demanded that Haiti compensate former French slaveowners for the value of all those slaves who set themselves free. Yes, France essentially demanded reverse slave reparations. In 1825, France sent warships to Haiti and demanded 150 million francs. Not only did the United States agree with this, but it backed up France's demands for the debt on the

---

* *To be fair, Dessalines did have some help defeating the French. Although the Haitian forces were fearsome, yellow fever was as much of a threat to white people on the island as any Black soldier. While the Black and mulatto Haitians had developed immunity, yellow fever had ravaged the white soldiers since their arrival.*

international stage, imploring European countries to ignore Haiti's existence until it paid this money.

One could argue that this debt, which thrust the new nation into poverty and took 122 years to pay, was at least half the fault of the European countries who silently allowed France to enact this racist policy. One could perhaps fault America for helping France to extort Haiti. The 1823 Monroe Doctrine had explicitly stated that "any attempt by a European power to oppress or control any nation in the Western Hemisphere would be viewed as a hostile act against the United States," which America overlooked in this particular case. We just let it slide, because—let's be honest—using violence or the threat of violence to extract wealth and labor from Black people is *kinda America's thing.* America reprimanding France for stealing from Haiti would be like the Rolling Stones calling out the Beatles for appropriating Black music.

When Haiti became an independent country in 1804, white Americans just about lost it. Having just witnessed the power of a Black revolt in the Revolutionary War, the newly formed white supremacist country ruled by rich plantation owners and Northern bankers feared that the Haitian uprising would inspire Black American slaves to do the same. Furthermore, they were threatened by the idea of a tropical paradise that could produce more crops than the U.S. agrarian economy. Prominent enslaver and American president Thomas Jefferson refused to recognize the self-freed country, a tradition of ignorance that continued until 1862, when Americans decided to take a different tack. Ever the colonizers, the United States sent troops to Haiti's doorstep seventeen times between 1862 and 1915. Andrew Johnson even wanted to annex Haiti and make it part of America—that's how badly they wanted to suppress and control this region.

And if a land grab didn't work, the next best thing that America could do was to economically destroy the nation. Yes: the most egregious part of the story is that the decline of Haiti's wealth was an entirely American proposition, beginning in America's greatest superstore—the slave market.

On December 7, 1711, New York City's Common Council passed one of its earliest zoning laws. It ruled that the city's official place for selling and renting humans would be at a wooden structure near the edge of the city under a buttonwood tree. The area was protected by a rampart built by Dutch settlers, who called it "De Waal Straat." By the end of the Haitian Revolution, George Washington had been inaugurated there, and the Bill of Rights had been passed at the very same spot. Alexander Hamilton, who constructed the country's financial regulatory system, is buried not far from the spot where this slave market once stood. On this piece of property, Black bodies evolved from a simple commodity for forced labor into an asset for investment, speculation, and security, traded the same as pork bellies and crude oil.

In 1792, twenty-four of New York's wealthiest men signed the document that would create the New York Stock Exchange. To commemorate its slave-trading past, the men named the charter after the site where they exchanged souls for money. They called it the Buttonwood Agreement. The location described by the Dutch moniker eventually evolved into a simpler name: Wall Street.

That's where all of Haiti's wealth lies.

Whenever Haiti couldn't make its payments to the French, the country would take out loans, sending it deeper into poverty, because the loans could only come from French banks. Over the years, French banks lent the Caribbean nation money so often that Haiti wasn't simply repaying its original reparations debt: it was paying the loans, interests, and fees. As late as 1915, nearly 80 percent of Haiti's government revenue was paid to service its debt. And by the time it made the last payment in 1947—eighty-four years after the Emancipation Proclamation and 143 years after dismantling the shackles of its own slaveowners—Haiti was still in debt. Those payments didn't include the money that was taken by U.S. Marines when they marched into the Haitian National Bank, took $500,000, and deposited it at 111 Wall Street, New York, N.Y., for "safekeeping" during a period of unrest in 1919. The cost of German soldiers who assisted the American army in occupying Haiti from 1915 to 1934 didn't count either. Neither did the 40 percent of Haiti's national income that it was forced to pay to the United States and France when the U.S. occupiers wrote the demand into Haiti's 1918 constitution.

By 1947, Haiti wasn't even paying France: it was paying an American bank that had bought all of Haiti's debt from French banks. Located at the same 111 Wall Street, the City Bank of New York was founded in 1812 and expanded by Moses Taylor, who made his fortune by illegally importing slaves to Cuban sugar plantations after slavery was outlawed in the United States. So when Haiti made its last payment for dismantling its slavery state, it was actually paying an American bank that was built on slave trafficking—a bank owned by a man who disregarded international law to build the City Bank of New York, an entity that built its power via the institution of slavery, with money partially stolen by an international conglomerate of white soldiers who occupied Haiti.

So don't believe the current narratives about Haiti's instability being the result of poor governance or corruption. Haiti is poor because it was forced to pay 90 million francs, the contemporary equivalent of $21 billion as of 2020, including billions in interest to the City Bank of New York. You probably know the bank by its current name: Citibank.

Of course, Citibank isn't the sole culprit. One corporation alone couldn't condemn a country to two centuries of poverty in opposition to the richest and most powerful nations in the world. The white world was not just complicit in the economic destruction of Haiti, they piled on. Despite repaying the independence debt in 1947, Haiti still owed billions to other countries and the World Bank until after the 2010 Haitian earthquake, when France's president forgave Haiti's non-independence debt.

In Black America, the legacy of the Haitian Revolution would outweigh any of the country's economic or political struggles. Haiti would serve as the gold standard for Black resistance until the day America finally decided to end the constitutional erasure of its African residents' humanity. It would be whispered in slave revolts and bellowed in speeches. Free Black communities would adopt its name and enslaved communities would embrace its tactics. Through the eyes of the enslaved, the people of Haiti undertook vengeance, and liberty and equality reigned in Saint-Domingue.

Haiti won.

They are free.

THREE LITTLE QUESTIONS

1. **The "Patriots" were:**
   a. British citizens who fought for their freedom against their oppressors.
   b. Black citizens who fought for their freedom against their oppressors.
   c. Thugs who looted, rioted, and hated their country.
   d. Pro-violent protesters.

2. **The Declaration of Independence was controversial because:**
   a. When they said "all people," it was figurative.
   b. Or maybe the "Creator" is white.
   c. Or maybe Black people forgot to "declare the causes which impel them to the separation."
   d. It wasn't *unanimous* unanimous.

3. **What is the difference between a revolution and an insurrection?**
   a. "Insurrection" is harder to spell.
   b. They're the same thing.
   c. If you lose, it's an insurrection.
   d. Insurrections rarely include royal families; Prince was in the Revolution.

ACTIVITY

Split into groups of two and choose one of these debates. Debate your partner. The person with the most convincing argument will be declared the winner.

DEBATE 1: Both of you are free white people. Person A should try to convince the group that they should fight alongside the Patriots. Person B should try to convince the group that they should fight alongside the British Loyalists.

DEBATE 2: Both of you are free Black people. Person A should try to convince the group that they should fight alongside the Patriots. Person B should try to convince the group that they should fight alongside the British Loyalists.

DEBATE 3: You are both enslaved in South Carolina. Person A should try to convince the group that they should fight alongside the Patriots. Person B should try to convince the group that person A is not crazy.

5

DRAPETOMANIACS

GET FREE OR DIE TRYING

Before preachers, life coaches, and self-help gurus proclaimed they could cure crack smoking, depression, and infidelity with vision boards, self-affirmations, and prayer cloths, Dr. Samuel Adolphus Cartwright mesmerized America with a pseudo-scientific breakthrough that would remain unmatched until the invention of the Shake Weight. Although he was previously best known for his staunch opposition to the wild idea that microscopic ghosts called "germs" caused disease,[1] in 1851, Cartwright would become most renowned for presenting a paper before the Medical Association of Louisiana proposing an explosive new mental illness called "drapetomania," or "the disease causing slaves to run away." In it, he wrote:

> *The cause in the most of cases, that induces the negro to run away from service, is as much a disease of the mind as any other species of mental alienation, and much more curable, as a general rule. With the advantages of proper medical advice, strictly followed, this troublesome practice that many negroes have of running away, can be almost entirely prevented, although the slaves be located on the borders of a free state, within a stone's throw of the abolitionists.*[2]

Cartwright's racist pseudo-psychology illustrates another delusion of whiteness: namely, the continued justification of oppression—state-sanctioned rape, murder, and unending torture—by portraying Black people's insatiable inclination toward freedom as a sickness or a criminal impulse. For everyone else, the irrepressible compulsion for liberty is viewed as a symptom of a craven, barbaric psychopathy. This nation's history is pockmarked with examples of the idea that freedom is for white people.

Although most Enlightenment-era thinkers agreed that freedom is the natural state of man, they somehow carved out an exception for their belligerent negroes because, in their white minds, property rights were as important as individual freedom. The race-based forced labor system that built America into an economic power could only exist through violence and the threat of violence. In places like South Carolina, where the captives outnumbered the free, this state-sanctioned institution of racial dehumanization required constant enforcement. But every speck of evidence reveals that resistance—both conscious and subconscious—was interwoven into the fabric of life as an enslaved person. Through acts large and small, organized and individual, the search for liberty was a way of life for Africans in America. It wasn't drapetomania, but a persistent and unyielding belief in their personhood that drove the enslaved Africans to seek out freedom.

Under Cartwright's asinine hypothesis, this imaginary illness manifested itself in many ways. Some sufferers ran away to freedom, while others were mad enough to physically resist oppression. The most unhinged drapetomaniacs did the unthinkable—they tried to eliminate the source of their oppression. But according to this medical diagnosis, the contagion's victims shared a common goal: to get free or die trying.

It was sometimes impossible to tell when an enslaved person was struck with freedom fever. While the most popular stories of resistance involve coordinated violent events, the most common form of resistance took place in small ways on a daily basis. All across America, Africans coerced into bondage used understated and not-so-subtle methods to counteract the brutality of slavery. Some undermined their evil overlords' financial goals by reducing productivity, sabotaging their work equipment, and planning labor strikes. Others played sick or worked in a slow, deliberate manner. When a generally dependable servant stopped taking pride in their work, drapetomania was a potential cause.

Of course, enslavers searched for cures for this malady. The city of Charleston, South Carolina, developed an entire "corrections" industry dedicated to punishing and reforming rebellious human property.[3] Slaveowners could send insolent slaves to the "Sugar House," an old sugar factory where city workers were paid to whip and reeducate the troublemakers and malingerers.[4] The first execution in the Massachusetts Colony took place in 1681 when Maria, a "negro servant to Joshua Lambe of Roxbury," set her master's house on fire, as well as a neighbor's. According to the Massachusetts Bay Colony's court records, Maria "wittingly, willingly and feloniously set on fire the dwelling house of Thomas Swann . . . and presently went and crept into a hole at a back doore of thy Masters Lambs house and set it on fier also."[5] Maybe Maria was a cold-blooded murderer. Perhaps the desire to be a full, independent human being had driven her into a state of pyromania. In any case, there was only one antidote for Maria's delirium. The compassionate people of Massachusetts had to burn her alive at the stake. They had no choice.

In a capitalist racket based on the theft of labor, intellect, and Black bodies, it may seem logical that Africans would resort to stealing things from the people who stole them, as well. But according to the rules of drapetomania, these people had a *medical disorder* that turned them into thieves. "One day, a group of us were working in the field," Cecelia Simmons Green recalls of her time on the Grimball Plantation on James Island, South Carolina. "We heard Mr. Hinson talking to another white man; he was telling him: 'You think them niggers stupid but they have plenty of sense. I think some of them been going in my fields at night stealing my vegetables and selling them in the market.' We would hold our heads down and laugh because we knew who was teafing the vegetables."[6] Apparently, in South Carolina, the person who sows, waters, weeds, and harvests a plant can somehow "steal" it from the people who did absolutely nothing to create it.

Since enslaved people were governed by property laws, running away to freedom was legally considered an act of theft, despite the ironic fact that the whole slavemaking industry was based on abduction. Sometimes these drapetomaniac slaves absconded to British-controlled Canada, free states, or wherever the Underground Railroad led them. But these weren't the only places to run. Some of the most popular escape destinations in America for the enslaved were just anywhere *away from white people.* Sallie Smith, a woman enslaved on a Louisiana plantation, says she "stayed in the woods" half of the time of her enslavement, depending on the kindness of the other enslaved people in the area.[7] Assuming her brother knew her whereabouts, Sallie's former captor tortured her brother until he, too, bolted from the plantation and joined her in the woods. Unfortunately, there were no peer-reviewed studies to investigate whether these recurring bouts of drapetomania were genetic.

The South was surprisingly also a viable option for some slaves who were infected with this ailment. There, entire communities were built that are still being discovered today, including Bas du Fleuve, a vast area between the mouth of the Mississippi and New Orleans that was controlled by runaways for most of the 1770s. During the colonial period, the all-Black town of Fort Mose in the Spanish-held Florida territory was a popular destination for those who wanted a permanent vacation from slavery. Spain had abolished slavery in the territory, and after the War of 1812, a fully armed British "Negro Fort" in Florida became the center of the Black resistance against the institution of slavery, forming its own army. The British Corps of Colonial Marines was made up of free Blacks and fugitive slaves who fought alongside Native Americans to protect the kind runaways who quarantined themselves to protect others from their contagious virus.

Perhaps the most remarkable of these oases of freedom was the Great Dismal Swamp, a million-acre area that covered southeastern Virginia and northeastern North Carolina. Historians still don't quite know how many escaped Africans built communities and lived free in the Great Dismal Swamp, but new research suggests that thousands may have lived there.[8]

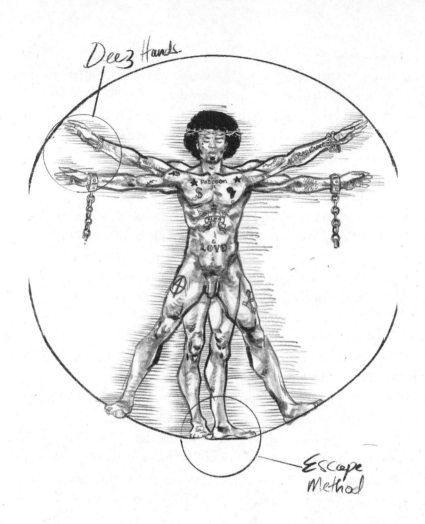

Deez Hands

Escape Method

Historians usually refer to these collective groups of unownable Africans as "maroons,"[9] but the nomenclature varied by region. In Alabama and Georgia, they were called people who lived "in the woods," but perhaps the most telling moniker for the self-emancipated Africans came from Virginia and Maryland, in that Great Dismal Swampland. Nicknamed the "outlands," the region was too treacherous to travel through by horse or canoe. Virginians ultimately reappropriated an adjective to describe unconquerable residents of the unconquered lands, calling these freedom-inclined Boyz n the Hood "outlandish."[10]

From colonial times on, many of these maroons kept themselves alive through the generosity of enslaved Africans on plantations, as well as by hunting, fishing, and raising their own crops. Some engaged in small-scale banditry and theft, but for the most part they didn't bother white people, so white people left them alone. Because tens of thousands of these outlandish Africans had fought against the Patriots in the Revolution, many had weapons, military training, and knowledge of how plantations worked. They also had no intention of working from sunup to sundown without a pay stub.

One of the longest-lasting of these communities flanked both sides of the Savannah River, in the area that separates Georgia from South Carolina. Maroons had lived there since the 1770s, but in 1786 the Grand Jury of Chatham County, Georgia, demanded that the local militia do something about the "large gangs of runaway negroes."[11] Early on the morning of October 11, 1786, militiamen attacked the settlement. Four white soldiers were wounded and four maroons were killed in the skirmish before the militia found themselves low on ammunition and retreated. Determined to return these free souls to bondage on behalf of the "land of the free," the militia gathered a few more white men and then attacked again at sunset. But the maroons were waiting and overwhelmed the militia, forcing them to back dat azz up again.

But you know these fools couldn't let the word out that they had been beaten by a group of ragtag negroes. Even a whiff of self-determination and resistance threatened the entire fabric of the slave-based society. The maroon hunters returned the next morning, hoping the can of whoop-ass opened by the former slaves had been depleted, unaware that Maroon Fight Club had four rules:

1. Do not talk about Maroon Club.
2. Do not talk about Maroon Club.
3. Only fight when it is absolutely necessary.
4. If white people keep showing up, there is no more Maroon Club.

When the white boys returned, the maroon settlement was empty. The militia destroyed the small encampment, including homes, farms, barns, fifteen boats, and thirty-four hundred pounds of rice. But still, the maroons survived, building another encampment. The next spring, a South Carolina militia overran and destroyed another community on the other side of the Savannah River. Within six months, the maroons had built another community. The new location had twenty-one homes protected by a four-foot wall. Thanks to the rules of Maroon Fight Club, maroonage could continue.

While many escaped slaves took to communities like these, some, like Harriet Jacobs, survived as a maroon wholly without community.

Harriet Jacobs was born a slave in 1813, on a legal technicality. According to the ancient Virginian principle of *partus sequitur ventrem*,[*] a child born to a slave was also a slave.[12] Harriet's grandmother Molly had been freed by her owner but was later kidnapped and reenslaved. Because of this, Harriet's mother was doomed for a life of slavery, as were Harriet and her brother John.

Harriet and her brother taught themselves how to read and vowed to escape after they were sold at auction and separated from their mother and grandmother. Harriet's grandmother was eventually freed again and allowed to live in a house on the plantation where Harriet and John were also living as slaves. When she was fifteen, Harriet's master began sexually harassing her. Hoping for protection, she began a relationship with Samuel Sawyer, a lawyer who would later become a U.S. congressman and father Harriet's two children. Harriet's master was so mad about the relationship that he sold Harriet to his brother, but Harriet eventually escaped and began living as a maroon. Meanwhile, Harriet's harassing master offered her children along with her brother at a discount to a slave trader, but only after the slave trader promised to separate them and sell them individually. The slave trader promised, but instead sold the entire family to Sawyer (the slave-raping congressman), who had promised Harriet that he'd free their kids and her brother. He, of course, never did. Sawyer did, however, send the kids to live with their great-grandmother Molly, who was still living on the plantation. This at least gave Harriet some relief, because she had the opportunity to watch her children grow up.

---

[*] *Literally "offspring follows belly."*

And if you're wondering how she did that if she was a runaway, well, Harriet was living right underneath her former master's nose. During the day, she would hide in a nearby swamp. At night, she hid out in Molly's attic, never revealing her presence to her kids. The attic had no light and at its highest point was three feet tall. Harriet managed to drill a hole in the cramped crawlspace so she could read the Bible and watch her children. She lived that way for seven years. Eventually, she escaped to New York, where she was reunited with her children and her brother, who had been sent north by Sawyer but still essentially lived as slaves.

Because of the fugitive slave laws, the evil enslaver still technically owned Harriet. Every so often, he would find out where Harriet lived, and she would have to go into hiding again. It wasn't until 1852, when Harriet was thirty-nine years old, that abolitionist Cornelia Grinnell Willis, for whom Harriet worked as a nanny, would purchase Harriet's freedom for $300. The rapist congressman, who still owned Harriet's children and brother, finally sent them to free states to live with Harriet. She spent the next five years writing the story of her life, but no one would publish it. In January 1861, *Incidents in the Life of a Slave Girl* was finally released, and Harriet became an abolitionist icon.

Some manifestations of the disease were so acute that they sparked unbelievable stories, like the Gullah-Geechee folktale of the Igbo people who can fly:

> Ain't you heard about um? Well, at that time Mr. Blue he was the overseer and . . . Mr. Blue he go down one mawnin with a long whip fuh tug whip them good . . . Anyway, he whipped them good, and dey gits togedduh an stick dugh hoe in duh fiel an den . . . riz up in the sky an tun heself into buzzuhds and flew right back to Africa![13]

In May 1803, a shipload of seventy-five captive Igbo people were purchased for $100 each to grow rice on forced labor plantations on St. Simons Island, Georgia. Apparently, the ship was infested with Cartwright's disease, because the shackled passengers screamed all the way to America. When the captain would send members of the crew down into the belly of the ship to quiet them, the crew members were terrified to realize that the captives weren't just screaming; they were saying one chant, over and over, in unison: "*Orimiri Omambala bu anyi bia. Orimiri Omambala ka anyi ga ejina.*"[14] When the ship got close to the shore, the chants grew louder. "*Orimiri Omambala bu anyi bia. Orimiri Omambala ka anyi ga ejina,*" they prayed in unison. Then, somehow, they broke the chains, and threw the entire crew overboard. Led by a captured chieftain, the Africans then walked calmly into the sea, chanting, "*Orimiri Omambala bu anyi bia. Orimiri Omambala ka anyi ga ejina,*" drowning themselves rather than be slaves.

Some say the number was seventy-five; other sources put the number at thirteen. One contemporaneous account described it as a terrible loss of the plantation owner's investment. Others describe the Igbo rebellion as a mass suicide. Whatever the case, witnesses watched while shackled slaves calmly walked into Dunbar Creek on St. Simons Island in Glynn County, Georgia, and drowned themselves, chanting, "The Water Spirit brought us here. The Water Spirit will take us home." They were free.

One of the worst incidents of drapetomania happened on January 28, 1856, when Margaret Garner, her husband, their four children, and eleven of their fellow enslaved freedom-seekers stole their master's horse, sleigh, and gun and absconded from their Boone County, Kentucky, plantation owner, Archibald K. Gaines. The family crossed the frozen Ohio River and split up. The other escapees eventually made it to freedom via the Underground Railroad, while the Garners hid out at the house of their uncle Elijah Kite, a free Black man.

Fugitive slave catchers eventually discovered the family's location and surrounded Uncle Kite's house, hoping to return them to their owner. Twenty-two-year-old Margaret knew they were done for. Described as a mulatto who was always "cross tempered,"[15] Margaret was likely the product of a slavemaster raping her mother. Historians say at least two of her own children had been conceived from the same rampant slavemaster's sexual assaults. Knowing the horrors that would undoubtedly befall her daughters, rather than see them suffer the same fate, Margaret grabbed a butcher knife and slit her two-year-old daughter's throat. To sacrifice the fruit born of one's own womb as a gift of liberty is a decision that only the most desperate freedom-seeker can know. Garner's story served as the basis for Toni Morrison's award-winning novel *Beloved.*

The insatiable desire to get free by any means necessary included the option of death. Of course, "Give me liberty or give me death" sounds perfectly rational when it comes from the lips of a white person. But logic, common sense, and the narcissistic delusion of whiteness dictates that Black people who would rather die than be enslaved must be mentally ill. Ask Dr. Cartwright. That's just science.

But the most famous and most belligerent of these drapetomaniacs terrified white people in the coastal region of South Carolina for years, while providing an unfettered example of resistance to the Black folks in the region. The undisputed king of the maroon bandits, escapees, and saboteurs was a man they called Forest Joe.

Couldn't nobody own Forest Joe.

Very little is known about Forest before he escaped from the Carroll plantation in South Carolina's Richland District, but by the spring of 1821, "the celebrated Bandit Joe" was becoming notorious for his brazen, charismatic leadership and his ability to vanish into thin air.[16] Chronically ill with stage 5 drapetomania, he was unapologetic about infecting enslaved people with his affliction. If Angela Davis had a baby with T'Challa and gave it up for adoption to be raised by Tupac, that baby would one day read about the first man to truly live the thug life and say, "That Forest Joe dude *be wildin'*!"

Joe was over six feet tall and light-skinned, with a scar on his cheek from when someone had bitten him during a fight and calves that were pockmarked from gunshot pellets he suffered during his encounters with fugitive slave hunters. To say that he was an intimidating presence would be an understatement.

Joe had a variety of tactics to help bolster that badass image. Unlike the clothes of most maroons and enslaved Africans, Joe's weren't made of osnaburg, a coarse, often white fabric used for slave garments. He had found a way to dye or stain his clothing different shades of brown. This makeshift camouflage helped him blend into the background, but it wasn't the most incredible part of Forest's gear. Joe had also fashioned himself an upper garment out of some material "through which no ball could well pass," or so it was said. That's right: Joe, in 1821, had created a bulletproof vest.

Joe ran with a tight gang of maroons that included women and children. One of Joe's best homeboys was a man named Jack, who stole himself from his master and walked two hundred miles to join Joe's crew. Joe's second-best homey was also named Jack.* Together, Joe, Jack, and the other Jack would form a clique that terrified white people more than Critical Race Theory, absentee voting, and affirmative action combined.

Like Freeway Ricky Ross, Frankie Beverly, and the concept of rhythm, most people in the Black community knew about Joe long before white people found out about him. An abundance of charisma, combined with his inability to give a damn about white people's laws, created an inflated mythos that endeared him to his already enslaved brothers and sisters throughout Georgia and South Carolina. Accomplices would also carry out many of the late-night "raids" but attribute them to Joe, Jack, and the rest of the maroon gangstas on those plantations. This precursor to the "no snitching" rule enhanced Joe's reputation as a master bandit of mythic proportions who could singlehandedly steal livestock, crops, and hundreds of pounds of lead to melt for ammunition.

Late on the night of May 21, 1821, Joe and the two Jacks were out killing cattle on George Ford's plantation. One of Ford's forty-nine enslaved Africans dry snitched on Joe, so Ford, "one or two of his negroes, and a white man, a carpenter employed by him," set out to stop Joe's raid.[17] Joe and his merry band of thugs were ready and waiting. When George pulled up on his late-model horse, Joe's gang ambushed George's crew. Walking Jack opened fire, shooting Ford in the head and chest. With only one gun between them, George's team ran for cover while Joe and the others were able to escape in a canoe they had hidden at the mouth of the Santee River. But of course, there's always one guy who messes everything up. Ford's killer would have remained a mystery, but apparently, Jack *really liked* oxtails. When he walked

---

* *Jack was a trendy name in the early 1800s, well before he became an advocate for "in the box" manufacturers and the beanstalk industry.*

back to retrieve the cattle, one of Ford's men was hiding behind the dead ox and captured him. Two weeks later, Jack was hanged, but not before confessing that Joe was the ringleader. To quell his constituents' concerns, Governor Thomas Bennett offered a bounty of $168.62 for Joe's head.[18] A group of militiamen formed a formal Joe-hunting committee and raised another $300 in reward money, instigating a manhunt that would last for years.

Instead of admitting that Joe could outsmart them, militiamen reported that he knew some kind of magic, or that he had extra-long legs that allowed him to cover distances very quickly. Some people believed he was impervious to bullets and could make himself invisible. The stories of Joe's escapes spread, worrying white South Carolinians while further securing his status as a hero to the enslaved population. As the chase for Joe consumed the state, the elusive fugitive also helped free scores of enslaved Africans, enlarging South Carolina's maroon population. Captives who stayed on plantations would even help him out with inside information and intelligence. For many, ensuring Joe's survival was a form of resistance in itself.

On the day of Jack's execution, Joe entered the Georgetown home of a free Black couple and "escaped" after the woman was "obliged" to give Joe a "considerable quantity" of bacon and corn. Unfortunately for the authorities, the unharmed couple had no idea which way Joe went. On June 22, another South Carolinian managed to set a trap for Joe. After encountering Joe stealing his lead, a gentleman retreated but made three of his "coloreds" wait for the bandit near the riverbed, where he kept a canoe and a raft. He would never see the boat or the raft again, and only one of his "coloreds" returned. Another enslaved woman was in her master's home when Joe burst in and somehow found all the owner's ammunition, guns, and powder. Some people thought it was pretty strange that she didn't scream or alert the neighbors to Joe's presence. Instead, she waited calmly, unharmed, until her now-unarmed enslaver returned home. In 1822, three men reported that they had severely wounded Joe, but he had made a miraculous recovery that no one could understand. Maybe it was Black magic. Perhaps Joe really was a witch. Or a ghost. Whatever he was, he was driving the white people crazy with fear and trepidation.

To be fair, the rumors weren't just coming from anxious whites. In November, the *Charleston City Gazette*[19] printed an account warning their readers that they had received reports of "armed runaway negroes" who were robbing people outside the city.[20] Apparently, "several negroes" were headed to town to buy supplies for their owners when they were stopped and robbed of their masters' money and goods. After keeping the victims "in custody till after night," the evil criminals, who somehow still had the morals not to harm the people they were accosting, decided to let the servants go, even giving them prepared statements to take back to their enslavers. The Black victims dutifully delivered these "insulting and menacing messages to the masters of those whom they had robbed."

I can hear him now:

"Some dude name Joe robbed us, took your money, made us hang out with him all day, and then he let us go. He told us to tell you not to come looking for him, or he'll do you like he did Ford! Also, he said you should give me a few days off, or he gon' kill you! Now, you know I love working in the fields, but that's what he said. And he looked *real* mad, too."

By 1823, Joe was a veritable superhero. Black people were looking out for him, fueling the aura of power around him, while others were joining him. When questioned by the militia, some enslaved Africans would say that they had spotted Joe just to throw them off the scent. Some embellished his status by perpetuating the myth that Joe was a voudou priest who drank the blood of his victims. Joe had somehow managed to create an intelligence network and a disinformation machine. The white population was scared out of their minds, and for good reason—sometimes old Forest outperformed even the wildest rumors.

Joe was reportedly steaming mad that an enslaved driver had "rescued" a woman whom Joe was holding for ransom.[21] Some people say she was Joe's mistress, and the two were running a scheme to extract money from the woman's master. (By "some people," I mean the woman, because as soon as this woman was freed, she escaped again, went back to Joe's camp, and stayed with him until his last day.) Regardless, you know Joe couldn't let some off-brand driver play him like that. It would ruin his street cred, so Joe vowed to kill the driver. Everyone begged him not to do it because the driver belonged to the former governor. But Joe wasn't known as a particularly cautious guy, and he would not be deterred.

In August 1823, over two years after he killed George Ford, Forest Joe walked onto the plantation of former South Carolina governor James Burchill Richardson in broad daylight. In front of the enslaved people, the plantation overseer, and everyone on the plantation, Forest pulled out a gun and shot the driver dead. And just for good measure, he turned and fired at the overseer. Of course, this just amplified Joe's legend—many of the other enslaved people considered drivers to be accomplices to white enslavers. And while he had been best known for his midnight raids and eluding his hunters under cover of darkness, to do this on a former governor's plantation meant there was no longer any further doubt that Joe was undeniably real.

Of course, the moment Joe started shooting at white people in broad daylight was the day everything changed. Desperate, the Joe-hunting militia decided to offer the rewards to "certain negroes" to snitch on Joe with the promise of no stitches. The group even agreed to free any slave who helped them find Forest Joe. For months, people kept quiet, until October, when an enslaved riverboat worker named Royal decided to take the money and lead a militia to Joe. After several days, the militia eventually found Joe near the Santee River, and a standoff ensued. Vowing he would never be taken alive, Joe was killed on the spot.

After his death, the South Carolina militia raided Joe's camps and killed many of the maroons, including a three-year-old. For added measure, they cut off Joe's head and put it on a stake at the mouth of the river "as a warning to vicious slaves." There is no record that Royal ever received his monetary reward or was even set free. But the South Carolina Joe-chasing militia that killed Forest Joe and swindled Royal would continue to hunt maroons and fugitive slaves and change the South forever.

Scholars and media outlets routinely cite Boston as creating the nation's first municipal law enforcement agency in 1838, which is technically correct.[22] However, over a decade prior on October 2, 1823, the citizens of Pineville, South Carolina, had met in the town library to "devise a plan for apprehending or dispersing a gang of desperate Runaways."[23] The group immediately began collecting money from the town's citizens to solve its maroon problem.

"One of the Number is a Fellow called Forest or Joe," wrote the committee's secretary and treasurer, Thomas Gaillard. "This Party, sheltered by the Difficulties of an approach to their camp and strengthened by Fire-Arms and other weapons of offence, have threatened the lives of many Individuals; by daring acts of villainy have disturbed the Peace of the community—and carry on unmolested a system of open violence and Robberies."[24]

The good citizens of South Carolina had no idea that they were treating a disease that wouldn't be discovered for more than a quarter century. Twenty-eight years before a bunk physician discovered the "disease causing slaves to run away," and fifteen years before the General Court of Boston passed a law to organize its Day Patrol,[25] the newly formed "Standing Committee" simultaneously came up with the cure for the diseased freedom-thirsters and an official name for its Forest Joe apprehension commission. The slave-hunting squad's name would eventually serve as a prescription for drapetomaniacs like Joe as well as define the relationship between Black Americans—free or enslaved—and law enforcement agencies for years to come.

They called themselves the Pineville Police Association.[26]

TO KILL WHITES

THE MULTICULTURAL REBELLION OF 1811

While sugar farmer James Brown[*] was purchasing a few items from the trading firm run by Stephen Henderson and William Kerner in the summer of 1806, he found an incredible bargain. For a mere $1,300, Brown purchased fifteen-year-old Kwaku and twenty-one-year-old Kwamina[1]—two healthy and powerfully built Africans imported from the Ashanti Kingdom. Because slavemasters rarely care about diction and pronunciation, Brown changed Kwaku's name—an Akan moniker usually given to people born on Wednesday—into "Kook," while Kwamina, which was reserved for men born on Saturday, would become "Quamana," a name that means "I own you; therefore it is my prerogative to erase your history and culture for something that fits neatly into my mouth." But regardless of whitewashed nomenclature, the important thing to know is that these two men would inspire a revolt that would change the Louisiana Territory forever.

As a major shipping port, New Orleans served as a hub for America's intra-national slave trade, eventually surpassing Charleston as the largest slave market in the United States. Kook

---

[*] *Not that one. The Godfather of Soul would never.*

and Quamana were among the 50 percent of captives who made it to the New World without committing suicide or dying along the way.[2] The two arrived to this foreign land in 1806 without any sense of the landscape or customs. They had no idea that the Louisiana Territory had only been part of America for three years and the federal government was not yet sure when or if it would become a state. They didn't know that France had sold the territory to America after Haiti's slave revolt forced France out of the New World colonization business. They were unaware that the plantations surrounding New Orleans were a veritable mixing pot of African cultures from across the diaspora. Some of the French who escaped the Haitian Revolution had sold their slaves in the territory. Other slaves were imports from various African kingdoms. All Kook and Quamana knew is that they wanted to be free.

There were also things that Brown himself was unaware of when he purchased his new human property. As an import from Kentucky, Brown was not accustomed to the Orleans Territory's demographics, which had so many free people of color that slave patrolling was virtually impossible. Brown had to acclimate himself to the idea that the local traditions dictated that his enslaved humans could visit other plantations and even patronize Black-owned bars and meetinghouses. Had Brown completed a thorough background check on his human chattel, he might have understood that the scars on Kook and Quamana meant they were likely raised as *okofokum*, West African soldiers trained in hand-to-hand combat, firearms usage, and war tactics from birth—and he might have guessed that maybe, just maybe, Kook and Quamana wouldn't be pleased with their circumstances.[3]

Brown, who kept a careful eye on his human property, was relieved to see that his new assets had become friends with Charles Deslondes, a Creole mulatto on Colonel Manuel Andry's nearby agricultural concentration camp. There was no better role model for the two newly arrived Africans than Deslondes. At just twenty-two years old, Deslondes was the

Andry plantation's primary slave supervisor, and was in charge of keeping the other bondsmen in check. He was known to be compliant, intelligent, and so trusted by his master that he was even allowed to exact brutal beatings on the men and women he supervised. The other enslaved Africans didn't even seem bothered by this power, or Deslondes's lighter skin, his larger hut, and the other fringe benefits that he enjoyed. Because the torture of slavery was inescapable, who would you rather have wielding the whip—a white man who was part of the society that saw you as subhuman property, or someone who was also subject to the horrors of this inhumane institution?

Colonel Andry seemed to trust Deslondes, permitting him to spend the night at his girlfriend's slave quarters on the nearby Trépagnier farm. Both slaveowners hoped the romance would result in offspring and the financial windfall of free human labor. A brutal and eccentric master, François Trépagnier was known to keep a small boy, Gustave, as a house pet to whom Trépagnier fed table scraps and treated like a human puppy. But now Gustave was getting older. Many of Trépagnier's slaves believed the next child born on the estate would replace Gustave as the Trépagnier pet.

Unlike Deslondes, Quamana and Kook didn't ask their master's permission to visit neighboring estates. Late at night, they would employ the techniques gleaned from their homeland's warrior training to abscond temporarily from the Brown farm. As Quamana crept through the tall sugarcanes from plantation to plantation, Kook would post in the tall trees as a lookout. It was there, in the forest, that they would spend their nights huddled with Charles Deslondes and Harry Kenner, learning the English language, familiarizing themselves with the cultural terrain, and plotting a rebellion that would change the history of New Orleans.

While transcripts of their conversations do not exist, Kook and Quamana probably recounted tales about being schooled in guerrilla warfare and military strategy, while Deslondes, a mixed-race Creole, likely shared stories of rebellion he heard from the thousands of French-speaking white immigrants who moved to the Orleans Territory after the Haitian Revolution. They unquestionably had to have heard about Juan San Maló, the iconic leader of a nearby maroon colony. After repelling anyone who dared enter the German Coast's swamps for years, Maló was finally captured by a Spanish militia in 1784 and hanged. And they had to have discussed how even the *ideology* of freedom was being policed during that time. In 1805, New Orleans's governors arrested a white French-speaking man for spreading the ideas of liberty and freedom among free and enslaved people of color. As a former French colony, the Louisiana Territory was teeming with stories about the slaves who had just beat the brakes off of white slaveowners, and white people took notice.

But these legendary stories of resistance were not their only impetus for rebellion. In the time between the Haitian Revolution and the Louisiana Purchase, 3,102 free people of color moved to New Orleans as French citizens. Deslondes and other slaves didn't have to dream about what it was like to be free; they witnessed people who looked and talked like them walking around and being treated as whole human beings. Unlike most enslaved communities, the subjugated population of New Orleans had an image of freedom that was not synonymous with whiteness. They saw what was possible, and they were going to take it for themselves. And so they plotted.

Their plan was multicultural from its inception. Kook and Quamana understood that a third-generation slave would not necessarily trust the plans of a warrior who barely spoke the language or a supervisor who carried out the wishes of a white man. Instead, they recruited various leaders, dividing them up according to their country of origin, language, background, and plantation. Tapping in local leaders to relay the plans and lay out strategies was immensely effective, as they could communicate in the language of the people they recruited. They also would be intimately familiar with the habits of the individual plantations and the obstacles they might face during a violent insurrection.

That allowed the leaders to know that some of the recruits were enslaved on the plantations of local militia who were off in Florida fighting the Spanish. Others pointed out that their masters were devout Catholics, which meant on the Feast of the Epiphany—the Christian holiday commemorating three wise men bringing the first gifts to the newborn child who would be revealed as God incarnate—they would be at church.[*] Effectively, insurrectionists had essentially organized individual battalions for an army of rebels.

On the night of Tuesday, January 8, 1811, Colonel Manuel Andry was one of the few white men in the area not celebrating Jesus's baby shower. In the middle of the night, he was stirred out of his sleep wondering why his most loyal slave was standing over him with an axe. As the fog of sleep lifted, Andry noticed that Deslondes was not alone. Just as Deslondes lifted his axe, Andry leaped out of his bed, bum-rushed his accosters, and escaped down the staircase, wounded but alive. As Andry exited his home, he caught a glimpse of the revolters hacking his son Gilbert to pieces.

Deslondes did not chase his fleeing master. Instead, the rebel leader directed twenty-five fellow revolutionaries from his unit to seize every weapon on the farm. Because both Colonel and Gilbert Andry were leaders of the local militia, there were plenty of muskets to distribute to the trained Africans. The men who were skilled with the blades required for sugarcane farming armed themselves with machetes and swords, while Deslondes rifled through Andry's closet and found what he was looking for—Andry's colonial army attire. In a few short minutes, the slave driver had transformed himself into the man he had secretly wished to be for years. He was now the uniformed military leader of one of America's greatest uprisings.

Word of the rebellion quickly spread up the coast. As they marched along the bank of the Mississippi River, ten more slaves

---

[*] *Legend has it that these "Three Wise Men" didn't even wrap their gifts. And, apparently, the Bethlehem Galleria Mall was out of everything except frankincense and myrrh.*

joined the ranks, bringing horses and munitions. By the time
Deslondes's procession united with Kook and Quamana's even
more militant squadron at the Brown farm, the Black army
numbered well over one hundred men. On horseback were
eleven leaders representing the diaspora of the enslaved, divided
into companies, including the Muslim Senegambian warriors,
the Sierra Leone insurgents, the native-born Black soldiers, and
the Akan infantry. They began to head toward the Trépagnier
forced labor camp.

Even as he heard the African war drums approaching,
Trépagnier did not fear being taken by the savages. His hands
held steady as he leveled his double-barreled musket in their
direction. The mist from his gun did not disturb him one bit,
even as it intermingled with the smoke from the fire set by the
mutineers. Perhaps that is why he did not notice the guerrillas
sneaking up from behind the plantation house.

By the time Kook began hacking the confident enslaver
into chunks, it was too late for fear. But suddenly the African
executioner stopped mid-thrust as a small figure approached the
scene. Kook stepped aside and watched as Trépagnier's worst
fear raised an axe to deliver the deathblow.

Gustave was no longer a pet.

The revolutionaries met at a designated spot and began
their march to New Orleans. As they marched toward freedom,
the rebellion grew. Because of the driving rain, the brigands
couldn't burn down the plantations they passed, but during the
march, maroons and free Black laborers continued to join in.
Although surviving records only account for twenty-four slaves
in the revolt, eyewitnesses say there were between two hundred
and five hundred revolters by the time they were holed up at the
Fortier estate, planning to invade New Orleans.

The next morning, the sentries at New Orleans awoke to
a huddled mass waiting at the gates. They were the survivors
who had somehow escaped the wrath of the multicultural army
and fled to the city for safety. Upon hearing that an army of

angry Black men was marching toward New Orleans, Governor William Claiborne immediately locked down the area. He forbade any male negro—free or enslaved—from being on the streets after 6 p.m. Knowing that most of his local militia were off fighting the Spanish, Claiborne was desperate to find any way to face down the rebellion.

Eventually, the news managed to reach the territory's top military leader, Brigadier General Wade Hampton, who also happened to be one of the largest slaveowners in America. Brigadier General Hampton knew he could easily overwhelm the ragtag band of rebels with superior firepower. Only half of the self-emancipated slaves were armed with muskets, and their ammunition was limited. When he discovered that the armed insurgents were at the Fortier place, Hampton ordered an attack, only to find that the coalition had retreated. Little did he know that Ashanti warriors were known for strategic retreats that lured their opponents into a false sense of security. The multicultural brigade was waiting in the nearby swamps, ready to attack. The desperados were all set to wipe the floor with Hampton when suddenly another force attacked them from behind.

It was Colonel Manuel Andry.

As the uprising's first target, Andry had not fled to New Orleans like the other victims of the insurrection. Instead, he had escaped across the Mississippi and assembled a militia of planters who lived on the other side of the river. The planters gathered every canoe they could find, rowed back across, and stumbled upon the Black soldiers. Andry's crew, flush with firepower, simply waited until the slaves ran out of ammunition before they hunted the insurgents down.

When they found Charles Deslondes, Andry's vigilante squad chopped off both of his hands, broke both of his legs at the thigh, shot him, and then burned his body on a bed of straw. Deslondes's death was repayment for Gilbert Andry, one of ultimately only two white men who died during the entire escapade. Its brutality was meant to serve as a reminder of what happened to a slave who had the audacity to undermine the institution that defined their existence.

After a series of interrogations and unsanctioned tribunals, many of the freedom-seekers confessed and gave up their co-conspirators. Quamana refused to name names, but Kook, however, admitted to the revolt's other casualty, proudly boasting that he was the man who had delivered death to the cruel François Trépagnier. The tribunal decreed "that the heads of the executed shall be cut off and placed atop a pole on the spot where all can see the punishment meted out for such crimes, also as a terrible example to all who would disturb the public tranquility in the future."[4] Apparently, enslavement was not a terrible enough example.

Governor Claiborne would use the uprising to successfully lobby for statehood, arguing that revolts and extrajudicial executions would continue to happen without federal oversight. The federal government capitulated. On April 30, 1812, the Territory of Orleans was admitted to the Union as the state of Louisiana.

On January 8, 1815, exactly four years after the day the enslaved men along the German Coast took up arms against their oppressors, the British Army would attack the American forces commanded by Major General Andrew Jackson in the Battle of New Orleans. Although the War of 1812 had technically been over for two weeks, news of the signing of the Treaty of Ghent had not yet reached the United States. For the three years prior, the British had won nearly every battle in the war, including the invasion of Washington, D.C. Jackson was woefully unprepared and significantly outnumbered, but he would enjoy the United States' one military advantage—the Brits were attacking a region that was now well equipped for quelling an uprising.

When Jackson sounded the alarm for volunteers, over a thousand well-armed Louisianans grabbed their guns and rushed to his aid. They were better trained than the federal forces, and were prepared to fight. It wasn't even a contest: the British suffered about two thousand casualties, while the United States had around sixty. The Battle of New Orleans was the only decisive American victory in the entire War of 1812.

Perhaps this is the most enduring legacy of the German Coast uprising—fear. The paranoia during a slave rebellion made plantation owners in the area take their militia duties seriously. Gun sales soared, and volunteer militia continued to train weekly even after Deslondes, Quamana, and Kook's rebellion had been put down. Everyone was armed and prepared for a slave war that never came. The federal government had even stationed an extra regiment of troops in the area and compensated the slaveowners for the executed property. Meanwhile, the city of New Orleans banned the sale of ammunition to Black people and outlawed slaves congregating at any event other than a funeral or a Sunday dance (*it still was New Orleans, after all*).

During the tribunals following the revolt back in 1811, many of the mutineers were asked what would have happened if they had succeeded. Most said they just wanted to form their own all-Black town. Like the legendary Juan San Maló, they had planned to build a republic on the German Coast and live by the words of the famous French Revolution motto recently co-opted by the state of New Hampshire: "*Vivre Libre ou Mourir*"—Live Free or Die.[5]

Even though Brown testified that he watched Kook, Quamana, Deslondes, and Kenner plan the rebellion, only Deslondes and one other man were ever fingered as "leaders" of the multicultural revolt. Deslondes's master had witnessed his treachery, and, of course, he was someone whom white people considered "intelligent," so he was an obvious choice. The other man was an enslaved named "Jupiter," whom no other enslaved person ever suggested was one of the revolt's principal architects. Perhaps the reason why "the jury noted that he was one of the leaders of the uprising" was that when the interrogators asked why he joined the insurrection, Jupiter's simple, straightforward answer was recorded in the trial proceedings and enshrined the source of fear that would forever follow the revolution of 1811.

"He said he wanted to go to the city to kill whites."[6]

THREE LITTLE QUESTIONS

1. **Which enslaved person was considered the most resistant?**
   a. A field slave.
   b. A house slave.
   c. A literate slave.
   d. An enslaved slave.

2. **What was the worst part of being enslaved?**
   a. The inescapability.
   b. The violence.
   c. The pay.
   d. The "being enslaved" part.

3. **What was unique about America's form of slavery?**
   a. It was color-based.
   b. It was inheritable.
   c. It was constitutional.
   d. All of the above.

ACTIVITY

SYSTEM UPGRADE

You are tasked with creating a humane system of enslavement that will not cause your human chattel to escape, revolt, or otherwise resist. In one million words or fewer, describe this system.

6

THE NEGRO, SPIRITUAL

There is a balm in Gilead
To make the wounded whole
There is a balm in Gilead
To heal the sin-sick soul[1]

Ninny* was tripping.

I was thirteen years old, and it was the last day of auditions for my eighth-grade talent show. I had tried every available mainstream medical remedy to overcome a bout of the flu that had muted my skills as a microphone fiend.[†] I had slathered myself in Vicks VapoRub, taken shots of Robitussin to the head, and lined my throat with so much honey that I'm still ashamed to look a bumblebee in the eye, but nothing worked. Since I was one of the top-ranked middle school emcees in the coastal region of South Carolina, my rap crew, the Fresh Force, was on pins and needles about whether I would make the audition. Luckily, my grandmother informed me of a surefire remedy that would solve all my problems: I had to drink my own pee.

---

* *A Gullah word meaning "one who has prayed for your mamma, aunts, uncles, and all your cousins."*
† *These skills were developed before I became a teen. And because I was lactose intolerant, I couldn't deal with ice cream either, Rakim.*

Yes, my grandmother, who had told me *on more than one occasion* that she loved me, wanted me to urinate in a cup, drink it, turn it upside down, put it on a table, and let her pray over the cup. I later learned that this was a traditional folk cure that dated back to slavery,[2] but my first instinct was to yell, "*Oh, hell no!*" However, I knew I couldn't use such language in front of a board-certified mother of the church who was saved, sanctified, and filled with the Holy Ghost child of God, because using such ungodly language would expose me to the possibility of a smiting. (I honestly don't know what that means, but Pastor Johnson talked a lot about the Lord "smiting" sinners, and my immune system was not in the position to fight off a smite from God *and* this mystery illness.)

My ninny was a praying woman whom I have seen pray the air back into a flat tire (that's a whole other story but, *I promise*, it happened). She was a product of what Black Southerners call "that old-time religion." She earned her graduate degree in the Holy Ghost long before I was born, back when she was a founding member of the Household of Faith Holiness Church of the Living God, Pillar, and Ground of Truth. And to her, the cure made perfect sense as a remedy, *and* as a test of my faith. Not only did she know how much I wanted to audition, but she also knew that my sisters would roast me forever for drinking my own pee, so she placed a small coffee mug on the dining room table and told me to pee in it, which I did. But she didn't make me drink it right there and then. Instead, she left it on the table. All I had to do was drink it and turn the cup upside down, and—if she came back and saw the empty cup turned upside down—she would pray over it and not tell anyone. But if the pee was untouched, then she (and God) would know that I didn't have enough faith.

Look, I know faith is the substance of things hoped for and the essence of things not seen, but I couldn't see myself drinking my body's factory-refurbished lemonade, so I walked past that pee cup all day. I *really wanted that audition*, but did God really require his children to walk around with urine sloshing in their stomachs before he healed them? And what if I liked it and became addicted? Was there a twelve-step program for drinking whizz? In the end, I decided to trust in the Lord, my grandma, and Tinkleholics Anonymous. I woke my grandmother up in the middle of the night (so my sisters wouldn't call me "pee-pee boy") and handed her the empty pee cup. Then my grandma began praying.

Oh, dear reader, my grandma said *all* the prayers. She prayed hard as anyone I've ever heard. She called on all *his holy names*: Jesus, King of Kings, Lord of Lords, Alpha, Omega, Bright and Morning Star, the Lamb of God, Almighty, Mos Def, H to the Izzo V to the Izzay (For shizzle my nizzle kicked the devil out of the way). And when I woke up the following day, guess what?

I was healed!

Although I was elated, I was not surprised in the least. After the Fresh Force took first place in the talent show, my faith in God and the ancestors was confirmed. Even my grandmother was proud of my "devil's music."

"See how God works things out?" she explained when I recounted the win to her. "God healed you and got you that money! That's what happens when you step out on faith! Don't forget to pay your tithes."

If you're wondering how this story relates to the history of Black people in America, it comes down to the power of "the church." Like many descendants of enslaved people in this country, I grew up in "the church," which means any account from my childhood generally involves houses of worship and the faith of my family and my community. Although our religion can be considered part of a Christian denomination, the American tradition of Black Christian theology is ultimately an amalgam of Protestantism, Catholicism, Judaism, Islam, and African traditions. In the Household of Faith, we considered ourselves the Children of Israel and knew we were blessed and highly favored. We celebrated Passover, ate halal, and knew God was good all the time and all the time God was good. Our choir marched into the sanctuary on pastors' anniversaries, and we kept the seventh-day sabbath. We shouted when the Holy Ghost came, and sat in the hierarchy of an African village. The "grown people" sat up front in the pews reserved for the elders; the children must earn a seat. One of the most tragic experiences of my youth was the shame I endured whenever my church would have a special service. If the church got too crowded, the children would be banished to a waiting area outside the sanctuary. My mother, however, insisted on keeping us in view. So during a special convocation, she would force my sisters and me to bring milk crates, position them in the aisle next to her designated seat, and spend the rest of the service dodging the Holy Ghost on these unwieldy plastic cages.

While unique, our church body was just one of many adaptations of the Black faith tradition sprinkled across America's religious landscape. Be they Pentecostal, Bible-Believing Baptist, African Methodist Episcopal, the Church of God in Christ, the Nation of Islam, or the thousands of non-affiliated congregations, perhaps the *only* way to understand any story of young Black America is through the lens of its communal faiths and religion, and how and why they developed.

Comprehending the complexity of Black faith begins with dismissing the notion of a "white man's religion," and any notion of obedient conversion during the early days of America.[*] Perhaps the best way to contextualize the contemporary Black tradition of faith is to realize that, for the most part, the new Black residents of America did not convert to Christianity or Islam; Christianity and Islam converted to African America, and morphed into new expressions of spirituality that combined African rituals, Christian theology, Muslim doctrine, and the essential precepts of survival and resistance.

* * *

> *I couldn't hear nobody pray, Lord.*
> *I couldn't hear nobody pray.*
> *See when I was way down yonder by myself*
> *I couldn't hear nobody pray.*[3]

In the beginning, Christianity was one of the main excuses used to justify the human trafficking industry that enslaved indigenous and Black people in the New World. Even though the Jamestown colony was originally founded as a get-rich-quick scheme, these capitalist

---

[*] *Including the relatively newfound Church of Marvell Harriot and Latter-day Grandchildren.*

dreams were hidden under the guise of "propagating of Christian religion to suche people as yet live in darkenesse and . . . to bring the infidels and salvages living in those parts to humane civilitie and to a setled and quiet govermente,"[4] according to the 1606 Virginia Charter. In theory, the English colonizers were supposed to introduce civilization to North America's indigenous natives by teaching them about the European version of an omnipotent deity. In practice, they mostly just stole land, resources, and, of course, labor.

Massachusetts's 1641 law expressly forbade slavery "unless it be lawfull captives taken in just warres, and such strangers as willingly selle themselves or are sold to us."[5] This statute was derived from the Levitical law, the portion of the Torah that informed the Jewish priesthood, which would become the book of Leviticus in the Christian Bible:

> *"Because the Israelites are my servants, whom I brought out of Egypt, they must not be sold as slaves. Do not rule over them ruthlessly, but fear your God.*
>
> *"Your male and female slaves are to come from the nations around you; from them you may buy slaves. You may also buy some of the temporary residents living among you and members of their clans born in your country, and they will become your property. You can bequeath them to your children as inherited property and can make them slaves for life, but you must not rule over your fellow Israelites ruthlessly."[6]*

Because the American Pilgrims considered themselves to be builders of the "New Jerusalem," in this case, "fellow Israelites" meant white people. No self-respecting Christian would enslave a fellow follower of Christ, so it made sense that Africans would have to be excluded from the colonizers' What-Would-White-Jesus-Do mandate. Therefore, rather quickly, early Americans had to give up their initial cover story of trying to spread the gospel, and became reluctant to introduce their enslaved property to Christianity, lest their double standards be exposed.

When Lorinda Goodwin and her family converted to her master's faith on a Georgia plantation, she quickly realized the unspoken limitations of Catholic practices for the enslaved.

"I'd tell the priest everything I did wicked,"[7] she explained. "But I tell you, one time I had a cousin who told the priest he wanted to get free and asked him to pray to God to set him free, and bless your soul ma'am, the priest was about to have my cousin hung. The priest told my cousin's marster about it and they was talking strong about hanging my cousin . . . From that day on, I could not follow my Catholic religion like I had."

While most European immigrants worshipped the blue-eyed Jesus with surfboard abs, there was no universal African religion. Some worshipped the gods of their homeland, while others converted to Catholicism before arriving in America. Others practiced Hoodoo or Santería, a mix of West African traditions and Catholicism developed in the Caribbean. Even early forms of Christianity incorporated elements from all of these individual practices. Their "Holy Ghost" manifested itself in Yoruba dances. In his biography, fugitive slave Charles Ball described men who believed "there were several gods; some of whom were good, and others evil, and they prayed as much to the latter as to the former."[8]

Historians say more than one-third of the Africans brought to America practiced Islam, a fact that is still stamped on the identity and religion of Black America.[9] However, very little has been recorded about Islam among enslaved Africans because many Muslims worshipped in secret, and non-Muslims often did not recognize the religion. "There was one man on this plantation, who prayed five times every day," explained Ball, "always turning his face to the east, when in the performance of his devotion." Ball was describing *salah*, the Muslim prayer. Among Sierra Leone's Mandingo people, Islam was so prevalent that slave traders eventually began using "Mandingo" to describe Muslim slaves. Because enslaved Muslims were more likely to be literate, many of the interpretations and translations of the Christian Bible came from Muslims. The Muslim practice of circling the Kaaba is still prevalent in Black churches during the collecting of tithes and praise breaks for dancing a "ring shout."

In some of Georgia's coastal communities, the majority of the enslaved practiced Islam. In the 1820s, Bilal Muhammad, enslaved on Sapelo Island in Georgia, wrote a thirteen-page text in Arabic. Belali and Hester Mohomet, also enslaved on Sapelo Island, reflected their family's Muslim beliefs in their children's names, in the family's use of Muslim prayer beads, and in how they observed their hours of prayer, explained their great-grandniece, Shad Hall:

> *Belali hab plenty daughtuhs, Medina, Yaruba, Fatima, Bentoo, Hestuh,*
> *Magret, and Chaalut . . . Magret an uh daughtuh Cotto use tuh say*
> *dat Belali an he wife Phoebe pray on duh bead. Dey wuz bery puhticluh*
> *bout duh time dey pray an dey bery regluh bout duh hour. Wen duh*
> *sun come up, wen it straight obuh head an wen it set, das duh time dey*
> *pray. Dey bow tuh duh sun an hab lill mat tuh kneel on. Duh beads is*
> *on a long string. Belali he pull bead an he say, "Belambi, Hakabara,*
> *Mahamadu." Phoebe she say, "Ameen, Ameen."[10]*

Ultimately, just prior to the Revolution, the new Americans realized that it was too late to un-convert people, and slowly came around to the idea of Black Christians. Remember, their self-serving laws had already made slavery intergenerational and perpetual—and on top of that, we'd get language like Virginia's 1667 law "declaring the baptisme of slaves doth not exempt them from bondage."[11] So this was not a benevolent act, but one that they had to accept.

To assuage the fears of the white faithful, the Anglican Church through the Society for the Propagation of the Gospel in Foreign Parts (the church's missionary arm) distributed ten thousand copies of two letters to the residents of the British colonies in 1727, assuring slaveowners that Christianity "does not make the least Alteration in Civil Property."[12] More relief came in 1794 when a group of well-meaning white liberals formed the Missionary Society for the Conversion of Negro Slaves. To further its prophetic cause, the group printed a Caucasian remix to the King James Bible that left out all the parts that might incite freedom in the hearts of the enslaved. The censored version removed 90 percent of the Old Testament and half of the New Testament,[13] eliminating potentially seditious passages such as the story of the Israelites' captivity and escape from Egypt, including Exodus 21:16 (King James Version), which reads, "And he that stealeth a man, and selleth him, or if he be found in his hand, he shall surely be put to death." Naturally, the curators of the Slavery Bible kept all the parts necessary to curate a crop of compliant negroes, including Ephesians 6:5 (King James Version): "Servants, be obedient to them that are your masters according to the flesh, with fear and trembling, in singleness of your heart, as unto Christ."

The logic here was that if Black people began to worship the exact same God as white people, they might want the same thing white people enjoyed: freedom. They might question, and rebel. This wasn't just a hypothesis. Charlotte Brooks, enslaved on a Louisiana plantation, wondered, "How could any Christian man believe it was right to sell and buy us poor people like wee was sheep?" The leaders of the Stono Rebellion revolted for this exact reason—the goal was always to reach Spanish Florida, where Catholic law forbade the enslavement of Christians. After Jemmy and his crew went on their white-people killing spree, colonial lawmakers across the South passed versions of South Carolina's "Bill for the better ordering and governing of Negroes and other slaves," banning the state's Black captives from writing, gathering in groups, and worshipping together. Many Africans were unmoved by such attempts to ban them from their new forms of faith. Some held on to their religion in secret, while others were openly defiant.

Just as the white version of Christianity was used to justify the divinity of European royalty, colonization, and, ultimately, the theft and bondage of human beings, the Black form of Christianity reinforced the universal concepts already ingrained in the culture of the new African America. Christianity did not replace the religion of the Africans; it morphed into a new, Afrocentric expression of the Christian faith that would be at once revolutionary, resistant, and laced with the remnants of devotion imported from the motherland. When congregants sang about falling "on my knees with my face to the rising sun," in the traditional negro spiritual "Let Us Break Bread Together," they were invoking the rituals of Islamic prayer; they were conjuring the memories of Christ's Last Supper; they were summoning the spirit of their homeland. This new creed also did not displace fusions of African folk beliefs and Abrahamic religions such as Santería, voudou, and the South Carolina Lowcountry's own version, *roots*, or Hoodoo. They were worshipping their new God in the ways they had worshipped their old gods. It was Christianity, reconstructed. As Du Bois noted, "African religion, both fetish and Islam, was transformed . . . carried out secretly and at night; but more often in open celebration which gradually became transmuted into Catholic and Protestant Christian rites."[14] Yes, the first thing we remixed was "the gospel."

* * *

After the Revolutionary War, the doors to the Black church began to open.

> *There's gonna be a meeting (meeting tonight)*
> *There's gonna be a meeting (meeting tonight)*
> *We're meeting on the old camp grounds*
> *There's gonna be singing (singing), shouting (shouting), praising the*
>   *Lord*
> *There's gonna be a meeting (a meeting on the old camp ground)*

"My daddy said although they had chains around their necks and ankles, they would walk miles to get to a prayer meeting," Aida White Moore recounts in Eugene Frazier's *James Island: Stories from Slave Descendants*. "When they sing that song 'There's a meeting tonight on the old camp ground,' everyone knew there was a service that night. Pappy, his family and the other slaves on the plantation hold prayer meeting in a bush tent near the river called 'Will Foot Run.' The bush tent was made with small tree branches and lined with paper bags. They used crates and boxes for seats."[15]

The Black church that emerged after the Revolution was a wholly new creation. The First African Baptist Church of Savannah; Silver Bluff Baptist in Aiken County, South Carolina; and First Baptist Church in Petersburg, Virginia. All claim the title of the oldest Black congregation in the United States. Most of these new congregations were founded by Black Loyalists, churchgoers who sided with the British during the Revolution. These were not just religious institutions; they were defiant oases of freedom that emerged as pillars of nearly every Black community—free or enslaved, Christian or Islamic.

Aside from being spaces for praise and worship, Black churches, and in particular the Black church in Philadelphia, served as the hub of African America. Aided by Pennsylvania's gradual abolition act, self-emancipated slaves, Haitian immigrants, and unclaimed Africans flocked to Philadelphia to find work and build lives after the Revolution. After a 1688 protest by four German settlers in the Philly suburb of Germantown, the Religious Society of Friends (or the Quaker community) started thinking that maybe Jesus didn't like this slavery thing. Quakers eventually abolished slavery among their members, bolstering the freedom movement in the state. Shortly before fifty-five white men, including about twenty-five slaveowners,[16] convened in Philadelphia in 1787 for the Constitutional Convention, two Black preachers—Richard Allen and Absalom Jones—founded the city's first Black religious organization, the Free African Society (FAS).

Although Jones was an Episcopal and Allen was connected to the Methodist Church, both of which were overwhelmingly white at the time, the work of the FAS was not just about religion; it also provided mutual aid, medical care, wealth-building education, and social services for "free Africans and their descendants" in Philadelphia. FAS caused so much consternation among whites in Pennsylvania that the two had been accused of everything from stealing money from whites to harboring a secret remedy that made Black people immune to yellow fever. They even had to write a book explaining how they helped Black people survive an epidemic of yellow fever in 1793.[17] Dismissing the racist allegations, they noted that Black Philadelphians died at the exact same rate as white Philadelphians.

Perhaps FAS's most troublesome act was their insistence on educating Black Americans. Starting with a reading class developed as part of Sunday school curriculum in 1795, members began opening up schools in homes, tents, and even their barns to members of their congregation. In 1802, Jones became the first African American to be ordained as a priest in the Episcopal Church, and his first move was to convince his church to open a school. Allen, however, wanted to continue worshipping in the Methodist tradition that focused on sacraments and the methodical practices of the faith without the dry services in the Quaker tradition. In 1816, he founded the African Methodist Episcopal Church, the first independent Black religious denomination in America.

By 1837, the FAS ran ten private Black schools in Philadelphia with financial support from Quakers. That same year, the Institute for Colored Youth was established with a $10,000 grant from Richard Humphreys, a Philadelphia Quaker. The school relocated to Delaware County in Pennsylvania and was eventually renamed Cheyney University, the first historically Black college or university in America. And the Philadelphia influence spread. In 1856, Cincinnati, Ohio's Methodist Episcopal Church opened Wilberforce University, the first Black-owned and -operated college. Many historically Black colleges and universities are the direct result of this involvement from the church.

In the South, the Black church played a significant role in the education and resistance movements of free and enslaved Black congregants. While Black churches in the North often grew out of established white congregations, the Southern process for forming churches was essentially to gather in a tent, building, or barn and declare, "We're a church now."[*] Reverend David George, a freedom-seeker who was among the Black Loyalists transported to Nova Scotia, founded Silver Bluff Baptist Church in Aiken in 1774 or 1775. The First African Baptist Church of Savannah didn't earn official recognition until 1788, but its core congregation had been meeting since 1773. First Baptist in Petersburg began meeting in a building on the Byrd plantation in 1774. But like my grandmother often said about the Household of Faith, which started in a tent, Black churches are not *buildings*, they are *people*.

As Southern states passed statutes banning reading and manumission—the act of freeing slaves—Black churches offered shelter on the Underground Railroad, and spaces where free and enslaved

---

[*] *As for ordaining ministers, the process was very similar. Instead of saying, "We're a church now," they replaced the word "church" with "preacher," "pastor," or "rev'n."*

African Americans could educate themselves. The Virginia Revised Code of 1819 said that "all meetings or assemblages of slaves, or free negroes or mulattoes mixing and associating with such slaves at any meeting-house or houses, &c., in the night; or at any SCHOOL OR SCHOOLS for teaching them READING OR WRITING, either in the day or night, under whatsoever pretext, shall be deemed and considered an UNLAWFUL ASSEMBLY" punishable by public lashing.[18] However, whites often overlooked literate Black clergymen, allowing them to spread the gospel among the enslaved.* When a large number of people attended Andrew Bryan's services in Savannah during the American Revolution, he was arrested for plotting a slave rebellion and his parishioners were whipped. That said, a Chatham County judge declared him innocent and released him after several white members of the community protested. That type of "benevolence" didn't last long. In 1831, an enslaved minister named Nat Turner organized a violent uprising in Virginia, prompting states to pass even harsher laws. North Carolina, whose laws were lax compared to Virginia's, disallowed its enslaved population from learning anything except how to count, even proscribing the ownership of books and pamphlets.

But the laws of man could not stop the enslaved. Du Bois estimates that 9 to 10 percent of the enslaved population secretly learned to read. While Thomas Jefferson opined about how "blacks, whether originally a distinct race, or made distinct by time and circumstances, are inferior to the whites in the endowments both of body and mind,"[19] the enslaved of Monticello were reading and writing. Carpenter John Hemmings, blacksmith Joseph Fossett, and cook James Hemings, all enslaved at Monticello, were literate. Peter Fossett, whom Jefferson also enslaved, was sold to another plantation and held classes teaching his fellow enslaved people to read and write. To be fair, these self-educated Black men and women had to keep their intelligence a secret, lest the noble Founding Fathers discover that all men were actually created equal.

---

* If you're wondering how enslaved Black people skirted literacy laws, remember, white people enforce the law as they see fit.

* * *

Steal Away.
Steal Away.
Steal Away.
Steal Away to Jesus.
Steal Away.
Steal Away home.
I ain't got long to stay here.

A literate Black person in America was considered a dangerous entity. Literacy could enable a slave to forge their freedom papers. Sohia Auld taught the alphabet to one of the enslaved children on her Maryland plantation until she was warned that "knowledge unfits a child to be a slave."[20] Undeterred, the young child continued to learn in secret and eventually held a weekly Sabbath School class that taught other enslaved men and women to read the Bible. When other slaveholders in Maryland discovered that dozens of Black men and women were learning to read and write, they burst into the makeshift

church and dispersed the congregation with bats and rocks, temporarily ending tutoring lessons of the illiterate slave turned volunteer teacher Frederick Douglass.

Meanwhile, educated free negroes increasingly used their accumulated knowledge to inform and inspire insurrection—especially among Black congregations invested in the growing abolition movement. In 1829, David Walker, a free Black man who was active in the AME Church, wrote and began circulating *Walker's Appeal to the Colored Citizens of the World.* This revolutionary pamphlet advocated for the overthrow of the institution of slavery by any means, including violence, if necessary. The four-part pamphlet openly challenged Jefferson's claims of white intellectual superiority, earning the manifesto and its author the honor of being banned in several Southern states. "The bare name of educating the coloured people scares our cruel oppressors almost to death," Walker wrote. "America is more our country, than it is the whites'—we have enriched it with our *blood and tears.*"[21] Labeled as "seditious," the *Appeal* was banned in cities across the South, and African Americans in New Orleans and Charleston faced jail time for having it in their possession. The state of Georgia placed a $10,000 bounty on Walker's head, $1,000 if someone did the dirty work themselves and turned over his dead body.

The freedom and autonomy offered in the Black church extended past the doors of the sanctuary and inspired the fight for God-given rights. In 1844, twenty-three-year-old William Still, a literate free man, moved from New Jersey to Philadelphia and began working as an abolitionist. He operated a stop on the Underground Railroad, owned businesses, and successfully lobbied for the desegregation of Pennsylvania streetcars. When the Pennsylvania Anti-Slavery Society hired Still as a clerk, he provided a connection between the free Black community and the city's white abolitionists. Still also had a few radical ideas. Instead of appealing to legislators and influential white people, he wanted to take the abolition movement to the streets, putting out the word that his group wanted to find a way to challenge the Fugitive Slave Act of 1850, which essentially made every white person in America a slave hunter by requiring them to help slaveowners catch escapees.

Still would become most famous for the "kidnapping" of Jane Johnson. Since slavery had been abolished in Pennsylvania, Still believed that any enslaved person who entered the state could choose freedom, even if they were passing through. On July 18, 1855, he received word that an enslaved woman named Jane Johnson, who was traveling through the city with her master, wanted to be free. As Johnson and her children boarded a ferry to leave with her master, Still ordered five Black dockworkers to hold her enslaver and ferreted her and her children away, hiding them from police, slave hunters, and even the white members of his group. A month later, Still and three of the five seamen were tried and acquitted for rioting and assaulting a white man when Johnson, under the protection of abolitionists and Pennsylvania authorities, testified on Still's behalf. "I went away [with Still] of my own free will," she told the court. "I always wished to be free and meant to be free when I came North."[22] Aided by Northern abolitionists, Jane Johnson settled in Boston and was never apprehended.

Perhaps Denmark Vesey's story best illustrates the role of the Black church in resistance and education. Enslaved before the Revolution, Vesey was literate in three languages before winning $1,500 in the Charleston lottery in 1799 at the age of thirty-two. He paid $600 for his freedom, opened a carpentry business, married an enslaved woman, and attended Second Presbyterian Church before leaving to help start Emanuel AME Church in Charleston. When authorities briefly closed the church's doors in 1818 for meeting after sunset, it was the second-largest AME congregation in the country, with 1,848 members.[23] The church was shut down once again in 1821 when the Charleston City Council learned that the church was becoming a "school for slaves."[24] Vesey began preaching that enslaved Africans were the current-day manifestation of the Children of Israel who were enslaved in Egypt.

A free, educated, and financially independent Black man, Vesey was dogged by the fact that his wife and children were enslaved. After repeated attempts to purchase his family's freedom, to no avail, he came up with a solution: he was going to set everyone free. Vesey recruited thousands of enslaved people throughout the Lowcountry as well as Haitian sailors working at Charleston Harbor to prepare for a revolt scheduled for July 14, 1822. Betrayed by slaves who heard of the revolt and feared the repercussions, Vesey and his co-conspirators were arrested and tried by a secret Charleston court. Over the next month, about 130 Black men, free and enslaved, were charged with taking part in the conspiracy. In July, sixty-seven were convicted, thirty-two were deported, and thirty-five of the alleged plotters were executed, including Vesey.

Charleston would never be the same. The atmosphere of white fear permeated the city. The government established a separate force to put down insurrections and built a facility to train slave-catchers and house weapons and ammunition. The South Carolina State Arsenal eventually became the Citadel, a private college that still trains soldiers for the U.S. military. But the worst fate was reserved for Mother Emanuel AME Church. The City Council razed the building and pastor Morris Brown was kicked out of the state. Charleston would not have an independent Black congregation until after the Civil War.

* * *

In 1849, James Bradley, a wealthy South Carolina businessman, knew his enslaved servant Ervin could read and write. Because of Ervin's considerable skills as a blacksmith, locals overlooked his literacy and his antagonistic attitude, even allowing the talented bondsman to preach on plantations in the Salem District of South Carolina. Before Ervin's enslaver died, he outlined his will, dividing more than a hundred slaves on two plantations between his children.[25] But the slaveowner did not want his children to spend their time dealing with a slave as cunning and rebellious as Ervin. Ignoring the state proclamation against manumission,* the wealthy enslaver issued one final set of instructions for the executors of his estate.

"My belligerous Negro Man Ervin is to have his own time," he

---

* Ignoring laws against manumission was so common that giving an enslaved person his or her "own time" was recognized in wills and legal documents.

explained in the 1849 will. "He is not to be appraised when my estate is valued and no further services is required of him."[26]

Ervin was freed, but was still allowed to preach to the enslaved. He eventually settled outside Bishopville, South Carolina, and during the Civil War would travel to nearby Darlington County to sell tobacco. Even though he had a small plot of land, he often sold more crops than many of the larger landowners, stirring curiosity among local farmers. It turns out that Ervin's enslaved parishioners had been stealing small portions of their masters' tobacco harvests and "donating" the crops to the blacksmith in exchange for his teaching them how to read. During one trip to the market, angry farmers "seized upon" Ervin and his son, Ervin Jr., killing the father, while the son escaped. Ervin's family was kicked out of the area and relocated to an area between Lee County and Darlington County.

Ervin Bradley's descendants would forever cherish their faith and their religion. His great-great-great-granddaughter would successfully petition the state legislature to establish the South Carolina African American Heritage Commission in 1993, charged with preserving African American culture and historic structures and creating the curriculum for the history of the state's Black population. Although they accomplished goals that Ervin could only dream of, in the mid-1980s, one of Ervin's descendants, Michael Harriot, ignored the tradition of faith and courage of his ancestors.

Every spring, my family would spend a week at my aunt Marvell's two-bedroom house located across the street from the Household of Faith Holiness Church's Camden headquarters, which was also located on the property formerly owned by Bonds Conway. Because my aunt's house was so small, my mother, two aunts, three sisters, five cousins, and I would cram ourselves onto the beds, floors, couches, and corners of this tiny brick house across from where we would worship all day and all night for an entire week. My aunt didn't have a television (everyone knows that televisions are nothing but instruction boxes for heathens), so instead of watching movies, the cousins would stay up all night playing board games and laughing as my oldest cousin, Reggie, mimicked the Holy Ghost shouts of every saved and sanctified member of the congregation. My aunts spent most of the time cooking.

Around the corner from my aunt's house lived Elder R. O. Johnson, the second in command of all seven churches that assembled during this Holy Week. And because my grandmother was a founding member of the Household of Faith, instead of staying at my aunt's house, she would bunk with Elder Johnson and his wife, a faithful woman who was almost as devout as my grandmother.

The problem with this arrangement was that I loved my grandmother and was not used to being apart from her for any extended period of time. So occasionally I would walk the half block to Elder Johnson's house and sit there quietly, just so I could be close to my grandmother.

Elder Johnson was a stern, intimidating man who seemed seven feet tall and was built like a fire hydrant. He made dry jokes, dreamed of becoming an auctioneer, and owned a furniture store/gas station/ extermination business that made most of its money selling candy and cold sodas. Elder Johnson would sometimes let me run the entire store when I was in town. He also taught me how to throw a punch and chop people in the throat, told me stories about fighting in Vietnam, and gave me a microphone for my eleventh birthday that encouraged me to launch my nascent music career. One time I even watched him fight a white man who called me a "moon cricket" for counting his change too slowly. Elder Johnson was the closest thing I had to a grandfather, as my grandfather died before I was born.

Elder Johnson's wife, Sister Johnson, always thought I would be an "important person" one day. So, aside from anointing my head with oil every year to keep me protected, she always urged me to read stuff from her collection of Christian books. Most of it was boring, but there was one series of books that I loved by a Puerto Rican gang member turned Christian author named Nicky Cruz.

One morning, during Convention Week, I was waiting to walk with my grandmother to church. She had been sick for a few weeks but insisted on walking the one block to church. I distinctly remember that there was a James Cleveland record blasting through the house on the hi-fi stereo. Elder Johnson was standing in front of me, tying his tie, when my grandmother sauntered out of the spare bedroom. Sister Johnson then noticed that my grandmother was not looking well and she asked my grandmother how she had slept, to which my grandmother replied:

"I'm pretty sure I fainted in my sleep."

I thought that was the funniest thing ever and couldn't stop laughing. As I giggled, my grandmother took a huge medicinal-grade gulp from a cup and walked to the bathroom and spit it out. When she returned, she placed the cup upside down on the table. As she brushed her teeth, Elder Johnson turned the stereo off, said a slow prayer, and continued tying his tie. I immediately stopped laughing and stared into the abyss. Everyone could see that I was upset, and my grandmother repeatedly asked what was wrong, but I could not explain how my faith had been shaken or that the elders had failed me. When Sister Johnson asked again, I just pointed at the upturned cup that now held prayer instead of urine and muttered softly:

"Wait . . . You're supposed to spit it out?"

Sister and Elder Johnson stared at me for a second, wondering what the hell I was talking about, until my grandmother broke the silence and tapped me on the head. "Come on, boy, let's go to church!" she said. "You obviously need Jesus." As I stood up, still shaken, my grandmother added: "Don't forget your crate."

* * *

Perhaps the greatest legacy of this African American institution lies in the subtle difference in language that separates *the* Black church from all others. In medieval England, any sacred place or house of worship offered immunity to fugitives, which is partly why a church is considered a sanctuary, defined as "a consecrated place" or "a place of refuge and protection." In America, that tradition did not apply to fugitive slaves or Black people in general. But the Black church is *not a place*, nor does it exist in the physical realm. It is a school with no address and a meeting space with no location. It is a political machine and a human rights organization. It is why, in sermons, songs of praise, and speaking among each other, Black people rarely refer to a church as "a sanctuary."

The Black church is "*the* sanctuary."

THE TOP-SECRET RECIPE TO AUNT PHYLLIS'S FRIED CHICKEN

1 chicken, cut into parts
Some Lawry's seasoned salt
Some pepper
Buttermilk
Egg
A big pot of used grease
Piggly Wiggly bag
2 cups of Red Band all-purpose flour

First of all, I know you're wondering how this is related to history. Although there is a dispute over whether the Scottish or West Africans invented fried chicken, there is no dispute that the African version was the one that had seasoning and batter.[1] We're making the one invented by Black people.[2] And joking about unseasoned chicken is actually an ethnic slur. I will not denigrate Scottish culture. They make great toilet paper.

And yes, it has to be a Piggly Wiggly bag. This is not to say the bag must come from Piggly Wiggly. In South Carolina, *all* grocery bags are Piggly Wiggly bags, no matter where they come from. Unless, of course, you're talking about a *paper bag*, which, of course, is technically called a "Kroger sack." But you can't make this chicken in a Kroger sack. Don't be stupid.

Next you need to salt it. Not with just any salt. You need the Lawry's seasoned salt, the salmon-colored goodness that your mama taught you to sprinkle on everything from collard greens to corn on the cob. Sprinkle that on the chicken, along with some pepper, whisk the egg and milk together, and dump the chicken in there while you wait for your grease to heat up.

Now here is the key: your grease can't be new. It has to be melted Crisco used from the last time you fried some of this chicken. I know what you're gonna say. "Well at some point the grease has to be new!" Look, I'm just telling you the recipe. If you want some metaphysical answer to which came first, the chicken or the grease, then you just ain't prepared for this. And don't EVER call it cooking oil. It's grease. Calling it cooking oil will make your chicken taste nasty.

Next you need some Red Band flour. Pour that Red Band flour into the Piggly Wiggly bag and then pour some pepper in there, with some more Lawry's seasoned salt. How much? I don't know—*until there's enough.* Who do I look like, Juan Garrido? I trust the ancestors to tell me when there's enough salt, so summon his spirit. Just make sure you don't use a measuring cup. It ceases being soul food when you use measuring utensils.

Now dump your chicken in the bag and shake it. Shake it for the task system, which allowed slaves to raise their own chickens. Shake it for all those chickens that slaves stole from masters who

Nutrition Facts		
6 servings per container		
Serving Size : All Black People		
Amount per serving		
Calories		**99**
		% Daily Value*
Total Phat		**10%**
Saturated Fat 1g		**5%**
Trans Fat 0g		
Perseverance 0mg		**82%**
Creativity 16mg		**34%**
Excellence 37g		**94%**
Blackness 1g		**100%**
Dietary Fiber 4g		14%
Total Sugars 12g		
Includes 10g Added Sugars		**20%**
White 3g		**0%**
Iron 8mg		5%
Potassium 40mg		6%

* Now I haven't eaten all day. How am I gonna do this man? Yeah don't wait for her man, don't wait for her I'll tell you what man: come with me now and you know

weren't paying attention. Shake it for every part of the chicken that sustained us, including the chicken feet and gizzards that we frown upon as "slave food," to which my grandmother always responded, "Slave food is what got you here. And you ain't even gotta pick no cotton!"

Now it's time to make sure your grease is the right temperature. I don't know what the right temperature is, but I do know if your grease is too hot, your chicken will burn before it's done. And if it's not hot enough, you'll get greasy, soggy chicken. My grandmother checked it by wetting her hands and flinging a few drops of water into the grease. If the grease smokes, it's too hot. If it sizzles, it's just right.

Then you ease your chicken into the grease and wait for it to float. Depending on the piece, it will take somewhere between eight minutes and four hundred years. When your chicken starts to float, wait a little bit longer. Then you take out your chicken, lay it on a paper towel, and do it all over again.

Don't forget to save your grease!

And enjoy.

THREE LITTLE QUESTIONS

1. **The first Black church in America was:**
   a. Probably in a secret location.
   b. Not likely Christian.
   c. Aboard a slave ship.
   d. Wherever two or three were gathered.

2. **The difference between "the Black religion" and mainstream Christianity is:**
   a. African spirituality is embedded in the religious traditions.
   b. Black churches clap on the one and the three.
   c. Jesus isn't white.
   d. Do white choirs march into the sanctuary?

3. **Negro spirituals:**
   a. Relayed coded messages.
   b. Were sources of affirmation.
   c. Birthed a new form of American music.
   d. All of the above.

ACTIVITY

HOW BLACK IS YOUR CHURCH?

Give yourself one point for each of the following that you have experienced. Use the answer key to determine the Blackness of your church.

1. Been baptized outside.
2. Bought an outfit for a specific church service.
3. Knew who every seat on the front row was reserved for.
4. Shouted.
5. Played an instrument in your church band.
6. Owned a tambourine.
7. Turned to your neighbor.
8. Yelled at someone to demand that "You better _____" (sing, preach, or "praise his name").
9. Turned an R&B/rap song into a gospel song.
10. Been anointed with extra virgin olive oil.
11. Used a church fan from a funeral home but you were not at a funeral.
12. Marched into the sanctuary with the choir.

13. Been disciplined for laughing, talking, or not having your eyes closed during prayer.

14. Served on a "board" (usher, deacon, mothers).

15. Used a tithes envelope.

16. Owned a choir robe.

17. Brought a song to choir rehearsal.

18. Put a shawl over someone who fainted while shouting.

19. Stood up when the choir got to "the good part."

20. Used a highlighter in a Bible.

21. Questioned whether someone was "saved."

22. Had multiple people simultaneously "lay hands" on you like Holy Voltron or a Jesus Soul Train.

23. Been on the "sick and shut-in" list.

24. Given money to a visiting pastor based on the quality of his preaching.

25. Rode in a church van.

26. Held one finger in the air to exit the sanctuary.

27. Been a member of a gospel group that was NOT the choir.

28. Served on a non-preaching "ministry" (music ministry, kitchen ministry, cleaning ministry).

29. Introduced yourself in front of a congregation by noting that you are a member of "_____, where _____ is the pastor."

30. Could identify women parishioners by their church hat.

31. Marched in line to pay your offering.

32. Been accused of being deaf by a preacher who insisted "y'all don't hear me."

33. Began a testimony by "giving honor" to people.

34. Played shouting music.

35. Knew which deacon prays the longest.

36. Could imitate church members' shouting style.

37. Evacuated a pew to avoid having your toe stepped on by someone who "caught the Holy Ghost."

38. Bought a gift for a pastor's anniversary and another for the "mother of the church."

39. Owned a pair of "church shoes."

KEY

0–10: NOT A BLACK CHURCH: Your church may have had Black members, but it was just a church. Instead of instinctively knowing the words to every church song, your congregation may have used hymnals, and the only musical accompaniment was an organ.

11–20: BLACK & BOUGIE: Your church was Black but y'all probably had really good air-conditioning, your pews were cushioned, and your church didn't have a fainting protocol. Y'all probably "hired" your pastor.

21–30: BLACK CHURCH: Your church had a drummer and a high-level deacon who was designated to read the scriptures to the sermon. Your church was controlled by a Black Illuminati board composed of men who wore Stacy Adams and women whose purses were filled with the most potent peppermints.

31–39: BLACK AF CHURCH: Your grandma had the Holy Ghost, didn't she? Your church is so Black, the ushers wore nurse shoes and white stockings. Your church is so Black, you often dined in the basement on the moistest pound cakes. Your church is so Black, you didn't even have a pastor—the "angel of your house" had the title of reverend or bishop. Your church is so Black, you know women with titles like "deaconess," "prophetess," and "Mother." Your church is so Black, you can't even finish this post without whispering the words:

"May the Lord watch, between me and thee . . ."

ONESIMUS SAVES THE WORLD

n 1706, Boston preacher Cotton Mather received a tremendous gift in the offering plate—a human being. When Mather opened his tithes envelope and saw the blessing, he said it was a "mighty smile of heaven upon my Family"[1] and decided to name the newly arrived African "Onesimus," after a biblical slave.[*][†] One would have to think that Onesimus found Mather to be a little dimwitted. After all, Mather wanted Onesimus to worship some white man named Jesus, who apparently hated witches and gave away slaves on his birthday. Mather disliked Onesimus because Onesimus also refused to convert from Islam to Christianity, and because Onesimus's intelligence made him seem "wicked" and "thievish."[2] At any rate, Cotton Mather didn't trust Onesimus, especially when the slave told Mather something impossible to believe: he knew how to cure smallpox.[3]

At the time, the disease was ravaging the colonies. When Mather asked his smart-mouthed slave if he had ever contracted smallpox, Onesimus answered, "Yes and no."[4] Onesimus showed his owner a scar on his arm and explained that he had undergone surgery in Africa that made him immune to smallpox. Mather balked; there was no way he was going to take some medical advice from a Black slave who didn't know that Jesus was white. Then, in 1716, Mather was reading Dr. Emanuel Timonius's writing *Philosophical Transactions*. Timonius was extolling the virtues of inoculation from Constantinople, which was under Muslim rule. That's where Onesimus was from! Could Onesimus have been telling the truth? Did Muslims know how to prevent smallpox?[5] And how come Jesus didn't know about this? Aside from another witch trial, there was only one way to find out if inoculation really worked . . . After questioning Onesimus further, Mather followed the African heathen's instructions to cut himself and rub the pus from a smallpox sore into the cut, in order to make himself immune.

After trying the cure on himself, Mather finally believed Onesimus and started telling doctors everywhere, even sending letters abroad, but American medical professionals thought Mather

---

[*] *Peter Cottontail, too. Yeah, I said it. Peter Cottontail is a bootleg Bugs Bunny.*
[†] *Mather was very unoriginal, as are most people named "Cotton."*

was out of his mind for taking advice from Africa. Boston's elite argued that it was immoral to interfere with divine providence. But one physician, Dr. Zabdiel Boylston,[*] took Onesimus's advice, pricking smallpox sores (which weren't too hard to find at the time) and injecting the pus under the skin of willing participants. In total, Boylston got around 280 people to participate in the quickest vaccine trials since "Operation Warp Speed." For their efforts, Mather and Boylston were pilloried by the local press, including the *New England Courant*'s publisher, James Franklin.

In 1721, smallpox killed about 14 percent of Boston's population, but only six of the people inoculated by Onesimus's recipe died. Massachusetts would quickly become the first state to promote public vaccination, helped by James Franklin's younger brother, who eventually became a bigwig. (Aside from spreading Onesimus's vaccination idea, I'm sure James's little brother, Benjamin Franklin, did some other stuff.) Having saved Mather's family and ultimately whole colonies, Onesimus tried to purchase his freedom from Mather shortly after the smallpox epidemic passed, even offering to buy another enslaved person to replace him. Mather refused, explaining that he couldn't send Onesimus out into the world as an unsaved soul. No self-respecting slaveowning, witch-burning Christian would do something so egregious.

---

[*] *No relation to the other Zabdiel Boylston.*

7

THE BLACK EMANCIPATION PROCLAMATION

A POEM

When in the Course of human events, it becomes necessary for one people to dissolve the bonds of servitude which have failed to define their existence, and to assume among the powers of the earth, the separate and equal station to which the Laws of Nature and of Nature's God entitle them, a decent respect to the opinions of history requires that they should declare the causes which impelled them to their actions.

Only we held these truths to be self-evident, that all men are created equal, that they are—no, that we are—endowed by their creator of all things with certain unalienable rights, that among these are life, liberty, and the pursuit of happiness. We are the only ones who ever believed that, to secure these rights, governments are instituted among men, deriving their authority from the consent of the governed. We do not consent.

Whenever any form of government becomes untenable of these ends, it has been the right of the people to alter or to abolish it, and to institute new government, laying its foundation on such principles and organizing its powers in such form, as to them shall seem most likely to effect their safety and happiness. Prudence, indeed, dictates that governments long established should not be changed for light and transient causes; and accordingly, all experience hath shewn, that mankind is more disposed to suffer, while evils are sufferable, than to right themselves by abolishing the forms to which they are accustomed. But when a long train of abuses and usurpations, pursuing invariably the same Object evinces a design to reduce them under absolute despotism, it has always been the right and the duty of the people to throw off such government, and to provide new guards for their future security.

Such was the simmering long-suffering of African people in America. Their existence on this continent is a story of enslavement, oppression, and the most prolonged, undemocratic, heartless treatment of men, women, and children in the history of the human species. In every stage of those oppressions, the subjugated people collectively petitioned for redress in the most humble of terms. Their repeated petitions were answered only by repeated injury. Thus, a country whose national character is marked by every act that may define tyranny is unfit to rule a people. Nor were the oppressed wanting in attention from White

America. The enslavers and their advocates were warned, from time to time, of attempts to extend the already unwarrantable jurisdiction over the permanently indentured population. They were reminded of the circumstances of their forcibly enslaved, who appealed to their native justice and magnanimity. The bondsmen conjured them by the ties of their freed kinsmen, their radical allies, and their common humanity to disavow the institution. Yet they too were deaf to the voice of justice and of consanguinity. And so, this immature infant nation being impervious to reason, logic, compassion, and self-realization, there came no other choice. The men for whom this country had withheld liberty and justice since the day it was founded had to save America from itself. They wanted that smoke.

—*"The Unanimous Declaration of 'These Hands'*
by the Black Folks of America"

* * *

As Black people are acutely aware of cultural appropriation, the term "after" holds a special meaning in the lexicon of poetry, specifically the African American spoken-word genre. When a writer bases a poem on an already existing work or premise, the writer credits the original work in the introduction of the derivative piece by citing the initial author. For example, when Najee Omar begins his 2015 spoken-word piece with "Poems are bullshit . . ." he references the groundbreaking work "Black Art" in the title, "The Anti-Poem (After Amiri Baraka)." No one would have accused NBC of whitewashing a Black sitcom and creating a hit show for Caucasian palates if the title card on the pilot episode of one of the most successful sitcoms in history would have read *"Friends*: After Yvette Lee Bowser's *Living Single."*

In 1935, historian William Edward Burghardt Du Bois presented an entirely new historical perspective with the publication of *Black Reconstruction in America: An Essay Toward a History of the Part Which Black Folk Played in the Attempt to Reconstruct Democracy in America, 1860–1880.* Challenging the notion of academics that portrayed Reconstruction as a failure, Du Bois posited that the post–Civil War era was a confrontation over economic and political power between the working class (enslaved people) and the elite (slaveowners).* The fourth chapter, titled "The General Strike," was an even more brilliant and radical historical interpretation. In it, this great thinker put forth a new thesis: that the enslaved Black men and women helped win the War for Eternal Slavery simply by removing themselves from the economy that funded their proposed white supremacist empire. It was an interpretation so radical that many considered it downright preposterous. But it was true.

This is How the Slaves Freed America (after W. E. B. Du Bois's "The General Strike").

In 1860, on the eve of what we call the Civil War, the four million enslaved Americans of African descent were the most powerful force in the country. Not only were these bondsmen essential to the production of food, cotton, rice, and church songs, but their simple existence had been leveraged to secure mortgages on real estate, businesses, and investment loans. More than 60 percent of the world's cotton came from the American South, as did the majority of American millionaires—all by-products of chattel slavery. Their combined worth of $3.5 billion made Black bodies the single largest asset in the national economy,[1] worth more than four times the combined total of all the money in America.[2] If you only counted the per capita wealth of the white population, eight of the ten wealthiest states held slaves. In less than a hundred years, the forced labor of Africans had created an economic juggernaut.

Now this rapidly expanding nation faced an existential crisis. No longer was the enslavement of human beings seen as a detestable but necessary evil—Canada, England, France, Spain, Portugal, and Mexico had abolished the institution more than a decade before the outbreak of the Civil War. It had not only become America's national shame, but was a threat to national security. Enemies of the state could potentially activate sleeper cells containing millions of dark-skinned allies with nothing but the promise of freedom, which had happened during the War of 1812 and the American Revolution.

---

* _Pronounced "hoo-why-itt."_

Remember that stuff you just learned about Denmark Vesey? It wasn't just a cool story. Vesey's supposed revolt sparked more crazy conspiracy theories than the illuminati and Barack Obama's birth certificate, the craziest of which is that Black shipworkers from around the world were ready to join Vesey's rebellion. It all came to a head in 1822, when South Carolina passed the Negro Seaman Act, requiring all Black sailors to be imprisoned when their ships were docked in South Carolina. Equating "the presence of a free negro flesh" with "a moral pestilence which is to destroy the subordination of the slave, and the state itself," the act even required sailors to pay for the time spent in the state's lovely jails or be sold into slavery.[3] When a circuit judge declared the law unconstitutional, South Carolina enforced it anyway, knowing it would never make it onto a Supreme Court docket because of one Southern conservative and champion of white supremacy—South Carolina's radical pro-slavery political giant John C. Calhoun.

Calhoun was arguably one of the most powerful men in antebellum politics, having served as a congressman, senator, secretary of war, secretary of state, and two terms as vice president. In 1828, Calhoun penned the *South Carolina Exposition and Protest*, which introduced the idea that states could nullify federal laws, including tariffs, treaties, and taxes that unfairly burdened the states that benefited from free labor—the earliest rumbles of the region's aversion to "big government" policies that interfere with "states' rights" and "the Southern way of life." If the South conceded to "big government" and the campaign against the institution of forced labor, then the federal government could theoretically outlaw human trafficking altogether. John Calhoun wouldn't have it. South Carolina had already effectively nullified a federal judge's anti-slavery decision and other states took notice.

Eventually, Georgia, North Carolina, Florida, Alabama, Mississippi, and Texas passed laws that were identical to the Negro Seaman Act, effectively nullifying a federal judge's decision. In the Kansas and Missouri Territories, a five-year war between 1854 and 1859 had erupted over the possibility of slavery expanding into new states. At the heart of the conflict was whether Kansas would outlaw slavery when it became a state or ban the institution like its southern neighbor Missouri. As Congress debated the matter, pro-slavery Border Ruffians went to war against anti-slavery "Free Staters" to voice their opinion on the issue in the most American way possible: killing anyone who disagreed. The white-on-white violence even erupted in Congress.

The "Radical" wing of the newly organized Republican Party was comprised of a few anti-slavery politicians who understood that war was the only way to eradicate such a profitable enterprise. While some white abolitionists opposed race-based servitude, most Republicans simply wanted to preserve the union of settler states they called "America." Contrary to the dominant *white-people-fought-to-end-slavery* narrative, few, if any, white men were willing to donate their lives to the cause of a free African American. Just as the Founding Fathers acquiesced to the South and excluded Black people from the "all men are created equal" when initiating the American experiment, most political leaders wanted to figure out a way to avoid a North vs. South showdown, even if it meant denying Black people's freedom. This centrist sentiment resulted in the election of President Abraham Lincoln, who admitted that his "paramount object in this struggle is to save the Union, and is not either to save or to destroy slavery."[4]

Lincoln calmed fears of disunion by insisting that he had no plans to elevate Black Americans, free or enslaved, to the status of white men. "I will say then that I am not, nor ever have been, in favor of bringing about in any way the social and political equality of the black and white races," he said in an 1858 speech. "I will say in addition to this that there is a physical difference between the white and black races which I believe will forever forbid the two races living together on terms of social and political equality. And inasmuch as they cannot so live, while they do remain together there must be the position of superior and inferior, and I as much as any other man am in favor of having the superior position assigned to the white race."[5]

Once again, I need to emphasize this: no one, not the Northern abolitionists, Lincoln, the Union army, the Confederate turncoats, or the slaves themselves, saw the inevitable showdown as a battle to end slavery. "Neither North nor South had before 1861 the slightest intention of going to war," wrote Du Bois. "The thought was in many respects ridiculous. They were not prepared for War. The national army was small, poorly equipped, and without experience. There was no file from which someone might draw plans of subjugation. When Northern armies entered the South, they became armies of emancipation. It was the last thing they planned to be. The North did not propose to attack property. It did not propose to free slaves. This was to be a white man's War to preserve the Union, and the Union must be preserved."[6]

To explain how the country broke this intractable stalemate, historians often point to Lincoln's election, the Nullification Crisis, Bleeding Kansas, the Missouri Compromise, or any number of social, political, and economic factors that supposedly set the nation on the path toward the War for White Rights. Rarely mentioned are the Black revolutionaries who escalated the national discord and further radicalized abolitionists and political figures of the period until the incongruity of a democracy that allowed human captivity could no longer be ignored.

There are some who cannot wait for change and pledge themselves to the cause of dismantling the status quo with their own hands. When they are white, we refer to them as "patriots" or "freedom fighters." When they are Black, these unswerving agitators are most frequently painted as "thugs" or criminals. But if the informal nation within a nation known as Black America ever existed, then the preternatural instinct for survival and resistance that resides in the souls of Black folk at that time must be described as a unique form of patriotism. They were more radical than all of the Republicans combined, and they were the driving force of the Southern economy. They were at once powerful and oppressed . . . until they freed themselves and, in doing so, saved America. They could not wait for deliverance, so they undid their own shackles. History is written by the victors, but it is made by the rebellious. This chapter is an ode to the great Black American Revolution: After Jemmy. After Denmark Vesey. After Nat Turner. After Black people, and each of their small-scale uprisings and individual acts of desertion. *All of them.*

Previously, we'd talked about the American Revolution as the largest Black uprising, but perhaps the greatest insurrection in America was ultimately the slow, steady trickle of men and women who used the Underground Railroad to secure their freedom. While history portrays the network of safe houses, abolitionists, and conspirators as clandestine and secretive, the *real* Underground Railroad used every available means, public and private, to transform slaves to free men. Sometimes they secreted slaves to Canada, while other times the buck contingent chose the path of knucking. The tactics of the Black abolitionists frequently escalated to the point where white abolitionists disavowed their more radical Black counterparts.

Take, for example, the case of Shadrach Minkins. When white abolitionist lawyers failed to successfully represent escapee Minkins, the first person in New England seized under the 1850 Fugitive Slave Act, Boston's Black leaders came up with a different plan. A gang of "outraged black men" burst into the courtroom, faces disguised, and wrestled Minkins away from federal marshals. Hiding him in a basement, the outlaws eventually helped the fugitive escape to Canada.[7] Nine "African American activists"[8]—including Robert Morris, the second Black man admitted to the Massachusetts bar—were indicted and tried for treason, but were ultimately acquitted on all counts. This type of action was the Underground Railroad, too.

Others, after Jemmy, Nat Turner, and Denmark Vesey, tried to jump-start nationwide revolts where Black captives took up arms and went Stono on the slaveholders. John Brown's brazen attack on the U.S. arsenal at Harpers Ferry, Virginia, on October 16, 1859, is often cited as the Civil War's first unofficial battle. Brown, a white abolitionist, alongside a crew of around twenty insurgents, attempted to initiate an uprising, but they were quickly snuffed out by a company of U.S. Marines. These freedom fighters were later tried, and Brown was hanged along with his co-conspirators.

Brown was perceived as a tragic but delusional white man by those who were too blind to see that a reckoning was coming. Many Southerners took the incident as proof their captive property was not interested in taking up arms to fight. "By the confession of Brown it appears that the slaves were not parties to the plot, which, however, was concocted with the expectation that they would rise by thousands, and join in it as soon as the first blow was struck; in which hope the conspirators were signally disappointed," read an editorial in the *Kentucky Commonwealth*. "For one, we do not believe that many even of the most radical Abolitionists were encouraged in it."[9]

If they only knew.

Harriet Tubman and Frederick Douglass, both of whom were self-liberated via the Underground Railroad, had quietly lent their support to Brown's mission. Brown had met with Douglass on more than one occasion, receiving messages, support, and money from him and his network. One of Brown's most trusted accomplices, Shields Green, actually met Brown while living at Douglass's home. Harriet Tubman provided strategic support, reconnaissance, and recruits for Brown's mission. She might have been with Brown if she had not fallen ill days before the Harpers Ferry raid. And just before Brown set out for Harpers Ferry, he met with Moses Dickson. Upon hearing Brown's plan, Dickson "tried to dissuade [Brown] by telling him that the time had not yet come."[10] If anyone would know, it would have been Moses Dickson.

Born free in 1824, Dickson trained as a barber and began touring the South at age sixteen before becoming an ordained clergyman in the AME Church. On August 12, 1846, he gathered eleven other Black men in order to develop a ten-year strategic plan for a national uprising that would end slavery. The Knights of Liberty took an oath, swearing, "I can die, but I cannot reveal the name of any member until the slaves are free."[11] The membership would eventually cover every slaveholding state but Texas and Missouri. Many of the founding members managed stops and funded the Underground Railroad, which also provided the Knights of Liberty with a system of messaging, recruiting, and freeing potential members. After ten years, the men had enrolled 47,240 "reliable, fearless" Knights of Liberty who had been drilled in military maneuvers and were "courageous, patient temperate and possessed of sound, common sense." They planned to have a concentration of forces in Atlanta, where they expected to have 200,000 forces march on the anti-American traitors from the South.[12]

"A day was set," Dickson explained, "but before the time came, it had become apparent to the leaders that the relations between the North and the South were becoming so strained that it was decided to postpone our rising."[13] Many of the members would join the Union fight and help freedom-seekers through the Underground Railroad. "After the war had settled the question of negro freedom, the name of the order was changed" to the International Order of Twelve Knights and Daughters of Tabor.[14]

Continued revolts, escapes, and acts of rebellion didn't just bring the country closer to civil war—these incidents helped secure victory for the Union, although that was never the main goal of the enslaved. Again, the slaves were on the side of freedom. Just as the throwdown between the Patriots and the Loyalists provided an excuse for Africans to liberate themselves during the Revolutionary War, the political and economic arguments between the Southern slavemasters and the Union preservationists were immaterial to the Black bondsmen held captive below the Mason-Dixon. For them, armed conflict provided the perfect opportunity for emancipation, by any means necessary.

Given a choice between being part of America and owning slaves, the South chose treason and secession, sending the nation into what still stands as the bloodiest war in the history of this country. This war was won through the efforts of the escaped slaves, whose mere absence would eventually cause the economic collapse of the Southern empire. Yet when their War for Unending Enslavement began, the South considered their human property an advantage. While there is no evidence of Black soldiers fighting on behalf of the Confederacy, enslaved men and women were used as cooks, laborers, and personal attendants in the military. In many respects, it was these very Black people they forced into labor who best undermined the Confederate States' military efforts.

Take, for example, the case of enslaved Charlestonian Robert Smalls. As soon as the war began, Smalls was assigned to helm the Confederate transport boat the CSS *Planter*. Although the color of his skin prevented him from becoming a wheelman, Smalls became one of the most experienced naval helmsmen in the Carolinas. For nearly a year, he steered the ship, surveying waterways, delivering troops, and carrying supplies throughout Georgia, Florida, and South Carolina. On May 12, 1862, while picking up four large guns in his hometown, he and the enslaved crew stayed on board the vessel while the white men luxuriated around Charleston. But Smalls had a surprise for everyone: they were getting the hell out of South Carolina.

Around 3 a.m., Smalls found the captain's uniform and straw hat, and calmly sailed past the Union blockade, replicating all the captain's signals at every checkpoint. He circled back to pick up his family, along with the families of his fellow crew. The other crewmen tried to convince Smalls to avoid Fort Sumter, the Confederate stronghold and site of the war's first battle, knowing it would be filled with soldiers and seamen. Smalls refused, insisting that he should take the normal route, lest he arouse suspicion. Instead, he flashed the signal to pass the Fort Sumter checkpoint. When there was no response, everyone on the boat dropped to their knees and began praying and crying. Robert did not. He kept going, and was allowed through. Before they reached the Union's naval blockade across the harbor, Smalls took a bedsheet, tied it to the flagpole, and hoisted it in the air, alerting the sailors of the Union vessel the *Onward* that they were not enemies. "When they discovered that we would not fire on them, there was a rush of contrabands out on her deck, some dancing, some singing, whistling, jumping; and others stood looking towards Fort Sumter, and muttering all sorts of maledictions against it, and 'de heart of de Souf,' generally," one of the *Onward*'s crew explained. "One of the Colored men stepped forward, and taking off his hat, shouted, 'Good morning, sir! I've brought you some of the old United States guns, sir!'"[15] That man would introduce himself as Robert Smalls.

A week later, using information provided by Smalls, the Union forces took the Stono Inlet and occupied it until the end of the war, eventually leading to the capture of South Carolina. Even Lincoln was impressed. Little could he imagine that Smalls would not only dismantle his edict against enlisting escaped slaves into the Union army but, in 1868, become one of the first Black men elected to Congress, undermining Lincoln's 1858 position against "making voters or jurors of negroes, nor of qualifying them to hold office."[16]

When the fighting started, Union military leaders were unprepared for the influx of escaped slaves ready to open long-preserved cans of whoop-ass on their pro-slavery taskmasters. The debate over the legal status of "contrabands" like Robert Smalls was as contentious as the ongoing debate over the value of Black Lives. In 1861, Frank Baker, James Townsend, and Shepard Mallory stole a skiff near the spot where the *White Lion* landed with the first enslaved Africans in America. The enslaved men had been leased to the Confederate army to defend batteries in Virginia; instead, they rowed to Union-occupied Fort Monroe and presented themselves to Major General Benjamin Butler. When scouts informed Confederate major John B. Cary about the escape, he requested the return of his leased "property." Butler refused.[*] Trained as an attorney, Butler explained to the un-American troop leader that since Virginia considered itself an enemy combatant, the rules of war dictated that the men were now property seized during formal hostilities. Following Butler's informal declaration, Congress passed the Confiscation Act of 1861, stripping Confederate volunteers and their co-conspirators of their enslaved property that managed to reach Union-occupied spaces.

A few months later, Union major general David Hunter issued General Order No. 11, declaring:

> *The three States of Georgia, Florida and South Carolina, comprising the military department of the South, having deliberately declared themselves no longer under the protection of the United States of America, and having taken up arms against the said United States, it becomes a military necessity to declare them under martial law. This was accordingly done on the 25th day of April, 1862. Slavery and martial law in a free country are altogether incompatible; the persons in these three States—Georgia, Florida and South Carolina—heretofore held as slaves, are therefore declared forever free.[17]*

According to established military tradition, Butler and Hunter were technically correct, but the implications were enormous. If the runaways were "contraband of war," then, by extension, the army, not Lincoln, held authority in the Confederate States of America. Butler and Hunter's acts incensed Lincoln. He had no intention of wading

---

[*] *To be fair, Cary didn't have his receipt.*

into the fight over slavery, knowing it would exacerbate the resistance of the already incorrigible slaveholding states. "If I could save the Union without freeing any slave I would do it," Lincoln explained to *New York Tribune* editor Horace Greeley, "and if I could save it by freeing all the slaves I would do it; and if I could save it by freeing some and leaving others alone, I would also do that. What I do about slavery and the colored race, I do because I believe it helps to save this Union; and what I forbear, I forbear because I do not believe it would help to save the Union."[18] Lincoln quickly rescinded Hunter's order, but it was too late. The Confederate States were officially recognized as a separate entity.

But General Hunter's controversial order that would eventually set Lincoln, Congress, and the Union forces on the path toward enlisting free Black recruits and emancipating slaves was not his own idea. Hunter often consulted with a battlefield nurse who had been helping slaves flee to freedom, enlarging Hunter's crew of renegade soldiers. Hunter had even been paying her, but after the army stopped Hunter from recruiting Black soldiers, she gave up her salary so she wouldn't be seen as Hunter's favorite. Instead, she baked pies in the evening to sell to the white soldiers. Reenter Harriet Tubman. The famed conductor of the Underground Railroad was instrumental in Hunter's success in the South. Tubman's years of experience facilitating escapes gave Hunter access to a veritable super-soldier. Tubman could map the terrain for other troops, gather intelligence from the enslaved, and lead reconnaissance missions without being detected. Clearly understanding the advantage Black soldiers gave the Union, Hunter continued to antagonize the treasonous Southerners, enlisting their fugitive slaves to fight against them.

In 1863, Hunter would ruffle even more feathers, writing Confederate president Jefferson Davis directly:

> *You say you are fighting for liberty. Yes you are fighting for liberty: liberty to keep four millions of your fellow-beings in ignorance and degradation;—liberty to separate parents and children, husband and wife, brother and sister;—liberty to steal the products of their labor, exacted with many a cruel lash and bitter tear;—liberty to seduce their*

*wives and daughters, and to sell your own children into bondage;—
liberty to kill these children with impunity, when the murder cannot be
proven by one of pure white blood. This is the kind of liberty—the
liberty to do wrong—which Satan, Chief of the fallen Angels, was
contending for when he was cast into Hell.[19]*

Jefferson Davis had already ordered Hunter to be executed, but he
evaded capture. The War Department and Congress eventually came
around to Hunter's line of thinking, and formally enacted legislation
through the two Confiscation Acts. The first Confiscation Act, signed
on December 2, 1861, authorized Union troops to seize rebel property, which of course included slaves. The act authorized the troops
to consider slaves as contraband but did not specify their status. The
second Confiscation Act of 1862 clarified the position of the escaped
slaves of anyone "engaged in rebellion against the government of the
United States," and the slaves of anyone "who shall in any way give
aid or comfort" to Confederate contraband, declaring that all escaped
slaves in Confederate territory "shall be deemed captives of war, and
shall be forever free of their servitude, and not again held as slaves."
With these acts signed into law, the Emancipation Proclamation—
enshrined in white history as the document that kick-started the freeing of slaves—was essentially a formality, a performative gesture by
a president who didn't have the authority, intentions, or backbone to
free the people he had deemed inferior.

By 1865, the Union army was managing more than one hundred
"contraband camps" to deal with the steady stream of escapees. Somewhere between eight and fifteen thousand freedom-seekers showed up
in New Bern, North Carolina, from which William Henry Singleton
recruited at least a thousand Black soldiers. After the Union capture of
Roanoke Island, North Carolina, freedmen established their own self-
sufficient town, the Roanoke Island Freedmen's Colony. But the largest of the refugee bases was at the site of a town west of Fort Monroe,
Virginia. After ten thousand slaves turned themselves into freedmen
by escaping to Phoebus, Virginia, Mary Peake, a free Black woman,
began gathering adults and children under an oak tree to teach them
how to read. By the time the formerly enslaved gathered under that

tree to hear Lincoln read the Emancipation Proclamation, they had transformed the Grand Contraband Camp into one of the first official self-contained Black communities in America.* Mary Peake's oak tree would become known as Emancipation Oak, and Peake's lessons would become the cornerstone for the historically Black institution Hampton University.

The ranks of the Union army swelled with freedmen willing to fight. Among the approximately 185,000 Black men who volunteered for the Union army, 93,796 were from Confederate states. Sixteen were awarded the military's most prestigious decoration, the Medal of Honor.[20] The 175 regiments of the United States Colored Troops (USCT) gave the Union a decided advantage. The contingent of Black Union forces included the 54th Massachusetts Volunteer Infantry Regiment, immortalized in the movie *Glory*, and the Corps d'Afrique—a Louisiana unit formed after landowning free Black men were banned from joining the Confederate army.

And it wasn't just the men who provided a military advantage. Everyone knows that Harriet Tubman had a thing against slavery, but most people don't know that during her time as a Civil War scout and nurse, she freed even more slaves than she did as a conductor on the Underground Railroad. On June 2, 1863, Tubman became the first woman—Black or white—to lead a U.S. military operation, directing an armed assault during the Combahee Ferry Raid. Leaving with 150 Black soldiers from Beaufort, South Carolina, Tubman provided reconnaissance and helped three gunboats dodge Confederate mines. Once they reached their destination, the men eased off the boats and attacked the Heyward, Middleton, and Lowndes plantations, three of the South's largest agricultural slave camps. They burned the rice plantations to the ground and filled the Union steamboats with more than seven hundred instantly freed bondsmen. Not one soldier was lost.†

---

* *Not including the Great Dismal Swamp, Forest Joe's camps, and other places white people didn't know about.*
† *Tubman also fed Colonel Robert Shaw his last meal before he led the 54th Massachusetts on their doomed Fort Wagner assault. While the infamous nurse Clara Barton took care of the white men wounded in the battle, Tubman was providing comfort and aid for the Black soldiers.*

Meanwhile, Mary Louvestre (sometimes Touvestre) not only helped millions of enslaved people taste freedom—she changed the history of warfare in the process.

The battle for naval supremacy was crucial in the War of Slaveholder Aggression. Prior to this era, sea battles were contests between easy-to-sink, extremely flammable wooden ships—and it likely would have stayed that way if not for Mary Louvestre, a free woman who was a talented artist. Not only could Louvestre sketch, but she was a gifted seamstress, which is how she wound up in the home of a Confederate engineer, whom she overheard discussing a plan to reinforce a salvaged Confederate ship with iron.

Louvestre knew that this idea could turn the war for the South, so she copied the drawings, hid them under her dress, and asked for permission to visit her previous owners. She traveled to the nation's capital, where she received a military escort to meet with officials from the Department of the Navy. When the commander of the Norfolk Station heard of her bravery, he asked the navy secretary to offer Louvestre "any reward which her services might be thought to merit" for her brilliant and courageous act.[21] The Union used the information to speed up the production of the USS *Monitor*, which would face off with the CSS *Virginia* (previously the USS *Merrimack*) in the world's first battle between two ironclad ships, signaling a new era of naval shipbuilding. The battle made worldwide news and ushered in a new era of water-based warfare that gave the Union navy a clear advantage on the seas. For her efforts, Mary received a thank-you letter.

Tubman, Louvestre, Smalls, Minkins, and countless other names lost to history risked their lives for Black America. The South would incur devastating financial losses because hundreds of thousands of slaves absconded from Confederate homes and forced labor camps. Remember: the Black servants were much more than just labor. They held the intellectual property that created the billion-dollar agricultural industry that would have made the Confederate States of America the fourth wealthiest in the world, ahead of every European country except Britain.[22] Their bodies secured the loans and mortgages that made the lower Mississippi valley home to more millionaires than anywhere else in the United States.[23] In terms of stopping the expansion of slavery, Denmark Vesey's revolt was actually success-ful. The Black free-staters ensured that Kansas was admitted as a free state. The people who were enslaved were the power and the might of the South.

The Union army never intended to free the slaves. Lincoln didn't want to free the slaves. The Emancipation Proclamation *couldn't* free the slaves. Black people freed themselves. And in doing so, they de-feated the Confederacy and freed America from its most undemo-cratic institution. They were less concerned with flags, taxation, or saving the Union than they were with saving their people. Still, the re-sult of their actions was a victory for America. The freed slaves would come to literally define what it means to be an American. We are the ones who continually push this country toward its goal of becoming more perfect. We are the reason it is still a union.

If our existence has a purpose, if the universe has meaning and is not a series of random things that happened, it *cannot* be a coincidence that the first "contrabands" rowed a stolen boat on the exact same path as the *White Lion*. Nor unfathomable that one of the first self-sustained Black communities began where the English colonizers established their first settlement. It is impossible to believe there is no significance to the capital of the slave trade's ultimate undoing coming from the cunning of slaves who trafficked themselves to freedom. If this was a work of historical fiction, having Harriet Tubman radicalize Gen-eral David Hunter into issuing a bootleg Emancipation Proclamation would be too unbelievable. The fact that Robert Smalls steered the *Planter* to Fort Sumter for the ceremonial raising of the American flag, signaling the end of the Civil War, would seem like a fairy tale if it were not true. Having him represent South Carolina in the House of Representatives is almost too much, especially considering that part of the reason he won was his ability to speak the Gullah language.[24] That he was the "leading colored delegate" to South Carolina's con-stitutional convention after the Civil War[25] is too on the nose. These stories seem like a metaphor for something exponentially larger. But this is a poem. And, remember: America is just a story.

And this is a poem . . .

After Black people.

THE LOST CAUSE, EXPLAINED

"Explain Like I'm a Racist 5-Year-Old"[1] began as a takeoff of the popular subreddit "Explain Like I'm 5," which simplifies complex issues into easily understandable, digestible bites. While it was meant to break down the complicated issues of race, economics, and politics into a conversational form that even a bigoted toddler could understand, the character only known as "Racist Baby" soon became one of my best friends. Although his parents seem a little bigoted, RB often stops by, unannounced, and peppers me with questions. I tolerate him because I feel it is my duty to prevent Racist Baby from becoming Racist Man.

Hey, Racist Baby! Why are you carrying a cape?

Well, my daddy keeps telling me "the South shall rise again." I'm from Mississippi and I just wanted to make sure I'm ready when I get the ability to fly.

No, my little baby bigot. I'm sorry to tell you this, but you're probably not going to grow wings. Your dad is talking about the Confederacy.

What is the Confederacy?

The Confederate States of America was created in 1861 when eleven Southern states decided that they no longer wanted to be part of America, so they took their ball (and by "ball" I mean slaves) and left, prompting the Civil War. They refer to it as "seceding," which sounds nobler than what it really was: treason. When I was twelve, I told my mother that I was no longer subject to her rules, and she had no dominion over my bedroom because I was seceding from the household.

Just as the Southern states found out, secession did not go well.

Why did they secede?

Slavery.

And . . . ?

That's it. Just slavery.

But my textbook says it was about states' rights, not slavery. How do I know you're correct?

Well, they actually wrote it down.

On December 20, 1860, South Carolina became the first state to commit treason by officially declaring that its citizens didn't want to be part of the United States if it meant they couldn't treat Black people as property. The Declaration of the Immediate Causes Which Induce and Justify the Secession of South Carolina from the Federal Union was written as if it were a sequel to the Declaration of Independence. But instead of spelling out their grievances against their version of the tyrannical Great Britain, their entire list was just variations of "Y'all won't let us have slaves!"

The government had "denounced as sinful the institution of slavery," the Carolinians whined. "They have permitted open establishment among them of societies, whose avowed object is to disturb the peace and to eloign the property of the citizens of other States. They have encouraged and assisted thousands of our slaves to leave their homes; and those who remain, have been incited by emissaries, books and pictures to servile insurrection."[2]

You know what? Now that I read that, you might be right. It wasn't *only* about slavery. South Carolina left the Union in part because Northern abolitionists apparently kept reading books and showing pictures to enslaved people. My bad. They probably promoted the myth of the Lost Cause.

How'd they lose their cars? I thought they rode horses back then!

No, RB. The Lost *Cause* is an ongoing ideology that promotes the Confederacy as a valiant cause undertaken by brave men. They believe the Civil War wasn't about slavery and the Confederates weren't racist.

But my dad says slavery wasn't racist because things were different back then.

Therein lies the problem. Even if your ancestors didn't think of it as evil back then—*we do now*! Championing a bygone era that fought for human bondage is like sitting back and fondly remembering the good old days when a man could beat his wife for burning the pot roast.

So Confederate symbols are racist because they symbolize slaveowning?

Not quite. Although the entire reason for the Confederacy's existence was to preserve the "peculiar institution" of Black people as human chattel, most Confederate symbols have absolutely nothing to do with the Civil War.

I don't think that's right. My grandpop has a Confederate flag and he says it represents our heritage. Wanna see a picture?

Oh, that's not the Confederate flag. The first Confederate flag looked almost exactly like the U.S. flag, except it had fewer stripes and stars. But the United Confederation of Slaveholders hated that flag because it resembled the American flag and in battle they were hard to tell apart. In fact, you've probably never seen any of the actual flags that officially represented the Confederate States of America.

The Confederate flag you're talking about originated from a

design by William Thompson in 1863. And for him, there was no confusion about the true meaning of the flag that has now come to represent "Southern heritage." He said, "As a people, we are fighting to maintain the heaven ordained supremacy of the white man over the inferior or colored race; a white flag would thus be emblematical of our cause." He called that flag the "White Man's Flag."[3] But that was revised into a third version. And the proliferation of that flag is all thanks to a group of white frat boys.

According to historian Leroy Stafford Boyd, in 1812, a group of University of North Carolina students founded the fraternity Kuklos Adelphon, "the official name of an order that also went under the names of Circle of Brothers, Kappa Alpha, KA and the Alpha Society."[4] Kappa Alpha began to emerge with independent chapters throughout the South, until the fraternity essentially went extinct just before the Civil War.

In October 1865, defeated Confederate general Robert E. Lee officially became president of Washington College, now Washington and Lee University, in Lexington, Virginia. Two months later, on December 21, 1865, a new Kappa Alpha Order was founded there. Confederate veteran Samuel Zenas Ammen is celebrated as the frat's "practical founder"[5] because of his idolization of Lee and the Confederacy, as described in early KA literature: "Southern in its loves, it took ['Stonewall'] Jackson and Lee as its favorite types of the perfect Knight. Caucasian in its sympathies, it excluded the African from membership."[6] And what better symbol for this fraternity than the star-sprinkled banner flown by the great white knights Lee and Jackson? The flag you know as the "Confederate flag" is actually the battle flag of the Army of Northern Virginia, under the command of General Robert E. Lee.

The new KA wasn't limited to college campuses, either; members could form chapters called "klans" in surrounding counties to create a "Circle of Brothers." Three days after Kappa Alpha 2.0's founding, six men, including former Confederate soldiers, gathered in Pulaski, Tennessee, and started a spin-off fraternity that, according to Leroy Stafford Boyd, was also based on the old Kappa Alpha rituals. This group modified the name of the original Kappa Alpha and translated it to the hillbilly pronunciation from the Greek, "Kyklos," meaning "ring or circle," and "Clan," meaning "brothers or family." They called themselves the "Klu Klux Klan."[*]

In multiple issues of the group's newsletter, *The Journal*, a heralded Kappa Alpha Order alumnus, Thomas J. Dixon Jr., insisted that "Kappa Alpha need not fear to claim credit for suggesting the movement that culminated in a Kuklux Empire."[7] Dixon would also famously start to get women involved in the organization.

Wait. I didn't see any ladies at my dad's meetings.

Well, my little kindergarten Klansman, that wasn't always the case. In 1894, about seventy miles from where the Klan was founded, a group of white women united disparate pro-Confederate groups under one umbrella called the United Daughters of the Confederacy (UDC). Instead of terrorist activities, these women had a more targeted approach in venerating the Confederate symbology. While the ladies affiliated with the UDC did not create or substantially contribute to the precepts of the Lost Cause mythology,[†] this group of white women was largely responsible for mainstreaming it.

In fact, here's a quote from Thomas J. Dixon speaking directly to the UDC:[8]

> *Every clubhouse of the United Daughters of the Confederacy should have a memorial tablet dedicated to the Ku Klux Klan; that would be a monument not to one man, but to five hundred and fifty thousand men, to whom all Southerners owe a debt of gratitude; for how our beloved Southland could have survived that reign of terror is a big question.*

The "Lost Cause" was always a part of clandestine white supremacist clubhouse dogma, but it was the United Daughters of the

---

[*] *It's how Greek sounds when you speak with a Southern accent. Have we discussed white people's struggle with names?*

[†] *The phrase "Lost Cause" first appeared in a book by pseudo-journalist and Confederate sympathizer Edward Pollard, whose book* The Lost Cause: A New Southern History of the War of the Confederates *explained that American-style slavery was "really the mildest in the world" because it "elevated the African . . . in the interest of human improvement." White people really be tripping.*

Confederacy who supercharged it with one of the most successful marketing campaigns in American history. Historian Karen L. Cox argues that the "Confederate tradition" as we know it was formed by these organized groups of white women who wanted to perpetuate the myth that "states' rights, not slavery, caused the Civil War"[9] by painting an "idealized portrait of the antebellum South, one that romanticized white paternalism and African American slavery and glorified the valor of Confederate soldiers."

And clearly, that belief has held. According to a 2019 *Washington Post*-SSRS poll, 41 percent of Americans believed the Civil War was about something other than slavery.[10] A July 2020 Morning Consult poll showed that 43 percent of Americans believed the Confederate flag was a symbol of Southern pride. Only 39 percent agreed that it was a symbol of racism.[11]

How did they do that?

By casting white supremacy as part of Southern values. They started by lionizing white supremacist turncoats as champions for Southern culture. Have you ever seen a Confederate monument?

Of course! I've seen a lot of them. That's what we do on vacations. They're like my Confederate army figurines, but bigger. My mommy says I should see them all before they're all torn down and our history is erased.

Well, it's gonna take a while. A 2016 analysis by the Southern Poverty Law Center found 718 monuments and statues to Confederate icons on public property across the country, the vast majority of which were funded by one group—the United Daughters of the Confederacy.[12] Most of these statues were erected more than fifty years after the Civil War. In fact, when the SPLC looked at the history of these monuments and places named after Confederate icons, they found that the surges in dedications and namings coincided with two periods. The first began around 1900 and includes the institution of Jim Crow laws and the nativist movement of the 1920s that revived the Klan after its immediate formation. The second began in the early 1950s through the late 1960s, during the segregationist backlash against the civil rights movement. Between those two eras, the UDC focused their efforts on fundraising, building their ranks, and spitting on Black kids who tried to integrate their schools.

The UDC partially funded the "largest shrine to white supremacy in the history of the world,"[13] a more than twelve-thousand-square-foot carving of Jefferson Davis, Robert E. Lee, and Thomas "Stonewall" Jackson located at a stone quarry just east of Atlanta. In 1915, at the place now known as Stone Mountain Park, landowner Samuel Venable granted perpetual rights to the Ku Klux Klan to hold meetings, formally kick-starting the modern era of the KKK. Helen Plane, the UDC charter member who conceived the Stone Mountain Memorial, initially intended for it to include the Klan, because, as she told the initial sculptor, "I feel it is due to the Klan which saved us from Negro domination and carpetbag rule,* that it be immortalized on Stone Mountain. Why not represent a small group of them in their knightly uniform approaching in the distance?"[14]

The first sculptor hired to carve Stone Mountain was selected to begin his work in 1916, but ran out of time and money. But after the Supreme Court's *Brown v. Board of Education* decision brought desegregation to Georgia, donations poured into the UDC's coffers, allowing them to complete their work. The park finally opened as a tourist attraction on April 14, 1965—exactly one hundred years to the day after President Abraham Lincoln was shot by a white supremacist.†[15]

Wow! That timing is a little funny. But maybe they really loved their veterans.

Aww, my little Confederate kiddo, the United Daughters of the Confederacy was as concerned about preserving the memory of Confederate soldiers as your dad's "choir" members are concerned with roasting marshmallows on flaming crosses. By the turn of the

---

* *"Carpetbagging" is an old Southern term applied to Northerners who moved to the South, also known as "Yankees," "outside agitators," and "white people who aren't racist enough."*
† *Probably a coincidence.*

twentieth century, many of the women who were actual wives and daughters of Civil War veterans were either dead or suffering from bouts of "the vapors." But instead of disintegrating, the UDC saw a surge in membership, fueled by the growing determination to separate the races with Jim Crow laws. At the fourteenth annual meeting of the North Carolina Division of the United Daughters of the Confederacy,[16] one of the speakers extolled the organization's virtues:

> *You were the song of the Old South: you are the theme of the New South; and to-day in this high hour of peace and commercialism, when men are prone to forget, we find you banded together, United Daughters of the Confederacy, all still loyal to Southern rights, democracy, and, thank God, to white supremacy.*

Hmmm. Are you saying that they brainwashed people into loving the Civil War's losing side by building statues and waving a flag?

The new generation of Southern belles were less concerned about memorializing veterans than they were about institutionalizing the tradition of white supremacy that the army of racists fought to uphold. And the statue thing was only one part of their campaign to brainwash people into venerating white supremacists.

The UDC's plan was multilayered. Their national history committee organized propaganda campaigns in school districts across the country, including its annual essay contests that rewarded children who wrote glowing reviews of the South's disbanded slaveowning utopia. They also sponsored parades, placed Confederate flags alongside the U.S. flag in schools across America, and even founded "Children of the Confederacy" chapters. But perhaps the Daughters' biggest impact was the way they shaped how kids like you learn about slavery.

No single organization influenced the way educators teach the antebellum South and the Civil War more than the UDC. By World War I, the UDC had more members than any teachers' union, parent-teacher association, or historical society in America.[17] The

UDC's history committee eventually became so powerful that they were not only allowed to choose which textbooks were acceptable for teaching history, but they began to write their own.

"[We realize] that the text-books in history and literature which the children of the South are now studying . . . [are] guilty not only of misrepresentations but of gross omissions, refusing to give the South credit for what she has accomplished," wrote Mildred Lewis Rutherford. "As Historian of the U. D. C., and one vitally interested in all that pertains to the South, I have prepared, as it were, a testing or measuring rod. Committees appointed by Boards of Education or heads of private institutions and their teachers can apply this test when books are presented for adoption, so that none who really desire the truth need be hampered in their recommendation for acceptance or rejection of such books."[18]

And so fictions were created and perpetuated in schools across the country. In 1922, after using David. S. Muzzey's *American History* textbook for more than a decade, the North Carolina Textbook Commission effectively banned the textbook from schools because it taught students that slavery caused the Civil War.[19] A 1957 UDC-sanctioned textbook claimed that Virginia's enslaved Africans were "generally happy" and insisted that "Negroes went about in a cheerful manner making a living for themselves and for those for whom they worked."[20] A fourth-grade textbook suggested that students draw pictures of the Klan and make replicas of the Confederate flag.

"The white people who had lived in Alabama before the war had no special protection," read *Exploring Alabama*, a 1970 textbook on the state's history. "They appeared helpless, and many of them were frightened . . . Finally some of the people took matters into their own hands. They organized secret societies to help protect their special interests. The best known of these was the Ku Klux Klan."[21]

But my daddy says the flag represents my Southern heritage. You're from the South. Why don't you like it?

Well, RB, in 1948, Southern Democrats walked out of the Democratic National Convention and formed their own party—the

States' Rights Democratic Party, more commonly referred to as the Dixiecrats—to protest integration. Soon, the flag we now know as the Confederate flag became a symbol that represented the staunch opposition to the "liberal values" that the civil rights movement was trying to impose on the Jim Crow states.

After the University of Alabama was ordered to integrate its campus, the college's Kappa Alpha chapter started flying the flag as a symbol of their "heritage" and the "Southern way of life," prompting most of the school's white fraternities to follow suit. In 1956, Georgia incorporated the banner into its state flag, even though it *never represented the state during the Confederacy*. South Carolina's general assembly passed a concurrent resolution to fly the flag at its statehouse in 1962.

None of these states ever mentioned the Civil War in their reasoning for hoisting a flag in honor of the defeated Whitekanda. Like the KKK, the Kappa Alpha Order, and the United Daughters of the Confederacy, their only concern was preserving white supremacy and segregation.

Oh, I heard about segregation. My daddy calls it "the natural order."

I'm sure he does, you brainwashed brat. Anyway, at first, the United Daughters of the Confederacy tried to prevent people from using the Lee flag—not because it was offensive, but because it was *inaccurate*. But they eventually gave up trying to correct the narrative.

Why'd they give up?

Because it was their fault!

They were the ones who had promoted the myth of states' rights, heritage, and this Southern culture. They were the ones who cloaked their anti-Black rhetoric in an ahistorical narrative. While the Klan was lynching and the Kappa Alpha members were institutionalizing racism, the United Daughters of the Confederacy were the ones who were rewriting the origin story that recast white supremacist villains as heroes.

But if people have been taught that the Confederate flag represents their heritage, then is it racist?

If your dad taught you that he believes two plus two equals five, does that mean that everyone else should accept it? Should we change all the calculators to accommodate your dad's incorrect math tutorial?

Wait, I'm still trying to add up two plus two.

My point is this: It doesn't matter what anyone believes. The truth is that Confederate monuments celebrate men who committed treason against this country. The current Confederate flag represents a war to preserve the practice of human trafficking, rape, and murder. The only reason it reemerged into the national consciousness is because segregationists wanted to deny Black people their constitutional rights.

But if it's so bad, then why does my dad love the Confederate symbols so much?

For the same reason forty-three-year-old dudes try to tell you about the time they scored 38 points in a high school basketball game, or how guys who pledged a fraternity twenty-seven years ago will throw out their backs trying to put on impromptu step shows at the club as if they're still in college. They have the same sickness that makes Mick Jagger wear skintight leather pants: a distorted, delusional self-image cemented in their glory days.

Some people stay stuck in the past because the present and future don't look that good. Eighteen sixty-five was about the last time white people were really winning. Since then, they have been engaged in a bunch of diversionary tactics to try to keep the playing field from being level and keep from having to compete against the rest of America without the advantages their whiteness has endowed them with. It is the dread of staring truth and reality in the face, and finding out that they are inadequate. It is fear.

So should everything having to do with the Civil War be banned?

Of course not. But celebrating the anguish, mistreatment, and subjugation of an entire people is also distasteful. When some people see Robert E. Lee, it reminds them of a deplorable part of American history. Imagine if your tax dollars went to maintaining symbols and history books that reinforce narratives of white supremacy, or having to see a physical representation every day that reminds you of America's continued injustice toward your people.

But once all the monuments to and symbols of the Confederacy become shameful, how are we, as Southerners, supposed to remember the Civil War?

The same way we remember the Revolutionary War, the War of 1812, World War I, World War II, and every other conflict in American history: *with books*. We don't need a statue of Saddam Hussein to remember Desert Storm. I don't think the lack of mustachioed enslavers will make us forget the deadliest war this country ever fought.

I know there are people who would rather whitewash the past and romanticize the antebellum days as Southern belles sitting on front porches sipping mint juleps, but they were also willing participants in an almost 250-year genocide.

Maybe one day, out of its racist stupor draped in rebel flags and white supremacist wet dreams, the South will rise again.

And then you can come with me to the marshmallow roasts!

Nah. Probably not.

THREE LITTLE QUESTIONS

1. **Which of the following did not cause the Civil War:**
   a. Greed.
   b. Slavery.
   c. White supremacy.
   d. Black people.

2. **The best two-word description of the Confederacy is:**
   a. States' rights.
   b. Whites' states.
   c. States' wrongs.
   d. Yeeee-hawwww!!!!

3. **What would have been the Confederate States of America's largest export?**
   a. Cotton.
   b. Runaway slaves.
   c. Banjo music.
   d. Whiteness.

ACTIVITY

RANK THE LOST CAUSES

Imagine that the Confederacy had won the Civil War, and rank these residual negative effects in order of worst to worse-er.

1. The Confederate economy would have collapsed from the lack of industrialization.
2. Third-world poverty would have been created from the disproportionately uneducated, unskilled white non-slaveowners.
3. No Outkast.
4. Zero NBA Championships, Super Bowls. However, the University of Alabama football team would have been . . . well, not much different.
5. The Confederate flag would have become a symbol for racist traitors who turned their back on their country.
6. The Confederacy would have been the largest non-democracy on the continent.
7. Once secession became precedent, any state could secede whenever they disagreed with federal laws.

8. Poor white "illegal aliens" would be streaming across the Southern border to take our jobs, give their kids a better education, and commit crimes. We'd probably have to build a wall or something.

9. We wouldn't have to deal with Florida.

10. The inevitable race war.

8

CONSTRUCTION

In describing the nation's post–Civil War era, the blood shed by innocent Black victims of white terrorism often becomes the focal point in
the retelling of Black history. For the first time since the inept English
searched for jewelfruit trees on the Virginia shore, the white men imagined a world that did not belong to them. Dispossessed of their human
property, their wealth, and their honor, the planters and the poor Confederates were left only with the solidarity of their skin. "He turned,
therefore, from war service to guerrilla warfare, particularly against
Negroes," Du Bois wrote. "He joined eagerly secret organizations, like
the Ku Klux Klan, which fed his vanity by making him co-worker with
the white planter, and gave him a chance to maintain his race superiority by killing and intimidating 'niggers'; and even in secret forays of
his own, he could drive away the planter's black help, leaving the land
open to white labor. Or he could murder too successful freedmen."[1]

But that is what they did *to us*; not what we did.

After the great war for white supremacy, our forefathers brought
forth on this continent a new nation. This Black America, conceived
in their hearts and built by their unchained hands, was at once the
paramount dream of the ex-slave and the ultimate realization of every
white Southerner's fears. At the negro's feet lay a tattered and smol-
dering South, yet ripe with the fruit of liberty and unending opportunity, ready to be redefined.

LAND OF THE THIEF, HOME OF THE SLAVE

Motherless children sees a hard time
When their mama's gone.
Motherless children sees a hard time
When their mama's gone.
Lord, why you make this world so cold?
They ain't got no place to go.
Motherless children sees a hard time
When their mama's gone.

If ever there was a metaphor for America, it is the story of the estate located at the intersection of the Ashley River, Wappoo Creek, and the Stono River.

When William Wallace McLeod purchased the estate in 1851, he had no idea that his new asset was already one of the most important plots of land in the history of America. The McLeod Plantation was on James Island, South Carolina, just outside Charleston, a short walk from where Jemmy started the Stono Rebellion in 1739. It served as the base for the Black Pioneers during the siege of Charleston in the American Revolution.

According to slave schedules, between 1851 and 1865, McLeod forced ninety-five different human beings to work six days a week on the new property roughly the size of the Harlem section of Manhattan.[2] Violence was necessary.[*]

After buying his new slice of earth for enslaving, Mr. McLeod transformed his new land into a producer of South Carolina's most lucrative product—Sea Island cotton. Unlike the more common varieties, Sea Island cotton can grow on stalks up to six feet tall, producing flowers as large as a human fist, with long, sturdy cotton fibers akin to the expensive Egyptian variety.[3] McLeod had never grown cotton before, but he owned Pompey Dawson, an enslaved man known for

---

[*] *Unlike their contemporaries farther south, the slave-dependent agricultural entrepreneurs on James Island did not employ overseers. Instead, the wealthy white entrepreneurs, their families, and the other 193 white residents of James Island collectively used violence or the threat of violence to extort free labor from James Island's 1,533 unpaid servants.*

singing his favorite negro spiritual, "Motherless Children Sees a Hard Time." He bellowed it as he worked in the marsh tending cotton until he became known as "Hardtime" Dawson. Although he had been enslaved for all of his life, Hardtime was one of America's foremost Sea Island cotton specialists.[4] Bolstered by Hardtime's intellectual property, McLeod's farm became one of the most prosperous forced labor enterprises in South Carolina. While it was just the fifth-largest plantation on James Island in acreage, it ranked third in the value of livestock, second in value of its produce harvest, and first in Sea Island cotton production.[5]

Hardtime was married with four children, the oldest of whom was William Dawson, who likely marched to McLeod Plantation blindfolded and barefoot, like most of the human beings McLeod purchased from Charleston Harbor, the country's busiest slave-trading port. Will's feet never recovered, and he walked with a limp all his life. But he inherited his father's knowledge of Sea Island cotton and was expected to carry on his father's legacy so that he could produce generational wealth for McLeod and progeny.

When the Civil War's first shots were fired across the river from the McLeod Plantation, William McLeod brought in his brother to run the farm, moved his family to a vacation home in Greenwood, South Carolina, and volunteered for active duty with the Charleston Light Dragoons, a Confederate army unit so elite it was known as the "Sons of Privilege."[6] Before he left to fight for his right to protect his slave camp, he "leased" a few of his slaves to the Confederate army. Little did he know that they would not be the last Black people from McLeod Plantation to serve in the Civil War.

FORTY ACRES AND A MULE

Although Reconstruction is generally considered to be the period after the Civil War, it began as early as 1862, when Confederate forces had suffered mounting losses, and Lincoln began establishing provisional governments in conquered Confederate territory. As soon as Union navy ships appeared across the river from the McLeod Plantation in

1862, nine of the individuals who were enslaved there emancipated themselves. Three weeks later, another captive fled slavery. No one knows what happened to the original nine Africans who absconded from the McLeod Plantation; however, because of military records, we do know what happened to the tenth. On May 25, 1862, a Black crew member volunteered on the USS *Pembina*, a Union navy gunboat patrolling the intersection of the Ashley River, Wappoo Creek, and the Stono River. He proved himself an invaluable navigator and served aboard the USS *Wabash*, a Union steam frigate, until October 1865. His name was William McCloud Dawson, the son of Hardtime.

Unlike the owner of the McLeod Plantation, by fighting for his country, Will immediately became acknowledged as an American citizen. By collectively deciding to kill their countrymen in order to continue the two-hundred-year tradition of terrorizing and owning Black people, the Confederates had formally renounced their citizenship to become citizens of the Confederate States of America. McLeod and others were now traitors in their own land.

Post-secession, in order to restore the Union he promised to keep intact, Lincoln had to decide how he could create a path to regaining citizenship for the Southern turncoats. The Radical Republicans proposed the Wade-Davis Bill, which said that in order for a state to be readmitted to the Union, it would need to institute a ban on slavery in its constitution and have a majority of its voters take an oath of allegiance. Yet after the Wade-Davis Bill passed the House and the Senate, Lincoln refused to sign it. Always the moderate, he proposed a more lenient idea. His Ten Percent Plan required one-tenth of a state's voting population to take the "Ironclad Oath":

> I _____ do solemnly swear (or affirm) that I have never voluntarily borne arms against the United States since I have been a citizen thereof; that I have voluntarily given no aid, countenance, counsel, or encouragement to persons engaged in armed hostility thereto; that I have neither sought nor accepted nor attempted to exercise the functions of any office whatever, under any authority or pretended authority in hostility to the United States; that I have not yielded a voluntary support to any pretended government, authority, power or constitution within the United

States, hostile or inimical thereto. And I do further swear (or affirm) that, to the best of my knowledge and ability, I will support and defend the Constitution of the United States, against all enemies, foreign and domestic; that I will bear true faith and allegiance to the same; that I take this obligation freely, without any mental reservation or purpose of evasion, and that I will well and faithfully discharge the duties of the office on which I am about to enter, so help me God.[7]

As this bill languished, the Radical Republicans' plan to require abolition as a term of readmission was rendered moot on January 31, 1865, when Congress passed the Thirteenth Amendment to the Constitution. The new amendment declared, "Neither slavery nor involuntary servitude, except as a punishment for crime whereof the party shall have been duly convicted, shall exist within the United States, or any place subject to their jurisdiction." This, not Lincoln's magical Emancipation Proclamation, is what, legally, finally outlawed slavery in the United States.[*] And with that came freedom, but also great ambiguity about the status of these newly freed men and women.

The Constitution had never defined citizenship, leaving the new freedmen with no national status, surrounded by an angry and violent white population that had been defeated, in part, by their former servants. Until this point, whether freed slaves could vote, own property, or even if they had rights had been defined by individual states. Rhode Island had allowed Black people to vote since 1842, while Pennsylvania had rescinded its state laws granting Black citizens access to the ballot because Philadelphia, the state's largest city, was becoming majority Black. And in the wake of the constitutional amendment, with its sweeping proposition of the illegal nature of slavery, an entirely new discussion needed to be had about these freed men and women.

On March 3, 1865, Congress created the Bureau of Refugees, Freedmen, and Abandoned Lands. Under the direction of the secretary of war, the Freedmen's Bureau was intended to last for one year

---

[*] *You might want to remember the "except as a punishment for crime" part. It seems kinda important.*

and "direct such issues of provisions, clothing, and fuel, as he may deem needful for the immediate and temporary shelter and supply of destitute and suffering refugees and freedmen and their wives and children."[8] The Union army seized the land and the Freedmen's Bureau set up their South Carolina office at a plantation just outside of Charleston, at the intersection of the Ashley River, Wappoo Creek, and the Stono River, on the McLeod Plantation.

As Lincoln was struggling to come up with a plan for how to discipline the unpatriotic white Southerners, Secretary of War Edwin Stanton and General William Sherman met with twenty Black ministers in Savannah, Georgia, to discuss the fate of the emancipated Americans. The main spokesperson, sixty-seven-year-old Garrison Frazier, had one request: "To have land, and turn it and till it by our own labor."[9] Of the twenty Black leaders, all but one confessed that their deepest desire was to live separate from whites.

Armed with the Freedmen's Bureau's language that gave him the "authority to set apart, for the use of loyal refugees and freedmen, such tracts of land within the insurrectionary states as shall have been abandoned . . . acquired title by confiscation or sale, or otherwise,"[10] in January 1865, General William Tecumseh Sherman, commander of the Military Division of the Mississippi, issued Special Field Orders No. 15. The military directive commandeered over four hundred thousand acres of land in South Carolina, Florida, and Georgia and proclaimed that "no white person whatsoever" would be permitted to reside on the lands," adding that "the sole and exclusive management of affairs will be left to the freed people themselves, subject only to the United States military authority and the acts of Congress."[11] With the help of the Freedmen's Bureau, Black America had seized the opportunity to fulfill the dreams they had imagined.

With respect to Charleston, South Carolina, Sherman's order specified that parcels of land would be given to the men and women who had been enslaved:

> *The islands from Charleston south, the abandoned rice-fields along the rivers for thirty miles back from the sea, and the country bordering the St. Johns River, Florida, are reserved and set apart for the settlement of the*

*negroes now made free by the acts of war and the proclamation of the
President of the United States.*

This was of special significance in Charleston County, where
2,880 slaveholders had held 37,290 enslaved Africans, making it the
highest county slave total in America.[12] After Robert E. Lee brought
the War of White Supremacy to an end by surrendering his troops
at the Appomattox Court House on April 9, 1865, the Freedmen's
Bureau set about carrying out Sherman's order in Charleston, with
Brigadier General Rufus Saxton leading the effort to distribute the
land. During the Civil War, Saxton was in charge of recruiting and
commanding the Union's Black soldiers. Although some assumed this
was an insult to Saxton, they had no idea that he had been raised by
a father who was a Unitarian minister, a staunch abolitionist, and a
feminist writer (yes, they existed back then). Saxton started to divide
the land into forty-acre plots and gave out land grants to the newly
freed Black Charlestonians.

Freedmen from all over the county flocked to McLeod Plantation,
an area that had the added benefit of protection courtesy of Massachusetts's all-Black 55th Regiment, who had turned the plantation into a
hospital during the war. When white men tried to visit, they "were
met by a party of Negroes, forty in number, who rushed to the landing [at McLeod Plantation] armed with guns and drove them away
with threats to kill them if they came to disturb them in their homes
again."[13] In 1865, Saxton's officials lined up the formerly enslaved,
many of whom had set up tents and temporary shacks at McLeod's
They handed each of the heads of the families a piece of paper, and
explained that the deeds they just received meant they now owned the
plantations they had spent their lives building for free. Some rejoiced,
while others collapsed in tears. One of the men—America's foremost
expert in Sea Island cotton—broke into song. For the first time in his
life, William "Hardtime" Dawson had a home of his own. But this joy
did not last.

On April 15, 1865, John Wilkes Booth assassinated Abraham Lincoln, leaving Confederate sympathizer Andrew Johnson as president.
Johnson was a Southerner, a slaveowner, and a Democrat who had

been chosen for the vice presidency in the hopes of stopping the South from seceding. As a former senator of the Great State of Tennessee, Johnson repeatedly let his Democrat friends know where he stood on the issue of freedmen: "As for the Negro I am for setting him free but at the same time, I assert that this is a white man's government,"[14] he said in an 1864 speech, reiterating his earlier promises of "a free, intelligent white constituency, instead of a negro aristocracy"[15] after the war. When Johnson ascended to the presidency, his first course of action was to stop that slaves-getting-land nonsense.

As second in charge of the new Bureau of Refugees, Freedmen, and Abandoned Lands, Brigadier General Saxton refused to comply with Johnson's orders, writing that "the faith of the Government is solemnly pledged to these people who have been faithful to it and we have no right now to dispossess them of their lands."[16]

Johnson fired him.

As soon as he became president, Johnson pardoned every Confederate traitor who was willing to swear their allegiance to the United States and gave them back their land. And because Sherman's order was only legal under the War Powers Act, as commander in chief, Johnson simply rescinded it. On March 7, 1866, the Charleston office of the bureau informed Charleston's white plantation owners who had been dispossessed of their real estate after becoming official traitors to their country that they could return to their plantations as long as they shared with the former slaves, issuing General Order No. 9:

1. The former owners of land upon the Sea Islands . . . will be permitted to return and occupy their lands, or a portion of them, subject to the terms and conditions hereinafter specified.
2. Neither owners of lands nor freed people will be allowed to make use of threats against each other or the authorities of the United States . . . or to do anything to disturb peace on said Islands; but all disputes will be referred to Major Cornelius for adjudication.
3. Grants of land made to the freed people in good faith, by proper authority, or occupied by them . . . will be

held as good and valid, until changed or modified by
competent authority. But Major Cornelius may set apart
and consolidate them contiguous to each other, on one
portion of the plantation . . . in such manner as to give the
freed people a part possessing average fertility and other
advantages.[17]

In July 1866, Congress agreed to reauthorize the Freedmen's Bureau while stipulating that all the confiscated lands would be returned to the original owners. For nearly two years, Black people in South Carolina's Lowcountry actually owned the land on which they had been enslaved. On James Island, America's slave capital, *most* of the land had been redistributed to the former slaves before it was taken away. But now these freedmen were surrounded by angry Confederates whose land had been taken by Black repo men. And in those two years, they had all tasted Black power.

BLACK POWER

The formerly enslaved knew what it took to sustain themselves in the country they now co-owned. It's not like the Black populace suddenly lost the skills they used to build the immense wealth for Southern slaveowners. They knew that farming could be profitable, and they were not afraid of the work. They understood that they had previously been forbidden to read because education was an essential component to success. They were aware that wealth came from landownership. They knew how to gain and maintain power.

Some of the formerly enslaved refused the compromise to work for their former masters. Some seized abandoned lands of Civil War soldiers who had died in the war. Others purchased property from the financially strapped former planter class. When President Andrew Johnson restored the land to the former enslavers, some had already earned enough money to move off of the McLeod farm. By 1867, all the white plantation owners of James Island had regained their property, except for the children of William Wallace McLeod. McLeod had died on his way home from the Civil War, and his estate was tied up in legal issues until 1880.

Luckily, the formerly enslaved folks of McLeod, including Will and Hardtime, had assistance fighting for what was rightfully theirs from the Freedmen's Bureau, which was then under the direction of General Oliver Howard, a Civil War hero. Congress had given Howard "almost unlimited authority," including legislative, judicial, and executive power, which he used to help African Americans create institutions they needed to sustain their communities. President Johnson hated Howard for his open allegiance to the equality of Black people. The bureau was building the kind of America he had vowed would never exist when he decided to stay loyal to the Union. But the line was already drawn. Because the commander in chief can't just undo federal funding, there was nothing the pro–white supremacy president could do about it.

Although the bureau could not undo Johnson's order reinstating Confederate land, Howard had a better idea. He introduced a set of minimum wages for Black laborers who still worked on their former owners' property. To further secure their financial independence, he formalized contracts between Black workers and their employers. Because of this, Hardtime was still able to purchase his own piece of land, and Will was able to get a pension while working as a laborer at the McLeod Plantation. They both kept their money in the Freedman's Savings Bank, which held the savings of approximately seventy thousand mostly Black depositors in more than thirty-seven locations across seventeen states.

One of the most significant components of the Freedmen's Bureau was its education initiative, which built more than a thousand Black schools throughout the nation and allocated $400,000 toward the training of their teachers. By the end of 1865, more than ninety thousand students attended freedmen's schools, with an attendance rate eclipsing 80 percent of the school-age population.[18] For some reason, the white administrators were astounded by the Black pupils' "natural thirst for knowledge."

General Howard didn't just fund these projects, he empowered Black communities, providing the resources for them to build and maintain these institutions for themselves. He was intentional about creating a class of Black teachers and theologians, essentially seeding the country with churches that would build more schools and educators to fill the vacancies. Freedmen's Bureau agents scouted organizations and churches that were already engaged in educating formerly enslaved people and funded their efforts. In conjunction with the American Missionary Association, the bureau sponsored two dozen institutions of higher learning for African Americans, including Fisk University, Clark Atlanta University, and, of course, Howard University.[*]

In 1869, on the land where they had at one point worshipped in a tent made with tree branches and paper bags, Pappy White and a few of the men and women who were formerly enslaved at McLeod's and the nearby plantations christened a platform and began building what is now known as Payne Reformed Methodist Union Episcopal Church (Payne RMUE), on Camp Road in James Island. They arranged to purchase the property from the owners of the Seabrook Plantation in 1875, paying a dollar a year for ninety-five years. Pappy White's granddaughter Aida White Moore learned how to read at Three Trees Elementary, a three-room school on James Island founded by former slaves. As Payne RMUE's researcher and historian, she preserved many of the records that we rely on today.[19]

By 1868, Charleston, a city that had thrived on slave trading and slave labor, was now being controlled by its Black majority. Africans took their own produce to the market. Workers unionized. Generations were becoming educated. They had financial independence and social mobility, which angered white men even more. "And beyond that," Du Bois explained of the white Southerners' fears, "if a free, educated black citizen and voter could be brought upon the stage this would in itself be the worst conceivable thing on earth; worse than shiftless, unprofitable labor; worse than ignorance, worse than crime. It would lead inevitably to a mulatto South and the eventual ruin of all civilization."[20]

---

[*] *As you read those words, you may have heard someone scream "H.U.!" Don't be alarmed; Howard alumni can't help themselves.*

The worst conceivable thing on earth happened. Because the Confederate states were not represented in the federal legislature, Radical Republicans dominated Congress, and on July 9, 1868, another constitutional amendment was ratified. For the first time in American history, the federal government explicitly defined American citizenship, declaring, "All persons born or naturalized in the United States, and subject to the jurisdiction thereof, are citizens of the United States and of the State wherein they reside." The ex-slaves were not just free; the Fourteenth Amendment constitutionally guaranteed them all the "equal protection of the laws" previously afforded to white men. Almost eight months later, the Fifteenth Amendment declared, "The right of citizens of the United States to vote shall not be denied or abridged by the United States or by any State on account of race, color, or previous condition of servitude."

African Americans registered to vote in droves. South Carolina's Black voters quickly outnumbered whites. In 1868, the Black majority elected Francis Lewis Cardozo as the South Carolina secretary of state. Howard and the American Missionary Association had sent Cardozo to the state to establish freedmen's schools in South Carolina before he became the first African American to hold a statewide office in the United States. Black voters also sent Richard Cain, superintendent of AME missions and pastor of the historic Emanuel AME Church in Charleston, to the South Carolina state senate. In the state house of representatives was Union veteran and hero the notorious Robert Smalls. By 1870, the lieutenant governor of South Carolina was Black. A Black man was on the state's supreme court. And the state house of representatives was *majority Black*. Forty-seven percent were from Charleston, and as soon as they ascended into office, they started exercising Black power. A Black aristocracy had entered the chat.

On March 27, 1869, State Senator Cain created the South Carolina Land Commission to help the freedmen own the property they were farming. Essentially, the state government bought the land, and the Black borrowers were only responsible for the interest and the taxes for the first three years. If the borrower paid the loan off in eight years, they received the title. If not, they could still lease the land. In seven years, fourteen thousand formerly enslaved African Americans owned land in South Carolina. Benjamin Randolph, another South Carolinian who became one of the first Black men to serve as a presidential elector, crowed about the success. Randolph eventually helped create the state's first universal public education system while working with the Freedmen's Bureau.

And this wasn't just a phenomenon in South Carolina. In Mississippi and Louisiana, Black voter registration exceeded 90 percent.[21] Hiram Rhodes Revel became the first Black man to serve in the U.S. Senate, representing Mississippi. In 1872, Louisiana's Pinckney Benton Stewart Pinchback became the first African American to govern a state. Between 1870 and 1884, fifteen Black men were elected to the U.S. House of Representatives, and more than three hundred served in state legislatures.[22]

Black power was not just limited to politics, either. After emancipation, the Southern economy had collapsed. The whites were left to pay off loans and mortgages with literal Confederate money, which was worthless. The collateral that secured their wealth was gone, and the slave economy was no more. Not only had the plantation owners lost their profit margins, but the poor, working-class whites had to compete against an increasingly educated population of Black Americans. Most slaveowners had no Plan B, and were truly shocked to discover that the men and women who had worked under the constant threat of violence were not about to acquiesce to their white tears. Meanwhile, thousands of negro soldiers received regular pensions, and others earned money working their own land.

Black power was real. The workers had organized. Religious and civic institutions were building Black middle and upper classes. They controlled the political power base in the cities and the states.

There was only one choice for the cowards. They summoned the mob.

SLICK WITH BLOOD

Building things is hard. Destroying things is easy. After America began to witness what Black people could do if they were simply left alone, the reshapers of their own destiny became the target of disgruntled ex-Confederates who regarded the sharing of power as a collective affront to the white race. For them, power was a zero-sum game. White America's continued existence depended on the eradication of Black power, and so the destruction began.

On July 30, 1866, angered by newly issued provisions that disenfranchised Black voters, a group of freedmen, including hundreds of Black veterans, gathered on the steps of the Mechanics Institute in New Orleans to protest during the Louisiana state constitutional convention. Expressing their outrage in the Blackest way possible, they paraded to the assembly with a marching band to show their displeasure with the exclusionary laws that would become known as the "Black Codes." As they marched, a mob of white supremacists, policemen, and ex-Confederates brutally attacked the demonstration, until the marchers sought refuge inside the Mechanics Institute, where, as Ron Chernow explained in *Grant,*

> *The whites stomped, kicked, and clubbed the black marchers mercilessly. Policemen smashed the institute's windows and fired into it indiscriminately until the floor grew slick with blood. They emptied their revolvers on the convention delegates, who desperately sought to escape. Some leaped from windows and were shot dead when they landed. Those lying wounded on the ground were stabbed repeatedly, their skulls bashed in with brickbats. The sadism was so wanton that men who kneeled and prayed for mercy were killed instantly, while dead bodies were stabbed and mutilated.*[23]

"The floor grew slick with blood."

I have never been able to rinse that phrase from my mind. The carnivorous reaction to Black people *existing* is a theme that runs throughout American history. As early as 1865, the military commanders and workers with the Freedmen's Bureau began receiving regular reports of "murders and outrages" committed by whites against freedmen. In the Abbeville district of South Carolina, a "desperate and ruffianly character by the name of Reuben Goldberg . . . deliberately, and without provocation, as plenty can testify, shot a Negro by the name of

A. Payton, who always bore a good character in this neighborhood and has always been free."[24] Reformer Benjamin Randolph was allegedly murdered in cold blood by a Klansman. Confederate officer D. Wyatt Aiken, a Klan leader, had called for Randolph's assassination, according to Freedmen's Bureau officials.[25] Aiken was arrested, released two days later, and never faced trial. When they heard about his crime, South Carolina's white community elected him to serve five terms in Congress.

While many historians describe Reconstruction as a period of "racial unrest" marked by lynchings and "race riots," it was undoubtedly a war. There were soldiers who wore uniforms, took oaths, and volunteered their service to organized, armed units. They had a common enemy and a plan to take them out. The network of terror cells that sprang up during Reconstruction went by many names, including the White League, the White Knights, the Knights of the White Camellia, and—the most famous of all—the "Circle of Brothers," otherwise known as the Ku Klux Klan. It was insurrection, ethnic cleansing, and terrorism with a little bit of guerrilla warfare mixed in for good measure. To enforce their goals, the loose confederation of historically white fraternities all had one common strategy: killing as many Black people as possible and overthrowing the government that had enabled their freedom.

In the 1868 election, Black citizens exercised their new right to vote and overwhelmingly supported Republican candidate Ulysses S. Grant. In Eutaw, Alabama, Black voters catapulted Grant to a two-thousand-vote margin in the county. Days before the 1870 midterm election, fearing the power of Black voters, Klansmen opened fire at a rally of twenty-eight hundred Black people, killing at least four and causing hundreds to stay home on election day. The Democratic gubernatorial candidate won the county by forty-three votes.

Ku Klux Klan members in North Carolina assassinated a state senator, murdered a Black town commissioner, and lynched so many Black voters in 1870 that Governor William Woods Holden declared an insurrection, suspended habeas corpus (the right against unlawful detention), and imposed martial law. But none of the more than a hundred terrorists arrested in what would become known as the

"Kirk-Holden War" was ever charged with a crime. Holden, however, was removed from office when Democrats gained control of the state legislature after African American voters were forced to choose between voting and their lives.

Many of the reports of these atrocities came directly from the Freedmen's Bureau. Even before the war's official end, bureau officers detailed "outrages," warning that white people were getting a little out of control. In describing a "freed boy" who was "dragged about three miles with a rope around his neck," residents of Caldwell Parish in Louisiana were told by the sheriff that if they signed a warrant, they would be "met by 50 armed men and killed." The bureau report ended by noting that "many colored people have been and are being killed in Parish on a/c of political opinions."[26] In Laurens, South Carolina, "ten or twelve persons" were slaughtered the day after the 1870 state elections. A congressional committee investigating Klan violence heard accounts of whites and Black ballot-casters being "waited upon" by a white supremacist mob.

On Easter Sunday in 1873, the Knights of the White Camellia, Klansmen, and Confederate sympathizers opened fire on Black voters in Colfax, Louisiana, burned the victims' bodies, and threw the corpses in a nearby river. No one knows how many people were murdered during this incident, but a military report lists eighty-one Black men; another fifteen to twenty bodies were fished out of the Red River, and another eighteen were secretly buried. "The bloodiest single instance of racial carnage in the Reconstruction era, the Colfax massacre taught many lessons," writes historian Eric Foner. "Including the lengths to which some opponents of Reconstruction would go to regain their accustomed authority."[27]

The white supremacist terrorism was not confined to violence. Almost every single state of the former Confederacy had begun enshrining Black Codes in their state constitutions in attempts to preserve the social and economic order that existed prior to emancipation. In South Carolina, farmworkers were required to work from "sun-rise to sun-set," and were mandated by law to refer to their supervisors as "master." The rules undermined the labor contracts instituted by the Freedmen's Bureau, and went as far as to forbid any person of color from learning a new trade, declaring, "No person of color shall pursue or practice the art, trade or business of an artisan, mechanic or shop-keeper, or any other trade, employment or business on his own account and for his own benefit, or in partnership with a white person, or as agent or servant of any persons, until he shall have obtained a license therefore from the Judge of the District Court."[28] Even worse, nine states passed or updated their vagrancy laws, essentially redefining "vagrancy" as "existing." In Mississippi, a Black person was breaking the law if he or she was "found unlawfully assembling themselves together either in the day or nighttime."[29] Kentucky filled up its jails by banning "rambling without a job" or "keeping a disorderly house." Tennessee laws withheld education from Black children by forcing them to work for free as "apprentices" under their former slavemasters.

Most often, whites used a combination of violence and technicalities to reclaim political and social status. In the 1866 election, when Georgia's Black voters elected three Black state senators and thirty state representatives, deemed the "Original 33," white supremacists flocked to the Peach State to expel the lawmakers under the new Black Codes. When the legislators challenged the laws in *White v. Clements*, the Georgia Supreme Court ruled, "After the most careful examination of this question, I am clearly of the opinion, that there is no existing law of this State which confers the right upon the colored citizens thereof to hold office, and consequently, that the defendant has no legal right to hold and exercise the duties of the office which he claims under *her authority*." For its violence and discrimination against Black people, Georgia was placed under military rule again in 1869.

Perhaps the most interesting part about the white supremacist tactics is that, in the long run, they still were unable to defeat the Black majority without cheating. Heading into the 1876 elections, in counties across South Carolina, white supremacist mobs threatened Black voters to vote for Democratic gubernatorial candidate Wade Hampton over Republican governor Daniel Chamberlain. In September 1876, a paramilitary group of five hundred white supremacists murdered about one hundred Black people in Aiken County, after threatening them that "their only safety from death or whipping lies in signing an agreement pledging to vote the democratic ticket at the coming election."[30] The Republican votes there somehow disappeared, but the Democratic votes quadrupled. In Edgefield, the vote total exceeded the voting-age population by more than two thousand.[31] The elections board threw out the suspicious counties' vote totals, which were upheld by a federal court. The Republican presidential candidate won South Carolina, as did the Republican governor.

Events in Louisiana and Florida had played out similarly as they had in South Carolina, with voter intimidation and suspicious vote totals throughout the state. In 1877, fifteen white men—five U.S. senators, five representatives, and five Supreme Court justices[*]—gathered in a Washington, D.C., room and decided to give the disputed electoral votes to Rutherford B. Hayes, the Republican candidate supported by Black voters, essentially making him the president. In exchange, the whites-only room also agreed to a plan that included three notable provisions:

- **REMOVAL OF TROOPS FROM THE CONFEDERATE STATES:** In many places in the South, especially Louisiana and South Carolina, the military presence was the only thing protecting Black freedmen from white supremacist violence.
- **FUNDS TO INDUSTRIALIZE THE SOUTH AND RESTORE ITS ECONOMY:** While this never really happened, it was clearly a nod to the white supremacists who couldn't compete with the Black laborers.
- **THE RIGHT TO HANDLE BLACK PEOPLE AS THEY WISHED:** The federal government agreed to essentially disregard the Constitution's equal protection clause.

The "right to handle Black people as they wish" became known as Jim Crow. Across the country—not just in the South—states passed segregation laws and disenfranchised Black people en masse. The

---

[*] *Remember there were fifteen Black members of the House and two Black senators between 1870 and 1890.*

Compromise of 1877 was the definition of white supremacy: Black voters had given Hayes the presidency, and in exchange, he and his white co-conspirators chose white supremacy over equality.

But there were some things they could not undo. By 1900, 42.8 percent of Charleston County's Black residents owned land and produced *most* of the cotton.[32] Historically Black colleges thrived, civic organizations flourished, and the religious institutions remained. The foundation created during this period of Black construction would form the framework for every movement for Black liberation going forward. What Black people created in the light of freedom could only be undone by trickery and evil. But that is not the lesson of Reconstruction.

Every single stereotype that remains about Black America was disproven after the Civil War. We were smarter. We worked harder. We were not the violent ones.

The criminal enterprise called America is nothing but a self-perpetuating white supremacy machine. The only parts that are good

and decent are the ones we shined with our spit. Everyone who calls themselves a citizen is a by-product of our determination to free ourselves. Due process exists because of us. The Founders only *said*, "All men are created equal"; we, the ones who made this country, prove it.

Still, that is also not the lesson of Reconstruction.

The lesson of Reconstruction *is us*. That we exist and breathe and love and sing and laugh and are still here is not a miracle or a revelation. It is a simple, unignorable fact that we cannot be extinguished. All the evil that the world has ever had to offer has been lobbed in our direction. They enslaved. They brainwashed. They lynched us separately and massacred us by the hundreds. They enslaved us by the boatload and sold our families in pieces. They mined our muscles and our minds for their profit and built an empire from it. And when we did the same without their help, they set it on fire.

This is America—a floor slick with blood.

But that is not who *we* are.

THREE LITTLE QUESTIONS

1. **After the Civil War, formerly enslaved people were rewarded with:**
   a. Nothing.
   b. Nada.
   c. Zilch.
   d. Citizenship, voting rights, and the constitutional protections they earned, which is technically not a "reward."

2. **What institutions did not exist in pre-emancipation America?**
   a. Constitutionally mandated public schools.
   b. A national system of state-funded colleges and universities.
   c. Universal male suffrage.
   d. Democracy.

3. **After emancipation, freedmen wanted . . .**
   a. To work for the same people who had brutally enslaved them.
   b. Revenge.
   c. To benefit from the labor that had been previously extracted through violence.
   d. White people to just leave them alone.

ACTIVITY

INHUMANE RESOURCES

You are a plantation owner with a hundred acres of cotton farmland. Write a recruiting letter to the people you formerly enslaved that will most effectively convince them to continue working with your organization.

9

SOMETHING ELSE

In 1948, James "Buck" Harriot, with cement blocks and his own two hands, built the homestead that would house every successive generation of his family. For most of his adult life, he worked a "good job" at a local paper factory while running a two-car taxi company on the side. When his family grew to six kids, he added a bedroom and turned the cement patio in the rear into a space from which he operated his cab company. Even after he moved his taxi stand to another location a block away, my family would still refer to that part of the house as the "back porch."

Separating the back porch area from the rest of the house was a hollow-core door made out of pressed wood. Since the 1950s, everyone who came to the house—strangers, family, and friends—signed that paper-thin shell of a door. When I eventually inherited the bedroom on the back porch as a teenager, some of my neighborhood friends would spot their grandparents' names scribbled in marker on both sides of the door. It documented teenage loves, high school football jerseys, and Black vernacular from "groovy" to "dope." At eye level, three square holes about the size of postage stamps pierce the wood of the back porch door. I always assumed the door had been damaged naturally, until my late grandmother recounted the story of how those holes came to be.

One time,[*] a crew of white men came to the house, outraged because my grandfather had been picking up people in the white community who called him for a ride, which was a no-no in the late '50s. The men somehow got on the back porch and started trashing things. My grandparents scuttled all six children into the bathtub, and my grandmother grabbed her pistol. When the first of three bullets pierced the back door, the intruders screamed, "Buck, you lucky!" Then an eerie silence fell.

Huddled in the tub, the entire family did not make a sound, other than my grandfather praying.[†] My grandmother said they stared at that back door for *hours*, not knowing what they'd find when they went out. Was his business trashed? Would there be a dead white man lying

---

[*] *All good Black stories began with "One time . . ."*
[†] *Ninety-seven-point-three percent of all prayers by Southern Black people are said out loud. We don't really pray in silence.*

on the ground? My grandfather eventually opened the door, and no one was there. The mob had destroyed the cab stand, but he eventually recovered from that loss. No one ever came back to harass them, and no one ever claimed responsibility.

I've always thought that we should remove the door and preserve it as a piece of our family history, but it still swings on the same hinges, unvarnished, the names and notes on it fading. Even when I argued that the door was too thin to offer any real protection, my grandmother would contemplate my argument before pointing to that single incident years ago. In her eyes, that splintering slab of pressboard saved the Harriot family. They would never replace it.

"They didn't take anything," I once pondered. "Do you think that they were just trying to scare y'all, or do you think they wanted something else?"

She answered without hesitation:

"Something else."

* * *

On November 4, 1890, the white citizens of South Carolina celebrated the election of serial killer turned governor Benjamin "Pitchfork Ben" Tillman. White South Carolinians were well aware of Tillman's penchant for mass murder, beginning with his time as a recruiter for the Sweetwater Sabre Club, a clandestine paramilitary fraternity devoted to killing as many Black people as they could. Tillman had already been indicted for murdering at least six Black men in Aiken County, South Carolina, after "the leading white men of Edgefield" decided "to provoke a riot and teach the Negroes a lesson" by "having the whites demonstrate their superiority by killing as many of them as was justifiable."[1] The future governor gained even more fame when his club members assassinated Black state representative Simon Coker as he knelt in prayer.

"The triumph of democracy and white supremacy over mongrelism and anarchy, of civilization over barbarism, has been most complete," said this king of the lynchmen to his inauguration crowd.

"The whites have absolute control of the State government, and we intend at any and all hazards to retain it. The intelligent exercise of the right of suffrage . . . is as yet beyond the capacity of the vast majority of colored men. We deny, without regard to color, that 'all men are created equal'; it is not true now, and was not true when Jefferson wrote it."[2]

Following his amateur career as a serial killer and his term as governor, Tillman represented South Carolina in the U.S. Senate until he died in 1918.[3]

Tillman was just one of many ethnic cleansers elected after Reconstruction. Georgia governor turned U.S. senator John Brown Gordon, one of the engineers of the Compromise of 1877,[*] was also commonly recognized as the head of Georgia's Ku Klux Klan.[4] Alabama's Klan leader, John Tyler Morgan, served in the Senate for three decades, from 1877 until 1907. Morgan fought to repeal the Fifteenth Amendment and introduced bills to "legalize the practice of racist vigilante murder [lynching] as a means of preserving white power in the Deep South."[5] Morgan served in the Senate alongside another Alabama Klan leader, Edmund Pettus, who represented the state for a decade until his death in 1907. Tennessee congressman George W. Gordon doubled as his state's Grand Dragon (and had written the precept for the Ku Klux Klan). Mississippi's "Great White Chief," Governor James K. Vardaman, was unapologetic about his pro-lynching stance:

> There is no use to equivocate or lie about the matter. Mississippi's constitutional convention of 1890 was held for no other purpose than to eliminate the nigger from politics. Not the "ignorant and vicious," as some of the apologists would have you believe, but the nigger . . . Let the world know it just as it is . . . In Mississippi we have in our constitution legislated against the racial peculiarities of the Negro . . . When that device fails, we will resort to something else.[6]

---

[*] Remember, the Compromise of 1877 gave Rutherford B. Hayes the presidency in exchange for Southern autonomy, or, as we know it, Jim Crow.

There is always "something else." After emancipation, the "something else" was the racial terrorism of Reconstruction. The Jim Crow era was the "something else" that followed citizenship, voting rights, and due process. The Klan was "something else." If American exceptionalism exists, perhaps it lies in this country's remarkable ability to conjure up "something else" to sate its appetite for Black bodies.

Du Bois believed the violent epidemic could be cured with an appeal to white men's sense of justice and fairness. He was determined to curb the mob murder fad that was overtaking America. On April 24, 1899, he left his home in his finest attire, his walking cane in one hand and a letter of introduction to the editor of Georgia's most prominent media outlet, the *Atlanta Constitution*, in the other. In truth, Du Bois needed no introduction. His reputation as the Harvard-educated scholar preceded him. He had taken a job at Atlanta University after finishing the first sociological case study of a Black community in the United States, *The Philadelphia Negro*, and was now engaged in groundbreaking research on the state of Blacks in the South, including the lynching problem. "It occurred to me," Du Bois wrote, "that I might go down to the *Atlanta Constitution* and talk with Joel Chandler Harris, and try to put before the South what happened in cases of this sort, and try to see if I couldn't start some sort of movement."[7] Armed only with his superior intellect, the great and honorable W. E. B. Du Bois was about to figure out what the hell was wrong with white people.

Instead of taking a segregated streetcar, Du Bois chose to walk to Chandler's Atlanta office. During his stroll, he discovered that a local retailer was offering a very distinct item for sale: the knuckles of Sam Hose, a recent victim of lynching. Du Bois stopped in his tracks, reversed course, and went back home. "I did not meet Joel Chandler Harris nor the editor of the *Constitution*," he wrote, explaining that his work was forever disrupted when he realized that "one could not be a calm, cool, and detached scientist while Negroes were lynched, murdered and starved."[8]

For two weeks, the story of Sam Hose had captivated the country. By all accounts, a brilliant, self-educated man, Hose had given up dreams of higher education to take care of his mother and intellectually disabled brother. While Hose was working as a fieldhand, on

April 12, 1899, his employer, Alfred Cranford, pointed a gun at him after he requested time off to visit his sick mother. To defend himself, Hose threw an ax at Cranford, killing him. When police arrived to investigate, Hose had already fled the scene. He knew he had no shot at justice. Something else was coming.

Over the next few days, police did not investigate the crime scene, collect evidence, or interview witnesses. Instead, Georgia's governor, the *Atlanta Constitution*, Coweta County authorities, and private citizens offered cash rewards for Hose's capture. Newspapers printed outlandish rumors, further instigating ire. Some reported that Hose had killed his boss after he was caught raping Cranford's wife in front of the couple's newborn child. They claimed Hose was insane from syphilis and continued his unfinished sexual assault after he hacked Cranford to pieces. A subsequent investigation by local officials found that Cranford's wife and child were unharmed.

When Hose was captured on April 23, a lynch mob of at least five hundred white people kidnapped him from deputies and took him to a field. People from across the state boarded trains to view the spectacle, but they did not lynch Hose immediately. First, the crowd took turns cutting off pieces of Hose's nose, ears, fingers, and genitals. Others used their knives to stab him repeatedly as onlookers cheered. Then they skinned him alive and doused him with kerosene while young children collected wood to build a pyre, before burning him alive, watching as his veins ruptured and his eyes withered. After the fire subsided, the crowd diced Hose's dead body into pieces and sold the remnants of their handiwork as souvenirs for those not fortunate enough to have attended the "barbecue." The festivities concluded with a prayer, and a sign marking the occasion, reading: "We Must Protect Our Southern Women."[9]

Between 1889 and 1922, the National Association for the Advancement of Colored People (NAACP) counted 3,436 lynchings, a rate of two Black people each week.[*10] Although this bloodlust was often characterized by mob violence, accusations of crimes, or hangings, white people would continue to implement increasingly brutal

---

* *We'll cover the NAACP later, I promise.*

new techniques in the great American pastime of murdering Black people in bulk. Their techniques varied so widely that the NAACP[*] eventually came up with four distinct qualities that defined lynching.

1. **SOMEONE HAD TO DIE FOR AN INCIDENT TO QUALIFY AS A LYNCHING.** I know this seems obvious, but when around twenty-five masked men dragged Jo Reed out of a Nashville jail cell, put a rope around his neck, threw him over a suspension bridge, and shot at his body until the rope broke, he technically wasn't a lynching victim because he survived.

2. **THREE OR MORE PEOPLE HAD TO TAKE PART IN THE KILLING.**[†] The makeshift rules didn't stipulate large crowds, like the one that appeared at sixteen-year-old Fred Rochelle's lynching. When a deputy handed the teenager to vigilantes in Bartow, Florida, in 1901, the mob kindly arranged for a special train to transport onlookers to the "barbecue" before forcing Rochelle onto a barrel, chaining him to a stake, dousing him with kerosene, and burning him alive.[11]

3. **ALL LYNCHINGS ARE ILLEGAL.** For instance, after a crowd of more than a hundred pursued Fred Sullivan and his wife, Jane, after their arrest, the couple confessed to burning down a barn in Byhalia, Mississippi. But it hadn't been legal for deputies to turn the pair over to "a committee of citizens." Especially since the deputy came back to discover "twenty men had organized a Judge Lynch court and carried out the execution with little formality."[12]

4. **WHETHER THE MURDER WAS FOR JUSTICE OR TRADITION, THERE HAD TO BE A REASON FOR THE LYNCHING.** David Walker was killed because he spoke disrespectfully to a white woman, a no-no in 1908 Hickman, Kentucky. The mob riddled Walker's wife, Annie, and infant child with bullets as they fled their burning house. The men shot three more of

---

[*] *In conjunction with the late historian Christopher Wallace.*
[†] *A Junior Mafia, if you will. What? My uncle Rob would think that's hilarious.*

Walker's children because they might tell. The oldest son stayed in the house, so the night riders set it on fire, just in case. See? There's always a reason.

The lynchings of Thomas Moss, Will Stewart, and Calvin Mc-Dowell in Memphis, Tennessee, in 1892 were a prime example of how Black death came resultant from this white furor.

Moss, a postal worker, was part owner of People's Grocery in the "Curve" neighborhood in South Memphis. Before Moss, Stewart, and McDowell joined eight other prominent Black men to open the store, William Barrett's grocery store had had Memphis's grocery game on lock. Barrett hated People's Grocery for infringing on his territory, even though Barrett's store had a reputation for gambling and selling bootleg liquor.* When People's opened across the street from Barrett's, even white customers patronized the Black-owned business.

On March 2, 1892, a young Black kid was outside People's playing marbles with a white boy. The two got into a fight over the game, and when the Black kid started winning, the white boy's father jumped in. Stewart and a few bystanders stopped the white man from "thrashing" the Black child, and a crowd gathered around. The next day, the father had let the incident go, but Barrett brought a Shelby County sheriff's deputy to People's to look for Stewart. When Barrett discovered Stewart wasn't working, he started ranting about how Black people were violent thieves. And to prove his point, he hit McDowell with a pistol. Apparently, white people in Memphis are really bad at fighting, because McDowell was able to recover, snatch Barrett's gun, and fire it at him. McDowell missed, but you know the white men don't take their butt-whippings like men. They issued warrants for McDowell, Stewart, and *even the little boy from the first fight*! The entire Black community was outraged and, during a neighborhood meeting, vowed to "clean out the white trash."[13]

Two days later, all of white Memphis had heard about the Black "conspiracy." On March 5, a law enforcement officer used the powers granted to him by whiteness to deputize five armed white civilians

---

* *That's why I don't shop at white-owned businesses. They are so ghetto!*

and cover the front and back of People's grocery.[*] But People's had already assembled a few Black men who were anticipating mob violence. They mopped the floor with Barrett's boys.[†] The white deputies then retreated back to Barrett's and sent *actual deputies* to arrest the Black crew. When the men at People's saw the uniforms, they readily surrendered their weapons and explained that they thought Barrett had brought some jackleg white thugs to the store to kill them. Even though Moss was in the back tending to the books, he was still arrested because, as a postal worker, he was said to be the leader of the anti-white conspiracy.[‡]

On March 9, seventy-five masked white men stormed the jailhouse, dragged Moss, Stewart, and McDowell out of their cells, and took them to a railroad yard outside of town. McDowell, who had whipped two white men, was shot four times in the face, leaving holes as big as fists. Stewart was shot in the neck and the eye. Moss, the owner, who had nothing to do with the alleged crimes, was shot in the neck. After the executions, a criminal court judge issued an order instructing the sheriff to "take a hundred men, go out to the Curve at once, and shoot down on sight any negro who appears to be making trouble." Armed white posses emptied local hardware stores of their guns and ammunition and heeded the judge's order. Evidence would later emerge that the judge may have even participated in the lynching. As the Black residents of the Curve hid in their homes, white residents looted People's Grocery, forever eliminating Barrett's Black-owned competitor.

Following the lynching, one specific quote began to filter through Memphis's Black neighborhoods. As he lay dying, Moss supposedly uttered his last words: "Tell my people to go West, there is no justice for them here."[14]

There was only one woman for the job of spreading that message.

---

[*] *Deputizing white men as law enforcement officers was a common practice during the lynching era, which absolved them from the repercussions of murdering Black people. Also, there were no repercussions for murdering Black people.*

[†] *Have I mentioned that the white gentlemen of Memphis are terrible at fighting?*

[‡] *In many Black communities, a post office job is one of the highest levels of employment, following teachers, preachers, and anyone who has the keys to the building in which they work.*

Although she was a transplant, she considered Moss and his wife to be the "best friends [she] had in town" and served as the godmother to their oldest daughter.[15] The brutal murders thrust her into the national spotlight, transforming a relatively well-known, outspoken journalist into one of the most fearless investigators and crusaders for justice in history: Ida B. Wells.

"The City of Memphis has demonstrated that neither character nor standing avails the Negro if he dares to protect himself against the white man or become his rival," wrote Wells in that week's edition of the *Memphis Free Speech*. "There is therefore only one thing left that we can do; save our money and leave a town which will neither protect our lives and property, nor give us a fair trial in the courts, but takes us out and murders us in cold blood when accused by white persons."[16]

And just like that, Memphis nearly ran out of Black people.

Wells was born enslaved in Holly Springs, Mississippi. After both her parents died from yellow fever, she assumed responsibility for her siblings at age sixteen. Despite these circumstances, she managed to achieve a formal education at Rust College and Fisk University, eventually landing a job as a schoolteacher in Memphis. In 1884, Wells sued the Chesapeake and Ohio Railway for dragging her off the train after she refused to give up her first-class seat to a white man. She won the lawsuit, but the Tennessee Supreme Court reversed it. When she was asked to write about her experiences in the local newspapers, outlets across the country noticed her talent. Her unapologetic willingness to take on Jim Crow made her a national favorite, earning her a one-third stake in the *Free Speech* and elevating it to one of the most radical and talked-about papers in the country.

A few weeks after the murders, the superintendent and the treasurer of the City Railway Company visited Wells at the newspaper office. Hearing about her influence in the Black community, they begged her to help them get Black patrons to ride the city streetcars. For some reason they couldn't explain, their most loyal customer base had suddenly disappeared. When Wells asked the men to posit a reason for the recent loss of Black customers, the men replied that they had been told that Black people were afraid of electricity, and assured her that the electricity was safe and reliable. Amused by the level of their Caucasity, Wells informed the businessmen that Black people had not suddenly become afraid of electricity in the last six weeks. "Why it was just six weeks ago that the lynching took place," she explained. "We have learned that every white man of any standing in town knew of the plan and consented to the lynching of our boys . . . The colored people feel that every white man in Memphis who consented to [Thomas Moss's] death is as guilty as those who fired the guns which took his life and they want to get away from this town. We told them the week after the lynching to save their nickels and dimes so that they could do so."[17]

A few days later, Wells published the entire conversation. By then, Black people were leaving Memphis in droves, heading west to Oklahoma. Hundreds of others were boycotting white-owned businesses. And Wells was just getting started. On May 21, 1892, in an editorial published in the *Free Speech* about a recent case of a Black man who had been falsely accused of raping a white woman, Wells called out "that old threadbare lie that Negro men rape white women. If Southern men are not careful, a conclusion might be reached which will be very damaging to the moral reputation of their women." In response, every white-owned newspaper in the city ran veiled threats to Wells. The *Evening Scimitar* wrote, "If the Negroes themselves do not apply the remedy without delay it will be the duty of those whom he has attacked to tie the wretch who utters these calumnies to a stake at the intersection of Main and Madison Sts., brand him in the forehead with a hot iron and perform upon him a surgical operation with a pair of tailor's shears."[18] That's "veiled," right?*

It would be the *Memphis Free Speech*'s final bow. A white mob destroyed the printing press and ran Wells's co-owner out of the city. Wells was out of town, visiting friends in New York, but locals warned her that men were stationed outside her house and at the train station watching for her arrival. She would never return to Memphis.

If Ida B. Wells had one gift, it was that she was born with what scientists have now identified as the genetic marker IDGAF. Wells's uncompromising stance, combined with her inability to accept even

---

* *When compared to a fist-sized hole from a shotgun shell.*

the slightest hint of racism and discrimination, is what made her one of the fiercest truth-tellers in the history of America. With her relentless reporting and unwavering advocacy, she became the undisputed leader of the anti-lynching movement. She didn't just call out white violence, either; Wells also fought for women's suffrage, children's rights, and labor reform. She called for peace *and armed self-defense.* She was Malcolm X and Martin Luther King Jr. And Oprah. And Beyoncé. Using a combination of statistical data, investigative techniques, and fearless truth-telling, she revolutionized journalism, and during her time, she was arguably the most famous Black woman in America, period.[*]

One of Wells's most frequent targets was her celebrity counterpart, the most famous and well-regarded Black man in the country, Booker T. Washington. She publicly called out Washington's "just be quiet and maybe they won't kill us" stance that favored fighting white supremacy by actually allowing white people to be supreme. In her criticism of Washington, Wells was always sure to point out that the oppression of the negro was not a Southern phenomenon, nor could it be cured by an industrial education and Black obedience. "They hail with acclaim the man who has made popular the unspoken thought of that part of the North which believes in the inherent inferiority of the Negro, and the always outspoken southern view to the same effect," she wrote of Washington. "This gospel of work is no new one for the Negro. It is the South's old slavery practice in a new dress. It was the only education the South gave the Negro for two and a half centuries she had absolute control of his body and soul."[19]

However, Wells wasn't as bothered by Washington's prescription for the lynching problem as much as she was with his characterization of Black men in general. As the foremost—and perhaps the only—lynching expert in America at the time, she often reminded her readers that the dismissive demonization of Black people as racists and criminals is what leads to mob justice. Wells knew that lynching had nothing to do with crime or justice; it was caused by *something else.* "Mr. Washington says, in substance: Give me money to educate the negro

---

[*] *I know there's a period at the end of the sentence, but you know how we do.*

and when he is taught how to work, he will not commit the crime for which lynching is done," Wells wrote. "Mr. Washington knows when he says this that lynching is not invoked to punish crime but color, and not even industrial education will change that."[20]

Washington wasn't the sole recipient of Wells's draggings. While she appreciated her white supporters, she issued not-so-gentle reminders to "forward-thinking" white women that they should watch their racist mouths, much to the delight of her Black fans.

As her notoriety grew, Wells became Black America's go-to person for dispelling racist stereotypes. In fact, one of her most famous beefs changed the way we viewed the lynching epidemic. During a tour of Britain, Frances Willard—a leading white suffragist and president of the Woman's Christian Temperance Union—advocated for the banning of alcohol by noting that the "colored race multiplies like the locusts of Egypt" because of it, adding that the saloon was Black America's "centre of power." Even before white people pushed forth the medical theory that racism lived in skeletal tissue, Willard insisted that not only didn't she have a racist bone in her body but, as she said, "So far as I know, I have not an atom of race prejudice."[21]

Still, Willard believed the "race problem" could be solved by Black people returning to Africa, and stopping the obviously stupid darkies from voting and drinking alcohol. "It is not fair that they should vote, nor is it fair that a plantation Negro, who can neither read nor write, whose ideas are bounded by the fence of his own field and the price of his own mule, should be entrusted with the ballot," Willard explained to the British press. "The Safety of women, of childhood, of the home, is menaced in a thousand localities at this moment, so that the men dare not go beyond the sight of their own roof-tree."[22] The notion that hypersexualized Black men find white women irresistible is one of the longest-running white ideations in White America, ranking right up there with Bob Dylan's singing ability and *Friends* being funny.

Y'all know Wells wasn't tolerating this nonsense. In her 1892 pamphlet *Southern Horrors: The Lynch Law in All Its Phases*, she dispelled the myth that lynchings were caused by rabid negro sexual predators, revealing that less than one-third of lynching victims had been accused of rape. Just before she departed for a speaking tour of England in 1894, Wells asked English newspapers to reprint Willard's interview, just so that she could destroy that white nonsense. "I find wherever I go that we are deprived the expression of condemnation such hangings and burnings deserve, because the world believes negro men are despoilers of the virtue of white women," she wrote in a column during her tour. "Unfortunately for the negro race and for themselves, Miss Frances E. Willard and Bishops Fitzgerald and Haygood have published utterances in confirmation of this slander."[23]

When Wells met Willard face-to-face in Britain, she asked her about it, noting after their conversation that Willard finally seemed to understand the error of her remarks. The next day, Wells was supposed to give a speech at the British Women's Temperance Association. When the organization heard that Wells had asked *Fraternity*, a Black-owned British magazine, to reprint Willard's racist remarks, they threatened to cancel the speech and make sure Wells wouldn't receive any more opportunities to speak during her trip if she didn't get the piece canceled. Wells made the speech and asked the BWTA to pass a resolution condemning lynching, which they did to quiet the controversy. A few days later, the issue of *Fraternity* proceeded with publishing Willard's entire interview.

Willard was mad AF. A Black woman criticizing her publicly? She wouldn't stand for it, *period*.[*] At the Woman's Christian Temperance Union's 1894 national convention,[†] Willard used her presidential address to attack Wells, who attended the conference but was not present for the address to white women. Instead of admitting that Wells's actual statistics proved Willard's ignorance, Willard said Wells's "zeal for her race" had clouded her perception of her friends. She defended her belief that Black men are pro-rape, while informing the audience that white men raping Black women "had largely ceased" once slavery ended, explaining that her white friends, who knew white people in the South, had told her as much.

"I make this statement on the testimony of well-informed Northerners who have long lived in the South, and who are, like myself, of

---

[*] *You know how they do.*
[†] *Can you imagine how boring Coachella for Karens must have been with no alcohol?*

New England ancestry and training, with all that those words imply," Willard explained to the white women in the audience. "An average colored man when sober is loyal to the purity of white women; but when under the influence of intoxicating liquors, the tendency in all men is a loss of self-control, and the ignorant and vicious, whether white or black, are the most dangerous characters." Willard ended by warning Wells to "banish from her vocabulary all such allusions" to white women having consensual sex with Black men. Wells, never the shrinking violet, responded to Willard's ignorance and threats with the ancient African aphorism: "I can show you better than I can tell you."

In 1895, Wells produced the hundred-page pamphlet *The Red Record*, which reframed the lynching epidemic as America's problem, not a Southern phenomenon. "Brave woman! you have done your people and mine a service which can neither be weighed nor measured," wrote Frederick Douglass in the preface of the pamphlet. "If the American conscience were only half alive, if the American church and clergy were only half christianized, if American moral sensibility were not hardened by persistent infliction of outrage and crime against colored people, a scream of horror, shame, and indignation would rise to Heaven wherever your pamphlet shall be read." Within, Wells used *sociology*, the relatively new academic approach pioneered in America by Du Bois, to dissect the nationwide, state-sanctioned crimes against humanity. *The Red Record* was straightforward and unrelentingly forthright—with the exception of one part.

Among the tabulated statistics and historical analysis, Wells addressed her nemesis in an unflinching takedown titled "Miss Willard's Attitude." After recounting the years-long quarrel, Wells challenged Willard and the Woman's Christian Temperance Union's supporters to prove that Wells had made a single incorrect or untrue statement. "I desire no quarrel with the W.C.T.U., but my love for the truth is greater than my regard for an alleged friend who, through ignorance or design misrepresents in the most harmful way the cause of a long suffering race," she explained. "When the lives of men, women and children are at stake, when the inhuman butchers of innocents attempt to justify their barbarism by fastening upon a whole race the obloquy of the most infamous of crimes, it is little less than criminal to apologize for the butchers today and tomorrow to repudiate the apology by declaring it a figure of speech." Willard didn't have much of a response after that. She just continued being white and ignorant.

Washington, Willard, and white women weren't the only ones for whom Wells had reserved a cache of "that smoke." Anybody could get it, including her friend and colleague the world-renowned scholar W. E. B. Du Bois.

When leaders from around the country converged in New York in 1909 to discuss a different approach to solving America's race issue, Wells accepted an invitation to attend. Du Bois, who had just returned from studying Germany, was the only Black person chosen for a subcommittee to select representatives to lead a new national organization. Wells, the most recognized anti-lynching advocate in America, was sure her name would be on it. Yet when Du Bois announced the list of forty representatives, Wells was not selected. Seething at what she called the "deliberate intention of Dr. Du Bois to ignore me and my work,"[24] she marched out of the meeting as others begged her to stay.

"I want to tell you that when that list of names left our hands and was given to Dr. Du Bois to read, your name led all the rest," explained John Millholland, who had also been on the selection team. "It is unthinkable that you, who have fought the battle against lynching for nearly twenty years singlehanded and alone when the rest of us were following our own selfish pursuits, should be left off such a committee."[25] A few minutes later, Du Bois confessed that he had removed Wells from the list and replaced her with one of his friends *who wasn't even at the meeting* because he thought Wells's efforts would be better represented by Celia Parker Woolley, a white woman. Realizing he had made a mistake, Du Bois amended the list of committee members to include Wells's name. She attended the group's next meeting with all expenses paid by the organization. At that conference, the group decided to put Du Bois in charge of publicity and research—his reputation as a well-known scholar and race advocate could help the group place articles and editorials into some of the country's most prestigious magazines and newspapers. Wells, however, argued that the group shouldn't have to submit to the whims and disposition of whites to have their voices heard. The executive committee agreed and immediately decided to launch their own magazine, *The Crisis*, under the organization's new name: the National Association for the Advancement of Colored People (NAACP).

Being named an "official negro leader" did not cure Wells's allergy to patriarchy and white nonsense. She criticized the other members of the NAACP for electing Mary White Ovington, a white woman, as chairman of the executive committee. Wells had previously taught Ovington a few investigative reporting techniques, which eventually led to Ovington's success in pushing through housing reform in New York City. But Wells noted the "air of triumph" and the "pleased look on her face" after Ovington participated in the deliberations that temporarily erased Wells from the list of the NAACP founders. "She has basked in the sunlight of the adoration of the few college-bred Negroes who have surrounded her, but has made little effort to know the soul of the Black woman," Wells wrote. "She has fallen far short of helping a race which has suffered as no white woman has ever been called upon to suffer or to understand."

To paint Ida B. Wells-Barnett with the oft-repeated trope of being "angry" is too simplistic. Perhaps Wells's dogged incorruptibility and that she openly criticized white benefactors (and the fact that she was a Black woman[*]) partially explain why she is not generally included as a titan of Black liberation on the same level as her more famous contemporaries. Booker T. Washington's approach is thought to be a relic of the past, but his legacy lives on. W. E. B. Du Bois is generally considered one of the fathers of Black history and sociology, partly because his approach was not as contentious as Wells's. But as Du Bois hypothesized that America's social, political, and economic structure enabled white supremacy, Wells contended, over and over again, that the problem was *white people*. While *Southern Horrors* and *The Red Record* would define how the NAACP and various other agencies approached racial terrorism for a century, Ida B. Wells is scarcely mentioned in the NAACP's early literature. Much of her newspaper reporting has

---

[*] *You know how y'all do.*

been lost to time. There is not a single copy of the *Memphis Free Speech* in existence. Still, Ida B. Wells remains the standard to which every Black journalist in America aspires, myself included.

* * *

In 1969, before I was born, my grandfather was killed in a traffic accident by a drunk driver as he drove his last customer home. The white teenagers were never prosecuted; all I know about him comes from other people's stories. I have seen pictures, so I know he smoked cigars, served in World War II, and often wore a white shirt. I cannot tell how tall he was or how his voice sounded, but he remains a mythic figure in my life.

I knew my grandmother well. She passed down my family history and protected her family's legacy. She could make ice cream from scratch and patiently put up with my constant haranguing for more stories. She worked the same "good job" at the same factory as my grandfather, yet she was not larger than life to most people.

One time, while waiting for biscuits to come out of the oven, I asked her if she was afraid on that night that the men could just kick that fragile door off its hinges. She insisted that she was not scared because my grandfather had assured her that his prayers were more powerful than all the men on all the porches in the world.

"You weren't praying, Grandma?" I asked.

She pinched her apron with her right hand, used it to pull the pan of biscuits out of the oven, and just shook her head from side to side. "No, Mikey," she said. She did not answer proudly, as if she wore her response as a badge of courage; she did it matter-of-factly, like doors and Black women sometimes will.

"I didn't wanna close my eyes," she said. "Not with that pistol in my hand."

She was something else.

THREE LITTLE QUESTIONS

1. **What caused the racial terrorism during Reconstruction?**
   a. White supremacy.
   b. White people asserting their political, economic, and social supremacy.
   c. Fear of white people not being supreme.
   d. Supreme whiteness.

2. **What is the biggest myth about lynching?**
   a. Lynching was rare.
   b. Lynching victims were usually criminals.
   c. Most lynching victims were hanged.
   d. Lynchings were a Southern phenomenon.

3. **Which one of these is not part of a lynch mob?**
   a. The person who falsely accuses a lynching victim.
   b. A Klansman who has never participated in an extrajudicial killing.
   c. A person who watches a lynching.
   d. A law enforcement officer who does not arrest a person who lynched someone.

ACTIVITY

LYNCHING OR NAH?

The NAACP defines a lynching as "the public killing of an individual who has not received any due process." Which one of these events should be considered a lynching?

1. A man is arrested for a crime, tried, convicted, and sentenced to death. Immediately after he is convicted, a mob takes him from the courtroom and hangs him.
2. An unarmed man is choked to death on a public sidewalk by a police officer while other officers do nothing.
3. A boy is walking through a neighborhood when a self-appointed neighborhood watchman tries to detain him. During the ensuing scuffle, the boy is shot in the chest.
4. A woman with a history of mental illness is tased to death inside a jail cell.
5. A man is falsely accused of a crime, convicted with manufactured evidence, sentenced, and executed by the state after his appeals are exhausted.

THE DIFFERENCE BETWEEN SOUL FOOD AND SOUTHERN CUISINE

Aside from holding an advanced degree in wypipology, I was raised in a family that owned a series of small soul food restaurants. I would therefore like to use my expertise to offer this handy guide to a few ways you can tell the difference between soul food and Southern food.

WHO COOKED IT?

This is the most important aspect. While anyone with a kitchen, a tub of butter, and a Paula Deen cookbook can make Southern cuisine, soul food requires certain things from the cook. First of all, all soul food technicians usually listen to gospel music when they are preparing the meals, preferably James Cleveland or the Mississippi Mass Choir. Their attire should consist of a pre-1993 family reunion T-shirt and house shoes (not to be confused with slippers; athletes and ballerinas also wear slippers).

To qualify for soul food consideration, the cook must also be an aunt, uncle, grandfather, or grandmother. Because of how the slave trade broke up families and forced new familial relationships such as playcousins, the cook doesn't have to be a *blood aunt*, but there must be someone who refers to the cook as

Aunt Wilma or Uncle Charles.* I make my candied yams the
same way my mother taught me when I was seventeen, but ever
since my sisters gifted me with nieces and nephews, my candied
yams have been *far superior* to my sister Comelita's. I do admit,
however, that there are actually no yams in America. The
mix-up happened during the slave trade, when enslavers packed
slave ships with yams to sustain their human cargo during
the Middle Passage.[1] It doesn't matter. Mine are better than
Comelita's because I have uncle status. It's also probably because
she kept her eyes open when she was praying in church.

SEASONING

Southern cuisine uses herbs and spices. Soul food uses *seasoning*. If
you are confused about whether something qualifies as a seasoning
or as a spice, there is an easy way to tell: spices grow in herb gardens,
while no one knows where seasonings come from. No one buys
seasoning; it just exists. I've been using the same bottle of Lawry's
seasoned salt since the George W. Bush administration, and it's only
half-gone. I run out of thyme all the . . .

Okay, no puns.

However, it should be noted that African American foods
traditionally used more seasoning not just to mask the foods
during slavery but because, in the South, salt was essential for
field laborers and sharecroppers who sweated all day.

RECIPES

Southern cuisine is concocted from recipes, while soul food is made
from knowledge. I once saw a recipe that said "season to taste" and
finally understood why white people's chicken tastes like a crisp fall
breeze blowing an American flag at a Toby Keith concert. Soul food
instructions come with measurements like "a little bit of nutmeg,"
"'bout this much butter," and "a bunch of sugar." I don't know how
you even measure a "pinch" or a "dash."

Because reading was illegal for our people for such a long

---

* *You know, I miss my uncle Charles, y'all.*

time, many soul food recipes were passed down by word of mouth. Plus, there are recipes that we simply created out of necessity. For instance, whoever discovered that cutting a slit in bologna will prevent it from bubbling up deserves a Nobel Prize.

CHICKEN

While we have already covered the art of fried chicken earlier in this book, here are a few additional things you need to know. Soul fool chicken is cut into individual parts, while there are only two pieces of Southern chicken: the breast and the quarter. If you order fried chicken in a Southern restaurant, you will either receive a breaded boneless, skinless chicken breast or one-fourth of the entire bird.

In a soul food restaurant, you can order a thigh and a wing. I contend that the thigh is the most underrated and least talked-about piece of chicken, yet it is never separated from the leg in Caucasian cuisine. Legs are trash. If you're over seven and you still eat legs, you need to grow up.

While the name and practice of barbecuing comes from a Taíno and native tradition, younger enslaved men learned how to smoke and barbecue under the tutelage of their elders who built and maintain BBQ pits, thus earning the title of a "pit master." Even when Southern restaurants bake or barbecue chicken, they surface-season their food. Soul food seasoning actually reaches the *soul* of the chicken and spreads itself through the meat.

JUICE

One of the easiest ways to tell whether a meal is Black-based is by examining the juice. I'm not referring to gravy here. *All soul food* makes its own juice. While collard green juice is perhaps my favorite, followed by the combination of black-eyed peas and candied-yam juice, some people prefer meat-based juices like turkey-wing juice. The juice at the bottom of a plate of soul food is exceeded only by Fruity Pebbles milk on the list of drinkable remnants.

There is one more thing I must add, but I must step back a few feet and turn on all caps: WHITE GRAVY IS NOT A THING!

White gravy is the devil's semen. There is no meat that turns gravy white, so stop doing that *right now*! And that's not racist, because people of color in New Orleans can teach you how to make a roux if you need it.

EDGES

The most noticeable difference between soul food and the Southern variety is the shape and condition of the food on the plate. Biscuits and cornbread may be served in both soul food and Southern-cuisine eateries, but Southern-cuisine biscuits are perfectly rounded, and their cornbread muffins sometimes include unnecessary stuff like corn. I don't need prizes in my cornbread! Soul food cornbread has right angles. How am I supposed to sop up my cabbage juice with a circular piece of bread? And don't come in here with that yeast-roll crap unless you want to get stabbed in the eye with this cornbread knife.

If you eat Southern cuisine, there is no difference between a macaroni edge and the center of the baked dish. Soul food, however, is an edge-centric art form. The burnt edges of baked macaroni are the best, followed closely by all crust-related desserts. I'm sure when Thomas Jefferson's enslaved, Paris-trained chef James Hemings created what they referred to as "a pie called macaroni" at a state dinner in 1802, the edge world was never the same.[2]

Not all soul foods have perfected the art of the edge yet, unfortunately. The centers of peach cobblers are trash. In the two thousand twenty-third year of our lord and savior Gladys Knight, why hasn't anyone figured out a way to make an all-edge peach cobbler? Apparently scientists are too busy focusing on idiotic time-wasters like sex robots and the cure for cancer to concentrate on *real issues*.

GREASE

This is a very important but underrecognized aspect of soul food. Southern cuisine uses vegetable or canola oil whenever a dish requires frying. But to be considered soul food, it must be fried in *grease* that someone saved from the last time you made the dish. Additionally, fish and chicken are the only soul foods that should be fried. Anything else is probably white-people-influenced fare. White people fry *everything*—butter, cotton candy, soda—especially at state fairs! Why are state fairs so frying-obsessed? Also, there is no such thing as chicken-fried steak. No one breads and fries a perfectly good steak.

And don't ever confuse the fish grease with the chicken grease. It's the cardinal rule of greasery.

UTENSILS

Southern restaurants will give you a knife, a spoon, and possibly two forks. You can get a fork with a plate of soul food and that's it. Soul food should be eaten with your hands or with another part of the meal. Biscuits are perfect for rounding up loose pieces of rice and gravy. And you should use *paper towels* from a roll when eating soul food, while napkins (cloth or paper) are allowed with Southern-based dishes.

I hope this disambiguation clears everything up. If you are still unclear whether your food is soul food or Southern food, just remember:

Any cook, Black or white, can make Southern cuisine . . .

But that doesn't mean they have soul.

10

WHITES GONE WILD

UNCLE ROB EXPLAINS "SEPARATE BUT EQUAL"

"Your mama, if you forgot to take the chicken out of the freezer."

I don't want to pat myself on the back, but you gotta admit that's a great answer. My response easily beat out the previous mundane answers such as Candyman, the police, and "the principal." If there was an all-Black version of *Family Feud*, I'm sure it would have shown up among the top five answers on the board when the host said, "Name something all Black people should be afraid of."

This was not a game show. Instead, I was sitting among a group of my friends, neighbors, and playcousins at an ancient African American ritual of respect known as a "settin' up." I was supremely confident in my witty reply until someone posed the question to my uncle Rob, who just happened to stroll by with the classic South Carolina settin' up plate—a piece of chicken, a spoonful of green beans, yellow rice, and a slice of pound cake. "Aye, Uncle Rob," my cousin Fred said while simultaneously offering Rob a nip.* "Name something that all Black people should always be afraid of."

Rob didn't even pause or look up before demonstrating why he

---

*   *A "nip" is a small quantity (approximately 1.8 to 2.9 ounces) of the beloved African American alcoholic beverage known as "brown likka." It is the second-lowest amount a person can drink and is more than a "taste" but less than a "lil teeny bit."*

held the title of Harriot Family Sage. I knew my response would soon be forgotten when he began giggling to himself in his traditional Uncle Rob-ian way, pushing wisps of air through his teeth like a tire leaking air. If he had a microphone, protocol would have dictated that he drop it when he lifted his head toward his assemblage of nieces and nephews and offered his contribution to the conversation. Sauntering away with his cup, his cake, and the number one answer on the board, Rob declared casually, almost too nonchalant to believe his response was unrehearsed:

"An American."

* * *

You wanna know something about history? I'll tell you about history. I taught my lil' nephew everything he knows. We were sitting here talking, and he said he had to run to the bathroom. I could tell by the look on his face and the sound coming from his stomach that he was gonna be a while, so I figure I'll help him out. You know he's lactose intolerant, right? That boy get the bubbleguts more than a vegetarian lion.

Oh, he's talking about post-Reconstruction? Bruh, if you want to know what happened after white people started acting the fool, sit down and let your uncle Rob tell you what you need to know. And you know your uncle Rob gon' keep it real with you.

I see he told my little joke up there. I better be getting some royalties from that.[*] And I know it might sound a little unpatriotic, but you're probably one of those people who conflate being an "American" with being a citizen. It's not the same thing. Americanism is an ephemeral, ever-evolving status that, historically, can only be bestowed by white people. He probably told you about how the Fourteenth Amendment established the legal definition of citizenship and explained how it gave Black people the same rights and privileges afforded white people. Now, that's what the books will tell you. But that's just a bunch of white nonsense. I tell you what—go buy yourself

---

[*] *Nope. He won't be getting royalties. When I was twelve, I found out that most jokes by Black uncles are just recycled Richard Pryor bits.*

one of those officially licensed Lakers jerseys and see if they will let you play with LeBron. They'll look at you the same way white people looked at Black folks when we demanded our rights way back in 1865. Or 1965. Or 2005. Nah, son. For most of this nation's history, lemme tell you how this country defined *American*:

"Not Black people."

That's right. Ever since the *White Lion* dropped Angela 'nem off in Jamestown, the subjugation of Black people has been *more common* than democracy and *more powerful* than that lil' Constitution those white folks are always raving about. That was written for them! And that's not a historical interpretation; it is an inarguable, objective fact. When it comes to the history of folks who look like us, there's two things I know. When it comes to singing, Frank Sinatra can't hold Luther Vandross's Jheri curl juice, and that white supremacy is this country's *most dominant* trait. That's a fact, Jack.*

Man, you don't have to believe me, just look at what they wrote! When those white boys wrote the Constitution, they said enslaved Africans were officially worth 60 percent of a white man. Then the first Congress limited naturalization to "any alien, other than an enemy alien, being a free white person . . . of good character."[1] Crazy, right? How can anyone of good character even write such gobbledygook? Plus, the people who were here when the white men arrived were not extended citizenship until the passage of the Indian Citizenship Act of 1924. Even though the Fifteenth Amendment technically gave us the right to vote, the arbiters of Americanism didn't even attempt to enforce the words contained in that document until the country was 189 years old. That's like . . . two years younger than God. You know who God is, right? Jesus's real daddy.

Now, I ain't gonna lie. I like the Constitution. It's a wondrous document that offers freedom and liberty to all Americans. But, while the eruption of post–Civil War racial terrorism was unconstitutional, it was not illegal for all intents and purposes. Laws are just words unless they are enforced. You are supposed to be arrested, tried, and punished for breaking laws, right? So, why didn't most of the white

---

* *I tried to tell Uncle Rob that I don't even know anyone named Jack, but he won't listen.*

supremacist groups that attacked Black citizens ever face any consequences for their actions?

Because they were Americans.

Take Louisiana, for instance. I know Mikey told y'all about the New Orleans Massacre because he loves talking about that "floor was slick with blood" nonsense. (Who do you think gave him that book?) But the Louisiana race war is the best example of how white supremacists overthrew the government at the end of Reconstruction. Don't worry; I'm finna break it down.

Louisiana's 1868 state constitution eradicated most of the Black Codes—the racially discriminatory laws governing Black Louisianians after the Civil War. It granted full citizenship and the right to vote to the formerly enslaved, as well as funding to integrated schools. It's not like white people suddenly started believing in democracy, freedom, or stuff white people yell about when they're about to do something foul. It's just that, once slavery was over, Louisiana suddenly had a majority-Black electorate. According to the 1870 census, 364,210 "free colored" lived in the Bayou State, compared to 362,065 whites.[2] Something had to be done. That "something" was the pandemic of racist rampages unleashed by Louisiana's white population during Reconstruction.

To dam the bloodshed, Congress passed the Enforcement Act of 1870, but it didn't work.[*] In 1871, they passed a second Enforcement Act that sent federal monitors to oversee all Southern elections. But white folks didn't pay it no nevermind. Congress tried again later that year. This time, they just outright called it the Ku Klux Klan Act and outlawed stuff like wearing masks in public, using guns to intimidate voters, and police participating in lynch mobs, all of which should have already made law. But the most significant provision in the third Enforcement Act gave the president the right to suspend habeas corpus—the right to be detained without a trial—and to use federal troops to suppress an insurrection. Union troops had already left many of the Southern states after the Civil

---

[*] *The first Enforcement Act banned mob violence or anyone who went "in disguise upon the public highways, or upon the premises of another" with the intention of violating citizens' constitutional rights. It was specifically aimed at the Klan.*

War, but after this passed, they had to return to stop white folks from killing Black people.

Man, the changes to the racial hierarchy burned white folks like they were frying bacon with no shirt on! The notion of the army protecting free, voting, politically empowered Black folks who *the white folks used to own* radicalized pro-white paramilitary insurgent groups like the Knights of the White Camellia, the Redeemers, and—the most unoriginal of them all—the White Man's League, who used violence, terror, and racism to overthrow the government long before the Proud Boys hopped on the insurrectionist bandwagon. And these were not the regular angry white folks like you read about at CPAC. Nah, these were organized military units composed of thousands of former Confederates and ordinary white men who frame their swords and eat "supper." Trust me, you don't wanna mess with white folks who eat supper. And unlike the Ku Klux Klansmen, the members of Louisiana's domestic terror cells didn't wear disguises. They wanted the freedmen to know they were the local politicians, bankers, police, and clergy that lived among them every day.

On July 5, 1874, all the men's lodges in New Orleans issued a call for volunteers and raised about 1,500 men for the Crescent City White League. Throughout the summer, they drilled, purchased munitions, and prepared for war. With officers embedded in the police department, they disarmed Black citizens and used media allies to perpetuate the fear of "Negro domination."[3] By the time they declared war on 3,600 police officers and state militiamen on September 14, 1874, the White League's forces had grown to 5,000. And they went wilder than folks at a Black Friday sale at Walmart! Federal troops eventually interceded and put down the insurrection, but the White League had made their point. The pro-white Democrats essentially set up their own alternative white supremacist legislature in a fraternity house in New Orleans. Run by alt-white governor John McEnery and lieutenant governor Davidson B. Penn,[*] the "rump" government collected taxes, passed laws, and controlled the state of Louisiana. At the same time, the constitutionally elected Republican officials only

---

[*] *Who undoubtedly ate supper.*

regulated a small part of New Orleans until 1877. To commemorate the event, the Fourteenth of September Monument Association and a pro-Confederate women's group erected the Battle of Liberty Place Monument, a thirty-five-foot obelisk with an inscription that read:

> *McEnery and Penn, having been elected governor and lieutenant-governor by the white people, were duly installed by this overthrow of carpetbag government, ousting the usurpers, Governor Kellogg (white) and Lieutenant-Governor Antoine (colored).*
>
> *United States troops took over the state government and reinstated the usurpers but the national election of November 1876 recognized white supremacy in the South and gave us our state.*

I hate to say "I told you so," but white supremacy was so inter-twined with Americanism that they etched it in stone!*

Now that troops were back in the South, how were white people going to assert their social and political dominance? Luckily, the high-falutin white people in the North had already solved that problem. While they looked down on the former Confederate states as racist savages, they provided the South with a template for white suprem-acy. Like the Bible says in Ephesians, "The only thing more racist than a Southern white supremacist is a Northerner who thinks they're racism-free."† White supremacy was never a Southern thing; it is *an American thing.*

Long before it was called "Jim Crow," the white citizens of the Northern United States had established a de facto system of segrega-tion that was, in many ways, more odious than the deep-fried rac-ism in the South.‡ The Northern form of American apartheid had less to do with property rights, economics, or fear of Black rule; it existed because whites sincerely believed they were *more human* than their Black counterparts. Pennsylvania disenfranchised Black voters in 1838 after initially allowing free Black men to vote. The Union army was divided into racial companies. Train companies in Boston,

---

* *Uncle Rob does not hate to say "I told you so."*
† *My cousin Ephesians used to write funny quotes in the Bible when she got bored in church.*
‡ *Odious means "stank."*

New York, and Michigan had racially segregated cars decades before the Civil War. In 1841, a young abolitionist showed out so bad about segregation policy that it took six men to oust him from the train. "In dragging me out, on this occasion, it must have cost the company twenty-five or thirty dollars," wrote the young abolitionist named Frederick Douglass. "For I tore up [the] seats and all."[4] This legacy did not disappear overnight.

In the meantime, the country tried one last thing to suppress the angry white mobs. In 1875, Congress passed the coincidentally named Civil Rights Act of 1875. The landmark legislation was enacted to uphold the "equality of all men before the law," banning racial discrimination with regards to "inns, public conveyances on land or water, theaters, and other places of public amusement."[5] Although the act was a reaffirmation of the Fourteenth and Fifteenth Amendments, there was one problem with the Civil Rights Act: *no one ever used it.* In the torrential cyclone of lynching and mobbing, President Ulysses S. Grant never invoked it, and the Department of Justice never even sent the text of the legislation to its U.S. attorneys!

I'm sure Mikey told y'all about how Rutherford B. Hayes did us with the Compromise of 1877, right? Yeah, that man rode a Black electoral wave to the White House and then sided with white supremacy, sticking to the racist arrangement made in a smoke-filled room, removing federal troops from the Southern states, and turning a blind eye to state-sponsored terrorism. You gotta give him credit, though. He was a visionary. Somehow, he threw Black people under the bus before buses were even invented! That's why the only Hayes I acknowledge is Isaac.

In 1883, the Supreme Court took its neglect for the welfare of America's Black builders to another level. The *Civil Rights Cases*—a decision that combined five different cases—dismantled the Civil Rights Act of 1875 by ruling that Congress didn't have the power to regulate the racist actions of individuals or to overrule racist state laws. "It would be running the slavery argument into the ground to make it apply to every act of discrimination which a person may see fit to make as to guests he will entertain, or as to the people he will take into his coach or cab or car; or admit to his concert or theater, or deal with in other matters of intercourse or business," wrote a white man who somehow earned the ironic title of a "justice," adding:

> *There were thousands of free colored people in this country before the abolition of slavery, enjoying all the fundamental rights of life, liberty, and property the same as white citizens; yet no one, at that time, thought that it was any invasion of their personal status as freemen because they were not admitted to all the privileges enjoyed by white citizens, or because they were subjected to discriminations in the enjoyment of accommodations in inns, public conveyances, and places of amusement. Mere discriminations on account of race or color were not regarded as badges of slavery.*[6]

With nothing but White America's sense of justice and fairness to prevent racial terrorism, white supremacist Democrats quickly gained control of state politics and declared open season on Black folks.

But Louisiana's racial reality was more complex than that of other states in the former Confederacy. Before the Civil War, many free people of color already attended integrated schools, and many were more educated than the lower classes of white citizens in the Big Easy. Take my light-skinned homeboy Louis Martinet, for instance. By 1890, Martinet, an Afro-Creole man, had already earned his law degree, served in the Louisiana House of Representatives, opened a newspaper called *The Crusader*, and was studying to become a doctor. Martinet hung out with his Creole homeboy Rodolphe Desdunes, who by comparison made Martinet look like he needed to do more with his life. Desdunes was a bilingual historian and poet who wrote in French, taught school, wrote in English for *The Crusader*, opened a school for Black children, served as a militiaman, and fought in the Battle of Liberty Place while running his own plantation. I'm not trying to start no mess, but these dudes were real superheroes. Bruce Wayne and Tony Stark *could never*.

These two were prominent in making the Big Easy become the cradle of the precursor to the civil rights movement, partly because everyone noticed that white people were about to start white people-ing. With the help of P. B. S. Pinchback, the first-ever African American governor of a state, Desdunes and Martinet formed their own pro-Black version of the Avengers called the American Citizens' Equal Rights Association (ACERA), which protested a legislative proposal, Section 3 of Act 111. Known as the "Separate Car Act," the law required "equal, but separate" railroad cars segregated by race. Despite ACERA's vigilance, the law passed anyway.

While the Separate Car Act was nearly identical to a Mississippi law, the legislation presented a bigger problem in Louisiana, because there weren't just two separate races, especially in New Orleans where there were Black people, white people, white Creoles, Cajuns, and people of all colors. Martinet, Desdunes, and sixteen other men from the Afro-Creole community came together to form the Comité des Citoyens (Citizens' Committee) to test the constitutionality of the Separate Car Act, and hired Albion Tourgée, a white attorney from upstate New York.

Tourgée was a former judge and advocate for Black rights, but he had no idea about the complexity of New Orleans's racial structure. All he knew was Black vs. white, so he wrote to the group suggesting that they get a Creole person who looked white to test the law. Martinet laughed at Tourgée's silly white idea, responding:

> It would be quite difficult to have a lady too nearly white refused admission to a "white" car. There are the strangest white people you ever saw here. Walking up and down our principal thoroughfare—Canal Street—you would [be] surprised to have persons pointed out to you, some as white & others as colored, and if you were not informed you would be sure to pick out the white for colored and colored for white. Besides, people of tolerably fair complexion, even if unmistakably colored, enjoy here a large degree of immunity from the accursed prejudice.[7]

They didn't want to do it for the Creole people; they wanted to do it for *all the people*, so they came up with a brilliant plan. They prepped Desdunes's son Daniel to board a white car. In preparation, they paid local police officers and had them prepare warrants with the specific infractions prelisted. They even approached the owners of the Louisville and Nashville Railroad to let them know they were going to test the constitutionality of the Separate Car Act. The railroad company was like, "Bruh, you think we like thinking about racism while we're trying to run a train company? Don't get me wrong; I'm not saying we're not racist. But this segregation thing is pretty expensive!"

And they did it! On February 24, 1892, Daniel Desdunes bought a ticket to Mobile, Alabama, and hopped on the "whites only" car. The car stopped at a predetermined spot where the group had detectives waiting. They went to court and prepared for a battle. When they arrived in court with their carefully strategized legal arguments ready, Judge John Ferguson told them there wouldn't be a hearing. The Louisiana Supreme Court had recently ruled that the Separate Car Act violated the Fourteenth Amendment so that it couldn't be applied to *interstate travel. The Crusader* declared that "Jim Crow was as dead as a door nail!" However, the ruling didn't apply to intra-state trains, so on June 7, 1892, the Citizens' Committee knew they had to do it all over again, and they needed to do it fast.

Once again, they bought the ticket. They hired the detectives. They told the train company. They staged the arrest. They filled out the warrants. So no one would suspect they were plotting, they decided not to use Desdunes's son again. Instead, they chose another young Afro-Creole man, Homer Plessy. They went before the same judge and asked him to dismiss the case on the grounds. But Ferguson disagreed. In the *State of Louisiana v. Homer Adolph Plessy*, Ferguson cited the *Civil Rights Cases* decision, explaining that railroads could be as racist as they pleased within state lines. They appealed and lost, which they expected. In denying the Citizens' Committee, the Supreme Court of Louisiana essentially said that Jim Crow laws were a product of the North, and now it was time for the South to get some of that good ol' white supremacy. "To assert separateness is not to declare inferiority," wrote the court, citing a Pennsylvania railroad law. "It is simply to say that following the order of Divine Providence, human authority ought not to compel these widely separated races to intermix."[8]

In other words, God believes in white supremacy.

The Citizens' Committee knew the stakes were high. If they lost at the federal level, it could mean segregation now, segregation tomorrow, and segregation forever.* The entire city of New Orleans was on edge. And on May 18, 1896, the U.S. Supreme Court established racial segregation as the law of the land. "Legislation is powerless to eradicate racial instincts or to abolish distinctions based upon physical differences," wrote Justice Henry Billings Brown.[9] "If one race be inferior to the other socially, the Constitution of the United States cannot put them upon the same plane." Now, some might call this a perfect example of white supremacy, but I wouldn't. However, I will have to ask Mikey about his cussing policy before I explain how I feel about the highest court in America essentially saying, "We can't do nothing about racism, bruh."

Of course, somehow they made this Black people's fault. The court reasoned that just because white people wanted to separate from Black people, it didn't necessarily mean that the whites believe Black people are inferior. According to this ruling, the idea that white society does not treat non-white people equally only exists because "the colored race chooses to put that construction upon it." Yes, they wrote that down. *On paper.*

Plessy v. Ferguson was more than the state's white minority had hoped for. The decision allowed them to create a two-tiered system that preserved white power. On May 12, 1898, a reconvened Louisiana constitutional convention adopted a new state constitution that enshrined all their racist imaginings into law. Convention president Ernest Kruttschnitt opened with a plea that foretold their purpose, saying, "May this hall, where thirty-two years ago, the negro first entered upon the unequal contest for supremacy, and which has been reddened with his blood, now witness the evolution of our organic law which will establish the relations between the races upon an everlasting foundation of right and justice. (Applause)."[10] The whites were at it again.

I know you think I'm finna tell you about poll taxes and literacy tests. Nah, bruh. They thought of *all the white things* to further suppress the Black population. The constitution used taxpayer money to pro-

---

* *Someone should write that down.*

vide pensions to Confederate soldiers. It included compulsory service to the state that could be waived if you paid your "road tax." They required a literacy test for all male voters, which could be waived if you were a "male person who was on January 1st, 1867, or at any date prior thereto, entitled to vote under the constitution or statutes of any State of the United States."*† The provision in Section 5 that would become known as the "grandfather clause" exempted the "son or grandson of any such person not less than twenty-one years of age at the date of the adoption of this Constitution."[11] They didn't have to hide it any longer. The only thing that would make their intentions more obvious is to restrict voting to "any male citizen over eighteen who has never used a jar of Murray's or a washcloth."

"We met here to establish the supremacy of the white race," remarked Judiciary Committee chairman Thomas Semmes during his closing remarks. "Our mission was, in the first place, to establish the supremacy of the white race in this State to the extent to which it could be legally and constitutionally done, and what has our ordinance on suffrage, the constitutional means by which we propose to maintain that ascendency, done? We have established throughout the State white manhood suffrage."[12]

The cocktail of racial terrorism, legal segregation, and constitutional white supremacy was a smashing success. In 1880, Louisiana's Black male voter registration rate was north of 90 percent. In the election of 1900, fewer than 3 percent of Black men were registered to vote.[13] Jim Crow had arrived. But it was not quite suppertime.

Now that you know what the white people were up to, lemme tell you what Black folks were doing. As White America struggled to rebuild its empire of racism, Black Americans were trying to accomplish the one goal they had been pursuing since 1620‡—having white people leave us alone.

Wait. Did you think we were clawing and scratching for the right

---

* In other words, white people.
† If they just said "white people," that would make them racist. But it wasn't their fault that this arbitrary cutoff date just happened to be the exact day when Black people gained the right to vote. I'm sure it was a coincidence.
‡ Most of 1619 was spent trying to figure out where the white people kept their seasoned salt. We're still looking.

to hang out in train cars and movie theaters with white people? Hold up, gimme a few minutes to stop laughing. Have you *met* white people? Think about it. If someone kidnapped you, made your family work for free, and murdered, raped, and brutalized your kin, who would want to kick it with them on the train? The fight against segregation had less to do with the proximity to whiteness and more about the social, political, and economic subjugation of Black people. Resisting Jim Crow was about our *humanity*. Plus, we had a sneaky suspicion that white people would soon forget about the "equal" part of "separate but equal." After all, white folks invented skiing, roller coasters, and bobsledding. They *love* a slippery slope.

This brings me to my man Booker T. Washington, who, even if he accomplished nothing in his life, would still rank in the top five Blackest names of all time along with D'Brickashaw Ferguson and Parliament-Funkadelic.

Booker T. was born into slavery and chose the last name Washington when he entered grade school. His mom would later tell him that she had already given him Taliaferro as a last name.[*] After working in the salt and coal mines of West Virginia, Washington attended Hampton Normal and Agricultural Institute under the recommendation of Hampton's founder, Samuel Armstrong. Washington would later move to Alabama and open Tuskegee Normal School, which would later become Tuskegee University. In building the school on a hundred-acre former plantation, Washington reassured Alabama's white supremacists that his institution would not challenge the economic or political domination of white society. Instead, his goal was to train teachers and provide an industrial and trade-based education to students, including agriculture, masonry, and domestic work. Using this model, Washington garnered support from Northern and Southern philanthropists at the school that would one day be famous for its students singing "Ball and Parlay" at every homecoming.[†]

Although he quietly supported political and civil rights efforts, Washington rarely publicly challenged white supremacy. Still, he

---

[*] *Although we could not find proper documentation, Uncle Rob swears this is the first time a Black mother asked someone if she looked like "Boo Boo the Fool."*

[†] *Look it up on YouTube.*

soon emerged as one of the key Black political figures and thought leaders in America, earning an invitation to speak at the prequel to Freaknik: the Cotton States and International Exposition at Piedmont Park in Atlanta.* Booker knew he had to kill it. There was a Southern war on Black people. Violence was rampant. If he got too radical, he could undo everything he had done at Tuskegee before they even had their first marching band. If he was too soft, he could lose credibility among his peers. Also, it was entirely possible that white people might just get mad and kill him if he said the wrong thing. Stuck in between a rock and a white place, Washington gave a speech that would later become known as the "Atlanta Compromise," which was essentially his plan to get white people to leave us alone.

Washington began the speech with a story about a ship lost at sea whose crew is dying of thirst. When they spot an oncoming vessel and beg for water, the other ship's crew repeatedly tell them to "cast down your bucket where you are!" Of course, the crew knows it can't drink ocean water, so they keep begging.† Finally, the unthirsty boat convinces the lost sailors to cast down their buckets and drink some of the water. It turns out, they were in the Amazon and not the ocean the whole time.

I know you're thinking that America ain't no sparkling river, but this was Washington's way of explaining that instead of fighting so hard for political equality, the relatively new freedmen should cast their metaphorical buckets down in trade, farming, and hard work. "Our greatest danger is that in the great leap from slavery to freedom, we may overlook the fact that the masses of us are to live by the productions of our hands and fail to keep in our mind that we shall prosper as we learn to dignify and glorify common labor. It is at the bottom of life we should begin and not the top," Washington explained.[14] Essentially, the educator proposed that Black people would chill out on the trying-to-be-equal stuff if white people just left us alone. In exchange for the gracious allowance of our existence, Black people wouldn't ask

---

* You thought I was kidding about the Freaknik thing?
† Hearing this speech at a young age is actually where I learned that seawater will kill you. Thanks, Mr. Washington!

for the right to vote, nor would they seek education beyond vocational training. The speech was seen by many as a total capitulation to white supremacy, as if white people haven't whited since the day the Jamestown settlers demanded that the Powhatans enroll the colonizers in their free lunch program.

Because white people have always believed there is one negro "leader" who speaks for all Black people, Washington soon became a favorite of the white establishment who favored Blacks who knew their place. He met with presidents Theodore Roosevelt and William Howard Taft, who both cared for Black people as much as Black people cared for the inventor of the noose. Many working-class and middle-class Black people admired Booker T. Washington's conservatism, but the intellectual class and the Black elite who didn't live in the South vociferously disagreed with him. That said, though he played the part, Washington secretly provided financial and political support for more radical desegregation and civil rights efforts.

Perhaps one of his biggest critics was W. E. B. Du Bois. Has Mikey mentioned him? I'm just kidding. I know nephew loves him some Du Bois. Initially, Du Bois told his counterpart that his Atlanta speech was a "phenomenal success" and a "word fitly spoken." But as time passed, Washington and Du Bois would throw subtle shade at each other about this intellectual impasse for years. The beef essentially boiled down to the fact that Booker T. Washington believed equality would come after Black folks gradually proved our worth through hard work and accommodating white rule. In his view, the highbrow thoughts of classical education and equal rights were folly if we hadn't established ourselves as real Americans. Until then, "in all things that are purely social we can be as separate as the fingers, yet one as the hand in all things essential to mutual progress."[15]

Du Bois, on the other hand, believed that education and equality went hand in hand, arguing that a "Talented Tenth" of educated Black elite would forge the path to negro freedom, if only the opportunity were allowed. "We have no right to sit silently by while the inevitable seeds are sown for a harvest of disaster to our children, black and white," Du Bois wrote in the diss track "Of Booker T. Washington and Others" in the seminal mixtape, *The Souls of Black Folk.*

"Washington's programme practically accepts the alleged inferiority of the Negro races."

This beef was bigger than Jay-Z vs. Nas; shadier than Michael Jackson vs. Prince; more contentious than sugar vs. salt in grits. Washington usually silenced his critics by smearing them in newspapers, but all the elite negroes loved Du Bois. He was light-skinned, had good hair, and went to Harvard. Plus, he wrote:

Mr. Washington distinctly asks that black people give up, at least for the present, three things,—

First, political power,
Second, insistence on civil rights,
Third, higher education of Negro youth,

—and concentrate all their energies on industrial education, the accumulation of wealth, and the conciliation of the South. This policy has been courageously and insistently advocated for over fifteen years and has been triumphant for perhaps ten years. As a result of this tender of the palm-branch, what has been the return? In these years, there have occurred:

1. *The disfranchisement of the Negro.*
2. *The legal creation of a distinct status of civil inferiority for the Negro.*
3. *The steady withdrawal of aid from institutions for the higher training of the Negro.*

These movements are not, to be sure, direct results of Mr. Washington's teachings; but his propaganda has, without a shadow of doubt, helped their speedier accomplishment.

Oh, snap! Did he just say Washington was helping white people?

At the heart of the dispute between these two historical giants lies the question of Black liberation: "How do we get free?" It is easy for a man like Du Bois, who grew up in an integrated community and studied all over the world, to criticize the tactics of millions of people like Washington, whose lives in the Deep South dangled at the end of a white man's whims on a daily basis. Booker T. Washington was a literal slave. For him and *most Black Americans*, the small amount of liberty and freedom afforded to Black people was abundantly better than being enslaved.

Still, I can't think of a single incidence where liberty has been achieved through gradual means, nor can I point to a single example of white people saying, "You know what? I think I'm gonna stop oppressing you." Perhaps the first step toward liberation begins with the dismantling of the idea that freedom is something that white people can give someone. Just sayin'.

In 1901, President Theodore Roosevelt invited Washington to the White House for dinner, which incensed many Caucasian Americans because . . . umm . . . I'mma go with the racism thing. Prior to Roosevelt's invitation, African Americans had visited the White House numerous times and even slept there. Sojourner Truth, Frederick Douglass, and many other people who switch to high-viscosity lotion in the winter had visited, dined, and even slept at the presidential residence before.[16] But, for whatever reason, Booker T. Washington eating dinner with the king of the whites infuriated people. Op-eds suggested that having breakfast or lunch would have been fine, but inviting a negro to dinner . . . outrageous!

"The action of President Roosevelt in entertaining that nigger will necessitate our killing a thousand niggers in the South before they will learn their place again," complained the senator Benjamin "Pitchfork Ben" Tillman of South Carolina.[17] Mississippi governor James K. Vardaman proclaimed that the White House was now "so saturated with the odor of nigger that the rats had taken refuge in the stable."[18] Papers across the country fueled fears that it would lead to more Black men raping white women because inviting a Black man to eat meant Roosevelt believed there was no reason "why the Anglo-Saxon may not mix negro blood with his blood." Others, including a trending poem called "Niggers in the White House," insisted that Roosevelt should just let Washington have sex with the first daughter because, as Ida B. Wells's old friends at the *Memphis Scimitar* wrote:

> *Any Nigger who happens to have a little more than the average amount*
> *of intelligence granted by the Creator of his race and cash enough to pay*

*the tailor and the barber, and the perfumer for scents enough to take away
the nigger smell, has a perfect right to be received by the daughter of the
white man among the guests in the parlor of his home.*

Even Black leaders criticized Washington for his respectability
politics. He was telling Black people in the South to submit to the
racial hierarchy while availing himself of the loopholes of Jim Crow
that fame afforded him. Ironically, the furor almost resulted in Washington's lynching when a "strange negro" was hurt jumping off the
train in Tuskegee. After the man recovered from his injuries at the
Tuskegee Institute Hospital, Washington revealed that he had nar-
rowly escaped a group of white men from Louisiana who had been
sent to murder him.[19] Even after those white boys tried to kill him,
Washington continued to push his narrative that the dignity gained
through hard work was the path to earning America's respect. Imagine trying to earn respect from people who don't use washcloths. It
don't make no sense.

Of course, W. E. B. Du Bois disagreed. His sociological research
showed lack of employment opportunities, disenfranchisement, and
the common ignorance of even the most well-meaning white people.
"They cannot 'understand' the Negro; they cannot protect him from
cheating and lynching," wrote Du Bois. "If he could defend himself
instead of having to depend on the chance sympathy of white citizens,
how much healthier a growth of democracy the South would have."[20]
Sadly, they couldn't start a Twitter beef or fight in a celebrity boxing
match. I kinda wish they—

Oh snap, Mikey's back!

* * *

Okay. Where was I?

Oh yeah, I was talking about my uncle Rob. He knows a lot about
history but he goes off on tangents sometimes. Please don't get him
talking about "separate but equal" or Booker T. Washington! He will
go on for hours! Anyway, when they said, "Name one thing all Black
people should be afraid of," Uncle Rob said, "An American," and ev-

erybody stopped laughing at my joke like his joke was funny or deep or something!

Anyway, I'm sorry if my uncle Rob talked your ear off. He's one of those old-school guys who jokes about everything. I tried to tell him that he shouldn't try to be funny when he's talking about important stuff like history and politics because people won't take you seriously when they're laughing. But he says I have no idea what I'm talking about.

Thank God I didn't inherit any of those traits.

THREE LITTLE QUESTIONS

1. **What is the flaw in the "separate but equal" argument?**
   a. If separation is based on race, it cannot be equal.
   b. Who separates things that are equal?
   c. It is theoretically possible, but practically improbable.
   d. The "but" part.

2. **What is the biggest myth about Jim Crow?**
   a. It was a Southern phenomenon.
   b. Black schools were not as good as their white counterparts.
   c. Segregated Black neighborhoods were poor.
   d. It ended.

3. **Which of these historical figure's traits was the most toxic?**
   a. W. E. B. Du Bois's elitism.
   b. Booker T. Washington's accommodationist ways.
   c. Ida B. Wells's lack of chill.
   d. America's racism.

ACTIVITY

CTRL+Z FOR RACISM

Construct a racially equitable education system.
   No, not on paper. Do it in real life.

FUNNY AF

THE MAN WHO INVENTED LAUGHTER

Most of the artistic creations commonly referred to as "American art" originated from the brains, hearts, and hands of Africans in America. Jazz is ours. We created the blues. Rock and roll belongs to us. Although most of these art forms evolved over time from a collection of intersecting sources, there is one uniquely quintessential American art form that every vaudeville historian and chronicler of American theater agrees was created by a Black man. While it might not sound so revolutionary now, the idea of a live entertainer of *any color* working without music, dancing, or tricks was simultaneously an act of pure hubris and a mark of a generational talent. And although he is not a household name, nearly every vaudeville historian and chronicler of American theater agrees:

Charles Case was the first stand-up comedian.

The product of an interracial relationship between an Irish woman and a Black musician, Charlie Case was born on August 27, 1858, in Lockport, New York.[1] His parents divorced when he was seventeen years old. The following year, he graduated from high school and began training with local attorneys to become a lawyer. After he opened his own firm above 75 Main

Street serving clients for five dollars per case, it quickly became apparent that Case wasn't cut out for the legal profession. Instead of relying on legal precedent, he dreamed up schemes to aid his clients' subversion of the law. When one of his clients was arrested for stealing a cow, Case advised him to feign insanity. Unfortunately, Case's client bragged about his strategy so much that the prosecutor caught wind of the plot. But something as inconsequential as the ethical standards of his profession could not stop Case's legal maneuvering. He took the case to trial, arguing that his client had found a rope on the ground and took it home before realizing there was a cow attached to it. Of course, the judge didn't buy it and sentenced the suspect to three years in Auburn state prison.

To be fair, Case spent more time playing the banjo and entertaining passersby than he did lawyering, which is probably why he couldn't keep a steady job. Still, he married, had two children, and eventually gave up the legal profession to become a traveling salesman. Some of the companies he represented refused to believe he was so bad at selling their products, because his prospective customers followed him everywhere he went. His bosses soon realized that the audiences were more interested in hearing Case's sales pitches and couldn't care less about the products.

Because of his light skin, Case could infiltrate segregated beer halls when he traveled, which is where he began to cultivate his talent for storytelling. He would often captivate local bars with long-winded rants that ended with him roasting everyone in attendance. His barroom antics entertained other traveling showmen, earning Case tickets to minstrel performances around New York. In the late 1880s, when one of his showbiz friends from the road fell ill, Case organized a talent show to raise money and decided to try his bar act.

A star was born.

Charlie Case didn't invent live comedy shows. Live performers have entertained audiences forever. The West African griot was an entertainer, musician, historian, and the keeper of the community's oral tradition. The Mali storytellers known as *jeli* were so culturally important, the term is literally derived from the Manding word for "blood." And of course, European cultures had jesters, clowns, and Bob Hope. But Case was different.

Between 1830 and the Civil War, minstrel shows had become America's most popular form of entertainment. Performances usually consisted of three acts that included burlesque dancing, musical performances, and comedic skits or speeches. The actors usually dressed in Blackface and performed sketches that almost always featured wisecracking stock characters, the most popular being a stereotypical version of the hapless Black "Sambo." The practice of white people dressing in Blackface was derided by men like Frederick Douglass, who called them "the filthy scum of white society, who have stolen from us a complexion denied to them by nature, in which to make money, and pander to the corrupt taste of their white fellow-citizens."[2] But minstrel shows had become so popular that Black performers began dressing in Blackface. Charlie Case entered show business just as minstrelsy was beginning to transition into what would become known as vaudeville. The vaudeville variety show lineup was much less dependent on single stars and usually featured as many as five different acts. With the crash of the banjo-playing ex-attorney market, Case had finally found a profession in which he could excel. By the 1880s, he commanded large audiences in nightclubs and theaters on the Loews circuit. He was called the "funniest human being who ever broke into vaudeville,"[3] and eventually became the highest-paid Blackface in America.

Like many entertainers during the era of minstrel shows, Case began his singing and dancing career with three partners, but it soon became evident that Charlie was a solo act. Curiously, he was a well-known neurotic who would fiddle with a string during his act to ease his nerves. Most of his stories were about his family—especially his father—and he usually peppered his tales with biting but hilarious lines. He would famously swing his arms to amplify the point of his hilariously fascinating but personal stories, which would soon become his signature. Artists who "borrowed" from Case would readily admit that he was the "greatest master of the unexpected statement in the world."[4] Although etymologists claim the origin of the term is unknown, vaudeville experts agree that he was the first person to call his technique a "punch line."

In the early 1900s, Case began having trouble. Some called it a "nervous breakdown," while those close to him insisted it was because of his profession. He often revealed the reason for his neurosis to his colleagues: he hated Blackface. But instead of quitting, Case changed his entire act. He stopped wearing costumes and Blackface. He no longer used partners or props. Except for an occasional parody song for which he was known, he did away with all the pretenses of music and live bands. After the switch, he became known as the "purest monologist of the vaudeville era," but the greatest marketers in show business didn't even know how to describe his act. Desperate for a title, they called him "The Man Who Talks About His Father."

"He stands in one place on the stage throughout his act," wrote one astounded reviewer in 1909. "Once in a while, he moves his hands but never his feet. He meanders from story to story, each one funnier than its predecessor and you are really wishing he would stop long enough for you to get your breath but he just keeps right on."

"Even though Mark Twain had worked with direct-address entertainment since 1857 and had been lecturing regularly since October 2, 1860,"[5] professor and theater historian Eddie Tafoya says, stand-up comedy was born when Case "took to the stage for the explicit purpose of telling jokes directly to the audience so as to elicit laughter." University of Calgary professor and humor researcher Dr. Robert Stebbins calls Case the "first pure stand-up comic" because he "came on stage dressed normally with no props"[6] and just told jokes.

Case died from a self-inflicted gunshot wound in 1916, just before his talent agency decided to get into the brand-new film industry by forming his managers at Metro-Goldwyn-Mayer, who would become known simply by their initials, MGM. When Case's wife heard of his death, she passed away from shock. Most of Case's white fans around the country read his obituary and were astounded to learn that he was Black, while white theater owners and show business insiders knew Case's African American heritage was an open secret.

"The inconsistent attitude of the white man on the color question was never more glaring than in the case of the deceased comedian," Lester Walton wrote in the *New York Age*, one of the most prominent Black newspapers in early-twentieth-century America. "Some believed the rumor that he was other than white untrue, others did not hesitate to express opinions in the affirmative; and yet no attempt was ever made to draw the color line."[7]

But Case's legacy remains. "Case suffered from more pirates than anyone in show biz," wrote vaudeville chronicler Joe Laurie Jr. in 1953, adding, "In fact, entertainers are still using his stuff on the radio and TV but it's not like it's Charlie Case."[8] Perhaps the most famous of the movie vaudevillians was W. C. Fields, the "comic genius" whose entire career was essentially a Charlie Case impersonation. In 1928, Fields copyrighted all his live sketches, including the sketch that later became the movie *The Fatal Glass of Beer*. The sketch, the movie, and even the song that opened the film were all created by Charlie Case.

In announcing his death, the reviewer for the *New York Evening World* said, "If all the minutes of joy he gave to the public could be added up it would cover hundreds of gladsome years."

11

SO DEVILISH A FIRE
THE BLACK WOMEN WHO STARTED
THE CIVIL RIGHTS MOVEMENT

> *Civilization must show two things: the glory and beauty of creating life
> and the need and duty of power and intelligence. This and this only
> will make the perfect marriage of love and work . . . but what of black
> women?*
>
> *The world that wills to worship womankind studiously forgets its
> darker sisters . . . I most sincerely doubt if any other race of women
> could have brought its fineness up through so devilish a fire.*
>
> —W. E. B. Du Bois

The history of Black America begins with Angela and ends with your mama. Between those two pillars lies all that this country is or ever will be.

When discussing the struggle for liberation and freedom, historians often date the campaign commonly known as the "civil rights movement" from the 1955 death of Emmitt Till until the Civil Rights Act of 1965. This overly broad description of the four-century effort to "get free" is usually confined to a list of names such as Martin Luther King Jr., Malcolm X, and Jackie Robinson, painting a picture as if Black people woke up in 1955 and discovered they were oppressed.

However, Black women's impact in politics, culture, and the collective reimagining of a free Black America formed the foundation of the modern civil rights movement. Even though they were doubly disenfranchised and marginalized by society, their impact was inversely proportionate to their social status. They were perhaps society's most underappreciated and discounted population, yet when it came to fighting for equality, they were arguably the most influential group in the country. It would be impossible to fully document Black women's contributions to this country, but to understand how Black people have not been consumed by the white-hot heat of America's flames, you must first understand the women who have shielded Black America from this forever-raging inferno.

MARY CHURCH TERRELL: FIRST

Mary Eliza Church was born in Memphis on September 23, 1863, to two recently emancipated slaves, Robert Reed Church and Louisa Ayres Church. When Mary was eleven, her parents sent her to Oberlin, Ohio, to attend Oberlin Public School, which also allowed her to escape the yellow fever epidemic that ravaged Memphis in 1878. Meanwhile, Robert spent his time purchasing the devalued property of deceased yellow fever victims and parlaying it into a real estate empire. When Mary returned to Memphis in 1879, the city had transformed. Her father opened restaurants, saloons, and state-of-the-art hotels that profited from the city's segregation laws, even using his immense wealth to open a bank that loaned money to Black residents. He transformed Memphis into one of the rare places where segregated facilities for Blacks were equal to, and sometimes better than, those that accommodated whites. Robert Church had become the South's only African American millionaire. (First.) Meanwhile, Mary's mother, Louisa, had an idea. She opened a posh beauty parlor that catered to Memphis's elite white women. (First.)

When Mary was seventeen years old, she graduated from high school and became one of the first Black women accepted into Oberlin College. As the first college in America to accept women, Oberlin created a course of study for female students that allowed them to graduate in two years. Mary said, "Nah," choosing the "gentlemen's path" that required four years of study, including learning to speak Greek. While there, she formed a tight clique of besties that included Anna Julia Cooper, the fourth Black woman in America to earn a Ph.D., and Ida Gibbs, who cofounded the first YWCA for Black women. After graduation, Mary earned her master's degree in education (another first) and began teaching modern languages at the historically Black Wilberforce University before moving to Europe to study, becoming fluent in French, German, and Italian.

After she returned to the States, Oberlin offered her a job as the registrar, which would have made her the first Black woman to hold the position. But Mary wasn't interested in sharing her talent to help white institutions prosper. Instead, she went to teach Latin at the infamous M Street School in Washington, D.C. (later renamed Paul Dunbar High). As soon as she got the job, the faculty at M Street set about trying to hook Mary up with one of their fellow teachers, Robert Terrell. It worked. Church eventually married Terrell, resigned her teaching post, and was named superintendent of the school.[*]

After her wedding, Terrell briefly considered leaving public life as an activist and educator. She was ready to focus on raising a family and engaging in community social work until one of her longtime friends, Thomas Moss—the postman and owner of People's Grocery in Memphis—was killed by a lynch mob. Terrell immediately joined her homegirl Ida B. Wells in the fight for anti-lynching laws, writing an article titled "Lynching from a Negro's Point of View" in 1904. Like Wells, Church became a prolific columnist and chronicler of Black life, always pushing for gender equality and civil rights. During a trip to the White House, the two pleaded for President Benjamin Harrison to address the lynching epidemic in his State of the Union speech, to no avail. Fortunately, Terrell's mentor convinced her that her talents were too immense for her to leave public life. After all, when your mentor is Frederick Douglass, you do whatever he says.[†]

---

[*] *For some reason, it was against the law for married women to teach. The reason was sexism.*
[†] *Frederick Douglass died shortly after walking home from a National Council of Negro Women meeting with Terrell.*

When Terrell was asked to speak at the 1904 International Congress of Women in Berlin (first), she gave the speech in German. Then she delivered it in French. Then she did it again in English. A staunch suffragist, Terrell cofounded the National Association of Colored Women, was a member of Delta Sigma Theta sorority,* and, along with Ida B. Wells, was one of the two Black women listed as founders of the NAACP. She penned numerous op-eds for the most important newspapers—Black and white—but did so under the pen name Euphemia Kirk.† Terrell often used her platform to share Wells's research to dispel the myth that lynching laws stopped Black men from becoming uncontrollable rapists.

"With one breath these spokes men for the South admit that during the war, when the men of that section generally speaking were on the battle field fighting to keep the iron heel of oppression upon the neck of their selves, the dusky bondmen, left behind on the plantations, protected the mothers, daughters and wives of their masters with a tenderness, a fidelity and sacredness of trust which the men of no race have ever surpassed," Terrell said in a 1905 speech. "With the next breath they insist that these men and their descendants have changed so radically in sentiment and conduct as to have become sexual degenerates and brutes, unable to control their passion for white women and unwilling to bridle their low desires."[1] If Terrell had dared address the historic fantasy of the sexually insatiable Black savage in modern times, they would have undoubtedly accused her of being a critical race theorist.

In a lifetime of incredible achievements, perhaps Terrell's most significant contribution to the movement occurred when she was eighty-seven years old. As one of America's most prominent Black women, she was named chair and spokesperson of the Coordinating Committee for the Enforcement of the D.C. Anti-Discrimination Laws, a group that pledged to fight segregation in the nation's capital. Before Terrell and her friends met at Thompson's Cafeteria on January 27, 1950, researchers at Howard University Law School had

---

* *Someone said "Ooo-Oop" as you were reading that.*
† *Kirk is a Scottish word that means "church," so the euphemism for Mary Church was literally "euphemism for church." Let's face it, she's smarter than us.*

informed the committee that the District had outlawed segregation in 1872, but it was never enforced. The manager greeted the party and informed them that they didn't serve coloreds. "Do you mean to tell me that you are not going to serve me?"[2] Terrell asked. When the manager confirmed that they were so racist they didn't even want Black people's money, an argument ensued. Terrell and her friends on the committee later returned to the restaurant to gather more information and were kicked out again, so the city filed a suit against the restaurant on their behalf.

Three years later, the U.S. Supreme Court unanimously ruled in *District of Columbia v. John R. Thompson Co.* that segregation was indeed against the law in the nation's capital, desegregating the city forever. By being kicked out of the restaurant, Mary Church Terrell kicked open the doors to equality.

MARY ELLEN PLEASANT: UNDERCOVER BILLIONAIRE

When abolitionist John Brown was hanged for treason after attempting a violent overthrow of the institution of slavery, there was a signed note in his pocket that read, "The ax is laid at the foot of the tree. When the first blow is struck, there will be more money to help. —WEP."[3] Army investigators desperately tried to find out who was responsible for aiding the armed insurrection, thinking it was a wealthy Northern abolitionist. They focused on the initials signed on the note, but they were reading them upside down. It turns out the note was written by one of the wealthiest and smartest Black women in American history.

Mary Ellen Pleasant was born circa 1814, but because her life is surrounded by mystery, no one knows where. Sometimes she claimed to have been born free, sometimes she claimed she was born in slavery and purchased her freedom, while other times she said she was a child of a voodoo priestess from the Caribbean. In any case, she wound up in Nantucket Island as a child, working as an indentured servant for a family of abolitionists. She never received a formal education, but said she "studied men and women a good deal,"[4] which may be how she married a wealthy Massachusetts business owner of Cuban descent, James Smith. Smith was a complicated figure—known to be an abusive man, he was also a staunch abolitionist. He died after four years of marriage, leaving Mary tens of thousands of dollars to fund her career as a "slave stealer" on the Underground Railroad.

While hanging out with abolitionists on Nantucket, Mary met and married John James Pleasant in 1848. Her new husband worked as a cook on a whaling ship, which enabled them to transport escaped slaves to Nova Scotia's Black communities. After the Fugitive Slave Act of 1850 made it too dangerous for Mary to continue her work, Mary and her husband moved to San Francisco just in time for the California Gold Rush, but not before stopping in New Orleans so Mary could take voodoo lessons from the infamous Voodoo Queen Marie Laveau. During her Louisiana stay, Mary and her husband arranged for escaped slaves to travel to California. When Mary arrived in San Francisco with a reported $15,000 in gold coins, she took a job as a domestic servant, even though she was worth nearly $500,000 in today's currency. Because the value of gold was at an all-time high, she exchanged her gold for silver, deposited the silver in the bank, and took out the money $1,000 at a time. Passing for white, Mary told the wealthy white men that she knew of a "speculator" who could loan money at a 10 percent interest rate. She used her position to eavesdrop on financial advice and, with the help of Thomas Bell, who worked at a local bank, invested in laundries, utility companies, brothels, and a string of boardinghouses. Her husband, meanwhile, continued to work at sea during the couple's thirty-year marriage.

Pleasant was one of the first investors in oil, and ended up owning so much land and real estate that California's governor took the oath of office in one of her boardinghouses. She used cunning instincts, blackmail, and her "exotic" looks to control the most powerful men in the city, writing in her unfinished autobiography that she was "a girl full of smartness" who "let books alone" and instead focused on learning how to influence people.[5] Because women weren't allowed to bank, she paid Bell handsomely to keep her deposits in his name. By 1875, Bell and Pleasant had made $30 million, nearly a billion dollars in today's currency.

Although she passed for white in the community at large, she didn't hide her race from her Black beneficiaries, explaining that she was the child of a Hawaiian and a "full-blooded Louisiana negress." As soon as the Fourteenth Amendment was signed, she officially changed her race to "black" and began funding civil rights cases.* Luckily, she faced little discrimination, partly because she used her connections and relationships to keep extensive records on the wealthy men who patronized her brothels, as well as detailed accounts of their illegitimate children and backroom political dealings. Pleasant reportedly even arranged marriages between wealthy men and young women whom she called her "protégées."

In San Francisco, Pleasant earned the nickname "the Harriet Tubman of California," funding the Underground Railroad and helping self-emancipated slaves to resettle,[6] hiring them at her numerous restaurants, boardinghouses, and horse stables. She was known to be a "one woman social agency" in California, providing relief for dozens of Black families. In 1858, Archy Lee, an enslaved man whose owner had brought him from Mississippi to California, escaped and declared himself free. Although California was a free state, Archy lost because as a Black man his testimony wasn't allowed in court. Mary paid for his legal fees and housing and worked to change the law that barred African Americans from testifying in court. By the time the case wound up in the federal court of appeals, the law was overturned, and Lee was declared a free man. In 1866, Pleasant filed a lawsuit against two companies after streetcar operators refused to let her ride. She withdrew one lawsuit when the Omnibus Railroad Company agreed to allow African Americans on their cars. The second case, *Pleasant v. North Beach & Mission Railroad Company*, outlawed segregation on San Francisco public transportation forever.

Pleasant died in 1904 after most of her resources were depleted by the widow of Thomas Bell, who claimed that Pleasant's money belonged to Bell. She still had her investments and property, but had spent much of her cash helping others. She spent her last years in a

---

* *You actually had to register your race back then.*

thirty-room mansion that spanned six blocks. Her underground activities were never known to whites until she dictated her autobiography and revealed her secrets, including the greatest one of all: "Before I pass away," she confessed, "I wish to clear the identity of the party who furnished John Brown with most of his money to start the fight at Harpers Ferry and who signed the letter found on him when he was arrested."[7] Mary's hate for inequality and love for her people were the sparks that fueled her life.

"Here was a colored woman who became one of the shrewdest business minds of the State. She anticipated the development in oil; she was the trusted confidante of many of the California pioneers . . . and for years was a power in San Francisco affairs," Du Bois said of Pleasant. "Yet, she held her memories, her hatreds, her deep designs, and throughout a life that was perhaps more than unconventional, she treasured a bitter hatred for slavery."[8] Amazingly, she managed to overcome every hurdle American society placed before her without losing her humanity or compromising her beliefs.

See? It's not impossible.

CALLIE GUY HOUSE: CHECK, PLEASE

The idea of reparations is not a new idea, nor has it ever been controversial until recently. After the Civil War, legislators, activists, and anyone with common sense attempted various forms of compensation for formerly enslaved African Americans. The Freedmen's Bureau was an acknowledgment of this sentiment, as was the Southern Homestead Act of 1866, which offered free land to ex-slaves.[*] Perhaps the most common proposal to create some form of economic security for ex-slaves was the freedmen's pension. Within the African American community, the National Ex-Slave Mutual Relief, Bounty and Pension Association (MRB&PA) quickly became the most popular grassroots effort to push the idea of compensation for former slaves. At the organization's first national conference in Nashville on November

---

[*] *White people took it all.*

28, 1898, the body elected Callie Guy House, a local washerwoman, as its assistant secretary.

Although the title might not seem impressive, House used her position to chart the course for the organization's future. She organized meetings in any place where white people weren't around. She visited churches. She contacted lawmakers. She talked to Black newspapers. She formed chapters and trained agents in states across the South. Taking inspiration directly from the government's pension structure for Civil War veterans, House created an organization so powerful that legislators were forced to listen to the group's demands. Between 1890 and 1903, six bills were introduced in Congress offering a lump sum, followed by monthly payments, to Black Americans who had outlasted slavery. But after Southern Democrats regained reputation in the federal legislature, anything that offered economic or political support for Black America was dead on arrival. After all, if they couldn't pass a law that made lynching illegal, reparations were a long shot. But they kept trying.

In 1915, the association filed a class-action lawsuit, *Johnson v. McAdoo*, in federal court for over $68 million, demanding the return of cotton taxes collected by the Treasury Department between 1862 and 1868. According to the suit, the money was due to former slaves and their ancestors for their unpaid labor. The suit eventually reached the U.S. Supreme Court, which claimed that the Treasury Department had governmental immunity because slavery was constitutional. In 1916, House was indicted for mail fraud on the grounds that she had sent bogus flyers through the mail. According to prosecutors, House had been soliciting donations from ex-slaves by falsely claiming that pensions had been secured for the ex-enslaved. Without evidence that House or any member of the organization had guaranteed or misled anyone to believe they would receive a pension, she was convicted by an all-white jury and sentenced to a year in prison.

During her trial, prosecutors revealed that intelligence officers from three different bureaus—the U.S. Post Office, the Justice Department, and the Pension Bureau—had been tracking House and the MRB&PA for years. Federal agents estimated that the group had three hundred thousand members organizing in churches, fraternities, sororities, and poor communities across the country, but some researchers, including historian Mary France Berry, believe the government's estimate may be on the low end. For comparison, in 1919, the NAACP had ninety thousand members. In less than twenty years, a thirty-six-year-old Tennessee washerwoman had organized the largest Black grassroots organization America had ever seen. The National Ex-Slave Mutual Relief, Bounty and Pension Association would dissolve after House's imprisonment, but the reparations movement that she championed would never die.

ELLA BAKER: BIGGER THAN A HAMBURGER

As a storyteller, I sometimes have to restrain myself from using hyperbole to point out the importance of certain historical events or figures. However, in this particular case, I am not faced with that problem. If one were to make a list of the most famous figures of the civil rights movement, including Martin Luther King Jr., Malcolm X, and the rest of the names that white people know, one humbly modest statement encapsulates the life of Ella Josephine Baker:

She is more important than *all* those guys.

Born in 1903, in 1930 Ella joined the Young Negroes Cooperative League to promote and teach Black economic power. She was protesting Italy's invasion of Ethiopia and fighting the unjust conviction of the Scottsboro Boys before Martin Luther King could even describe his dreams. She was named the NAACP's director of branches in 1943, and in 1952 she became the first female president of the New York City chapter. Baker was instrumental in founding every major civil rights organization during the 1950s and 1960s. In 1957, after the success of the Montgomery bus boycott, she moved to Atlanta to help form the Southern Christian Leadership Conference (SCLC). It was Baker's management and ideas that formed the framework of the organization's efforts. However, the group's patriarchal leader, Martin Luther King Jr., blocked her from public leadership roles.

Three years later, Baker was growing tired of the sexism of the ministers in the SCLC when she heard about the explosion of small sit-ins popping up across North Carolina. Knowing young people were the key to forming a more democratic movement, she invited students to a meeting at her alma mater, Shaw University. She convinced King to co-sign the invite and use up the SCLC's funds to finance the conference. The audience was filled with "126 delegates from 58 sit-in centers in 12 states" who would become known as the faces of the civil rights movement, including future congressman and Freedom Rider John Lewis, D.C. mayor Marion Barry, and the infamous Black Power champion Stokely Carmichael.

As always, the meeting was dominated by male leaders. But this time it was Baker's turn to talk. After King spoke about adopting non-violence and the need for strong leadership, Baker stood up and gave a speech titled "Bigger Than a Hamburger." She fired the students up by telling them to forget what had just been said, and instead to move toward more radical action, explaining that a youth-oriented, grassroots movement that was more democratic and leaderless could achieve more than just a few integrated lunch counters.

"I can remember her warning against entanglement with adults," civil rights leader Julian Bond explained. "But just to keep our movement pure. That we had started it, we had carried it forward, and we could carry it on by ourselves . . . She didn't say, 'Don't let Martin Luther King tell you what to do,' but you got the real feeling that that's what she meant. You know, 'He's a good man and so on, but don't let him tell you what to do.'"[9]

Thus began the Student Nonviolent Coordinating Committee (SNCC), one of the most effective bodies in the freedom struggle. After the meeting, Baker resigned from King's SCLC and became one of SNCC's most trusted advisors. She convinced the new group to form two distinct wings—one using nonviolent direct action and one organizing voting and political strategies. She helped build a partnership with the Congress of Racial Equality (CORE) and helped coordinate the Freedom Rides. She was a key figure in organizing the Mississippi Freedom Democratic Party, which offered an alternative to the all-white Democratic Party in the state. She accompanied the group that forced the Democratic Party to seat Black delegates at its national convention. She rejected the messianic traditional male leadership roles and promoted a "participatory democracy." The results of her actions influenced organizers throughout the country, recasting the disparate fights for equality as one unified civil rights movement.

In the 1940s, during her time as an NAACP leader, Baker helped organize leadership training sessions for young people interested in community activism. One of her youngest workshop participants would eventually rise to become secretary of her local NAACP chapter. Inspired by Baker, a young woman named Rosa Parks volunteered for a project that required her to sit down on a Montgomery bus and say, "Nah, I'm good."

Ella Baker's battle plans were as important as the foot soldiers who stood on the front lines in the fight for equality and civil rights. Yet because she was a victim of the inequality she fought against, her name is not as well known as those of her contemporaries. Perhaps she would be more famous if she had someone like Ella Baker to champion her cause. Then again, there is only one Ella Baker.

AMELIA BOYNTON WILL BE THERE

Amelia Boynton was everywhere.

In 1961, when civil rights advocates began the early push to expand voting rights in Dallas County, Alabama, a number of different strategies were brought to the table. First, they needed to know how many Black people in Selma and the surrounding areas had been disenfranchised. Knowing that children might not be suspected of subverting the Jim Crow laws, local activist Amelia Boynton had already organized kids in Dallas County to go door-to-door handing out surveys, concluding that of the fifteen thousand voting-age Black residents, just 242 were registered to vote. Because Alabama forced Black voters to prove their ability to read and knowledge of the Constitution, activists also needed to educate Black residents on how to pass the literacy tests required to register. Amelia Boynton had started the charge on that way back in 1935, teaching classes about how to pass the racist test after she became one of the first Black folks in the state to do so. Boynton was a trailblazer, and now she was getting key support from the movement. By 1965, Martin Luther King, John Lewis, and every major civil rights activist in America were sitting in Amelia Boynton's living room planning to overthrow Jim Crow in Selma, Alabama.

Born in 1911, Boynton attended Georgia State Industrial College (now Savannah State University) before transferring to the Tuskegee Institute, where she hung out with George Washington Carver—even naming a son after him—and earned a degree in home economics. As a U.S. Department of Agriculture home demonstration agent, she spent years traveling across rural Alabama teaching Blacks about homemaking, nutrition, and navigating rural life.

In Southern communities like Selma, there is often one community leader who serves the Black population's business needs. Some of the more common professions for this community leader include insurance agent, funeral director, or postal employee, but the one thing they usually have in common is that they are a notary public. So when the Ku Klux Klan ran the town's only Black notary public out of town, making it impossible to register to vote, Amelia convinced her husband to start an insurance agency, become a notary, and take over the organization the man had started, the Dallas County Voters League (DCVL). After she and Samuel acquired a building in downtown Selma, the couple held NAACP meetings in their tiny office, fighting the Klan, the state and local governments, and the notoriously racist local sheriff, Jim Clark. And she even fought hand-to-hand: when a well-known racist attacked the Boyntons in their downtown office in 1954, she grabbed a stick and stood right there, demonstrating the ancient African tradition of wishing a MF would.

In 1958, a young Howard Law School student was riding the bus to Selma for Christmas break when the bus stopped at a Trailways bus station in Virginia to allow the passengers to eat. Bruce, the law student, posted up at the "whites only" counter just like everyone else. When authorities told him to leave, Bruce wouldn't budge. He was arrested and convicted, but he wouldn't stop until his conviction was overturned. His mother called an NAACP lawyer she knew and made that friend promise to fight for her son, even if they had to go to the

Supreme Court. Those cops had no idea that Bruce Boynton's mother was infamous organizer Amelia Boynton, and that lawyer pal was none other than Thurgood Marshall. The landmark Supreme Court case of *Bruce George Washington Carver Boynton v. Virginia* overturned segregation on interstate commerce, changing the course of history forever. Shortly thereafter, young activists Ralph Abernathy, Stokely Carmichael, John Lewis, and others gained prominence on the Freedom Rides—a joint effort by CORE and the SNCC to enforce *Boynton v. Virginia*.

By 1964, Amelia had given up her leadership position in the DCVL to run for Congress, making her the first Black woman in the state of Alabama to run for Congress and the first woman of *any race* to run as a Democrat. After she lost, she didn't stop fighting for justice; she became even more deeply invested in the cause after Jimmie Lee Jackson, a twenty-six-year-old Black deacon, was beaten, shot, and killed by Alabama state troopers during a peaceful protest on February 18, 1965. Boynton rejoined the DCVL and invited the most prominent civil rights leaders of the time to the tiny town of Selma. While many of the league's members were dubious that any of them would show up, Amelia was there in her living room with Martin Luther King and James Bevel, along with organizers from the SCLC and SNCC, planning how to defeat segregation. There, they organized a march to the state capital in Montgomery to talk to Governor George Wallace about Jackson's death, but of course, Wallace dispatched his club-toting troopers to the march that became known as Bloody Sunday. When officers cracked John Lewis's skull on the Edmund Pettus Bridge during the demonstration, Amelia did not run. The viral picture of the protest was a photo of Amelia Boynton being gassed and beaten by police officers. *That* was one of the photos that turned public sentiment and convinced President Lyndon Johnson to sign the Voting Rights Act.

One of the coolest stories about Amelia Boynton's life was discovered only recently. For years, historians believed Cudjo Lewis, who was immortalized in writer Zora Neale Hurston's posthumous bestseller *Barracoon*, was the last living survivor of the slave trade. In 1860, Timothy Meaher, a wealthy Mobile, Alabama, plantation owner, made a bet with his friends that he could sneak a shipment of slaves into the country. Fifty-two years after the importation of human chattel was outlawed in the United States, the *Clotilda*, a two-masted schooner, snuck into Mobile Bay, returning from a secret mission in Benin, Africa. Captained by William Foster, the *Clotilda* unloaded its precious cargo: around 112 kidnapped human beings.

To hide their misdeeds, Foster rushed to the *Clotilda* and set it on fire. The vessel sank to the bottom. The stolen Africans were eventually sold and worked as slaves until they were emancipated in 1865. When they were denied reparations, Lewis and a group of slaves put their money together and founded the African-centered town of Africatown, located a few miles from Mobile.

In 2019, a British researcher discovered archival footage of Redoshi, a formerly enslaved woman who was sold to forced labor camp owner Washington Smith in Dallas County, Alabama. Redoshi lived two years longer than Cudjo Lewis and was even active during the infancy of the civil rights movement. And the story of how that archival footage emerged? One day, a USDA agent named Amelia Boynton visited Redoshi on her rural farm and began listening to the stories of her capture, enslavement, and emancipation. Excited, Boynton convinced the Department of Agriculture to bring a film crew out to "Aunt Sally's" farm and interview her about her experiences. Thus Amelia Boynton's influence spans from the transatlantic slave trade to this very moment . . .

Amelia Boynton was always there.

She still is.

THE WOMEN WHO DESEGREGATED MONTGOMERY BUSES

Claudette Colvin was mad.

On March 2, 1955, the outspoken fifteen-year-old high school student stepped onto a Montgomery city bus. Because Colvin's family didn't own a car, she took the Capitol Heights bus home from school every day. She was already sitting in the colored section when the driver, Robert Clare, demanded that she and three friends give their seats to white women who were standing up. Colvin thought about the paper on the unfair practices of segregation that she had just turned in to her teacher. She thought about how she couldn't even try on clothes at local department stores lest she sully the items with her Black skin. But most of all, she thought about her friend Jeremiah.

Jeremiah Reeves was so good-looking and cool, all the girls at Booker T. Washington High School had a crush on him. He played in the school's jazz band, and he already had a job delivering groceries to white neighborhoods. In 1952, the white residents in one Montgomery neighborhood confirmed their suspicions that Reeves was having an affair with a white woman when they peeked in a window and saw the couple undressing. The woman, however, claimed that Reeves was raping her. Police arrested Reeves, took him to a nearby prison, and strapped him into the electric chair for two days until he finally confessed.[10] Because Montgomery's Black citizens were not allowed to vote, an all-white jury sentenced Reeves to death. This is what radicalized Claudette Colvin.

When police officers dragged her off the bus and took her to jail, she had already joined the NAACP's Youth Council. As the cops made jokes about her bra size and body parts, Colvin screamed about her constitutional rights. She felt the echoes of injustice and the touch of her ancestors. "History kept me stuck to my seat," Colvin would later say. "I felt the hand of Harriet Tubman pushing down on one shoulder and Sojourner Truth pushing down on the other."

Aurelia Browder would be next.

A widower with six children, Browder didn't complete her high school education until she was in her thirties. She later enrolled at Alabama State University, where she met Jo Ann Gibson Robinson, a professor in the English Department. Robinson inspired Browder to get involved in the civil rights movement, and on April 19, 1955, Browder was arrested for sitting in the white section of a Montgomery bus. She would later graduate from Alabama State with honors, earning a bachelor's degree in science.

Susie McDonald, known around Montgomery as "Miss Sue," owned a pavilion in the city where Black residents could gather without fear of racial intimidation. When Miss Sue was arrested for violating Montgomery's bus rules on October 21, 1955, she was in her seventies and could pass for white. McDonald, however, had made sure to inform the driver that she was indeed a Black woman before she sat down. That same day, eighteen-year-old Mary Louise Smith was arrested for sitting in the whites-only section. Jeanetta Reese was arrested for the same offense. Finally, on Thursday, December 1, 1955, Rosa Parks did it too.

Unlike Colvin, Browder, McDonald, Smith, and Reese, Parks planned her protest. She served as the secretary for the Montgomery chapter of the NAACP and had participated in civil rights activism for more than a decade. Part of the reason Rosa was selected to publicize the injustice of segregation was because of her presentation. The leaders had already rejected Claudette Colvin because she was dark-skinned and outspoken, and was pregnant and unmarried. Parks, on the other hand, was fair-skinned, reserved, and had "good hair."

When Professor Robinson heard about Parks's arrest, she was fed up. After her prized student Browder had been arrested for the same thing, Robinson tried to convince her organization, the Women's Political Council, to organize a citywide bus boycott. Robinson called a few students and colleagues at Alabama State, and they printed thirty-five thousand flyers calling for a one-day citywide boycott and passed them out at local churches.

"Another woman has been arrested and thrown in jail because she refused to get up out of her seat on the bus for a white person to sit down," read the typewritten flyer. "It is the second time since the Claudette Colvin case that a Negro woman has been arrested for the same thing.

"This has to be stopped. Negroes have rights too, for if Negroes did not ride the buses, they could not operate. Three-fourths of the riders are Negro, yet we are arrested or have to stand over empty seats. If we do not do something to stop these arrests, they will continue. The next time it may be you, or your daughter, or mother. This woman's case will come up on Monday. We are, therefore, asking every Negro to stay off the buses Monday in protest of the arrest and trial. Don't ride the buses to work, to town, to school, or anywhere on Monday. You can afford to stay out of school for one day if you have no other way to go except by bus. You can also afford to stay out of town for one day. If you work, take a cab, or walk. But please, children and grown-ups, don't ride the bus at all on Monday. Please stay off all buses Monday."[11]

On December 5, 1955, a group of leaders formed the Montgomery Improvement Association (MIA) and asked Robinson to lead it. Robinson declined because of her job at Alabama State, so the next logical choice was E. D. Nixon. A thorn in white Montgomery's side, Nixon had been organizing civil rights campaigns as early as 1940 and was the unelected mayor of Black Montgomery. Because the early civil rights movement was entrenched in sexism, Nixon and others wouldn't even consider a woman leader. Rosa Parks wasn't even allowed to speak at the meeting. Nixon suggested a younger face for the movement, nominating the new pastor at Dexter Avenue Baptist Church: the Reverend Martin Luther King Jr.

Unlike the women who had stood up for their rights, King was reluctant. He wanted a more low-key position that would not upset the city's leadership. But after Nixon threatened to expose him as a coward, King accepted the role with a few conditions. As the leader of the Montgomery Improvement Association, King *did not demand* that the city integrate buses. The MIA called for a first-come, first-served seating, more African American drivers on predominantly Black routes, and courteous treatment of Black residents.

NAACP attorney Fred Gray decided to get involved. He tracked down Colvin, Crowder, McDonald, Reese, and Smith to file a civil rights lawsuit against the city. Reese eventually dropped out of the lawsuit because she was being harassed by whites in Montgomery, but Claudette, Aurelia, Miss Sue, and Mary were down. Gray won the case in U.S. district court, but the city appealed to the Supreme Court. On December 17, 1956, the Supreme Court rejected the city's appeals, affirming the district court's ruling in *Aurelia S. Browder, et al. v. W. A. Gayle, et al.* Segregation was unconstitutional on Montgomery city transportation, and on December 20, 1956, the Montgomery bus boycott ended.

MARY MCLEOD BETHUNE: MILITARY GENIUS

Not far from the plantation where my ancestors were enslaved in Sumter and Lee Counties sits a Mayesville, South Carolina, rice and cotton farm where Mary Jane McLeod was born.* Everyone knows that Mary McLeod Bethune would eventually take $1.50 and create the Daytona Literary and Industrial Training School for Negro Girls, a historically Black institution that later became Bethune-Cookman University.† After becoming the first Black woman to serve as a college president, she cofounded the United Negro College Fund, which has provided scholarships to more than five hundred thousand Black students. During this time, she forged a friendship with President Franklin Roosevelt's wife and used her status as Eleanor Roosevelt's "closest friend in [her] age group"[12] to push the president on his civil rights agenda.

Let's be clear: regardless of whether he did it for political expediency or his own white supremacist leanings, Frankie D. was a racist. He refused to support anti-lynching legislation. He nominated a Klansman to the Supreme Court.‡ He interned American citizens in concentration camps. And when he introduced his New Deal that made it rain billions on White America to lift the country out of the Great Depression, he largely excluded Black citizens. But behind the scenes, Bethune was one of the few people who could speak to Franklin in the African American dialect known as "keeping it real," successfully using her influence with the First Lady to push for economic and political progress for Black America.

Because he rarely came in contact with people of the negro persuasion,§ Roosevelt thought Bethune was one of the smartest

---

*   *According to the third transitive law of negrodynamics, this technically makes her my playcousin.*
† *How remarkable was this? One hundred years later, Tupac Shakur would still be "trying to make a dollar out of fifteen cents (a dime and a nickel)."*
‡ *Hugo Black wasn't just a Klansman with no judicial experience; Birmingham's Robert E. Lee Klan No. 1 awarded Black with a lifetime membership before he temporarily resigned to run for the Senate.*
§ *It's not white people's fault that they didn't know capable Black candidates. Remember, Jim Crow laws had segregated society. Also remember, Jim Crow was white people's fault.*

women who ever lived. As the director of the Division of Negro Affairs of the National Youth Administration, she convinced the president to set aside three hundred thousand public works jobs for African Americans. In 1936, Roosevelt tapped Bethune to organize the Federal Council of Negro Affairs. Known as the "Black Cabinet,"[13] the group of scholars, activists, and leaders wasn't an official government-sanctioned entity—they took no notes and usually gathered in Bethune's apartment or her office as a back channel on policy for Black America. One of the group's first orders of business was to discuss recent union protests led by union organizer Asa Philip Randolph, who was demanding an end to discrimination in defense industries. Because he was a socialist and a radical, Randolph wasn't a member of the Black Cabinet, but the brain trust knew the power and influence he wielded among the Black working class. The president was kinda preoccupied with this little thing called World War II, so he dismissed Randolph's threats of a large-scale protest in Washington until Bethune said, "Trust me, you wanna listen to ol' boy."

Roosevelt put the Black Cabinet in charge of addressing the issue. Rayford Logan, a member of the council and a history professor from Howard University, drafted Executive Order 8802, declaring that "there shall be no discrimination in the employment of workers in the defense industries or government because of race, creed, color, or national origin."[14] The order also established the Fair Employment Practice Committee to enforce equality in the defense industry.

With such a momentous victory under her belt, one would assume Bethune would leave well enough alone. "But more can be done," she wrote in a letter to Roosevelt on November 27, 1939. "One of the sorest points among Negroes which I have encountered is the flagrant discrimination against Negroes in all the armed forces of the United States. Forthright action on your part to lessen discrimination and segregation and particularly in affording opportunities for the training of Negro pilots for the air corps would gain tremendous good will, perhaps even out of proportion to the significance of such action."[15] Bethune didn't just make the suggestion that Roosevelt introduce Black pilots to the army's newly created air force, she laid out a plan on how to get it done without ruffling feathers.

Among the army's top brass, Black pilots flying airplanes was a ludicrous idea. There hadn't been an African American pilot in the history of the U.S. armed forces. And if you thought white people hated seeing uniformed Blacks being treated as heroes after World War I, can you imagine how furious they would be about Black pilots flying the most sophisticated aircraft in the world?* Commanding general Henry "Hap" Arnold was in dire need of pilots but admitted that a crew of African American airmen "would result in Negro officers serving over white enlisted men creating an impossible social situation."[16] To quell the controversy, Arnold commissioned a report that concluded that because of Roosevelt's executive order, the army couldn't turn away qualified Black pilots. However, there were only 124 African American pilots in the entire country. And since the army was segregated, there was no place to train them and no funds to build an entirely new training facility.

Black leaders felt betrayed. The July 1940 cover of *The Crisis* explained the controversy perfectly: "Warplanes—Negro Americans may not build them, repair them, or fly them, but they must help pay for them."[17] Bethune, however, was fine about the army's decision . . . because she had already found a solution to this inequity.

Unbeknownst to most of America, Bethune had privately convinced the White House to tack a benign provision—Public Law 18—onto a military appropriations bill intended to prepare the nation's armed forces for war. The addendum included funds for Black colleges and required the establishment of the Civilian Pilot Training Program (CPTP), a non-military aviation program that found qualified civilians and trained them as pilots. Because the Civilian Pilot Training Program wasn't technically part of the military, the historically Black colleges had been sending prospective pilots to train at the Tuskegee Institute, which used funds from Public Law 18 to recruit, test, and train Black pilots using the exact same methods employed at nearby Maxwell Field in Montgomery. Still, they needed a platform to prove they were as good as the white boys. And, naturally, Bethune had a literal ace up her sleeve.

---

* *Yes. Yes, we can imagine.*

On March 29, 1941, Eleanor arrived in Tuskegee to attend a trustee meeting for the Rosenwald Fund, a charity that donated millions to Black educational institutions, including Bethune-Cookman College. After her morning meetings, the First Lady took a day trip to Tuskegee's flight training site, where she met C. Alfred "Chief" Anderson, a Black pilot. Ignoring the protests of her Secret Service officers, Eleanor asked Anderson to take her on a short flight. Forty minutes later, the First Lady told Anderson, "Well, you can fly alright."

Four months later, on July 19, 1941, the army welcomed Class 42-C, the U.S. military's first all-Black class to train as combat pilots. Even though Tuskegee had identified, trained, and qualified the Black civilian pilots for flight school, the army still resisted. Citing the military's segregation policy, the top brass still insisted there was no place to complete their military training. But this is where Bethune's seemingly innocuous plan came together.

Remember Eleanor's meeting for the Rosenwald Fund? After her flight, the First Lady arranged for a loan to build Moten Field in Tuskegee, where the soldiers could complete their first phase of training. And because Randolph's Executive Order 8802 forbade discrimination in awarding defense contracts, Black-owned construction firm McKissack and McKissack won the contract to build a state-of-the-art training facility. Using a design by African American architect Hilyard Robinson, labor from two thousand of those Black public works employees that Bethune had lobbied for, and the funds from Public Law 18, McKissack and McKissack completed Tuskegee Army Air Field in just six months, making it the only army site that hosted three phases of pilot training (basic, advanced, and transition) at a single location.

On June 11, 1943, German and Italian troops surrendered the Mediterranean island of Pantelleria. In the entire military history of the world, a land force had never been defeated by an air-only assault until the very first mission of the 99th Pursuit Squadron of the U.S. Army Air Force—or as we call them, the Tuskegee Airmen. Mary McLeod Bethune's legacy extended into every section of Black life, in politics, education, economics, and social life. And all it took was wisdom, courage, intelligence, and a measly $1.50.

THREE LITTLE QUESTIONS

1. **How did Black women contribute to the civil rights movement?**
    a. They started it.
    b. They only provided the strategy, tactics, legwork, vision, and manpower.
    c. According to census data, the vast majority of Black activists were birthed by Black women.
    d. By being Black women.

2. **Who was more famous during her lifetime?**
    a. Ida B. Wells.
    b. Harriet Tubman.
    c. Mary McLeod Bethune.
    d. Lisa, Angela, Pamela, Renee (Tie).

3. **Which one of these benefited from the work of Black women?**
    a. Universal white male suffrage.
    b. Universal white female suffrage.
    c. Black male suffrage.
    d. All of the above.

ACTIVITY

MORE FIRE

Read about these Black women:

- **Daisy Bates**
- **Josephine Baker**
- **Elaine Brown**
- **Septima Clark**
- **Shirley Chisholm**
- **Anna Julia Cooper**
- **Angela Davis**
- **Charlotte Dupuy**
- **The Edmonson sisters**
- **Fannie Lou Hamer**
- **Dorothy Height**
- **Claudia Jones**
- **Barbara Jordan**
- **Marsha P. Johnson**
- **Pauli Murray**
- **Sojourner Truth**
- **Madam C. J. Walker**

SISTER ROSETTA THARPE

THE QUEER BLACK WOMAN WHO INVENTED ROCK AND ROLL

t is as simple as this: What we know as rock and roll did not exist before Sister Rosetta Tharpe. She came before Elvis and Johnny Cash. She preceded Chuck Berry and Little Richard. When most music historians are asked who invented this class of music, many will name one of the previously mentioned rock stars. The most respectful and thoughtful will say it was a combination of these men.

But every single one of those men, including Little Richard, will tell you that the *first person* from whom they heard the sound with which we have become familiar was Rosetta Tharpe. In his induction into the Rock and Roll Hall of Fame, Johnny Cash said that she was his favorite singer growing up. Little Richard called her his greatest influence. Chuck Berry said that his entire career was just "one long Rosetta Tharpe impersonation." A PBS documentary on her life called her the "godmother of rock and roll." She is still called the "forgotten mother"[1] of the genre and "the most influential artist ever."

In 1963, a collection of Black musicians traveled around the world with the Blues and Gospel tour. The bill featured artists such as Sonny Terry and Brownie McGhee, Cousin Joe, Otis

Spann, and Muddy Waters—all household names in America but relative unknowns in Europe. In fact, the only venue in the United Kingdom that booked the tour was in Manchester. As their train arrived in Manchester, one of the artists—Sister Rosetta Tharpe—asked the promoter if she could change her opening number to the gospel classic "Didn't It Rain." When she strapped on the guitar and played her unique mix of blues and gospel, it blew the audience's mind and influenced musicians in the area for decades, especially a group who traveled from London in a small bus together—some dude named Eric Clapton, a kid named Jimmy Page, and the members of a very obscure garage band called the Rolling Stones.[2]

Maybe she is overlooked because she was technically a gospel singer (because rock didn't exist yet, remember?). Perhaps Tharpe's Blackness has something to do with the fact that she wasn't elected to the Rock and Roll Hall of Fame until 2017. Or her queerness. Or the fact that she was a woman. Music authorities argue about a handful of songs recorded between 1946 and 1952 when discussing what might be the first rock and roll song ever, the most popular of which is "Rocket 88" by Jackie Brenston and His Delta Cats, recorded in 1951.

Music authorities be lying. It is all Rosetta.

* * *

Rosetta Nubin was born in 1915 in Cotton Plant, Arkansas. By the time she was six years old, she was performing in churches around the South with her mother. At that same age, she and her mother moved to Chicago. In 1934, she married a Church of God in Christ (COGIC) preacher named Thomas Tharpe, after she became a renowned gospel musician in the COGIC community. Rosetta would divorce her husband after a few years, but she kept the surname as her stage moniker. During a time when the idea of a guitar-playing woman was nonexistent, not only did Rosetta Tharpe erase this line by mastering the symbol of musical masculinity, but her blend of gospel and secular music was seen as earth-shattering. Her willingness to play "God's music" in the devil's den of nightclubs and music halls caused an uproar. She was one of the first artists to use heavy distortion on her electric guitar, long before the blues artists tried it.

After a move to New York, Tharpe began playing with some of the biggest bands in the country, including Duke Ellington's. By the time she was twenty-three, she had a recording contract, and recorded Decca Records' first gospel songs. In October 1938, when Elvis was three years old, when Chuck Berry was twelve, when Little Richard was six years old, and when Jackie Brenston and His Delta Cats were still kittens, Sister Rosetta Tharpe recorded "This Train," a gospel song that would become a mainstream hit. But the other side of that record featured Tharpe playing an electric guitar in a wailing, blues-inspired tempo that no one had ever heard before. The song was called "Rock Me."

Tharpe's 1945 hit "Strange Things Happening Every Day" was the first gospel record to cross over to the *Billboard* "race record" chart, eventually reaching number two. "Strange Things" poked fun at religion and opened with a riff that would typify guitar solos a decade later. It became a favorite of Memphis deejay Dewey Phillips and his protégé—a little-known white dude named Elvis something. The recording is now referred to as a "rock and roll" record and has been covered by Bruce Springsteen.[3]

Even though she was playing venues like Carnegie Hall and the Cotton Club with legendary acts such as Cab Calloway, Tharpe longed to get back to the gospel music circuit. After meeting gospel singer Marie Knight in 1946, Tharpe entered into a relationship with her and they lived openly as a queer couple until it ended in 1951. And this was major, as Sister Rosetta Tharpe was not an unknown, hidden little secret. She was such a huge star that she had her third wedding *in a stadium* where twenty-five thousand people attended. Yet with the move to folk music and the British invasion that rejuvenated musicians of her era in the 1960s and 1970s, Tharpe didn't get the same bump that male blues musicians did, because she continued to stick to gospel-themed music. She died on October 9, 1973, after suffering a second stroke.

Rock and roll did not exist before Rosetta Tharpe, but to say she "invented" it may be a little presumptuous. Yet she was somehow erased from the history of music. Most reasonable music historians will tell you that *one person* shouldn't receive credit for an entire genre. While it is true that not every single musician who ever played rock and roll was inspired by Rosetta Tharpe, it is also true that there is not a single rock musician playing in the current era doing something that Rosetta Tharpe wasn't doing eighty years ago. She did it *first*.

Just for the sake of clarity, let's see how Merriam-Webster defines "invent."

> **Invent:** *to produce (something, such as a useful device or process) for the first time through the use of the imagination or of ingenious thinking and experiment.*

Well, I guess that settles that.

12

THE RACE WAR III

THE CONSPIRACY THEORY THAT WAS TRUE

Johnny got the job.

It was 1913, and Johnny, a recent high school graduate, secured his first employment assignment at the Library of Congress, which was located a few blocks away from his childhood home. The position was also within walking distance of George Washington University, where Johnny had just enrolled as a freshman. Because of a stutter that had earned him the nickname "Speed," prospective employers had rebuffed Johnny, but this new gig didn't require face-to-face communication. Instead, Johnny mostly sat at a desk, typing memos and learning the library's filing system. By the time Johnny earned his master of law in 1917, he had become one of the federal institution's most diligent workers, impressing supervisors with his work ethic and his expertise in cataloging the institution's massive book collections. Speed would later say that his time at the Library of Congress trained him in "the value of collating material" and gave him "an excellent foundation" for assembling information and evidence.[1] After he graduated, Speed took his talents to his new gig, hunting potential enemies in the United States for the Justice Department's War Emergency Division, where he earned $900 a year.[2]

Speed's boss Thomas was a virulent segregationist who rose from academia's ranks to become one of the country's most respected white supremacists. In his previous job as president of a prestigious university, Thomas successfully ensured that his beloved Princeton would be the last Ivy League university to admit Black students.[3] Thomas had also famously written one of the more popular American history books that reinforced the national belief in Black racial inferiority. In it, he argued that the racial terrorism of Reconstruction was caused by white supremacists' "instinct of self-preservation to rid themselves, by fair means or foul, of the intolerable burden of governments sustained by the votes of ignorant negroes."[4]

Thomas was progressive in one aspect, however. He loved new gadgets. In 1915, Thomas invited Speed's frat brother Thomas Dixon Jr., a Klansman, writer, and "great-granddaddy of white nationalism,"[5] to host a screening of the film adaptation of his novel *The Clansman*. The movie is generally considered the first Hollywood blockbuster. Perhaps nothing was more of a catalyst for the Ku Klux Klan's resurgence in the 1920s than this movie night for one of the most racist films in the history of American cinema.[6] And its theatrical debut took place at 1600 Pennsylvania Avenue in Washington, D.C.

Speed's boss? None other than the president of the United States, Thomas Woodrow Wilson.

When Thomas Woodrow Wilson, the twenty-eighth president, held the White House's first movie screening for *The Birth of a Nation*, he said it was "like writing history with lightning."[7] Thomas and Speed were kindred spirits: they loved America, and both harbored a deep affection for white supremacy. And emboldened by his boss's call to smoke out secret radical organizations, Speed took to his job with fervor.

In 1917, as the United States was embroiled in the "Great War," Congress authorized the Espionage Act. The legislation gave the Bureau of Investigation the authority to investigate, interrogate, and surveil Americans suspected of "disloyalty."[8] In a few months, Speed had compiled thousands of files on American citizens who were suspected of being "subversive." His knack for meticulously collecting and storing information landed him a promotion to head of the "Radical Division"—the department's new General Intelligence Division. But in 1918, a few months after Speed's promotion, the First World War ended. Still, he found a way to make himself useful.

At twenty-nine years old, Speed became director of the most advanced non-military intelligence operation in the known universe—the Bureau of Investigation. What started with a job in the Library of Congress eventually evolved into a grand conspiracy that is still being uncovered to this day. Ultimately, Speed would use his position to collect, process, and catalog detailed bits of information to identify "radicals" and attempt to stop every movement for freedom and equality for the next half century.

Speed was *very good* at his job.

After World War I, many of the almost four hundred thousand[9] African Americans who served in the armed forces returned to the Jim Crow South with an entirely new perspective on the world. This group of men, who dubbed themselves the "New Negro," insisted on asserting their rights and speaking out against injustices. Naturally, they came back to a country that not only did not valorize them as war heroes, but approached them with increased suspicion. As Senator James K. Vardaman warned the Senate in 1917, "Impress the negro with the fact that he is defending the flag, inflate his untutored soul with military airs, teach him that it is his duty to keep the emblem of the Nation flying triumphantly in the air. It is but a short step to the conclusion that his political rights must be respected."[10]

Vardaman was one of many Americans who despised the New Negro phenomenon. Known as the "Great White Chief," the pro-murder white supremacist rose to national prominence on a populist stance that included his position that "if it is necessary, every Negro in the state will be lynched; it will be done to maintain white supremacy."[11] When Vardaman ran for Mississippi's Senate seat in 1912, his "redneck" followers wore "bloodstained" neckerchiefs.

The anti-immigrant movement[*] was just beginning in post-war America when presidential-inspired Klansmania was taking over the country. By the summer of 1919, the *original* anti–Black Lives Matter

---

[*] *The movement emerged against Asian, Catholic, Italian, and Irish immigrants who threatened the white way of life.*

movement had mushroomed into a full-on race war. Between April and September 1919 alone, sociologist, scholar, and all-around Black genius George Haynes reported forty-three lynchings, including sixteen hangings and eight men who were burned at the stake.[12] Tuskegee University counts seventy-six, with many of these events still being discovered.[13] That tally doesn't include the Elaine massacre, in which as many as eight hundred Black people were murdered when Klansmen convened on the Arkansas town for a good old-fashioned killing spree. But it does include:

- **MARCH 18, 1919:** When the NAACP asked Florida governor Sidney J. Catts to prosecute the mob who lynched Bud Johnson, he replied, "This would be impossible to do as conditions are now in Florida, for when a Negro brute, or a white man, ravishes a white woman in the State of Florida, there is no use having the people who see that this man meets death brought to trial, even if you could find who they are: the citizenship will not stand for it."[14]
- **APRIL 4, 1919:** Residents of Blakely, Georgia, were so "unsettled" by the appearance of Private Wilbur Little's army uniform, they asked him to stop wearing it. Because he had no other clothes to wear, he ignored them. He was found beaten to death. His death was announced, in the *Chicago Defender*, on his twenty-second birthday. No one was ever arrested.[15]
- **APRIL 5, 1919:** Daniel Mack, a Black veteran, brushed up against a man on market day. They sentenced him to thirty days on a chain gang. A white mob broke into the jail and took him to the edge of town, beating him all the way there. Mack survived by playing dead. No one was ever arrested, and it never made the newspapers because—as it turns out—the people of Sylvester, Georgia, "rioted" all the time.[16]
- **JUNE 7, 1919:** In Macon, Mississippi, a white mob beat a principal, a businessman, and other prominent Black people because they heard that Black workers had asked

for better working conditions and brought up a crazy idea called a "minimum wage." They whipped all the Blacks and literally turned the town all-white.[17]

- **JULY 10, 1919:** After a Longview, Texas, lynch mob killed Lemuel Longview for making "indecent advances" toward a white woman, whites attacked a Black man whom they believed had reported the incident to the *Chicago Defender*. They then set the Black neighborhood on fire, and killed at least four men.[18] The governor eventually ended the "riot" by declaring martial law . . . and arresting twenty-one Black people.[19]

- **AUGUST 29, 1919:** In Caldwell, Georgia, whites burned three Black churches and a lodge, killing at least one person, because they heard a rumor that a Black leader would "rise up and wipe out the white people."[20]

And hate-filled events weren't just limited to the South. On July 14, 1919, an army of more than two hundred white boys attacked the Garfield Park neighborhood in Indianapolis because they assumed a few Black boys were following them.[21] There were two riots against Black people who tried to move into white neighborhoods in New York and at least five in Philadelphia. Out west, the Bisbee, Arizona, police department got into a shootout with Black veterans because the soldiers had the audacity to parade around town in their uniforms. To be fair, the famed "Buffalo Soldiers" were in town to march in an *actual Fourth of July parade.*

We can't cover every event because . . . well, *no one knows* how many lynchings took place in the "Red Summer" of 1919. During this period that white people refer to as "racial unrest," few mainstream newspapers covered these disparate incidents or couched them as part of a greater trend. Some Black newspapers, like the *Chicago Defender* and the *Richmond Times*, reported on the terrorism trend. But no one covered this phenomenon like Marcus Garvey's *Negro World.*

Born in 1887 in Jamaica, Marcus Mosiah Garvey Jr. became one of the most controversial figures of his time for his views on racial separatism. His Universal Negro Improvement Association's "Back to

Africa" movement was one of the most influential Black movements of its time. In 1919, the UNIA's *Negro World* weekly publication boasted more readers than the *Washington Post*, the *Boston Globe*, and many other "mainstream" papers. And the *Negro World* reported the events of 1919 as one unified singular event of racial terrorism.

Speed was taking notes.

As the Red Summer raged, Speed was still investigating "subversives." But with no foreign war to build a reputation on and no formal experience in policing or detective work, he had to find a new way to keep his status as a rising star in the Bureau of Investigation. And he soon did, by casting white terrorism as a response to Black "subversive" activity.

To convey his growing power, Speed decided to adopt a more dignified persona. He was now known as J. Edgar Hoover.

On August 15, 1919, Hoover instructed his officers in New York to compile their surveillance of Garvey and find "at the earliest moment, a case for deportation." A Senate report on communist activity in the United States quoted the *Negro World* more than any other source. Hoover's files repeatedly referred to a *Negro World* article insisting that "Black men all over the world should prepare to protect themselves. Negroes should match fire with hell fire . . . The Negro must now organize all over the world, 400,000,000 strong, to administer our oppressors' Waterloo."[22]* This sounded too much like Black power. You know what was about to happen.

In April 1921, twenty-six-year-old J. Edgar Hoover became deputy head of the Bureau of Investigation. The following year, Marcus Mosiah Garvey was charged with mail fraud.[23] Garvey was convicted for mailing a radical leaflet to a Hoover informant. However, no one ever presented this brochure in court, and the informant could never quite recall what was in the envelope obtained by prosecutors. Garvey was free on appeal until March 1925, nine months after Hoover was named director of the Federal Bureau of Investigation, when he was imprisoned in the Atlanta Federal Penitentiary. When he was released

---

* *Waterloo is what the English call toilets. I'm pretty sure that's right. It might be a yodeling technique.*

in 1927, he was deported to Jamaica, where he was elected to serve on Kingston's city council and established the country's first modern political party.

Marcus Garvey would not be the last Black revolutionary targeted by Hoover.

Rosa McCauley was six years old during the Red Summer. She recalled nights staying up late with her grandfather as he sat by the door with a shotgun, protecting the family during Klan raids in rural Alabama. But McCauley was not afraid. When asked by a biographer why she couldn't sleep, she said she was waiting for her grandfather, a devout member of the Universal Negro Improvement Association, to fulfill one of her childhood dreams.

"I wanted to see him kill a Ku-Kluxer," she explained. "He declared that the first to invade our home would surely die."[24]

The injustices suffered by Garvey would guide McCauley's life. As a young woman, she said she "talked and talked of everything I know about the white man's inhuman treatment of the negro."[25] Thirty-six years after the summer of evil, she would board a Montgomery bus and change the world. By then, that Garveyite was known by her married name: Rosa Parks.

Bus rides would become a recurring theme of the civil rights movement. Segregation on public transportation was outlawed by the Supreme Court cases *Morgan v. Virginia* and *Boynton v. Virginia*; however, states, cities, and the South in general refused to enforce the laws. Peaceful protests were organized by the Congress of Racial Equality and the Student Nonviolent Coordinating Committee to test these laws in 1961. It was a brilliant move, because the Freedom Riders were a strategically diverse coalition. On each bus were:

- One interracial couple sitting together.
- One Black person sitting up front in the "whites-only" section.
- One person sitting in the back abiding by the white supremacist segregation rules.
- Other activists scattered throughout the bus.

Every Freedom Rider had a specific task in the action. Police officers wouldn't necessarily arrest people for breaking segregation laws—not because it was too overtly racist,[*] but because segregation on interstate transportation had already been deemed unconstitutional—so Southern cops would arrest Black people who dared break the rules of Southern inhospitality for "disturbing the peace" and other made-up rules. However, they couldn't press charges if a Black and white couple were *willingly* sitting together. Plus, nothing makes a racist madder than seeing interracial unity.

The person stationed in the back abiding by the rules was tasked with calling the Congress of Racial Equality in case the shit hit the fan. And shit *always* hit the fan. (Back then, 86 percent of fans were involved in shit-hitting episodes.) For instance, when the first Freedom Ride bus arrived in Anniston, Alabama, in 1961, policemen organized a welcoming committee with the Ku Klux Klan. Before they attempted to murder people for the crime of bus-riding, many of the Klansmen had just come from church. This holy group attacked the Freedom Riders on Mother's Day.

These terrorists started by throwing a homemade firebomb on the bus. When the Freedom Riders ran out to escape, a mob of local white people was waiting to do *moblike activities.*[†] They attacked the Riders en masse, hospitalizing some. The mob waited outside the hospital, eager to further harass their victims, when out of nowhere came the Blackest, bravest hero of them all: Reverend Fred Shuttlesworth.

Reverend Fred Shuttlesworth is one of the greatest civil rights heroes you've never heard of. He spoke at the March on Washington and helped organize the Selma-to-Montgomery march that ended with an attack by Alabama state troopers. Klansmen beat him with bats and chains for trying to enroll his daughter in a white school. White supremacists bombed his house . . . *twice.* (In all fairness, Shuttlesworth was accustomed to being bombed. He lived in "Bombingham," a city that Klansmen bombed at least forty times during the civil rights era,

---

[*] *"Too overtly racist" has never been a thing in America.*

[†] *Aside from flash mobs and Martin Scorsese movies, mobs aren't generally known for their benign group activities. Unfortunately, there are very few mob choirs.*

including the notorious terrorist bombing at the 16th Street Baptist Church.)[26]

Shuttlesworth took no guff from anyone, including from fellow civil rights leaders. He knew Martin Luther King from back when they were cellmates—the very era when MLK wrote the famous "Letter from a Birmingham Jail." When MLK attempted to negotiate a truce with Birmingham's white segregationists in 1963, Shuttlesworth wrote King from his hospital bed, as he had been hit with the full force of a fire hose. "Go ahead and call it off," he told King. "When I see it on T.V., that you have called it off, I will get up out of this, my sickbed, with what little ounce of strength I have, and lead them back into the street. And your name'll be Mud."[27]

When Fred heard about the attack on the Freedom Riders, he pulled up. He left Birmingham and quite literally pulled up to the hospital with an armed convoy of what he called "foot soldiers." Shuttlesworth dared the white mob to do something—and you better believe those cowards fled.

Shuttlesworth's convoy protected the bus along the way to the next stop in Birmingham, where more cops and Klansmen were waiting with bats, axe handles, pipes, and bicycle chains. Meanwhile, Birmingham's commissioner of public safety, Bull Connor, offered his protection . . . to the KKK. By the time the bus reached Montgomery, the white mob had grown so large that state troopers couldn't stop them. More firebombs were thrown, and more beatings ensued. Shuttlesworth called Attorney General Robert Kennedy, who had to call in the National Guard to protect the riders. The original group ended the first round and, in May, another group left Nashville, headed for Jackson, Mississippi, where they were arrested and sent to the Mississippi State Penitentiary (also known as Parchman Prison and Parchman Farm) for—and I can't stress this enough—*riding a bus*. This time, however, the white mob didn't beat them because there was a powerful group protecting them that even the Klan didn't mess with: Black women.

Womanpower Unlimited, a group of mostly Black women, raised the money to bail out the protesters. When the Freedom Riders were released, the Black women provided them clothes, toiletries, places to bathe, and food. Do you know how good Mississippi macaroni must taste after you've been in the center of a Klan rally? JFK asked CORE to cool off for the rest of the summer because it was getting too dangerous, but CORE refused. But the two buses of Freedom Riders didn't immediately leave Mississippi because something crazy started happening: Freedom Rides started forming *everywhere*.

The racist opposition to the simple act of sitting down on a bus had become a national story. All across the country, people started forming their own version of Freedom Rides. They boarded buses, sat down in segregated restaurants, protested injustice, and developed a multiracial coalition.

Speed was watching.

On Wednesday, July 12, 1961, five defendants in a Little Rock, Arkansas, courtroom had a decision to make. Standing in front of municipal court judge Quinn Glover were twenty-seven-year-old minister John C. Raines, twenty-three-year-old teacher Bliss Anne Malone, twenty-three-year-old artist and housewife Janet Reinitz, eighteen-year-old student Annie Lumpkin, and thirty-year-old minister Benjamin Elton Cox. After lecturing the group for their "assault" on the city, Glover presented the five Freedom Riders with a proposition that seemed as if it was ripped from the pages of a dime-store novel: they could pay a fine of $500 and spend six months in jail, or the local police could escort them to the edge of town.

Raines and Reinitz were white, while Malone, Lumpkin, and Cox were Black. Each had been charged with breach of peace for participating in the Freedom Rides. Glover's offer seemed like a deal. The defendants had already been assaulted by a crowd of more than three hundred people and spent two nights in jail. The group discussed the offer, and Raines informed officials that he—along with the others—had made a decision.

They chose jail.

The fines and sentences were ultimately suspended after an apology to the city, but the experience left a bitter taste in Raines's mouth. Raines had joined the Freedom Rides after reading about how Klansmen attacked, beat, and firebombed Freedom Riders in Anniston and Birmingham, Alabama. He was told to expect resistance from

Klansmen, but couldn't help wondering how the white supremacists always seemed to pick the right bus. As one fellow Freedom Rider—a guy named John Lewis—asked, "How do they be knowing?" Two years later, on September 15, 1963, Raines lent his support again after Klansmen bombed Birmingham's 16th Street Baptist Church, killing fourteen-year-olds Addie Mae Collins, Cynthia Wesley, and Carole Robertson, along with eleven-year-old Carol Denise McNair. Raines and hundreds of civil rights activists converged on Oxford, Ohio, on June 13, 1964, to train for the Student Nonviolent Coordinating Committee's "Freedom Summer," an attempt to register voters in a state notorious for using terrorism to disenfranchise Black voters. Six civil rights activists would be murdered that summer, including James Chaney, Andrew Goodman, and Michael Schwerner. Thirty-five more would be shot, eighty would be beaten, and more than a thousand would be arrested. Almost 90 percent who showed up for the registration were white.

After Freedom Summer, Stokely Carmichael, one of the original Freedom Riders, moved to Mississippi to register voters there. The young activist then moved to Selma to participate in the Selma-to-Montgomery marches. Viola Liuzzo, a white woman who had seen the Freedom Rides, also traveled to Selma to help with the demonstration. She provided first aid, and after entertainers performed for the civil rights protesters, she volunteered to drive activists to the airport. That's when a group of Klansmen saw her with a nineteen-year-old Black man in the car and opened fire, killing her. White residents in the area, however, dismissed the outrage, because Liuzzo was rumored to have driven down to Selma because she had a penchant for Black men.

During Selma's march for voting rights, Carmichael grew disillusioned of watching peaceful protesters get brutalized and decided to replicate the success of the Mississippi Freedom Party in Alabama's "Bloody Lowndes" County, a county that was 80 percent Black. Because of white violence and a history of lynching, as well as apathy from local judges, less than 1 percent of the county's Black residents were registered to vote. While organizing the Lowndes County Freedom Party (LCFP), the young organizer noticed that Black people in the county all carried guns for self-defense, a move organizers saw as just common sense. Because of their grassroots organizing, door-to-door registration efforts, and biweekly political workshops, by the spring of 1966, Lowndes County's electorate was majority Black. With their help, the Black voters eventually elected the county's first Black sheriff, John Hulett, in 1970.[28] Hulett would later become Lowndes County's first Black probate judge.

By the time Carmichael left Alabama, people were using one of his morale-building phrases that he had been chanting since the Freedom Rides: "Black Power." The LCFP eventually merged with the Democratic Party, and the young organizer would be named chairman of the SNCC. Another group would later get permission to use the LCFP's mascot Carmichael created to counterbalance the Democratic Party's rooster logo—the Black Panther.

On March 8, 1964, Malcolm X announced that he was leaving the Nation of Islam to start his own Black nationalist movement. The decision was closely monitored by Speed and his crew: the Black Muslim leader had been surveilled by the FBI for at least a decade, with the Bureau putting him in their Communist Index in 1953, noting that members of the Muslim Cult of Islam referred to white men as "devils."[29] In April 1964, he completed his pilgrimage to Mecca, and on May 8 the *New York Times* published a letter explaining Malcolm's new position. "If white Americans would accept the religion of Islam, if they would accept the Oneness of God (Allah), then they could also sincerely accept the Oneness of Man, and they would cease to measure others always in terms of their 'differences in color,'" he wrote. "I do believe that whites of the younger generation, in the colleges and universities, through their own young, less hampered intellect, will see the 'handwriting on the wall' and turn for spiritual salvation to the religion of Islam and force the older generation of American whites to turn with them." Malcolm's goal was to unite American whites, Blacks, and people of color from all countries to fight oppression. The announcement stunned many people—Black and white. Here was the Black nationalist, "white man is the devil" guy calling for a multicultural coalition. It was a shock—and the feds took notice.

In April 1964, one month after Malcolm left the Nation of Islam, the NYPD's Bureau of Special Services and Investigations (BOSSI) hired a Black undercover agent, Ray Wood, to infiltrate Black organizations. Shortly thereafter, journalists across the country reported a story about "a small group of negro extremists" and their plan to blow up the Statue of Liberty and the Liberty Bell. *Time* reported the story this way:

> *According to charges brought by New York police last week, the mastermind—if that is the word—of the plot was one Robert Steele Collier, 28, a library clerk who visited Cuba early last summer and returned to organize the Black Liberation Front.* * *Also charged were Walter Augustus Bowe, 32, a onetime trumpet player who used to lead a combo called "The Angry Black Men," but more recently has worked as a $50-a-week New York settlement-house youth leader, and boyish-looking Khaleel Sul-tarn Sayyed, 22, son of an Arab-descended Negro who runs a Brooklyn delicatessen. And then there was husky (6 ft. 1 in., 201 lbs.) Raymond A. Wood, 31, a former Chester, S.C., high school football star.*
>
> *The plotters were seeking to create a spectacular sort of disturbance that would dramatize the troubles of U.S. Negroes. Bowe, Sayyed and Wood started scouting around last month, visiting the 300-ft.-high, 225-ton Statue of Liberty in New York harbor. Obviously, blowing up the Statue of Liberty would be as spectacular an event as anyone could wish for.[30]*

That June, FBI director J. Edgar Hoover sent a telegram to the New York FBI offices that simply said, "Do something about Malcolm X." He was no longer a marginal figure in an obscure religion. He was speaking at Oxford University, meeting with heads of state from around the world, and had been invited to serve in the governments of three African countries—Ghana, Algeria, and Egypt.

---

* *The Black Liberation Front was an underground arm of the Black Power revolution that proposed to take up arms in the struggle for liberation. For some reason, they thought that a well-regulated militia was necessary to the security of a free people. I have no idea where they got that from.*

On February 14, 1965, Malcolm X's house was firebombed while he and his children slept. By the time Malcolm's bodyguards arrived, the police were there. Malcolm suspected that the Nation of Islam was behind the bombing and wanted him dead because he was being openly critical of Elijah Muhammad. As Malcolm sat in a police car with his bodyguard, he repeatedly told the police that he ran to grab his firearm after a Molotov cocktail crashed through his window. He knew he was under surveillance by the FBI and the local police force. Yet he insisted on telling the police that he, a felon, was in possession of not one but two firearms. But, for some reason, they wouldn't take him into custody. It was almost as if they wanted him on the streets. A week later, on February 21, 1965, three men charged the Audubon Ballroom stage at a meeting for the new Black nationalist group the Organization of Afro-American Unity. The armed infiltrators stood up and released a barrage of bullets from two semiautomatic handguns and a sawed-off shotgun. Wood quickly left the scene, and the iconic leader El-Hajj Malik El-Shabazz (Malcolm X) was rushed to a nearby hospital. Malcolm X was dead.

Speed was still not satisfied.

Around the time of the Freedom Rides, a young student named Fred Hampton joined the NAACP, assuming a leadership role within his local chapter that led him to grow Chicago's West Suburban Branch's Youth Council to five hundred members. Hampton had long been involved in on-the-ground activism; he started his own free lunch program at ten years old, cooking meals for neighborhood children. When Black students were excluded from his high school's homecoming contest, Hampton organized a walkout. The attention from the protests forced his high school to hire more Black teachers and diversify the administration. But his opposition to the Vietnam War led him to look for something more powerful. That's when he found the Black Panther Party. Well, actually, the Black Panther Party found Hampton. And by the time Hampton attended his first Black Panther meeting in November 1968 as a founding member of the chapter, Hoover had already opened a file on him. Hampton's phone had been tapped for nine months, and he had been designated as a "key leader" in the FBI's "agitator index" for five months.[31]

Six months after joining Chicago's Black Panther chapter, Hampton brokered a nonaggression pact with every gang in Chicago, and started teaching them the intricacies of the law. The coalition of Black gangs would shut down construction sites and other white-owned businesses unless they hired Black workers. He also upset the city hospitals when he convinced doctors to volunteer and give free medical care. Bob Brown, one of the founders of the Illinois chapter, soon left the party to work with Stokely Carmichael, making Hampton the party's national deputy chairman. Speed was watching.

In 1968, Fred had a brilliant idea—one that would ultimately lead to even more surveillance from Speed and the government.

Hampton was a follower of Malcolm X and had been active in Black organizations his entire life. Fred knew that power came from unity, so he started a mission to unite all the gangs of Chicago through his powerful rhetoric. He convinced the gangs to pool their money and start supporting Black candidates for political office. The street gangs formed a truce and united to monitor the police in Black neighborhoods. In 1969, Hampton organized the United Front Against Fascism conference. Calling the conglomerate the "Rainbow Coalition," the group included Black gangs, Puerto Rican gangs, and others. The multiracial collective united under the principles of economic kinsmanship. From July 18 to 21, 1969,[32] more than five thousand organizers from across the United States attended the conference, including lawyers, politicians, and civil rights activists from all walks of life. The coalition was united under the idea that universal freedom couldn't be achieved until Black liberation became a reality, and that Black liberation could only be achieved through armed self-defense and community control of the police.

During this conference, the Puerto Rican Young Lords promised solidarity, as did the Red Guard, a Chinese American group. And here is why Fred was dangerous: of the five thousand who were in attendance, more than three thousand were white.[33] Think how charismatic Hampton must have been to convince white people to essentially agree that the lives of Black people actually mattered.[*]

---

[*] *Someone should do something with that phrase.*

Fred was creating a national coalition for armed resistance against racism. Even the Young Patriots adopted the Panthers' ten-point plan, which was astounding to many in attendance, because the Young Patriots was a group of white Southerners who were trying to reclaim the old Southern slur "redneck" and turn it into a badge of honor.

Fred was organizing the next phase in the civil rights movement, and of course, Speed was taking notes.

Knowing that the FBI was watching his every move, Hampton had a bodyguard. William O'Neal was the director of chapter security and wouldn't let Fred out of his sight, even renting an apartment for Hampton. Sometimes O'Neal was a little too dedicated to the movement, like the time he started a gunfight against the Blackstone Rangers, one of the deadliest gangs in Chicago. Hampton spent countless hours trying to mend those fences, but Jeff Fort, founder of the Rangers, never trusted Hampton again. To make matters worse, in November 1969, while Fred was meeting with the Black Panther Party's national spokesperson in California, O'Neal instigated a shootout with local police officers.

On the night of December 3, 1969, Hampton had just finished teaching a class on politics and law at a local church. After O'Neal fixed dinner, Fred lay down with his wife, who was nine months pregnant, and fell asleep midsentence. O'Neal left, and Mark Clark, another Panther, was guarding the door in his absence. Around 4 a.m., police officers burst in and opened fire on Fred and the Panthers. They said it was a "raid," but an investigation showed that the police fired between ninety and ninety-nine bullets, and the Panthers only fired one round. When officers checked Hampton's body, they discovered he was still alive. Then, according to his wife, who survived the incident, two more shots rang out, and another officer said, "He's good and dead now."[34]

Hampton was twenty-one years old.

On December 9, 1969—five days after Hampton's death—aided by a map drawn by government informant Melvin Cotton Smith, the Los Angeles Police Department's brand-new Special Weapons and Tactics (SWAT) team released a barrage of bullets at another bed.

Smith had informed officials that Geronimo Pratt, the Los Angeles Black Panther Party's deputy minister of defense, would be sleeping there. Pratt was instead asleep on the floor. After a furious gun battle, Pratt and other Panthers were arrested. Three years later, Pratt would be placed in prison for a murder conviction that would be eventually overturned twenty-seven years later.

It is possible that more Panthers would have been targeted if not for Alice Faye Williams, a section leader in the Panthers' Harlem chapter who successfully led a disinformation campaign to fool the FBI that the Panthers' influence was fading. Her close ties to Pratt eventually made her a target. On April 2, 1969, Williams, along with Richard Earl Moore, Lumumba Shakur, Ali Bey Hassan, Michael Tabor, Eddie Joseph, Abayama Katara, Baba Odinga, Joan Bird, Robert Collier, Sundiata Acoli, Lonnie Epps, Curtis Powell, Kuwasi Balagoon, Richard Harris, Lee Berry, Shaba Om, and Kwando Kinshasa, was indicted for a Panther terrorist plot to bomb two New York City police stations and a government building. Facing three hundred years in prison and nine months pregnant, Williams decided to represent herself. During the longest political trial in New York history, she eventually got Ralph White, an undercover police officer who had infiltrated the Panthers, to admit under cross-examination that law enforcement officials had created the entire plot after he misrepresented their activities to his police bosses. The influence of Speed was buckling.

Over time, it became clear that the government was trying to frame everyone in the Black Panthers' ranks. Panther cofounder Huey Newton faced four trials for two different murders. His 1968 conviction for killing a police officer would be overturned, and he would be acquitted of killing a white woman in 1974. Officials charged Panther cofounder Bobby Seale with murder because he happened to be in town for a few hours when the death took place. Seale would beat the case, but not before he faced conspiracy charges for organizing an anti-war protest in 1968. Seale was found not guilty, but served four years in prison for contempt of court. The conviction was later reversed. During his murder trial in 1969, Seale was bound and gagged. The offenses were so egregious that a young law student organized law school students to document violations of Seale's civil liberties. That student? None other than Hillary Clinton.

By 1971, the white Freedom Rider John C. Raines had settled down, married, had children, and was a minister and professor at Temple University. Raines rarely talked about his time in the civil rights movement, because he always ended up sounding like a conspiracy nut. He had come to believe the FBI and the CIA were using "dirty tricks" to derail the movement for equality, and were responsible for the deaths of its Black leaders.

By then, many had even declared the era of civil rights to be a thing of the past. But some people still remembered. One night that March, while the world was enraptured with the boxing match between Muhammad Ali and Joe Frazier, a group of anonymous activists broke into an FBI office in Media, Pennsylvania, and stole a treasure trove of documents.[35] As they left to look through the pile of papers, Raines stopped by a pay phone and delivered the following statement to a journalist at Reuters:

> *On the night of March 8, 1971, the Citizens' Commission to Investigate the FBI removed files from the Media, Pennsylvania, office of the FBI. These files will now be studied to determine: one, the nature and extent of surveillance and intimidation carried on by this office of the FBI, particularly against groups and individuals working for a more just, humane and peaceful society. Two, to determine how much of the FBI's efforts are spent on relatively minor crimes by the poor and the powerless against whom they can get a more glamorous conviction rate. Instead of investigating truly serious crimes by those with money and influence which cause great damage to the lives of many people—crimes such as war profiteering, monopolistic practices, institutional racism, organized crime, and the mass distribution of lethal drugs. Finally, three, the extent of illegal practices by the FBI, such as eavesdropping, entrapment, and the use of provocateurs and informers.*
>
> *As this study proceeds, the results obtained along with the FBI documents pertaining to them will be sent to people in public life who*

have demonstrated the integrity, courage and commitment to democratic values which are necessary to effectively challenge the repressive policies of the FBI.

As long as the United States government wages war against Indochina in defiance of the vast majority who want all troops and weapons withdrawn this year, and extends that war and suffering under the guise of reducing it, as long as great economic and political power remains concentrated in the hands of a small clique not subject to democratic scrutiny and control. Then repression, intimidation, and entrapment are to be expected. We do not believe that this destruction of democracy and democratic society results simply from the evilness, egoism or senility of some leaders. Rather, this destruction is the result of certain undemocratic social, economic, and political institutions.[36]

The documents would reveal that John Edgar Hoover had used his skills to create a fifty-year intelligence-gathering and surveillance project that evolved into COINTELPRO, the counterintelligence program that targeted every Black leader during the civil rights struggle. Its stated goal was to:

1. Prevent the COALITION of militant black nationalist groups . . .
2. Prevent the RISE OF A "MESSIAH" who could unify, and electrify, the militant black nationalist movement . . .
3. Prevent VIOLENCE on the part of black nationalist groups.
4. Prevent militant black nationalist groups and leaders from gaining RESPECTABILITY, by discrediting them to three separate segments of the community . . .
5. Prevent the long-range GROWTH of militant black organizations, especially among youth.[37]

This is how we know that William O'Neal, Hampton's body-guard, was an FBI informant.[38] This is how we know that the FBI believed Stokely Carmichael had "the necessary charisma to be a real threat in this way" because, during the Freedom Rides, he began using the phrase "Black Power."[39] This is how we know that the FBI sent a "suicide package" to Martin Luther King Jr. after Hoover heard the "I Have a Dream" speech and told agents, "We must mark him now if we have not done so before, as the most dangerous Negro of the future in this nation."[40]

And this is how we know about Gary Rowe.

In 1960, twenty-six-year-old Gary Rowe joined the Eastview Klavern of the Ku Klux Klan, the most violent chapter in Klan history.[41] In 1961, Rowe was on the scene with a bat when Birmingham police commissioner Bull Connor and Sergeant Tom Cook gave Klansmen fifteen minutes of uninterrupted violence with the Freedom Riders. When he put the attack together in Birmingham, he used an iron pipe. Two years later, Rowe helped plan the bombing of the 16th Street Baptist Church. He was in the car with the Klansmen who shot Viola Liuzzo in Selma and helped spread the rumor that she was involved with Black men. But back in April 1960, Rowe was just a regular citizen before Barrett G. Kemp offered him money if he would join the Ku Klux Klan.

Barrett Kemp was a special agent for the FBI.[42]

Not all of this information was in the files recovered by the Citizens' Commission, but it was later determined that in 1965, prosecutors knew the names of the men responsible for the 16th Street bombing, including Rowe's. At that point, Hoover *personally intervened* and blocked any arrests, detention, and prosecution of the suspects.[43] He kept all of these files sealed and refused to participate in any investigations with state and local agencies, except one.

In 1969, William O'Neal gave the FBI a detailed floor plan of the apartment he was renting for Fred Hampton. Hoover authorized his agents to share that floor plan with Illinois state attorney Ed Hanrahan, who organized the predawn raid on Hampton. While searching through the document in 1971, the Citizens' Commission found a copy of the floor plan and noticed that, like many of the painstakingly detailed papers, it contained the acronym COINTELPRO.

In the book *The Burglary: The Discovery of J. Edgar Hoover's Secret FBI*, Betty Medsger writes:

*More than anything, the Media files offered "the public and Congress
an unprecedented glimpse of how the U.S. government watches its
citizens—particularly black citizens," wrote* Washington Post
*journalist William Greider in an analysis of all the files the summer
after the burglary. Despite the fact that the files had been removed from
a very small bureau office in a predominantly white area, they revealed
details of the bureau's policies and actions that made it clear the FBI
conducted massive spying on African Americans, most of it unjustified.*

*The overall impression in the Media files of how the FBI regarded
black people was that they were dangerous and must be watched
continuously. To become targets of the FBI, it wasn't necessary for
African Americans to engage in violent behavior. It wasn't necessary for
them to be radical or subversive. Being black was enough.*[44]

Although there have been numerous congressional hearings and
historical exhumations of the FBI documents, for some, the word
COINTELPRO evokes an automatic eye roll. To be fair, the idea
that the FBI monitored and demonized every Black movement in the
history of this country sounds like a harebrained conspiracy theory
to me, too. It's almost too dark to believe. And of course, to insinuate
that it is happening now would sound outrageous. But to know history
is to know the present. This chapter is not even about J. Edgar Hoover.

This chapter is about America.

THREE LITTLE QUESTIONS

1. **Which of the following conspiracy theories is not true?**

   a. COINTELPRO.

   b. The Compromise of 1877.

   c. The Tuskegee Syphilis Study.

   d. Rakim wrote "Summertime."

2. **How many foreign communist agents did the FBI eventually discover in the civil rights movement?**

   a. Ummmm . . .

   b. Why does that matter?

   c. Including the ones they made up?

   d. Fewer than one.

3. **J. Edgar Hoover was:**

   a. Kinda racist.

   b. A corrupt police officer.

   c. Just doing his job.

   d. Actually committing un-American activities.

ACTIVITY

WHITEMARE

Write an essay describing the worst-case scenario that white people imagined civil rights activists were attempting to create.

13

THUG LIFE

THE OTHER CIVIL RIGHTS MOVEMENT

In the sweltering August heat of Ferguson, Missouri, less than a stone's throw from where Officer Darren Wilson had pumped six bullets into the body of Michael Brown Jr., I clenched the rock-tossing hand of a nineteen-year-old kid I had met a few hours earlier. A few feet away, a multifarious conglomerate of long-gun-wielding cops, Missouri state troopers, and actual soldiers stood ready to use any means necessary to suppress any unrest. Earlier that day, this same kid had described how Ferguson cops terrorized young Black men in the neighborhood where Mike Brown died. Now he was ready to set it off.

I reminded him how he complained about "the media" describing protesters as "thugs." I pointed to a woman in a wheelchair and said that he was putting everyone in danger, begging him not to toss the first stone. I explained how the authorities and the media would ascribe his actions to all the peaceful protesters. "Like that sh—t matters," he replied with eyes full of water and desperation. "Can't you see? They gon' kill us anyway."

We stood there for a second . . . or a minute . . . or forever, with my hand around his wrist, his frustration in his palm. A millisecond before I decided to let his arm go, a brick sailed over our head into the armed brigade. As they began marching toward us, we both bolted.

I paused to put on a gas mask and spotted him through the noxious fumes. Perhaps he was only checking his surroundings, but I could swear that he was staring directly at me.

As he disappeared into the smoke and chaos, I ran away knowing the world would ignore the hundreds of peaceful protesters and attribute this civil unrest to "thugs."

* * *

Nearly two years later, two Department of Justice civil rights investigations forced the Ferguson City Council to accept a consent decree implementing new use-of-force policies and deescalation training, along with restructuring the municipal court system. Darren Wilson was never brought to justice, but the peaceful protests had partially worked. It was evidence that reasonable people can collectively force change.

Or maybe it was the thugs that helped push it all forward.

If we believed the whitewashed, safe-for-work version of the civil rights struggle, we would believe that a lone white man killed Emmett Till, jolting Black people out of a dreamlike state to suddenly realize that we didn't have all the rights afforded to us by the U.S. Constitution. In response, Martin Luther King convinced everyone to hold hands and march peacefully until he could remember his dream. When he told the world about it at the March on Washington, America suddenly saw the error if its ways and handed Black people their humanity and everyone lived happily ever after.

That is the CliffsNotes version of the civil rights struggle that exists in our collective whitewashed memory and is sold in social studies classes across America. Through a complex combination of whitewashing, guilt, and an intentional recasting of history that absolves them of their hatred, our historical translators have painted a sanitized, impressionist portrait of a struggle for Black liberation that was eventually fulfilled by America's unwavering commitment to justice and equality. Out of whole cloth, they managed to fabricate a fantastic ahistorical myth that somehow became truth. They remember a socially conservative, respectable campaign of racial reconciliation, not a movement of anti-establishment revolutionaries. And for their sake, the doctrine of nonviolent resistance was eventually reduced to simple "nonviolence." They never speak of the "resisting."

As long as America has existed, Black men and women have been engaged in a fight for full equality and liberty. But unlike the fairy-tale version would have you believe, the struggle has never been passive, nor has Black resistance been nonviolent. In their quest to "get free," Black people have always availed themselves of the right to self-defense and armed resistance. Of course, this would lead to them being characterized as criminals or malcontents. There is a difference between how one chooses to defend oneself and how one chooses to address social, economic, and political inequality through protest. The former is a personal choice, while the latter is an organizing strategy. The truth is, peaceful protest was just *one tactic* used by a small arm of what we call the civil rights movement.

Essie Harris became a leader of Chatham County, North Carolina's Black community by shooting it out with the Klan. Although he was not interested in politics, Harris attended a few meetings of his local Loyal League—a Black political group that organized voters. When Klansmen attacked his home a few days after Christmas 1870 to take his gun and warn him about voting, Harris initially complied. But when they shot up his home, wounding him in the arm and riddling his house with bullets, Harris figured his wife and five children were dead. He grabbed an axe and chopped one of the Klansmen in the head, then picked up his gun to finish off the rest of the mob. "They always said in my country that a man could not kill a Ku Klux," Harris told an 1871 joint committee investigating the white supremacist insurrection in the South. "They said that they could not be hit; that if they were, the ball would bounce back and kill you. I thought though that I would try it and see if my gun would hit one."

Even though Harris had never loaded his shotgun with anything deadlier than squirrelshot, he blasted one of the Klansmen in the face.

It worked! The shots did not bounce back and kill him. When he realized that the KKK were not impervious to any kind of bullet, Harris wanted to try it again, telling legislators:

> They said they were going to set my house on fire; that they did not intend to leave there till they had done it. I thought they were going to do it. I was just as certain as they were as that I was in there. I had some shot. I have often heard people talk about a man being so scared that he could not shoot people; but they had been there so long my fear was over; I had no fear at all by that time—not a bit. I went to my little wallet where I kept my shot and powder. The men were standing behind the chimney waiting for them to carry off the shot one, I reckon . . . Some eight or ten of them staid [sic] after the rest had started, saying they were going to set my house on fire . . . I loaded my gun again; I put an uncommon load in it—a dangerous load . . . After I had got it almost loaded I said, "Give me hold of my five-shooter." They said: "Boys, the old man is calling for his five-shooter, and loading his gun; let us leave." Upon that, they went off.[1]

Essie Harris then walked fourteen miles to the next county with a bullet in his arm to file a warrant against the Klansmen. He went back home and waited for them to be arrested. "I was the last man who shot a gun at my house," he said.[2]

Using guns to face the ongoing terrorist threat posed by white supremacy wasn't limited to Klan violence; it also figured heavily in the ongoing struggle against police brutality. On Monday, July 23, 1900, Robert Charles was sitting on the porch of a New Orleans house with his roommate when three white police officers began investigating reports of "two suspicious-looking negroes" roaming around the predominantly white neighborhood.[3] When the officers asked them what they were doing there, Charles stood up, as any Southern gentleman would in the presence of their would-be brutalizers. One of the cops, August T. Mora, took it as a sign of aggression and grabbed Charles. But Charles was no punk, and he fought back. When Mora grabbed his sidearm, Charles grabbed his own. Or maybe Charles grabbed his gun first. Mora told conflicting stories.* Both fired, hitting each other in the leg. Charles ran and left a trail of blood. When two officers came to his home and attempted to arrest him, he shot and killed them both. The manhunt was on.

New Orleans's white-owned newspapers wrote stories blaming the officers' deaths on the criminal element in the city's Black community. And because Charles was a member of several Black organizations, including a society promoting a return to Africa, New Orleans's white community took up arms at the so-called conspiracy. On July 25, a white mob called for the lynching of Charles's roommate, who had committed the crime of being Black and present. When their calls went unanswered, they proceeded to go on a Black people hunt, shooting at streetcars and in Black-owned hair salons, killing at least six Black people and injuring dozens. For some reason, the white mobs didn't think Black people would retaliate, but many were injured during the melee. When the police discovered Charles's whereabouts that Friday, the fugitive killed two more police officers who tried to apprehend him. A white mob gathered outside, so Charles started shooting them too. The mayor summoned the state militia, but Charles didn't care. Anybody could get it. By the time a firefighter eventually snuck into the home where Charles was holed up and set a mattress on fire around 5 p.m., Charles had killed or fatally wounded five law enforcement officers and wounded another nineteen members of the white mob. As he tried to escape, a member of the militia shot and killed him. After he dropped his rifle, the brave policemen riddled his body with bullets as the mob was allowed to beat the corpse.

But the white people weren't done. They attempted to burn down every school in the city, successfully razing "the best negro schoolhouse in Louisiana."[4] Black students wouldn't have access to a school for seventeen years. After that feat, the white people were sure they had taught New Orleans's Black population a valuable lesson. They had not. Robert Charles became a hero to Black residents in the city.

"He would have died had not he raised his hand to resent unprovoked assault and unlawful arrest that fateful Monday night," wrote

---

* *You know how it is when white people "fear for their lives."*

Ida B. Wells in the definitive account, *Mob Rule in New Orleans: Robert Charles and His Fight to Death, the Story of His Life, Burning Human Beings Alive, Other Lynching Statistics.* "The white people of this country may charge that he was a desperado, but to the people of his own race Robert Charles will always be regarded as the 'Hero of New Orleans.'"[5]

As the most prominent anti-lynching crusader in America, Wells often advised every Black person in the South to arm themselves against the epidemic of lynching, as she did after the lynching of her friend Thomas Moss, because, as she said, "I felt that one had better die fighting against injustice than to die like a dog or rat in a trap." Similarly, in Richmond, Virginia, polymath John Mitchell Jr. made himself into a national figure by pushing for armed self-defense in his newspaper, the *Richmond Planet.*

Born as a slave in 1863 in Richmond, Mitchell soon proved himself to be a young man of many talents. During high school, he won a slew of oratory contests, graduated first in his class, and also demonstrated an uncanny ability to draw maps by hand, as he showed while applying for an apprenticeship at the Bureau of Engraving and Printing.* After he learned the printing game, he settled down in the Black area of town at age twenty-one, when he was named editor of the *Richmond Planet.* Mitchell's status as the "King of Jackson Ward" may have come from the fact that he founded the Mechanics Savings Bank in 1902 and served as its president for twenty years. Or maybe it was his work as a teacher that made him more popular. Perhaps he was so well known for another reason:

Johnny wanted *all the smoke.*

Mitchell made his newspaper one of the most respected in the country by traveling around Virginia reporting on lynchings. But he didn't just write about the incidents—he advocated for armed resistance and made sure he practiced what he preached. When a Black Jackson Ward resident died during an encounter with a Richmond police officer, Mitchell was indicted for slandering the officer by calling him a murderer. Undeterred, Mitchell went to court and accused

---

* *He did have some help, though: some dude named Frederick Douglass noticed his talent and wrote him a very nice letter of recommendation.*

the officer *again*, insisting that he had evidence that the victim had been beaten to death by the cop. The court refused to let him inspect the body, but Mitchell forced his way into the University of Virginia to see the body himself. The charges were dropped. And when he publicly condemned an 1886 lynching in Southside Virginia, racists sent a letter informing him that he would be hanged if he decided to "poke that infernal head of yours in this county long enough for us to do it."[6]

Believing in the old negro principle of "eff around and find out," Mitchell replied to the threat with a quote from Shakespeare: "There are no terrors, Cassius, in your threats, for I am so strong in honesty that they pass me by like the idle winds, which I respect not."[7] The brazen journalist grabbed his twin Smith & Wesson pistols, hopped on a train, walked five miles to the site of the lynching, and waited for the cowards to come for him. Of course, no one ever showed up.

And it didn't stop there. Mitchell wrote that "the best remedy for a lyncher or a cursed mid-night rider is a 16-shot Winchester rifle in the hands of a dead-shot Negro who has nerve enough to pull the trigger."[8] He was proud of his status as the "Fighting Negro Editor," explaining that it was his job to "howl, yes howl loudly, until the American people hear our cries." His popularity earned him the ear of the governor, admiration from his fellow citizens, and a dedicated readership. Mitchell died at his desk on December 3, 1929, and was buried under a tombstone that reads: EDITOR, BANKER, ALDERMAN AND PIONEER OF CIVIL RIGHTS / "A MAN WHO WOULD WALK INTO THE JAW OF DEATH TO SERVE HIS RACE."

Black leaders publicly advocating for armed resistance and self-defense was not rare. When he began his work in Montgomery as a pastor and advocate, Martin Luther King Jr. kept a firearm with him. Mitchell often referred to armed self-defense as "natural law." Medgar Evers, the Lowndes County Freedom Organization, W. E. B. Du Bois, and others were known to "keep that thang on them."

Although organized efforts for equal rights began even before slavery ended, perhaps the origin of the modern civil rights campaign started when Black veterans returned from World War I. Beginning in 1914, thirty-one-year-old Hubert Harrison, who is alternately called "Black Socrates," the "father of Harlem Radicalism," and the "foremost intellect of his time," left the mostly white socialist movement and founded the New Negro movement. Hubert's intellectual radicalism advocated for a race-conscious, international movement for Black political, economic, and social power and inspired the Black thinkers who would become the leaders during the civil rights era, including Marcus Garvey, A. Philip Randolph, Bayard Rustin, and Malcolm X. The New Negro movement preached armed self-defense and became contagious among the Black World War I veterans who had seen the world and now refused to subject themselves to the racial terrorism that plagued post–Civil War America.

This staunch refusal to bow to white supremacy was taken as an affront by white Southerners, prompting the mass racial violence known as the Red Summer of 1919. But while many of these "race riots" were one-sided attacks by white lynch mobs, Black people refused to lie down and die silently. In July 1919, a fourteen-year-old girl was allegedly attacked by a Black man in Coatesville, Pennsylvania, a town where several white men had been acquitted of lynching an African American steelworker in 1911. When a rumor surfaced that the police had arrested another Black man and were preparing to lynch him, members of the town's Black community grabbed their guns, bats, and sticks and went to the town jail. When the mayor and police chief assured them that they hadn't arrested anyone, they marched to the city hall and stormed the building just to make sure. Not only hasn't there been a lynching in the entire state of Pennsylvania since that day, but for some reason, after the "Coatesville Call to Arms," the city became majority Black. I wonder why.

A few days after the Coatesville Call to Arms, the white wife of a civilian naval employee was assaulted in Washington, D.C. The local newspapers jumped on it, having riled up local veterans with tales of a "negro fiend" who was attacking the wives of sailors. On July 19, 1919, a mob of white veterans tried to lynch the Black man accused of the crime, but the crazy white troublemakers took it a step further and tried to bumrush a Black neighborhood in D.C. armed with bats and sticks. They tried to do their lil' lynching thingamajig, but the Black neighbors actually had guns and the Caucasian criminals went back to regroup. They organized more mob violence for the second night but, once again, Terrorists' Night Out didn't go as planned. Black churches, civic organizations, and regular citizens somehow raised $14,000 in one day to purchase guns and ammunition, and stationed sharpshooters on roofs and strategic areas. The unmelanated mob suddenly lost interest when the entire city started shooting at *everybody white*. Seventeen-year-old Carrie Johnson was arrested and charged with shooting and killing a white police officer from her apartment window during the "riots." But when she went to trial, the judge actually believed that she was protecting herself and dropped all charges.

Robert F. Williams may have been the biggest badass of them all. Born in 1925, Williams served in the Marines before returning to his hometown in Monroe, North Carolina, in 1955 and joining the NAACP. The press estimates that more than half of Monroe's twelve thousand residents were members of the KKK. So Williams applied to the National Rifle Association to charter a chapter and formed the Black Guard. Made up of around sixty men who were mostly veterans, they charged themselves with protecting Monroe's Black neighborhoods from the white boys in the pointy hats. In 1957, the Klan tried to attack the home of local NAACP vice president Dr. Albert E. Perry, but the Black Guard had fortified the house with sandbags, and the two groups engaged in a Wild West–style shootout. The Klan never returned, and the city of Monroe banned Klan motorcades.

Williams's bold tactics were not just deployed by men in town, either. When Dr. Perry was arrested on charges of "criminal abortion on a white woman," Williams led a group of armed women to the police station as they "surged against the doors, fingering their guns and knives until Perry was produced."[9]

And his words were just as radical as his actions. In response to the acquittal of a white man charged with raping Mary Reed, a Black woman, Williams said:

> *We cannot rely on the law. We can get no justice under the present system. If we feel that injustice is done, we must right then and there on the spot be prepared to inflict punishment on these people . . . Since the federal government will not bring a halt to lynching in the South and since the so-called courts lynch our people legally, if it's necessary to stop*

lynching with lynching, then we must be willing to resort to that method.
We must meet violence with violence.[10]

The statement, made on the courthouse steps in Monroe, prompted the NAACP to suspend him from the organization. But Williams wasn't cast out; he essentially became the de facto security guard for some of the largest civil rights protests. During a 1961 protest for the Freedom Rides, a white mob held Monroe's Black community under siege. In the mayhem, a white couple made a wrong turn and wound up in Williams's neighborhood. Williams offered them a place to stay and warned them that he couldn't guarantee their safety if they tried to leave. After a few hours they left unharmed, but law enforcement agents convinced the couple to say that Williams had kidnapped them, forcing his family to flee the state. On August 28, 1961, the FBI issued a warrant for Williams, charging him with unlawful interstate flight to avoid prosecution, warning agencies that he "has advocated and threatened violence" and should be considered armed and dangerous.[11] Williams fled to Cuba, where he established a radio station urging Black soldiers to participate in an insurrection against the United States. He returned in 1969 and was extradited to North Carolina, and the state immediately dropped all charges.

Williams's legacy loomed large. He always noted that his proudest accomplishment was that during the entire existence of the armed guard, no Black person under their protection lost their life to racial violence. At his 1996 funeral, Rosa Parks said he "should go down in history and never be forgotten."[12]

Even religious leaders of the time advocated for armed resistance. When five churches, a Masonic hall, and a community center were torched in Jonesboro, Louisiana, two different groups united to form the Deacons for Defense and Justice. In 1965, when students picketed the local high school for integration, Klan-affiliated police officers ordered the fire department to turn their hoses on the students. But the firemen quickly changed their mind when four Deacons showed up with loaded shotguns. The Deacons were the reason why Louisiana governor John McKeithan became the first Southern governor to capitulate to a civil rights demand by a civil rights organization, facilitating integration in the town's city government. But the Deacons weren't just fighting the Klan, they also patrolled their own streets, keeping Jonesboro's Black neighborhoods safe. In 1965, when a terrorist cell from the Ku Klux Klan came to Jonesboro to retaliate against Black students who finally integrated the high school, the terrorists were turned around by a local chiropractor named James Malcolm Edwards, who just happened to be the Grand Dragon of the Louisiana Realm of the United Klans of America.[13] Edwards hadn't suddenly turned into an anti-racist; he just didn't want any smoke with the Deacons.

The Deacons helped African American communities form chapters around the country, which of course landed them a spot in the FBI's COINTELPRO program. According to one report in the FBI's six-hundred-page file, the Deacons were "inclined to use violence in dealing with any violent opposition encountered in civil rights matters."[14] Speed and his team were hyper-focused on any incidents of arms possession within the Black community. California's Mulford Act repealed the right to carry firearms in public after Huey Newton and members of the Black Panthers marched on the state capitol on May 2, 1967. The FBI claimed they were a threat to law enforcement officers, too.

In 2017, the FBI issued a similar warning about a new threat called "Black Identity Extremists." In its report, the agency concluded that it is "very likely Black Identity Extremists (BIE) perceptions of police brutality against African Americans spurred an increase in premeditated, retaliatory lethal violence against law enforcement and will very likely serve as justification for such violence."[15] More than five years later, the FBI still cannot list a single murder caused by a Black Identity Extremist. In fact, only one person remotely prosecuted was a man named Christopher Daniels (known as Rakem Balogun). According to a court transcript, in twenty-five months of FBI monitoring, Daniels had not engaged in a single act of violence against an officer or another human being. When the judge asked the FBI if Daniels had resisted arrest, the agent replied that he hadn't. The federal agent admitted to the judge that Daniels had never said he wanted to harm a police officer or stated that he planned on doing so. In fact, the only evidence that the FBI offered for Daniels being the subject of twenty-five months of federal surveillance was his anti-police rhetoric on social media and a few chants at rallies. But the FBI noted that they assessed Daniels as a threat because they had discovered three things when they searched his home:

1. He legally bought firearms.
2. He was a founding member of the Huey P. Newton Gun Club.
3. He owned a copy of *Negroes with Guns*—the book that is called the "single most important intellectual influence" on Black Panthers founder Huey P. Newton. It was written by Robert F. Williams.

It is possible that Daniels just likes Black history. Or maybe he's afraid of losing his civil rights.

Oh, wait . . .

THREE LITTLE QUESTIONS

1. **Armed self-defense is:**
   a. Not incompatible with nonviolent resistance.
   b. Literally in the Constitution.
   c. Scary when Black people do it.
   d. A fancy way of saying "eff around and find out."

2. **Black Americans who died practicing self-defense were usually armed with:**
   a. Their Second Amendment rights.
   b. Reverse racism.
   c. The desire to be free.
   d. Black skin.

3. **_____ is an example of a nonviolent white national movement:**
   a. The American independence movement.
   b. The slaveowners' rights movement.
   c. The pro-lynching movement.
   d. The anti-integration movement.

ACTIVITY

SOME OF THE GOOD ONES

List ten protest methods, tactics, or efforts for liberty and equality that were embraced by a majority of white Americans in real time.

Okay, maybe five?

One?

ALL-THE-WAY FREE

Dear Tyran,

I know you rarely get letters when you're locked up, so I thought I'd write you this one and fill it with some good memories. The last time we saw each other, you were just finished with a bid, and I assumed I'd get to see my closest cousin all the time. I remember how shocked I was when we were sitting in a hotel room and you told me that you had spent over half your life in state prisons. I guess I hadn't calculated the years. Or maybe I just think of you the same way I did when we were younger—as the talented cousin who could cook, sing, draw, paint, and play music. That's probably it. I think of you as free.

When I think of being free, I think of those few hours we spent on the run in New Jersey. I remember I was about ten, which means you were about nine. You, Geet, Eric, and I spent the summer at Jannie's huge three-story house in New Jersey. Remember how—even though we were all cousins—we told everyone we met that we were brothers because, honestly, we really weren't pretending? I *know* you remember that we each had our own bedroom but we would sleep in the mother-in-law suite on the third floor every night. Man, we even had our own kitchen, which was *great*, because you had just learned how to make French toast. Bruh, I guarantee we went through a loaf of bread and a dozen eggs a day, every day, for an entire summer. We were on a strict French toast diet. Plus, Aunt Jannie had cable *with HBO*! And she bought us an Atari. And since I am the ONLY one of the male cousins who can't play the drums, of course, we had a drum set. And then Uncle Robert Harriot gave us four sets of boxing gloves. No boxing lessons, no training. Just boxing gloves for us to beat the hell out of each other. And Geet and Rob had hands like bricks but, since they were the oldest, they beat us up every day. Man, that was the best summer!

I loved when we'd go to the garment district in New York and Jannie would drag us around to the most uninteresting part of New York while she shopped for purses and luggage to sell at Black conferences around the country. Oh, do you remember the matches? During Aunt Jannie's travels, she collected matchbooks from hotels, restaurants, bars, etc. and filled a fishbowl with them—until we found them. And when she went to work her regular job at Essex Community College, she'd make us go to the library and you said it was like the Library at Alexandria.

That was also the summer I discovered one of the most glorious things that ever existed—walking around with your shirt off! Jannie was like: "Why would you put a shirt on if you ain't going nowhere? That's just unnecessary." How come no one ever told us we could just walk around scrawny and barechested all day? He-Man was the only person we'd ever seen do this but, still, Castle Greyskull was in a very secluded area and we were in downtown East Orange, NJ, balling with our shirt off running up and down three flights of stairs while dribbling a basketball *while wearing boxing gloves*! It was the greatest summer ever!

The only thing we couldn't do was go outside. Aunt Jannie barely let us sit on the porch. She even bought us a basketball hoop and put it in the house. We had no idea that crack was just coming out and she was just trying to keep us safe, but we moaned and groaned about it all summer. I don't know how Aunt Jannie survived. Can you imagine dealing with four preteen boys with no bedtimes, hopped up on syrupbread, running around unrestrained, fighting, dribbling a basketball, sweating, arguing, banging drums, watching R-rated movies into the wee hours of the morning while literally playing with fire all day and night?

We used to laugh at how Aunt Jannie wasn't born with the ability to modulate the volume of her voice, so she literally screams at *everything*. The third floor probably smelled like teenage armpits and cinnamon, but we would never clean up because Jannie was gonna yell anyway! Like you said, God gave her two outside voices and no inside voice, so when she'd tell us to clean up, we'd never do it. Remember that time she came up to vacuum the shag carpeting and got a puzzled look on her face, like: "Why is the vacuum picking up all these matches? What is going on?"

Man, she hit notes I've only heard high-level sopranos hit. She chased us around that house, but she had no realistic shot of catching us. She put us on punishment, which is to say we had to stay in the house and play video games and eat more French toast and play more basketball and fight more and bang on more drums. Basically, the only thing that changed was we couldn't get our popsicles. She also took the cable box, which meant we couldn't watch the original *Clash of the Titans*, which was debuting on HBO. And we were *outraged*! How were we supposed to survive with no HBO and no popsicles? This was America! We had rights! We thought about calling protective services, but do you remember what we did instead?

We ran away!

From the French toast house! From the shirts-optional house! From free trips to the Big Apple and unlimited books! From a castle with basketball and video games and late-night breasts and all the syrup we could eat!

I remember how we stopped at a bodega in a sketchy-looking neighborhood and put our money together to buy a bunch of popsicles in those clear plastic sleeves. Geet had on flip-flops and he said his toemeat was burning, which made me laugh uncontrollably. So we sat on the curb, sucking on popsicles, watching a rap battle between a bunch of dudes who said "fresh" a lot. All summer, Geet would force me to write raps for him, so he convinced me to battle that one dude, and I won! Then, all those street dudes from "up north" gathered around us and started asking us what South Carolina was like and if we rode horses or owned pigs. And then, with no map, a bagful of melting popsicles, and a rapidly deteriorating flip-flop toe injury, we continued our journey.

We were free.

I don't know how we made it to Uncle Rob's house, which was in the next town over, in Newark. We had barely made it into his apartment when Jannie burst through the door screaming (which was to say she was using her normal voice) about how her nephews had been kidnapped. But when she saw us, she broke down crying. Oh, she said she was gonna whip our asses, but she was crying, too! Aside from when she caught the Holy Ghost at church, I had never seen her cry. I will never forget that. On the ride back, she railed about how she had given us everything we could want while we sat there silently. She went on and on about how we were ungrateful and no one else would run away from such a luxurious life. When she asked us how we ran away from so much freedom, no one had an answer, until you pierced that silence and said:

"Cuz we ain't *all-the-way* free."

I think about that a lot.

I wonder what *all-the-way free* means, and if there is such a thing as *kinda free.*

I'm sure White America considered the formerly enslaved as all-the-way free when they abolished slavery, while creating a loophole that just allowed them to enslave non-whites without calling it slavery. You can read it for yourself. It's written in this little-known document called the Constitution of the United States of America, whose Thirteenth Amendment says, "Neither slavery nor involuntary servitude, except as a punishment for crime whereof the party shall have been duly convicted, shall exist within the United States, or any place subject to their jurisdiction."

Except as a punishment for a crime.

Now, instead of calling it slavery or involuntary servitude, they could call it "mass incarceration." Instead of private individuals forcing people of color to work for profit, they could force Black people to work for the profit of private individuals. To understand how this works, you gotta go back to a period that the great historian Richard Martin Lloyd Walters calls "Once upon a time, not long ago; when people wore pajamas and lived life slow."

In colonial America, if you were convicted of a crime, you were fined, whipped, banished from the community, or—in the worst-case scenario—you were sent to the gallows for capital punishment. You know what a gallows is, right? I don't know how much news you get in there, but a few historical reenactors recently built one in front of the U.S. Capitol building just before they stormed in. The good people in Charleston, South Carolina, came up with a better solution. They monetized slave-whipping. The city offered a menu and a price list to send belligerent or misbehaving Africans to the "sugar house"—a municipal building staffed with people who were authorized to inflict violence on enslaved Black people for a small fee. But trust me, cuzzo, these professional torturers didn't use boxing gloves.[1] When Southern cities like Savannah adopted this profitable system, they came up with an official-sounding name: the Department of Corrections.

In 1787, the Philadelphia Society for Alleviating the Miseries of Public Prisons met in Benjamin Franklin's home and came up with the plan for the first modern prison system. Instead of punishing criminals, they encouraged the prisoners to ask for forgiveness or "penitence," so they called it a *penitentiary*. The prisoners were kept in solitary confinement, and when they weren't subject to this inhumane treatment, they worked, prayed, and reflected on their behavior without contact or communication with other prisoners. Even when they were together, they were forced to wear masks so they couldn't see each other. The prison system that was built in Auburn, New York, on the other hand, used corporal punishment, hard work, and silence to rehabilitate prisoners. Inmates were allowed to congregate, but they weren't allowed to talk.

By the 1840s every prison system in America used either the Pennsylvania system or the Auburn system, but regardless of what method they chose to deploy, they all had one thing in common: free labor. Curiously, most of those prisoners were poor white men and white immigrants. In the days before the Civil War, foreign-born immigrants made up 3 percent of the South's population but up to one-third of the prison system in Southern states.*[2] Luckily, the Thirteenth Amendment solved this rampant white-on-white crime committed by "urban youth" by creating a new loophole. They called them "Black Codes."

After slaves were freed, every Southern state passed "vagrancy" laws that made it a crime to be unemployed. States like Georgia, Alabama, and Mississippi also made it illegal to learn a skill or trade without the permission of a white man. Louisiana's Black Code of 1865 required every Black person "to be in the regular service of some white person, or former owner, who shall be held responsible for the conduct of said negro."[3] Texas declared, "It shall be the duty of all Sheriffs, Justices of the Peace, and other civil officers of the several counties of the State, to report to the Judge of the County Court of their respective counties, at any time, all indigent or vagrant minors, within their respective counties or precincts, and, also, all minors whose parent or parents have not the means, or who refuse to support said minor."[4] When Black citizens inevitably broke these laws, they were sold to plantations and factory owners to work for free. Remember, slavery was abolished "except as a punishment for a crime," so, technically, this "convict lease system" didn't violate the Thirteenth Amendment.

Cuzzo, this bootleg form of slavery soon became the most profitable industry in America. We were only "kinda free."

The Tennessee Coal, Iron and Railroad Company (TCI) became one of the original twelve companies listed in the Dow Jones Industrial Average by using a workforce composed mostly of Black prison laborers convicted of petty crimes. When TCI was bought by United States Steel, the largest corporation on the planet, in 1907, the company went all in on penal labor.[5] Nationally, convict leasing averaged profits of 267 percent and was used to mitigate the growing demands of an increasingly unionized workforce in the early 1900s.[6] And the profit wasn't restricted to private entities. In 1898, 73 percent of Alabama's entire state budget came from convict leasing.[7] Following that example, in 1934, the U.S. government created a wholly owned government corporation called Federal Prison Industries to profit

---

* *Italians, Jews, and Eastern Europeans had not yet become white.*

from prison labor. Because these corporations were not required to offer a minimum standard of human rights to their enslaved souls, torture, abuse, and sexual assault were rampant. Malaria, pneumonia, and tuberculosis ravaged the prison population. Forty-one percent of Alabama's convict lessees died during their terms of incarceration in 1870, and Mississippi's prison death rate in the 1880s was nine times the rate of prisons in the North.[8] Still, the death rate would have been higher if states didn't have a policy of releasing terminally ill inmates so the prison system wouldn't have to bear the burden of burying its enslaved profit-makers. When states began outlawing convict leasing between 1925 and 1930, guess what happened, Tye? The Black incarceration rate plummeted to the lowest rate since slavery ended. But we were only a *little bit* free.

You know they had something up their sleeves, and it wasn't no popsicle! In 1971, President Nixon fixed the profit problem by declaring a "war on drugs." In 1970, almost 200,000 Americans were in prison. By 1985, there were almost 482,000.[9] By the end of 2019, there were 1.4 million people locked up in U.S. prisons, and Black Americans were incarcerated at nearly five times the rate of whites. Private prisons aren't the only ones profiting from this stolen labor. It's the $1.3 billion earned by telecom companies that have exclusive contracts with prison systems. It's the food companies that make $1.6 billion from prison commissaries. It's the insurance industry that makes $1.4 billion in bail fees. And it's not just the federal government. California uses prison labor to fight wildfires. Your favorite fast-food restaurant uses prison labor to process meat. Your furniture, license plate, and many of your clothes are made by prison labor.

I know I don't have to tell you this. You're in South Carolina, where Black people make up around 28 percent of the population and 58 percent of the state's incarcerated people.[10] I remember you told me that you work in the kitchen, so you probably aren't one of the people who make between 35 cents and $2 per hour making mattresses, golf carts, and office furniture for the state. I wonder what would happen if the state of South Carolina put the $59.61 it spends per prisoner every day toward drug treatment, education, and criminal justice reform?[11]

Trust me, cuz, I'm not saying people shouldn't be held responsible for committing crimes. But I can't help but wonder how Black people are incarcerated for drugs at three times the rate of whites when white people use more drugs. According to the Substance Abuse and Mental Health Services Administration's 2020 National Survey on Drug Use and Health, 48.7 percent of Black adults had used illegal drugs in their lifetime, compared to 58.9 percent of non-Hispanic whites.[12] How is it that Black people are arrested for 26 percent of the crimes but are incarcerated in state prisons at five times the rate of whites?[13] I know you don't have the answers. I'm just asking why we are always *kinda free*.

I know it's not fair because I can remember when I almost went to jail for you. Don't act like you don't remember when the police beat me up for the Kwanzaa cup. All I was trying to do was see you sing with your boy band, Mass Appeal, which I'm sure you can admit now was basically a knockoff of New Edition without the Jheri curls or the hit songs. It was the night before Christmas, and Mass Appeal was set to battle the notorious rap group Posse in the huge Christmas Eve talent show. The talent show was an EVENT: high-schoolers from near and far (mostly near) went to witness the year's hottest entertainment event. (I still remember you saying it wasn't "*the Posse*," stupid. Just "*Posse*.")

Basically, bruh, it was the first Verzuz battle. The Christmas talent show was the most anticipated show of the year and I *had* to be there to support you. I promise, it was *not* about the high school girls who were going to be there, that I would get to be the "cousin from out of town," or the fact that there was going to be a high school afterparty where students could grind their pelvic bones into dust slow-dancing to Guy featuring Teddy Riley. This was all about supporting *you*. There was only one problem: I was broke and I didn't have a ride. Luckily, I had a solution for this.

You know our family celebrates Kwanzaa as if it's negro Christmas. Well, I still had to get my Kwanzaa presents. My plan was to take the money my mom gave me for Kwanzaa shopping, buy some cheap BS, and use the rest to ball out at your talent show. Luckily, I found a ride with my classmate Lydell Hawkins. You remember Lydell: big dude, football player. He drove that 1977 Plymouth Volare with a burgundy top. Every drug dealer in town offered him money for that car because it was clean and in vintage shape. Because his name also began with an

H, Lydell and I had been friends for years because we had homeroom together every year since seventh grade. So on Kwanzaa Eve *eve*, we went to the Magnolia Mall, which was crazy crowded, and I found the perfect gift—a Kwanzaa cup! It was basically a coffee mug where the Kwanzaa principles would appear when the cup had hot liquid in it. Having secured the Kwanzaa bag, we headed to the show. There were a million acts that night, but only two mattered: Posse and Mass Appeal. Everyone knew what Posse was going to do. First of all, Posse had more members than a Baptist church choir and their members changed *all the time*. Their entire schtick was that each member would rap about anything they wanted, but the chorus was always the same:

> Heeeey We want some Poss-sayyyy
> Whatchu want, girl?
> Heeeey We want some Poss-sayyyy
> What you need, girl?
> Heeeey We want some Poss-sayyyy

Posse wouldn't sing the chorus. They would select the finest tenth- and eleventh-grade girls to chant the chorus and dance as "Posse Girls." Yes, Posse had its own cheerleading team as backup dancers. Didn't you used to go with a Posse Girl at one time? Man, dating a Posse Girl was like dating one of Destiny's children back then. They were basically the Victoria's Secret models of our youth. Anyway, Posse killed it. You know I love you, bruh, but I gotta be honest. Posse was dope that night. I felt sorry for y'all. Ain't no way Mass Appeal was gonna outdo the Wu-Tang Clan. But when it was time for Mass Appeal, y'all did an entire medley of hit R&B songs beginning with Bell Biv DeVoe's warning to never trust a big butt and a smile and ending with Hi-Five's "I Like the Way (The Kissing Game)," all while wearing the BBD airbrushed overall shorts and the Malcolm X hats. (Look, it was the '90s!) In case you didn't know, the only thing women like more than clever puns (women like puns, right?) is dudes who can sing falsetto. And I won't lie, y'all *sang*. If I wasn't trying to be cool and pull a stray Posse Girl, I definitely would have cheered for Mass Appeal. But y'all won anyway!

Even Lydell got some action. (And by "getting some action," I mean walking a girl outside and getting her phone number, because that meant you were *really* doing it in the eleventh grade!) Basking in all that high school glory, I totally forgot my curfew and I knew I was going to be in trouble. There was the small possibility that I could sneak into my room, which had its own door that led to the outside, without Mama hearing me, so I instructed Lydell to let me out on the corner and I would walk home, eliminating the chance that his loud-ass old-school car would stir my mom out of her Kwanzaa Eve slumber. Lydell didn't even make it a block before he noticed that I'd left the Kwanzaa cup in his car. He swooped around, pulled up next to me, handed my Kwanzaa gift through the car window, and drove away, while I started my walk back home.

Back then, our childhood home was one block away from the street that was basically a Walmart for crack. Eighth Street had every variety of crack: The crack rocks. The crack cookies. The crack that was whack. The crack that killed Applejack. *All the cracks.* So, at 1 a.m. on Kwanzaa Eve, what looked like a strange dope boy's car pulled up next to me, handed me something through the window, and disappeared into the night. Now that I think about it, I can see how that looked suspicious.

To be fair, when the cops jumped out of nowhere, I probably looked like I was a little high off cocaine. My clothes were askew. I was tired. I was coming from Eighth Street and was yelling some nonsense about being careful with my "package." As they searched for the crack I had *obviously thrown away*, with one officer keeping his knee on my back, I didn't even try to argue. All I could do was try to save my own life. I begged and I pleaded with everything I had. Oh, I didn't care if they shot me in the head or anything, I just didn't want them to break my mama's Kwanzaa cup. When they smashed my Kwanzaa cup to bits and let me go, I was devastated. I swear to you, of all the things I have ever seen police do—and I have seen police *kill people*—the saddest, most pitiful I have ever felt is walking that two hundred yards or so after the cops stomped on my mother's six-dollar Kwanzaa cup.

When I got home, my mom was waiting and I didn't even try to defend myself. I just listened to my mother yell at me. She yelled at me for being late. Then she yelled at me for being selfish and spending money on a talent show. My mother can lay a guilt trip with the best of them, and it was worse than having a knee at my neck. Even worse, everything she said was right. All she ever tried to do was to make us happy. She never cared about a Kwanzaa gift, but I'm sure she was upset that her only son would rather slow-dance with second-string Posse Girls than get her a damn Kwanzaa gift. I had *one job*. When my sisters gave my mom her Kwanzaa gifts that year, I felt so bad because the Kwanzaa gift for Mom was not only an in-house competition; it was a tradition. I know my mom was hurt because I could see it in her eyes.

A few days later, or maybe even the next day, a neighbor who saw the entire incident with the cops told my mom that the police had beat me up. She tried to file a complaint, but nothing ever came of it. When she calmed down, she let loose another rant about hanging out in the streets late at night. And halfway through her lecture, she started crying. I tried to tell her that I had just gone to see you in the talent show, but she didn't stop her Jannie-level soprano rant.

That's when I realized that my mom wasn't worried about the dope boys. She knew those dudes on the corner of Eighth Street wouldn't bother me. If anything, they'd protect me. She wasn't lecturing me about the danger of drugs. She knew I wasn't using "the cracks," as she called it. She wasn't even going off about missing my curfew. She was concerned about what *the cops* could have done to me.

"What if they had taken you to jail?" she asked. "Do you want to throw your life away? Being innocent doesn't mean anything to the police. You think they care? To them, you're just another Black boy in America!"

I think about that a lot.

I think about *you* a lot. You are the closest thing I will ever have to a brother. Now that I can see the different trajectories our lives have taken, I understand the privilege of contemplating absolute freedom. You are in a state-sanctioned loophole that legalized enslavement, and I am just a Black man in America.

And neither one of us is *all-the-way* free.

I love you, cuz.

Mikey

THREE LITTLE QUESTIONS

1. **Why did the mass incarceration system accelerate after slavery was outlawed?**
   a. To continue profiting from free labor.
   b. Because states created laws targeting Black people.
   c. It's probably a coincidence.
   d. Wait . . . When was slavery outlawed?

2. **The United States has the highest incarceration rate in the world. Why doesn't it have the lowest crime rate?**
   a. Because incarceration doesn't stop crime.
   b. Crime is caused by poverty, not lack of cages.
   c. It's probably a coincidence.
   d. Seriously, was slavery outlawed?

3. **Who profits from mass incarceration?**
   a. Corporate-run private prisons that receive state and federal funding.
   b. The people who get free labor.
   c. No one.
   d. Seriously, you mentioned earlier that slavery was outlawed. Did that seriously happen?

ACTIVITY

ONE GOOD REASON

Aside from America's racial history, give a logical, evidence-based reason why Black Americans are incarcerated at higher rates than any other group in America.

14

THE GREAT WHITE HEIST

Hello again, Racist Baby! What are you doing here?

Well, now that Jesus is about to come to get all the Black people, I just wanted to tell you I appreciate all the time you took to explain racism to me.

Wait . . . Who told you Jesus is coming back? And why would he only come back for Black people?

Well, I've heard my dad talking, and he was pretty upset. He said Democrats are talking about Black Revelations. We discussed that book of the Bible in racist Sunday school, but I didn't know there was a separate Bible for Black people.

No, Racist Baby. Those people aren't talking about *Revelation*, the last book of the New Testament, they're talking about *Black reparations*.

What's reparations?

Reparations is "the making of amends for a wrong one has done, by paying money to or otherwise helping those who have been wronged."

In this case, we are talking about reparations for slavery, Jim Crow, and the cumulative aftereffects.

My father told me that he's tired of hearing about slavery because it happened a long time ago and he had nothing to do with it. Plus, it was legal. How can you ask for redecoration for something that wasn't a crime?

It's *reparations*, RB. And your father is right. But just because enslaving and stealing labor from Black people was perfectly legal prior to 1868, America should not get to ignore the calls for issuing dividends to the descendants of the people who supplied this nation with 246 years of unpaid labor. However, there is a more compelling argument that may be more irrefutable. Namely, that slavery was just one small part of a loan that Black people invested into America for which we never reaped the dividends or the principal. At the center of this argument is how this country became and remained an economic superpower due in large part to the contributions of Black America's sweat equity and actual funds.

But a lot of white people didn't own slaves! So how is this their fault?

Again, that's true. Seventy-five percent of white families didn't own slaves and 1 percent owned forty or more.[1] But all those people still participated in the institution of slavery and benefited from the theft of labor, from the shipbuilders to the textile industry, the international traders to the national defense. This free labor propped up the entire national economy. But that was only a drop in the bucket when it comes to estimating what America owes Black people in reparations. If the Fourteenth Amendment was meant to function as a reset button to offer the American dream to the millions of Black hostages whose involuntary sweat equity built this country into a superpower, then the time since July 9, 1868, can only be described as a period of illegal theft.

According to the Brookings Institution, in 2016, the typical white family's net wealth was $171,000, while the net wealth of a typical Black family was $17,150.[2] The reason for this staggering wealth disparity is not just due to slavery, Jim Crow, or even America's unique form of racism. Since the moment the Fourteenth Amendment was ratified, America has been engaged in a Robin

Hood–like heist. But instead of taking from the rich and giving to the poor, the United States has circumvented the Fourteenth Amendment by stealing Black America's wealth and giving it to white people. Every white person in America—rich or poor, liberal or conservative, Democrat or Republican—has benefited from stolen goods that were hijacked from Black America.

Wait, are you saying all the white people back then were thieves? My mom would never steal!

Yes, all white people. To illustrate what I'm saying, let me tell you a story about where I'm from.

In 1948, when only sixteen states in America had outlawed segregated public schools, Black students in the tiny hamlet of Summerton, South Carolina, where three out of every four residents were Black, finally got tired of being robbed by white people.[3]

Every day, these young Summertonians maneuvered through one obstacle course after another, only to be rewarded with an inferior education. If the children were lucky, they walked as far as nine miles to attend one of the segregated schools in Clarendon County's District 22. On other days, rain would force students as young as six years old to wade across a stream to attend school. Often, when the water was particularly high, someone would provide a raft to row their way across the Lake Marion reservoir. When they arrived at school, they would have to collect wood for their unheated classrooms . . . if they arrived. Sometimes a student would just drown on the way.

This may sound like a rough life for impoverished rural students, but Summerton was not a poor town. The vast majority of Summerton's Black citizens were employed. Many owned businesses or worked at well-paying jobs in local factories. Their employers withheld federal, state, and local taxes from their paychecks just like their white counterparts. Summerton's Black residents were not exempt from paying property taxes, sales taxes, or any other assessment their government deemed necessary. Naturally, Black parents were outraged when they discovered the white children didn't have to make the same daily trek as their children because the district had purchased thirty buses to chauffeur them to school. Incensed, a group of parents begged school board chairman Roderick W. Elliott for just one bus, to serve the county's Black students.

He said no.

So, Harry and Eliza Briggs, along with nineteen other Black families, contacted the NAACP and eventually filed *Briggs v. Elliott*, the first of five cases that would later be combined and become known as *Brown v. Board of Education of Topeka*. But even before their case dismantled the Supreme Court's "separate but equal" precedent, the parents of District 22 fully understood why their children lived this precariously treacherous existence: white people in the district were stealing their money.

The white Summertonians who rode on school buses bought, in part, with the taxes paid by Black residents whose children crossed a river of racism are a perfect example of this theft. Those white children arrived at school well rested and ready to learn, while their Black counterparts endured inequities laid out in the initial *Briggs v. Elliott* complaint, including unhealthy and inadequate facilities, an insufficient number of teachers and classroom space, and inadequate resources.

The Black parents were disproportionately paying for white students' beautiful new schools and the comfort in which they engaged in learning. And this phenomenon wasn't unique to Summerton. Even though South Carolina was 40 percent Black in 1948, statewide, Black schools were valued at $12.9 million while white schools were worth $68.4 million.[4] If those white students succeeded in their resource-filled schools, they could go on to one of more than a dozen public institutions of higher learning in South Carolina.

However, if the Black graduates wanted to attend a state college, because of state segregation laws there was only one choice—South Carolina State College, the only four-year public Black college in the state. This detail wouldn't matter as much except for three important facts about the taxpayers whose money actually funded South Carolina's whites-only state post-secondary schools and the one publicly funded Black college, post emancipation:

- South Carolina taxpayers paid for seven whites-only colleges.
- South Carolina taxpayers paid for zero Black colleges. (South Carolina State College was a land-grant college, which meant it was founded with federal money after the Civil War.)
- The majority of South Carolina taxpayers were Black. (According to U.S. census workers, most of the school-age population, taxpayers, and wage earners in the Palmetto State were Black.)

Every Black person in South Carolina was being robbed, and every white person in South Carolina benefited from it.

Okay, I can kinda see your point, but my dad didn't even go to college. He can't even help me with my homework!

I'm sorry about that, RB. But the theft of Black wealth wasn't just limited to education. Four years before Summerton's Black parents filed suit against their children's school district, President Franklin Delano Roosevelt signed the Servicemen's Readjustment Act of 1944. Commonly known as the G.I. Bill, the law offered government-guaranteed home loans and paid tuition costs for World War II veterans . . . unless you were Black.

In the book *When Affirmative Action Was White*, Ira Katznelson notes that of the sixty-seven thousand mortgages approved under the G.I. Bill in New York and northern New Jersey suburbs, fewer than a hundred of the homebuying veterans were not white. A banker in Corpus Christi, Texas, reportedly explicitly told one Black veteran, "It is almost impossible for a colored man to get a loan."

When it came to college loans, even colleges in the North rejected Black veterans, and because historically Black colleges and universities were packed to the gills with students who couldn't attend white schools in the South, in 1946, only 20 percent of the former Black soldiers who applied for education benefits had enrolled in college, according to Hilary Herbold in "Never a Level Playing Field: Blacks and the GI Bill." "Though Congress granted all soldiers the same benefits theoretically," writes Herbold, "the segregationist principles of almost every institution of higher learning effectively disbarred a huge proportion of Black veterans from earning a college degree." And many of the G.I. Bill's home loan denials were based on a government policy that may be the most important contributor to the racial wealth gap: redlining.

Wait . . . Even when my dad *tries* to help me with my math homework, my teacher marks a lot of the answers with a red line. Are you saying my teacher is racist?

No, that's a different kind of redlining, my future fascist. You're talking about dumblining.

For most of America's history, metropolitan neighborhoods were organically configured, primarily by economics. Rich people lived in rich neighborhoods, and poor people lived in places that smelled a little bit like garlic. Even Irish, Jewish, and Italian enclaves, while ethnically homogeneous, were characterized by residents of similar socioeconomic standing. Poor Irish lived alongside poor Irish. Middle-class Italians lived with other middle-class Italians. Not only did these groups have the chance to advance economically, but they were also afforded the opportunity to achieve whiteness. And with that assimilation came integration.

In the mid-1930s, the federal government sponsored the New Deal, which created huge economic programs to lift America out of the Great Depression. The government mechanized farms, funded businesses, built suburbs, gave out jobs to any able-bodied American, and created a national minimum wage. The new Social Security Administration (SSA) gave people financial security in their old age. The Works Progress Administration (WPA) gave people jobs. Most important, the Home Owners' Loan Corporation (HOLC) refinanced mortgages at low interest rates to prevent foreclosures.

New Deal legislation was a massive investment in America's future, and although it was costly, it helped reduce poverty and charted a path out of the Great Depression. More than any other group of legislation in American history, the jobs, social programs, and guaranteed loans created by the New Deal are responsible for building what we now call the "middle class." There was only one problem: Black people were overwhelmingly excluded from the most impactful parts of the New Deal.

To ensure that these guaranteed mortgages were not risky, the HOLC created color-coded "residential security maps" of 239 cities. The maps essentially highlighted the neighborhoods that were good investments versus neighborhoods that were poor investments. The "risky" neighborhoods were highlighted in red, including every one of the 239 cities' Black neighborhoods. In fact, even upscale Black neighborhoods like LaVilla and Sugar Hill in Jacksonville, Florida, visited by Duke Ellington, Ella Fitzgerald, and Zora Neale Hurston, were deemed "too risky" by the HOLC. And instead of solely using these maps for government-backed home loans (which would have been racist in and of itself), banks began using these maps for *all home purchases and refinancing*. Because of this, as generations of Americans lifted themselves out of poverty, Black people could not take part in America's primary driver of wealth—homeownership.

Redlining was outlawed in 1968 by the Fair Housing Act, but it still affects almost every economic aspect of Black communities to this day. Nearly every calculable effect of institutional inequality can be traced back to this eighty-five-year-old government policy. Redlining explains why researchers at the Brookings Institution found that homes in neighborhoods where the population is majority Black are valued, on average, $48,000 less than homes in white neighborhoods. The result is a $156 billion cumulative loss in Black-owned property values, even when the white neighborhoods have the same amenities, crime rates, and resources as the Black neighborhoods.[5]

About 36 percent of education funding comes from local property taxes, the "single largest source of local revenue for schools in the United States." These lower home values,[6] which are the direct result of redlining, mean that schools in Black neighborhoods receive less funding. Therefore, redlining is why Edbuild reports that majority-white school districts receive $2,226 more per student than non-white districts: a theft of $23 billion.[7]

Residents who live in formerly redlined areas pay higher interest rates and are denied mortgages more often than whites with the same credit and income, according to reporting by the Center for Investigative Journalism. They also pay higher auto insurance rates, pay more for fresh food, have less access to medical care, pay higher interest rates on loans, receive more parking violations, pay higher bail amounts, and wait longer to vote. The white people who built their fortunes from low-interest loans, cheap food, and high home values don't pay more taxes. Yet they are benefiting from current and past policies that have taken money from Black taxpayers and handed it over to whites.

Doesn't that sound like theft to you? At the very least, it's receiving stolen goods.

But if Jim Crow ended, why should white people pay for regulations?

Why is it so hard for you to say "reparations"? Also, no one has suggested that white people pay; they think *America* should pay, which includes my tax dollars as well as your dad's. But let's say your point was valid. Aside from being a racist, what does your father do for a living?

I don't know. I think he's a real estate agent, because he's always talking about keeping the Black man in his place.

Okay, my little baby bigot. It doesn't really matter. Let's say that your father discovered that the people he worked for had been underpaying him his entire career. Let's say he worked thousands of hours for which he wasn't paid. Should his employer pay him back?

Of course they should!

But what if your father died and *you* discovered that he had been underpaid? Should your father's employer pay you what they owed your father?

Yes! That could have been my college tuition, my inheritance, or my Junior Klansman dues. I want my money!

But what if you discovered it, and then *you* died? Should those people pay your children what was owed?

Yep. They should. I might have passed down more money to them if I had my father's money. Plus, my Junior Klansman dues are late.

Okay, last question: What if you discovered that your father was never paid for countless hours of work because there was a rule that said employers had to pay everyone who worked, except for your father? What if—because of this law—the company made millions and became a global superpower? Years later, if someone challenged that company and determined that the anti–father payment rule was wrong, should the company repay the people who worked, essentially for free, even if the people currently at the company are not responsible for what the company did in the past?

Hmm, the company is still benefiting from the labor of my father. I say they owe me something.

Well, America is that company.

From 1619 until today, white people have benefited from institutional national theft.

Well, when you put it like that, I guess you have a point. But has anyone ever received refutations from like what you're talking about?

Yes. As recently as 1988, the United States paid $20,000 to each survivor of Japanese American internment camps during World War II. The Tuskegee Experiment participants and their descendants were paid a total of $10 million in reparations by the U.S. government, and the state of North Carolina paid $10 million to the victims of forced sterilizations. Florida paid $2.1 million to the victims' descendants and the survivors of a 1923 massacre in Rosewood. The United States has also supported German payments to victims of the Holocaust, and the treaties that ended World War I and World War II included reparations. And when Haiti took its independence from the French, the United States sent warships to ensure that *slaveowners* received reparations. And most recently, in 2021, the United States agreed to pay reparations to some of the families of people who suffered trauma while being detained in immigration detention centers.

Also, the word is *reparations*, RB! Come on, kid!

But how can America just cut every black person a check? Who's going to pay for it? After all, the government's money is basically our money, right?

Well, remember that Great Depression I was just talking about? We somehow found $4 trillion to pay for World War II, the most expensive war in U.S. history just a few years later.[8] We conjure up around three-quarters of a trillion dollars every year for a military budget that's over twice as big as China's. When COVID-19 hit the United States, we found a trillion dollars lying under the country's couch cushions. Americans can somehow find billions to fund Medicare, Social Security, and Kardashian-related reality shows, but we never seem to have enough to repay the debt that America owes to Black people.

So who would receive these renovations?

Come on, little tongue-tied tyrant, you know it's *reparations*. And who receives reparations is still up for debate. The logical conclusion is that the American Descendants of Slavery (ADOS) should receive the bulk of reparations, which has sparked the #ADOS movement and hashtag. Others disagree, saying that *all* Black people in America are subject to the effects of slavery, Jim Crow, and anti-Black discrimination. White supremacy doesn't distinguish between someone whose great-great-grandmother was stolen and a third-generation Nigerian immigrant. Plus, if we tied reparations to the lineage, white people might get the bulk of the funds. Mathematically, *most* descendants of the enslaved are living as white people even though they have at least one person of African descent in their family tree. And remember how good they are at finding loopholes!

There is also an argument for generational-based reparations. Namely, any fourth-generation African American whose parents lived in the country before the passage of the Civil Rights Act of 1965 would be compensated, with an increasing amount distributed for each generation of their family that resided in America. Of course, there are also problems with that plan. Could the descendant of a person who emigrated to Nova Scotia in the 1850s petition for payment? How about the maroons who absconded from plantations as soon as they arrived in America and were never enslaved? What about someone who can't trace their lineage because their ancestor escaped slavery and changed their family name? Should we include Haitians who came to the Louisiana Territory as free people of color? They were never enslaved but their descendants were subject to the same inequality, terrorism, and subjugation as the small minority of Africans who were manumitted in their first generation of being enslaved.

I guess it comes down to what reparations mean. Are they a back payment for the free labor for which slaves were never compensated? Or are reparations a compensation for slavery, housing discrimination, Jim Crow, unequal schools, lynchings, redlining, and the cumulative effects of four hundred years of codified, anti-Black white supremacy?

My dad says Black people already get all his tax money in government handouts and welfare. Why should he pay instead of giving his money to me?

If your dad really cared about you, he'd want you to live in a world with less economic inequality, better schools, and fewer poor people. The value of the property he passed on to you would increase if there were fewer poor neighborhoods in your town. Studies show that crime is linked to poverty and economic inequality, so you'd be able to live in a safer world if we repaid the debt that caused much of those disparities.[9] He wouldn't have to worry about

Black people taking his tax dollars if he repaid the debt that caused those problems. And remember when your dad said he was tired of hearing Black people whine about slavery and racism?

Imagine how tired Black people must be.

But my mom says America will never give Black people reparations. Do you think she's wrong?

We have to remember one thing: your mom is a racist.

Ida B. Wells spent her entire life fighting for a lynching law, and it never happened. Martin Luther King Jr. said, "We can never be satisfied as long as the Negro is the victim of the unspeakable horrors of police brutality."[10]* Has that happened yet? Although many people in the Black community have dropped it like it's hot, few Americans have referred to Juvenile as "Big Daddy" while simultaneously backing dat azz up. My point is, you can't stop trying to do something just because you don't think it will happen.

Justice demands restitution, and until there are reparations, there can be no justice. Until there are reparations, anyone who pledges their allegiance to the flag that stands for a country with "liberty and justice for all" is a liar *and a thief*.

---

* *We are still unsatisfied.*

Okay, I get it. Well, I have to go now. I told my dad I was going to find out about Black Revelations, not reparations.

Okay, my little mini-Nazi. You might want to make sure your dad doesn't read the original book of Revelation.

Why not?

Because when he finds out that Jesus is Black, he's probably going to be pretty upset.

THREE LITTLE QUESTIONS

1. **What is the most valid argument for reparations?**

   a. It would decrease the racial wealth gap and wealth inequality.

   b. Reparations are an economic stimulus for the economically depressed.

   c. Black people are still paying for something that happened before they were born.

   d. America already has a huge deficit. Why not increase it even more?

2. **What is the most valid argument against reparations?**

   a. Reparations would decrease the racial wealth gap and wealth inequality.

   b. Reparations are an economic stimulus for the economically depressed.

   c. White people shouldn't have to pay for something that happened before they were born.

   d. America already has a huge deficit. Why increase it even more?

3. **What would the founders say about paying reparations?**

   a. "Allow a government to decline paying its debts and you overthrow all public morality." —Alexander Hamilton

   b. "It is incumbent on every generation to pay its own debts as it goes." —Thomas Jefferson

   c. Nothing. They're dead.

   d. "You freed *what*!?!"

ACTIVITY

ARE YOU INVESTED IN INEQUALITY?

Even if your forefathers didn't own slaves, you might benefit from slavery, Jim Crow, or racial discrimination if you have ever done any of the following things:

1. **ATTENDED COLLEGE:** Aside from colleges like Yale, Harvard, and the University of Virginia that have ties to slavery, institutions of higher education benefited from systemic white supremacy in a number of ways—from segregation to investing endowments into slave trading.[11]

2. **PUT YOUR MONEY IN A BANK:** Every single one of the five largest banks in America either has ties to slavery, used redlining maps in non-government transactions, or has been sued for charging higher interest rates and denying loan requests for Black clients.

3. **HAVE AN INSURANCE POLICY:** America's oldest insurance companies allowed slaveowners to insure their human chattel. Others allowed the use of enslaved people as collateral for mortgages, loans, and slave

ships. Car insurance and homeowners' insurance companies charge higher rates for people who live in Black neighborhoods.

4. **GO TO CHURCH:** The Catholic Church and many other early American congregations invested in the transatlantic human trafficking system, used slave labor to build facilities, and even purchased slaves with money from tithes and offerings.[12]

5. **VISIT A DOCTOR:** If you live in a majority white zip code, you are more likely to have access to a primary care physician. Black newborns are three times more likely to die when they are cared for by a white doctor.[13]

6. **LIVE IN A HOUSE:** Black borrowers with the same income and credit history are denied mortgage loans at higher rates. Homes in white neighborhoods are valued, on average, about $48,000 more than homes in majority-Black neighborhoods. Because banks don't have an unlimited supply of capital, white homeowners benefit from this discrimination.

7. **DRIVE A CAR:** Car lenders charge higher rates to Black buyers.[14] Same with car insurance companies. Essentially, Black buyers subsidize lower rates for white buyers.[15]

8. **EAT FOOD:** Black neighborhoods have fewer grocery stores and fewer healthy food options. Even when these stores are available, Black consumers pay higher prices to offset the costs in other areas. To be clear, this is not about poverty. In fact, according to a 2014 study, "At equal levels of poverty, black census tracts had the fewest supermarkets, white tracts had the most, and integrated tracts were intermediate."[16]

9. **DRINK WATER:** Black Americans pay higher water bills but white Americans are more likely to have clean tap water. According to a national data analysis, "race is the strongest predictor of water and sanitation access."[17] Even when Black neighborhoods have clean water, the Black residents are essentially subsidizing water for white neighborhoods.[18]

10. **LIVE IN AMERICA:** If you're a white U.S. citizen, chances are you've benefited from voter suppression, tax laws, policing policies, segregation, economic inequality, hiring practices, the racial wage gap, and more. Also, if your president lives in the White House or your elected official has an office in the U.S. Capitol building, enslaved people built that.

THE BLACK WOMEN WHO WON REPARATIONS

While reparations have become a popular topic in the national conversation in the past few years, the struggle for holding America accountable for the injustices this country perpetrated against its Black citizens actually began before there was even a place called the "United States of America." And as usual, Black women have led the way.

When Betty Slew, a free white woman, gave birth to Jenny Slew in 1719, there was no question that Jenny was free. Even though Jenny's father was a Black man who was more than likely a slave, Massachusetts Colony laws dictated that a child's legal status was determined by the birth mother. But on January 29, 1762, John Whipple, an evil white man in Ipswich, Massachusetts, decided Jenny was a slave. He didn't buy her or argue her status. Whipple "with force and arms took her held and kept her in servitude as a slave in his service and thus restrained her of her lawful liberty . . . and did other injuries to the amount of £25," according to the civil suit *Jenny Slew, Spinster, versus John Whipple Jr., Gentleman.*[1]

The court dismissed Jenny's case because Whipple argued that Jenny was married, which meant she couldn't legally call herself a "spinster" (under Massachusetts law, a woman had no legal identity apart from her husband). But Jenny appealed her case, informing the Salem, Massachusetts, Superior Court she had been married, more than once, to enslaved men. And since the law didn't recognize the marriages of enslaved people, she was technically a "spinster."

Jenny's lawyer, Benjamin Kent, was an early abolitionist who was known for fighting in court on behalf of enslaved people. Historians know about Slew's trial because Kent's best friend was in court every day and wrote about it in his diary. This friend was a pretty big deal—some dude named John Adams. Jenny Slew won, and was the first enslaved person in America to be granted her freedom in a trial by jury. Not only did she win her freedom, but the jury awarded her the cost of her previous trials and £4 in damages. The judge declared, "This is a contest between liberty and property—both of great consequence, but liberty of most importance of the two."[2] After the trial, Kent helped his bestie with a project and suggested he include a phrase that he used in Jenny's trial. When Adams finished his lil' project, the Massachusetts Constitution—the world's oldest still-functioning constitution—he included the phrase inspired by Jenny Slew. The phrase would be revised by Benjamin Franklin and used in another one of Adams's projects: the Declaration of Independence.

That's how a Black woman inspired this little phrase in the part of the Massachusetts Constitution known as the "Declaration of the Rights of the Inhabitants of the Commonwealth of Massachusetts": "All men are born free and equal, and have certain natural, essential, and unalienable rights; among which may be reckoned the right of enjoying and defending their lives and liberties; that of acquiring, possessing, and protecting property; in fine, that of seeking and obtaining their safety and happiness."[3]

Does that sound familiar?

When Adams and Kent were working on the Massachusetts Constitution, they met in the home of Colonel John Ashley of Sheffield, Massachusetts, a well-respected, Yale-educated lawyer. One day, one of the enslaved women working in Ashley's home overheard them reading the newly ratified Massachusetts Constitution, and the "all men are born free and equal" line stuck out to her. The woman, known as "Mum Bett," would use the precedent set by Jenny Not-from-the-Auction-Block to free every slave in the state.

Born in 1742, Elizabeth "Mum Bett" Freeman once tried to stop her cruel slavemistress, Hanna Ashley, from hitting Bett's little sister with a heated shovel. Bett blocked the blow with her arm, scarring her. For the rest of her life, she refused to cover the burn mark. When curious people asked about the scar, Bett would shrug, stare at Ashley, and say, "Ask the Missus!" Yes, Betty was petty. She left the house, refused to return, and eventually sued for her freedom.

After she heard that she was born "free and equal," Mum contacted Thomas Sedgwick, an abolitionist lawyer. According to Sedgwick's wife, Mum explained, "I heard that paper read yesterday, that says, all men are created equal, and that every man has a right to freedom. I'm not a dumb critter; won't the law give me my freedom?"[4]

Sedgwick was ready to put up a fight, filing a case in the Great Barrington Court of Common Pleas on behalf of Bett and Brom, an enslaved man. In May 1781, a Massachusetts jury took one day to decide that Mum Bett should be emancipated, but Colonel Ashley decided to appeal. So on August 22, 1781, Massachusetts Supreme Court chief justice William Cushing was ready to issue his decision on *Bett and Brom v. Ashley* when Ashley dropped his challenge. Legal experts agree that Ashley understood that instead of his breaking a particular law, the challenge was to the existence of slavery under the state's constitution, so he had no path to victory. Bett's actions had summarily emancipated every enslaved person in Massachusetts. The court also awarded Bett 30 shillings, the equivalent of $763 today. Bett changed her name to Elizabeth, chucked the deuces to Ashley, and spent the rest of her life working for Sedgwick— for pay, of course.

And maybe you're saying, "Those previous cases were important. But should the proceeds from lawsuits be considered reparations? Maybe they're just legally awarded damages." Well, Belinda Sutton (previously Belinda Royall) has now entered the chat.

Belinda was stolen by an "armed band of white men" from the place we now call Ghana. Her master, Isaac Royall, sided with Britain in the championship round of the American Revolution.[5] After the war, he fled to Nova Scotia, figuring New England's "Patriots" might be mad at him (this was before Belichick took over the team). In 1783, seventy-year-old Belinda petitioned the Massachusetts General Court for a pension for herself and her daughter, writing:

> *Fifty years her faithful hands have been compelled to ignoble servitude for the benefit of an Isaac Royall, until, as if Nations must be agitated, and the world convulsed for the preservation of the freedom which the Almighty Father intended for all the human Race, the present war was Commenced . . .*
>
> *The face of your Petitioner, is now marked with the furrows of time, and her frame bending under the oppression of years, while she, by the Laws of the Land, is denied the employment of one morsel of that immense wealth, apart whereof hath been accumilated [sic] by her own industry, and the whole augmented by her servitude.*
>
> *WHEREFORE, casting herself at your feet if your honours, as to a body of men, formed for the extirpation of vassalage, for the reward of Virtue, and the just return of honest industry—she prays, that such allowance may be made her out of the Estate of Colonel Royall, as will prevent her, and her more infirm daughter, from misery in the greatest extreme, and scatter comfort over the short and downward path of their lives.[6]*

Belinda and her daughter were awarded the equivalent of $2,500 per year. But here's the thing: the "Massachusetts General Court" wasn't a judicial body. It was the name of the state's legislative body. She had won her reparations by a legislative act.

In 1818, Winny sued her enslavers in the Missouri courts. But instead of arguing her slave status, Winny charged her master Phebe Whitesides (Pruitt) with assault and battery and unlawful imprisonment for holding her against her will. Winny contended that since slavery wasn't allowed in the Missouri Territory or the Northwest Territory, the moment they brought twelve-year-old enslaved Winny to the Northwest Territory in 1793, she was legally free. The Whitesides lived there for three or four years before moving to the Missouri Territory, holding Winny as a prisoner for about twenty years. Winny was awarded damages of $167.50, or $4,102 in 2022 dollars. Whitesides appealed, and the Missouri Supreme Court case *Winny v. Whitesides* eventually set the standard for freedom petitions.

But Winny, Jenny, and Mum Bett had nothing on Henrietta Wood, who won the largest U.S. verdict specifically for reparations. Wood was born around 1818 and sold to a New Orleans–based Frenchman when she was a teenager. When Wood's master returned to France, his wife brought Wood to Ohio and registered her as free. Wood found a job and went about her life as a free woman. But in 1853, Josephine and Robert White, the daughter and son-in-law of Wood's former master, hired a deputy sheriff to kidnap Wood and sell her *back into slavery*. Wood sued for her freedom but lost because she couldn't produce documents that proved she was freed. She was sold again and eventually ended up on a Texas plantation, where she remained enslaved until the end of the Civil War.

But Henrietta wouldn't let Josephine and Robert's reenslavement stunt slide. In 1870, Wood filed suit against the deputy, asking for $20,000. The jury sided with her, awarding her $2,500 (about $67,000 in 2022). Wood used the money to help pay for her son's education. He became one of the first Black graduates of the Northwestern University Law School.

Henrietta still wishes a motherf—

Nah, too easy.

15

THE RACE OF POLITICS

UNCLE ROB EXPLAINS THE TWO-PARTY SYSTEM

As you consume this collection of stories about the Black experience, you will invariably have questions. For instance, you might notice that for the first half of America's history, the Democrats were the bad guys who fought to uphold the institutions of slavery, Jim Crow, and legalized racial subjugation; then, all of a sudden, the Democrats became the good guys. One of the favorite assertions of Candace Owens, and other Black people who happily let white people touch their hair, is that negroes have been bamboozled by the Democratic Party. They often ask why the Democratic Party tends to get the Black vote by default. I'm sure you've heard some variation of this argument. With a false sense of superiority bestowed upon them by conservative negro-whisperers, they will say that Black voters are stuck on the "Democratic plantation." They argue that Democrats started the Ku Klux Klan and supported segregation while Republicans are the party of Lincoln, self-determination, and, most of all, "bootstraps." But how did it happen?

It's actually a valid question. Until Carol Moseley Braun's election in 1992, every African American who served in the U.S. Senate belonged to the Republican Party.[1] Twenty-one Black men served in the House of Representatives as Republicans before a Black Democrat was elected. The Democratic Party, on the other hand, was, until the

1960s, the party of the South. It was the party of social conservatism. It wanted to preserve slavery and segregation. The party's Southern contingent generally opposed the Civil Rights Act and the Voting Rights Act. It was the party of states' rights, small government, and Jim Crow. They wouldn't even allow Black people to be present at their convention until 1924.

So what happened? Why is it that 80 percent of Black voters have consistently identified as Democrat over the last twenty-five years, while the GOP electorate has been at least 80 percent white?[2] Why hasn't a Republican presidential candidate won a majority of Black voters in fifty years? What happened to make America's two-party system so racially polarized?

To show the evolution of the current two-party system, perhaps it would be useful to examine a few quotes from important historical figures of our past.

* * *

What's up, everybody? It's your boy, Uncle Rob!

Mikey's in there looking through some books. He said something about finding some quotes from Black historical figures about voting, and you know what? I'm Black and I was born in 1949, which makes me a historical figure! Plus, who knows more about politics than your favorite uncle? I don't know why that boy thinks you want to hear from some dudes in old black-and-white photographs instead of people who were actually affected by it. Then again, that boy reads too much. I bet he didn't tell you that he pronounced W. E. B. Du Bois's name as "dew bwah" for years until I told him that it's pronounced "do boys." I blame his mama. She went to that uppity all-Black boarding school and came back speaking fluent French.* But you know who can give you the real lowdown on the history of white politics?

Moi.

Before I was born, Black voters were as likely to identify as Demo-

---

* *My mother attended the Boylan-Haven-Mather Academy, an all-Black boarding school founded in 1867 to teach the children of former slaves.*

crats as they were Republicans.[3] In the South, it was a little different. Like many voters in the South, my mama 'nem identified as Republicans because they said Southern Democrats were kinda racist. And when they said "kinda racist," you gotta keep in mind that Southern folk think the sun is "kinda hot." Black folks in the South never say what they mean. Like when a Black woman tells you that she has "a trick for yo' ass," she is not about to teach you magic. Your best bet is to disappear like Black folks did from the Republican Party. And I heard you wanted to know why that happened.

If I was writing a history book, I would start by explaining that Federalists like Alexander Hamilton wanted a strong central government, a national bank, and a federal army and navy. Democrat-Republicans like Thomas Jefferson, on the other hand, who saw "big government" as a threat to their individual liberties, favored low taxes and a concept called "states' rights." Mikey's probably told you some gobbledygook about the dispute over the formation of a national bank, international policy, and national credit.[*] But to understand the politics of Baby America, all you have to know is one fact:

White supremacy is the defining characteristic of America's politics.

While other political, economic, and social issues have mattered more or less over the years, white supremacy has been the organizing principle of American politics before America even existed. Of course, your raggedy history book will explain how the nation's first two political factions, the *Federalists* and the *Anti-Federalists*, was about representation, states' rights, and taxation, and not humanity or white supremacy. They'll say the Federalists wanted a strong federal government, a national army, and a central bank that handled the country's debts, while the Anti-Federalists favored states' rights, a weaker executive branch, and a government that wasn't dominated by New England merchants and Northern aristocrats.

But a lot of the beef was about slavery. Even though many Federalists owned slaves, Anti-Federalists were afraid that a strong federal government dominated by Northern aristocrats could essentially ban

---

[*] *Okay, Uncle Rob isn't wrong, but "gobbledygook" is a strong word. Plus, it sounds kinda racist.*

the institution. They wanted their new nation to treat in the manner suggested by a more beloved group of men known as the Isley Brothers once suggested, "It's your thing, do what you wanna do." And so they compromised. Ultimately, the new Constitution of the United States of America actually told the states who to sock it to.

After the Founders signed away two-fifths of Black people's humanity in exchange for political expediency, the Federalists and the Anti-Federalists formed into two parties. The Federalists became the Federalist Party. They were religiously puritanical, pro–big government, and strong in New England. The Anti-Federalists became the Democrat-Republicans, a party that favored an agrarian economy, smaller government, and states retaining more rights.* It is important to note that neither party was overly concerned with the *abolition* of slavery. Each had anti-slavery factions, but aside from the New England states that had abolished slavery, the Democrat-Republican Party dominated early American politics. By the election of 1824, the Federalist Party had collapsed, and the Democrat-Republicans had splintered into factions.

Andrew Jackson actually won the popular vote in 1824 and had more electoral votes, but because none of the candidates (all of whom were Democrat-Republicans) won a majority of electoral votes, the House of Representatives elected New Englander John Quincy Adams as president. After the "corrupt bargain," Jackson desperately wanted a rematch against John Q. But Johnny was already the Democrat-Republican nominee, so Jackson's homeboys from Tennessee took their horses down to Old Town Road and nominated him for president under the banner of the Jackson party. When Jackson beat the brakes off John Quincy Adams in the rematch, Jackson's conservative, pro-slavery supporters created a political organization called the "Democrats." At their inaugural convention in 1840, the Democratic Party adopted its first official platform, resolving that "all efforts of the abolitionists or others, made to induce Congress to interfere with questions of slavery . . . have an inevitable tendency to diminish the happiness of the people, and endanger the stability and perma-

---

* *Has Mikey mentioned how bad white people are at naming things?*

nency of the Union, and ought not to be countenanced by any friend of our political institutions."[4] The Democrats' main platform centered around the concept of "nullification"—the idea that states had the right to invalidate laws they deemed unconstitutional. Of course, the only law they wanted to nullify was the one about owning human beings. Democrats thought the federal government should leave those decisions up to the states.[*]

It is true that the Republican Party was founded on the principles of anti-slavery. Founded in 1854, the GOP's only real concern was stopping the expansion of owning men.[†] They were so in favor of ending America's peculiar institution that members were often called "Black Republicans" as a slur. And trust me, they weren't talking about Kanye West. Republicans also elected the first woman to Congress, supported Black suffrage, and pushed for civil rights legislation before Martin Luther King was born.[5] The Civil War, in effect, was a clash over the evolution of America's two political parties—one that wanted the right to own men and another that vehemently opposed the possession of human beings by others.

In 1870, the United States ratified the Fifteenth Amendment, declaring, "The right of citizens of the United States to vote shall not be denied or abridged by the United States or by any State on account of race, color, or previous condition of servitude." Although most historians focused on the formerly enslaved Black voters in the South, before the Fifteenth Amendment, states like New York and New Jersey forbade African Americans from voting.[‡]

After the Civil War, Black voters formed "Union Leagues," secret advocacy groups that met in Black churches or schools to discuss civic and political issues. Aside from practicing a new popular dance called the Electric Slide, these leagues usually supported Republican candidates, and encouraged millions of Black men to register to

---

[*] *In America, "leave it up to the states" has always been code for "we don't want anyone but white men to have rights." See slavery. See segregation. See voting rights. See abortion. See women's suffrage.*

[†] *Not for moral reasons. The pro-slavery, "states' rights" Democrats controlled the South and the Republican Party didn't want their political and economic power to grow.*

[‡] *New York rescinded its ratification of the Fifteenth when legislators realized Black people were included in the word "citizens."*

vote (women were not yet allowed). After the Civil War, Mississippi's voting-eligible population was suddenly majority Black, and the Black voter registration rate was more than 96.7 percent.[6] The South's white minority couldn't stand it. After the Compromise of 1877 formally allowed the Democrat-controlled white minority to disenfranchise Black people, the state's Black voter registration dropped to less than 6 percent by 1892.[7] This is why the highest turnout in the history of presidential politics happened in 1876, when Black voter suppression tactics were not yet enshrined into law.

Of course, white Republicans began to get antsy about the growing Black majority ruling their party, too. They eventually formed an all-white faction of the party.* In 1888, the Texan Norris Wright Cuney, a Black Republican, began to fight against white party leaders who wanted to use the Jim Crow laws to oust Black elected officials from the state convention, calling the faction the "Lily-White" movement, not to be confused with Lil Wyte, a Caucasian Soundcloud rapper that I've never heard but am sure exists.

By 1890, the Lily-Whites had successfully created two factions of the Republican Party, distancing themselves from efforts to protect civil rights and joining Democrats to suppress Black voters throughout the South. Meanwhile, a "Black-and-Tan" faction emerged, because organized white supremacist violence helped the Lily-Whites gain power. In the early twentieth century, white Republicans often ran as Lily-Whites in state and local elections, while Black candidates ran under the Black-and-Tan banner. Composed of Black voters and the few white politicians who had not sided with white supremacy, the Black-and-Tan movement soon became a minority within the Southern GOP. In 1921, Richmond, Virginia's Maggie Lena Walker—the first Black woman to open a bank—ran for state superintendent of schools under Virginia's Lily-Black ticket with gubernatorial candidate John Mitchell Jr., who owned a bank in a section of Richmond known as Black Wall Street. The moguls eschewed the Black-and-Tan ticket partly to point out the party's hypocrisy after Virginia's Republican Party banned Blacks from attending the state convention.

---

* *Kinda like the modern-day Tea Party, but racist. Okay, just like the modern-day Tea Party.*

The Republican Party tried every imaginable tactic to lure Southern white voters to their side, even outlawing seasoned chicken at their conventions. A few whites joined the GOP when William Taft's 1908 presidential campaign pushed his "Southern Policy" promise to not appoint African Americans to federal jobs in areas where it would lead to racial conflict. When Democrat Woodrow Wilson won the election of 1912 on a promise of rolling back any gains African Americans had made since emancipation, Du Bois said: "It is no exaggeration to say that every enemy of the Negro race is greatly encouraged; that every man who dreams of making the Negro race a group of menials and pariahs is alert and hopeful."[8] The dividing line in American politics was suddenly clear. The party that won the votes of conservative white racists would win the South and Midwest.

African American voters overwhelmingly supported Franklin Roosevelt's four presidential campaigns in 1932, 1936, 1940, and 1944, but for other contests, as many Blacks identified as Republican as Democrat. Then, in 1948, disgusted with Democrat Harry Truman's order to desegregate the U.S. Army and the Democratic Party's support for anti–Jim Crow laws, thirty-five delegates from the Deep South walked out of the Democratic National Convention and formed the States' Rights Democratic Party (Dixiecrats). Black voters flocked to the Democratic Party. To be clear, Black people didn't *switch parties*. Their votes had always been split between the two political factions; they just stopped voting for Republicans. Indeed, they had a trick for the racist Republicans' collective ass.

But, as Saint Jerome said in the Bible, "White people gon' white."* For the most part, Southern whites kept voting for Democrats and Republicans couldn't get a foothold in the South. Republican Dwight Eisenhower won everywhere *but* the "Solid South" in 1952 and 1956. Then, in September 1957, Eisenhower sent federal troops into Arkansas to enforce the desegregation of Little Rock Central High School. In 1963, John F. Kennedy, a Democrat, broke with the party ideology and used Eisenhower's playbook to send in the white storm troopers—the Alabama National Guard—to force desegregation at

---

* *It's the third chapter of Niggalations, one of the lesser books.*

the University of Alabama. Then came the breaking point that would basically change the party affiliation of Southern voters. Shortly before the election of 1964, Democrat Lyndon B. Johnson signed the Civil Rights Act.

Aside from Jimmy Carter in 1976, the Solid South would never vote for a Democratic president again.

Those good ol' Republicans who never read a white lie they didn't like would like you to believe that Republicans supported the Civil Rights Act of 1964 and Democrats opposed it, which is only partially true. To understand the change in both parties' ideology, all one has to do is count the votes.[9]

- There were ninety-four Southern Democrats in the House of Representatives. Eight voted for the bill.
- There were eleven Southern Republicans in the House of Representatives. Zero voted for the bill.
- The Northern House Democrats voted in favor of the bill 145–9.
- The Northern House Republicans favored the bill 138–24.
- Of the twenty-one Southern senators (Democrat or Republican), only one voted in favor of the Civil Rights Act (a Texas Democrat).

As you can see, it wasn't the Democrats who opposed the Civil Rights Act and the Republicans who favored it. *Everyone* supported the Civil Rights Act except representatives from the South. Southern politicians from *both* parties voted against the legislation; and even further, every poll for the era shows that Southern whites opposed the law.

The Civil Rights Act was signed on July 2, 1964. In the presidential elections that year, 94 percent of non-white voters voted for Democratic candidate Lyndon Johnson, boosting him to a win over Barry Goldwater. But Goldwater, a Republican, managed to win five Southern states in that election, which was unheard of for a Republican. How did Goldwater do that? He won those states by opposing the Civil Rights Act. He knew that a majority of white Southerners felt "negro rights groups were asking for too much" on civil rights, while the rest of the country felt the groups were asking for "about what they should."[10] And just before the election, his vice presidential running mate and Republican National Committee chairman, William E. Miller, gave a speech warning America that the civil rights protests were the "payoff of the soft-on-crime, society-is-to-blame breed."[11] Breed! I haven't heard anything as racist as "breed" until forty years later, when I was called a "dindoo," as in: "When the police arrest Black guys, they always say, 'I dindoo nuffin!'" Say what you will about Republicans, but they are inventive when it comes to euphemisms for the n-word.

In 1968, Strom Thurmond teamed up with Richard Nixon, the 1968 Republican presidential candidate who was convinced that a Republican could win the South if he was willing to dog-whistle racism to the Southern voters. Along with H. R. Haldeman, they developed the "Southern Strategy" by emphasizing Nixon's belief that "the whole problem is really the blacks. The key is to devise a system that recognizes this while not appearing to."[12] Nixon won the 1968 election by carrying seven former Confederate states, a remarkable feat for a Republican. In his 1972 reelection, he doubled down on the racist rhetoric and won every single state in the South. Since that election, only Jimmy Carter won a majority of the old Confederate states formerly known as the Solid South. The old Confederate states fused into a Republican voting bloc few Democrats have been able to penetrate.

In 1981, Lee Atwater, the political campaign architect who refined the Southern Strategy for Ronald Reagan and George H. W. Bush, described the Republican Party's winning template:

> You start out in 1954 by saying: "Nigger, nigger, nigger." By 1968, you can't say "nigger"—that hurts you, backfires. So, you say stuff like, uh, forced busing, states' rights, and all that stuff, and you're getting so abstract. Now you're talking about cutting taxes, and all these things you're talking about are totally economic things, and a byproduct of them is, blacks get hurt worse than whites . . . "We want to cut this" is much more abstract than even the busing thing, uh, and a hell of a lot more abstract than "Nigger, nigger."[13]

On August 3, 1980, a new Republican presidential hopeful was searching for a spot to make a big political statement. Instead of speaking in his home state of California, he chose a place that was sure to rile up his base of angry white Southern supporters: the Neshoba County Fair in Philadelphia, Mississippi, which happened to be the site of Emmett Till's murder. In 1964, when members of the White Knights of the Ku Klux Klan abducted and murdered James Chaney, Andrew Goodman, and Michael Schwerner, Klan organizer Edgar Ray Killen was arrested and charged with the murders, but his first trial ended in a hung jury. On August 4, 1964, forty-four days after they disappeared, authorities found the bodies buried in a dam on the Old Jolly Farm, a stone's throw from the open field where Reagan chose to give his speech. As the mostly white crowd that included members of the Klan looked on, Reagan gave a thirty-three-paragraph, dog-whistle-filled speech about the dangers of welfare and "outsiders" to a rousing round of applause. That man knew what he was doing by conjuring up the worst elements of whiteness. He believed that he could employ the Southern Strategy and cement the South as Republican territory. More than fifteen thousand people showed up. I'm not saying this was racist . . .

Because I don't have to.

"I believe in states' rights," explained the man who would become the Conservative Beyoncé. "And I believe that we've distorted the balance of our government today by giving powers that were never intended in the Constitution to that federal establishment. And if I do get the job I'm looking for, I'm going to devote myself to trying to reorder those priorities and to restore to the states and local communities those functions which properly belong there."[14]

The "States' Rights" speech would become part of political history. Three months later, that candidate, Ronald Reagan, enjoyed one of the biggest presidential landslides in American history, completing his party's century-long switcheroo. In the 2020 presidential election, Republicans won 70 percent of white voters in the former Confederate states.[15] The GOP is like a Black cookout: a whole lot of whiting.

Oh, Mikey's back. I guess he can take it from here.

* * *

Wait. Did my uncle Rob just hijack my book again? I bet he told you about the Lily-Whites, didn't he? Did he make the fedora joke? Please don't tell me he made the fish fry joke. Oh, man. I'm sorry. It could be worse. He could have told you what "dindoo" means.

Aside from the jokes from 1979, Uncle Rob is right. Republicans are now the party of the alt-right. It is the party of economic anxiety and birtherism. It is the party of Donald Trump, the "Muslim ban," the border wall, David Duke, and all the white supremacists running for election on the Republican ticket in the 2022 midterms. Republican leaders now spout white supremacist theories, asking what non-whites have done for civilization.[16] They appeal to Islamophobia and its anti-immigrant base by repeating rhetoric that has no basis in fact. They rally right-wing support under the guise of "patriots" and "American values." It is the party of white people.

And lest one think the Democrats have emerged as anti-racist heroes, they are not so much *for* Black people as they are *the opposition party* for the GOP. Since the Civil Rights Act, 98 percent of the Democratic senators and 82 percent of the men and women appointed to the federal judiciary have been white.[17] Democrats have never elected a Black Speaker of the House or Senate majority leader. While its base is inarguably more diverse, the Democratic Party is still run by the brand of white men who compromised two-fifths of Black people's humanity for the sake of national unity.

An official ballot that offers two choices:
"White Supremacy"
"Liberty and Justice for All"

No, the GOP is not more racist than the Democratic Party. A party is just a name and a logo. There has always been a party that served as the home for white supremacy, and the Republican Party is just the *current* base. You can call it the Democratic, Republican, conservative, or MAGA, but among Southern whites there ain't but one party—the anti-Black party. So while future history books might one day credit Sean "Puffy/P. Diddy/Diddy/Puff Daddy/Brother Love" Combs with convincing people to wear bleached linen outfits to shindigs, America is the originator of the white party. The country has always had a two-party political system:

1. White people.
2. Everybody else.

Until the presidential election of 1948, the Democratic Party was the party of Jim Crow, segregation, and the Ku Klux Klan. In all the presidential elections between 1880 and 1947, Herbert Hoover (who ran against Catholic New York Democrat Al Smith) was the only Republican to win more than three of the Southern slaveholding states, which included Alabama, Arkansas, Florida, Georgia, Kentucky, Louisiana, Maryland, Mississippi, North Carolina, Oklahoma, South Carolina, Tennessee, Texas, Virginia, and West Virginia.* But this doesn't mean the Republican Party was welcoming to Black voters.

The Dixiecrats selected Strom Thurmond (who was only forty-six years old at the time) as their presidential candidate and based their new party's platform on segregation. In the 1948 presidential election, the Dixiecrat Party's platform of strict segregation won four Southern states and placed second in a fifth, ending the solidly Democratic South.

But something interesting happened. In 1964, Republicans nominated Barry Goldwater, an Arizona senator and GOP chairman who showed his adherence to white supremacy by voting against the Civil Rights Act. Goldwater chose New York congressman William E. Miller

---

* *More commonly known as the "Sweet Tea States."*

for a running mate, who warned against Democratic candidates being "soft on crime"—a reference to civil rights protesters staging demonstrations in cities across the country. The tactic didn't win the election, but the party of Lincoln made significant inroads in the South for the first time since the Civil War. Not only were the pro-segregationist states the *only states they won*, but literally, to this day, the Democratic Party has never regained control of the South.

Since then, every Republican president has gone all in on the Southern Strategy by dog-whistling to white voters. Richard Nixon promised a "war on crime" to keep the Blacks in line. Ronald Reagan proved he wasn't soft on crime by doubling the prison population during his time in office. Maybe the most famous "soft on crime" ad was George H. W. Bush's racist Willie Horton ad. Or the time he pulled crack cocaine out in the Oval Office to explain why "we need more prisons." While that might sound like I'm calling these presidents racist, I'm not.

We don't know what's in the hearts and minds of politicians. We can only judge them by what they do. And, just as they demonized civil rights protests by connecting them to crime, right-wing conservatives continue to weaponize white fear as a cattle prod to herd white voters under the GOP tent. After Reagan manufactured the scourge of nonexistent "welfare queens," George H. W. Bush ramped up mass incarceration and the war on drugs to protect the American people from the coming horde of negro crack babies, despite the fact that "three times as many whites had ever used crack as blacks."[18] In the 1990s, Newt Gingrich updated the Republican Party's anti-Black rhetoric by convincing middle America that "political correctness" was going to make their bigotry illegal and affirmative action would steal their jobs. Three decades later, fentanyl, Mexican caravans, Colin Kaepernick, CRT, cancel culture, and the "woke mob" have replaced crack babies, communist protesters, Black Power, secret Marxist protesters, and political correctness. But none of these things proves that the Republican Party is racist.

They prove that America is racist.

Over time, these racial dog whistles and culture wars have proven themselves as effective political techniques. Republicans couldn't win

elections consistently if these bigoted ideas weren't shared by a majority of White America.

It is entirely possible that Republican politicians aren't racist. It is
not reasonable to believe that most white people are not. But just like
the slaveholding declarers of independence and the white nationalists
who started an uncivil race war and the Reconstruction-era terrorists and the white women who advocated for the necessity of lynching
and the segregationists and the mass incarcerators and the vote sup-
pressors and the election-denying insurrectionists who just wanted to
make America great again, they will deny that white supremacy is
their ultimate goal. But their votes show it. The success of politicians
who openly espouse the premises of white supremacy shows it. This
country's history shows it. The ones who claim they want to make
America great again have never lifted a finger to transform this make-
believe democracy into a more perfect union.

They dindoo nuffin.

THREE LITTLE QUESTIONS

1. **Since the signing of the Voting Rights Act in 1965, no presidential candidate has won a majority of Black voters and a majority of white voters. Why?**
   a. Is this a serious question? You know why.
   b. I have no idea why white voters have different political goals than every other racial and ethnic demographic of voters in America, but I'm sure there's a reason.
   c. Maybe you should ask white people.
   d. Racism.

2. **Which term best describes the pre-Goldwater Democrats and the modern-day Republican Party?**
   a. Southern conservatives.
   b. Right-wing.
   c. Anti-Black.
   d. Pro-white.

3. **When did America become a democracy?**
   a. When all white men won the right to vote.
   b. When white women won the right to vote.
   c. When Black people won the right to vote.
   d. I'll let you know.

ACTIVITY

IDENTITY POLITICS

Euphemisms are often used to describe political groups. With no research whatsoever, guess whether the following euphemism is used to describe a group that is mostly:

(W) White

(B) Black

(E) Equally proportionate

1. Red states
2. States' rights
3. Dixiecrats
4. Evangelicals

5. Goldwater Republicans
6. Alt-right
7. Reagan
8. Family values
9. Silent majority
10. Christian conservatives
11. Black voters
12. Soccer moms
13. NASCAR dads
14. The negro vote
15. Suburban voters
16. Economically anxious
17. MAGAs
18. Urban voters
19. Liberals
20. Independent voters
21. College-educated voters
22. Conservatives

CHICKEN BOG VS. PERLO

The biggest dispute you've never heard of is between two African-inspired dishes that are rooted in slavery and the Gullah-Geechee community. Although they both originated in South Carolina and are often confused with each other, they are two entirely different things with entirely different cultures: enter chicken bog vs. chicken perlo.

WHAT IS CHICKEN BOG?

Chicken bog originated in the coastal region of South Carolina, near the Pee Dee River. Legend has it that in the mid-1800s, two slaves, Gibbie and Pody, lived on a plantation owned by Henry Buck, who owned more than a hundred slaves. The pair would boil chicken, sausage, onions, peppers, seasoning, and anything else they could find. Once the chicken became soft, they would remove the bones, throw in some rice, and have enough to feed dozens of enslaved people. That's still the recipe for chicken bog. It's said to be called that because the chicken is "bogged down" in the rice. Others say the name comes from the boggy land in the area, while my aunt Earlene says the name comes from what you get when you eat too much chicken bog: a big ol' gut.

WHAT IS CHICKEN PERLO?

Chicken perlo is a Lowcountry dish that is kinda like chicken bog, except it is not "wet." While chicken perlo is the predominant form of perlo-ing, there is also seafood perlo, "errthang" perlo, and I'm sure there's someone who is being frowned upon by the ancestors for making vegetarian perlo. Perlo is basically akin to the West African jollof, and relies less on the flavor of the chicken than a bog. And I know what you're thinking, but you're wrong. No, a chicken bog is *not* just a moist perlo, nor is a perlo a dry bog.

WHY IS THIS EVEN IN A BOOK?

In South Carolina's African American communities, this topic is as important as sugar vs. salt on grits, sugar in cornbread, or whether or not all cakes are just bougie pound cakes. Chicken bogs are the number one form of fund-raising in South Carolina. They fund baseball teams and send dance crews to state competitions. If a kid sells you a ticket to a bog, you can just stop by on the bog date and pick up a plate. It's basically like a raffle where everyone wins. Every year, the small town of Loris, South Carolina, holds a chicken bog festival because that's where chicken bog was supposedly invented.

YOU SEEM VERY BOG-BIASED

I come from bog people, so I am admittedly chicken-bog-biased. (And you don't make "*some* chicken bog," you make *a* chicken bog. The entire pot is one singular thing, like *a school of fish* or *a mob of white people*.) But perlo has its advantages. The problem is, unless you know a woman from the Charleston area who speaks Geechee, knows a little bit of roots, and wears a bonnet more than she wears shoes, finding great perlo is very rare. It's a skill. And people in Charleston will not hesitate to perlo-shame people for having inadequate perlo. On the other hand, *anyone* can make a good bog, even white people.*

---

* *You might need to add a little seasoning to Caucasian bog, but it's very hard to mess up a bog.*

SO WHICH IS BETTER?

This might not be satisfying but here is the answer: If you had to sample one of these dishes from a random person, you can't go wrong with chicken bog. But the best perlo wins against the best bog any day of the week. It doesn't matter because I think you see where I'm going here:

South Carolina is just better than everywhere else.

THE END OF THE MULTIRACIAL COALITION

L eading up to North Carolina's 1898 election, Wilmington, North Carolina, was a majority-Black town where African Americans held political positions and economic power. While North Carolina politics was dominated by white Democrats, white Republicans and populists in Wilmington sided with Black Republicans and formed the Fusion Coalition on a platform that included free public education and voting rights for Black men.

Nine white men, upset with being subject to "negro rule," started a campaign to unseat the Fusionists, while the Democratic Party chairman declared, "North Carolina is a WHITE MAN'S STATE and WHITE MEN will rule it, and they will crush the party of Negro domination beneath a majority so overwhelming that no other party will ever dare to attempt to establish negro rule here."[1] Another party leader boasted[2] that the election would be the "meanest, vilest, dirtiest campaign since 1876. The slogan of the Democratic party from the mountains to the sea will be but one word . . . 'Nigger'!"

They declared that Wilmington's white minority needed to unite and enforce the law through lynching if they wanted to stop the city's epidemic of Black men raping white women. To reinforce their point, they pointed to a speech by Rebecca L. Felton, a prominent feminist in Georgia, who in August 1897 expressed the most concern for the nonexistent plague of white women being raped by ravenous Black men, explaining, "If it needs lynching to protect woman's dearest possession from the ravening human beasts—then I say lynch, a thousand times a week if necessary."

Alexander Manly, who co-owned the *Daily Record*, Wilmington's only daily Black-owned newspaper, decided to refute the allegation. In the editorial usually attributed to Manly, the writer pointed out that Wilmington was filled with mixed-race children because *white men* were, more often than not, the interracial rapists, adding that white women were really having consensual sex with Black men because they couldn't be sexually satisfied by white men.

"Meetings of this kind go on for some time until the woman's infatuation, or the man's boldness, bring attention to them, and the man is lynched for rape," the editorial continued. "Every Negro lynched is called a 'big burly, black brute,' when in fact many of those who have thus been dealt with had white men for their fathers, and were not only not 'black' and 'burly' but were sufficiently attractive for white girls of culture and refinement to fall in love with them as is very well known to all . . . Don't ever think that your women will remain pure while you are debauching ours," added the writer. "You sow the seed—the harvest will come in due time."[3]

White Wilmington was *furious*. After holding a political rally that was literally called the "White Supremacy Convention," the white residents loaded the ballot box with fake votes and warned African Americans what would happen if they voted. By election day, many Black Wilmingtonians had decided not to vote, hoping to avoid violence.

The Fusionists won anyway.

On the morning of the election, the white supremacy party issued a "White Declaration of Independence" and demanded that the Black residents of Wilmington hand over Manly or make him leave town within twenty-four hours of the issuance of the declaration. They also declared that their superior intelligence should be recognized by allowing them to be in charge, regardless of votes. The Black leaders wrote a letter explaining that they were just as outraged by Manly's editorial as everyone else. They hadn't even voted, so it must have been *white people* who wanted the Fusionists to remain in power. Plus, they had already sent Manly on his way, so there was no need for violence.

The next morning, about five hundred white Wilmingtonians went to the armory, armed themselves, and burned down the office of Manly's newspaper. By the time they reached the Black section of town, the mob had grown to around two thousand. After killing a few Black people on the way, they forced the Fusionist mayor, police chief, and aldermen to resign at gunpoint. As Blacks fled the city, the terrorists dragged the most prominent Black businessmen to the train station and, in front of a crowd of applauding white people, forced them to board the train. Since 1898, Wilmington has been a majority-white town ruled by a white majority. In 1900, North Carolina inserted a poll tax, a grandfather clause, and a literacy test clause in the state's constitution, disenfranchising the next two generations of Black voters.

16

HOMEWORK

All the stories about my family that you have read in this book are true. They have been fact-checked via group texts, Zoom calls, and phone conversations with my sisters, aunts, cousins, and friends. Although they didn't give me express permission to document these anecdotes and reveal them to the world, I have no reason to think they will object, because I was raised with three of the greatest snitches in history. My three sisters—Comelita, Robin, and Sean—have never competed in track and field, but they were world-class athletes when it came to running and telling.

The funny thing about this was, even though they always ratted me out, they knew I would *never* do it to them. They would reveal a secret to me knowing I wouldn't share it with anyone, but they would never keep my secrets. They were so dependable in that regard that I actually respect their snitch game. I don't even blame them for their shortcomings because I know they can't *not snitch*. They *have to run and tell it*. To this day, if they discover something I was trying to hide, they will casually say, with no shame whatsoever:

"You know I'mma tell Mama, right?"

I don't blame my mother for my sisters' propensity for tattling. It wasn't a family trait. In fact, my mother disliked it as much as I did, which is why my sisters had to figure out how to snitch in an overt way. They eventually honed their backdoor tattletale tactics down to a science by uttering one phrase that would invariably pique my mother's curiosity:

"Something is wrong with Mike."

There was nothing I could do about this because there was a "no hitting" rule in our house that precluded all others. And of course, living with the Snitch Squad, you couldn't dare break the rules if I even plucked them on the earlobe. Because of how we were raised, we respected the code of the Harriot streets. But if any one of us ever found a workaround to a rule, we would argue the technicalities among each other. And besides turning in each other for violations of the house rules, my sisters were *great* at finding loopholes, which is why the discovery of "I was doing this first" upended the Harriot house for years to come.

I'd love to tell you that I discovered "IWDTF," but I can't lie, I don't know which one of us discovered this brilliant tactical loophole (probably Robin). But it was a way to make someone actually choose violence. Here's how it worked:

Say you were in the corner of a room, lying on a bed or anywhere else you couldn't escape. According to the precedent set in the landmark case *Harriot v. Harriot*, I was legally permitted to use my arms, a stick, or anything that could block your path. And if you ran into my arm, a broom, or an object that was already in motion, it wasn't my fault you got the snot knocked out of you.

The best time to do it was when someone had to pee. When I or one of my sisters had wronged another one of us, we waited until the offending party went into the bathroom, then we grabbed the broom and started waving it in front of the door. When the offender exited the bathroom, they would have to face the broom gauntlet, knowing that "I was doing this first." I can't tell you how many times my sisters and I have nearly beaten each other to death with a broomstick. I'm also not sure if my mother even knew this loophole existed, because if you got hit with the broom when someone was "doing this first," you simply didn't tell. In our prepubescent minds, "doing this first" was not a breach of the rules because, technically, the victim was choosing to suffer the consequences by interfering in an activity that was clearly in progress. Also, we figured we weren't technically "hitting" the victim of the broom gauntlet—the broom was doing the hitting. I can't tell you who discovered this idiotic rule, but I can tell you the moment when it ended. As I said, my sisters were forbidden from hitting each other, but there was one thing we also knew about my sisters:

They can fight.

It's not like they fought well "for a girl." They fight well for a middleweight MMA champion. They weren't mean and they didn't fight a lot. Most people have never seen them fight. Everyone just knows. There are a few grown men from my neighborhood who can attest to the Harriot girls' kicking-ass capabilities.

I don't know what started the drama, although I think it was about whose turn it was to wash dishes. All I heard is Robin in the living room yelling, "I was doing this first!" I entered the kitchen just as Robin smushed Sean in the face with a moist, Pine-Sol-soaked sponge mop. I got that bubblegut feeling that the Ayllón expeditioners probably felt when drinking that feces-laden water. But I didn't go to the bathroom because Sean was balling up her fists . . . in the Harriot house! As Robin waved the broom and gave her legal disclaimer that she "was doing this first," Sean uttered five words that would forever change the IWDTF game:

"Okay . . . Well I'm doing *this*!"

She swung on Robin. Thankfully, she missed, because she was about the length of a mop handle away from Robin. I wanted to stop it and I also wanted to see the fight and I also didn't want to die in a helicopter fist accident and I also didn't want them to kill each other. As they stood, face-to-face, smoke emanating from their noses, I knew I had to stop them. I thought about placing a bet on the winner, but I kinda like my sisters and didn't want them to perish in mutual combat. Plus, we had not yet come up with a Harriot concussion protocol. Frazzled, I ran into the middle room where my mother was sitting, unaware of the kitchen hostilities. Sensing something was amiss, she looked up and asked why I had the look of desperation on my face. I didn't know what to say. I was not used to this telling-on-people stuff, and according to our predetermined rules, Robin was not at fault for clocking Sean upside the head with a sponge mop. In what would later stand as a seminal moment in Harriot history, I joined the sister-snitching movement by reluctantly whispering:

"Something is wrong with Sean."

Two years after the passage of the Civil Rights Act—barely a year after the passage of the landmark Voting Rights Act—54 percent of white Americans said they thought the civil rights marches were "not justified," according to an August 1966 Harris poll.[1] In October, 85 percent of whites responded that the "demonstrations by negroes on civil rights" hurt the "advancement of negro rights."[2] By June 1969, only 32 percent of respondents felt Black protesters were "trying to be helpful."[3] Because of the civil rights movement, the country finally began to address the disparities, inequality, and terrorism that were the by-product of a quadruple century of racial oppression. But when all was said and done, the majority of white people in America had reached one conclusion:

Something was wrong with Black people.

And to fix America's racial problem, all this country needed to do was to fix Black people. To address the drugs, crime, and poverty caused by wealth disparities, unequal employment, and lack of community resources, they decided to police, arrest, and imprison the people who were subjected to redlining, segregation, and systemic discrimination. While the whitewashing of history has led us to believe that, at the time, we simply didn't understand that mass incarceration does not stop crime, we always knew it wouldn't work. Black people knew that America needed an economic solution to address racial inequities. Criminologists and sociologists knew that crime is a socioeconomic phenomenon. We have always known that arresting drug dealers and drug users doesn't affect the proliferation of drugs.

We weren't buying it. In the 1980 presidential election, when the Black unemployment rate was 15.1 percent and the white unemployment rate was 6.5 percent, 56 percent of the white electorate voted for Ronald Reagan, who proposed that welfare, affirmative action, and government handouts were causing all of America's economic woes. Nine percent of Black voters cast ballots for Reagan to have a second term, which is less than the 11 percent who voted for George H. W. Bush in 1988. In 1992, when Bill Clinton was elected, he won 83 percent of the Black vote but only 39 percent of the white vote. Clinton vowed to address racial disparities, but because the Blame Black People philosophy had become so enshrined in white identity politics, Clinton rejected progressive ideas in favor of the narrative that had become political fact: fix Black people and you can fix racism. By the presidential election of 2000, only 9 percent of Black voters voted for George W. Bush.[4] After Bush completed two terms as president, in 2008, America came up with a new solution.

Let's try a Black guy.

When Barack Obama declared his presidential campaign, all the racism you read about in previous chapters emerged. A furious search for his birth certificate was premised on the claim that he was secretly an immigrant from Africa. He had to resign from Trinity United Church of Christ, where his pastor, Reverend Jeremiah Wright, a graduate of historically Black Howard University who served in the Marine Corps and the navy, preached radical "Black liberation theology." Obama was accused of being a Muslim, consorting with radical left-wing extremists, and being anti-white. He was not a "real" American. His church was plotting against white people. He was a carpetbagger.

To America, Barack Obama was, and will always be, a "Black president."

And with him came some crazy ideas. If one were to catalog all the progressive ideas that have become mainstream over the past fifty years, they are just recycled versions of proposals that Black people have championed and White America has rejected. When the U.S. Department of Agriculture made its School Breakfast Program permanent in 1975, the Black Panthers had been doing it for a decade as part of their ten-point program that included:

- Land cooperatives using government aid to provide adequate housing.
- An education system "that teaches us our true history and our role in the present-day society."
- An end to police brutality.
- Criminal justice reform and an end to mass incarceration.
- Full employment.

It wasn't just the Black Panthers. Before his death, Martin Luther King Jr.'s Poor People's Campaign advocated for full employment and an early version of Universal Basic Income that has now become popular. The platform for Jesse Jackson's 1988 presidential campaign included provisions for LGBT rights, increasing infrastructure spending, reprioritizing the war on drugs, taxing the wealthiest 10 percent, free community college, reparations, universal health care, and voting rights reform. The only meaningful gun control legislation ever passed in America came at the behest of the Congressional Black Caucus, who opposed the 1993 crime bill, offering an alternative version that addressed the cocaine epidemic with drug treatment, asked for $3 billion for early crime intervention, and included the Racial Justice Act to highlight and solve the disparities in sentencing.[5]

These requests were considered too radical back then, because we had already decided that something was wrong with Black people. Therefore, America's racial problem could easily be solved if Black people just focused on themselves. Meanwhile, White America could help Black people by locking up criminals in the Black communities that emerged as a result of redlining and segregation, telling them how to focus on education in the unequal schools that Jim Crow built, and showing them how to pull themselves up by the bootstraps that white people bought with New Deal dollars.

Unfortunately, Barack Obama couldn't fix America.

By simply being the Black president, he became the symbol for what America could achieve. Even if most white people didn't vote for Barack Obama, "I voted for Obama" has become the rallying cry for people who believe in a post-racial America. The fact that his tenure as head of state did not reverse four hundred years of entrenched white supremacy shows that he was just a president. But while there are valid criticisms of Obama's two administrations from Black and white, liberal and conservative, perhaps his most important legacy is that the result of his presidency proved that there is nothing wrong with Black people.

There is something wrong with America.

Eight years, two months, and sixteen days after the election of Barack Obama, Donald J. Trump became president of the United

States of America. If one were to create a sentient being out of America's past and present, it would look like Donald Trump. It would hate anyone who is not white. It would believe itself to be an infallible "stable genius." It would hide secrets. It would whitewash its past. It would lie incessantly. It would rip brown babies from their mothers' arms. It would criminalize Muslims. It would mirror the intellect and sentiment of the vast majority of people who fill the country from sea to shining sea.

Donald Trump is America.

Donald Trump is a rich, powerful man who has convinced the world that his empire was earned through hard work, not a sordid past that includes, but is not limited to, taking advantage of his privilege. He made his fortune like America made its fortune: taking land, profiting off financial malfeasance, conning the masses, and refusing to pay Black and brown people for their work. He became the world's most powerful man in the world's most powerful country through a system that rewards white men for being white men. He has no particular intelligence or expertise, yet he has convinced his poor Caucasian co-conspirators that the only way they can succeed is by placing their foot on the neck of the people who don't look like them. The brown people. The Black people. The non-Christians.

Isn't that the most American idea of them all?

And like America, most people were willing to ignore his racism for the sake of self-preservation. Unlike the white people who claimed Obama was proof of a post-racial America even though most white voters didn't vote for him, Trump voters proudly admit that they cast their ballots for an unapologetic bigot just like the white supremacists of Reconstruction and the white nationalists of the civil rights era proudly proclaimed their objections to racial equality. They overlooked the inherent evil of his immigration policy, his fight against Critical Race Theory, and his championing of whiteness just like this country overlooked Jim Crow, segregation, lynching, and the evil that remains in every sector of society. They have forgotten how Trump excused a white supremacist murder in Charlottesville, Virginia, just like America excuses white supremacy as an institutional reality.

And he lies . . . like America lies.

Despite what the numbers say, he claimed his inauguration was the biggest inauguration in the history of inaugurations. He claimed he passed more legislation than any president ever. He said he won the Electoral College by a record amount. He said he was reelected. Truth be damned; facts didn't matter.

And according to Trump, America is the greatest country on earth, despite what the numbers say. We are a beacon of freedom and liberty even though we rank first in the world's prison population. We are the smartest nation in the world, despite ranking fourteenth in education and second in ignorance. We believe in equality and tolerance, despite ranking number one on the list of the most racist countries in the world.

See? I told you we were number one.

Trump promised he would fix our health care system, like America has been telling us for decades, but he made it worse. He preached prosperity for the middle class but his policies benefited the wealthy. He promised peace but started petty conflicts around the world. And just like this country has done since its inception, America is all too willing to remain blind to his transgressions, even with definitive proof. This country was willing to watch Trump and his minion of secondhand liars tell bald-faced lies to the American public without penalty.

And *that* is America.

Like its history, this nation is a mirage. Its greatness is a figment of a collective white imagination that envisions a bright, shining star where there is only a dumpster fire. America is a con artist. It is a counterfeit farce of a white country convinced of its own supremacy. It is a boot on every Black throat and noose on every negro neck.

Yet we remain.

Like the perseverance that overcomes white supremacy. Like the love that conquers hate. Like the truth that outshines injustice. Like the backs and hands and muscles and minds of the beloved Black diaspora that will collectively build this imperfect union into a home. If this nation ever truly becomes a post-racial society with liberty and justice for all, let the history of Black people in America reflect:

We were doing it first.

THREE LITTLE QUESTIONS

1. **Racism ended when . . .**
   a. The Thirteenth Amendment ended slavery.
   b. Congress passed the Civil Rights Act.
   c. Obama became president.
   d. America had a racial reckoning in 2020.

2. **What is the biggest myth in American history?**
   a. White supremacy.
   b. America is a democracy.
   c. "Liberty and justice for all."
   d. The "history" part.

3. **What is the main difference between "American history" and "Black history"?**
   a. Who writes the books.
   b. Same difference between fact and fiction.
   c. Black history is American history.
   d. There is no such thing as America.

ACTIVITY

FINAL EXAM

Create a "post-racial America."

ACKNOWLEDGMENTS

I did not write this book.

Everything that I am is because of Dorothy Harriot, who filled my heart, mind, and lungs with the stories of the living and the memories of the ancestors whose stories fill the pages of this book. The hands, souls, and elbows that shaped me into whatever I am or will become belong to the people of Hartsville, South Carolina. The teachers and the dope boys. The street scholars and the preachers. The dirt under the fingernails of factory workers and the cookies I bought from candy ladies. They gave me stuff and taught me things. They prayed for me. I belong to them. I *am them.*

This book would not be possible without the scholarship, guidance, and patience of Blair Kelley, whose syllabus provided the template for the storytelling contained in this project. Tanya McKinnon made me believe this was possible and Kate Napolitano shared my vision for a book about Black people. By creating Knubia and Knarrative, Dr. Greg Carr and Karen Hunter unknowingly served as my mentors. Kawan J. Allen's research and fact-checking were immeasurably valuable and Jibola Fagbamiye's art breathed life into the pages. I hope any judgment of this book lives up to Sarah Huny Young's cover design. Jenny Xu and Stuart Roberts stepped in and kept me on task.

I also thank my sisters, Comelita, Seandra, Robin, and Nikey; my aunts, Jannie, Marvell, Phyllis, Earlene, and Joyce; my uncles, Rob and James; my cousins, nieces, nephews, and all the extended members of the Harriot family for at least pretending to listen to my stories before they made it to a page. Anicca, Charles, and Josephine had no choice.

And Black people.
We wrote this book.
We *are this book.*
K

WORKS NOT CITED

BLACK AF HISTORY HACKS

We're not doing the "works cited" thing (there's a whole section of endnotes).

However, I often receive requests, tweets, and emails asking about books people should read if they want to know more about Black history, to which I usually reply: "All of them." If you, like me, don't have the time to read every book that was ever written, here are some specific works, databases, and publicly available resources that aided in the research for this book, even if they were not directly cited. Not only will these help you gain a deeper understanding about the past, they also offer an unwhitewashed version of Black America's untold story.

TEN ESSENTIAL BOOKS

Lerone Bennett. *Before the Mayflower: A History of the Negro in America, 1619–1962.* Eastford, CT: Martino Fine Books, 2016.

Keisha N. Blain, Ibram X. Kendi, eds. *Four Hundred Souls: A Community History of African America, 1619–2019.* New York: Random House, 2021.

Frantz Fanon. *The Wretched of the Earth.* New York: Grove Press, 1963.

Ibram X. Kendi. *Stamped from the Beginning: The Definitive History of Racist Ideas in America.* New York: PublicAffairs, 2016.

Middleton A. Harris, Morris Levitt, Roger Furman, Ernest Smith. *The Black Book.* New York: Random House, 2019.

Ivan Van Sertima. *They Came Before Columbus: The African Presence in Ancient America.* New York: Random House, 2003.

Gerald Horne. *The Apocalypse of Settler Colonialism: The Roots of Slavery, White Supremacy, and Capitalism in Seventeenth-Century North America and the Caribbean.* New York: Monthly Review Press, 2018.

John Hope Franklin. *Reconstruction after the Civil War.* Chicago: University of Chicago Press, 1961.

Ronald W. Waters. *Pan Africanism in the African Diaspora: An Analysis of Modern Afrocentric Political Movements.* Detroit, MI: Wayne State University Press, 1997.

Rayford W. Logan. *The Negro in American Life and Thought: The Nadir, 1877–1901.* New York: Dial Press, 1954.

ONLINE RESOURCES

I don't know if you've heard about this thing called the internet, but it's a great source for digging into history. Instead of simply googling a fact, investigate these sites:

- **BLACK NEWSPAPERS:** Google News, Newspapers.com, and a number of individual newspaper publishers offer digitized archives of Black newspapers that date as far back as the 1700s. Not only can you find the primary source, you can also read the contemporaneous reports of Black journalists.
- **U.S. CENSUS BUREAU:** The census doesn't just count people, it records financial data, geographic information, and voting data that create statistical snapshots of the past.
- **LIBRARY OF CONGRESS:** Read firsthand narratives of people who survived enslavement from the Federal Writers' Project. Listen to recordings of a Frederick Douglass speech. Hear an old blues recording. And it's free!
- **NATIONAL ARCHIVES:** You can download slave schedules, birth certificates, military records, and digitized transcripts from the Freedmen's Bureau archives.
- **ARCHIVE.ORG:** This is a valuable research tool that allows users to borrow out-of-print writings, old encyclopedias, and school textbooks.
- **TRANSATLANTIC SLAVE TRADE DATABASE:** Originally a CD-ROM, this online repository contains information on more

than 35,000 human trafficking expeditions that carried more than 12 million Africans to the Americas between 1520 and 1866.

- **GENEALOGY WEBSITES:** For-profit ancestry companies don't just do DNA tests. Many have created online access to birth records, death certificates, wills, newspapers, and other resources.

BLACK HISTORY TREASURE TROVES

Black history doesn't just live in books; it's all around you, waiting to be excavated. Some of the lesser-known hiding places include:

- **OTHER BOOKSTORES:** Many Black-owned, independent, and secondhand bookstores stock books that large chains usually overlook. Some will even have self-published works by local authors that were never available nationwide.
- **COLLEGES AND UNIVERSITIES:** Institutions of higher learning often invest in special collections and archives that preserve important documents and historical records. Many also host free lectures and events that are open to the public.
- **MUSEUMS:** Never leave a historical site without visiting the gift shop. You'll find art, audio recordings, oral histories, and research from people who may not be nationally recognized.
- **COURTHOUSES:** Every county's clerk of court is a treasure chest of history. Aside from wills, birth records, and death certificates, local governments archive proclamations, deeds to real estate, and transactions from the sale of human property.
- **BIG "SECOND" CHURCHES:** In most towns, the "First" church of a particular denomination is usually the white church. Any large church whose name includes the word "Second" probably has a Black congregation that formed pre-

emancipation or shortly thereafter (AME churches are the exception). If you attend one of these churches, I'd bet your tithes and offerings there's a repository the deacons simply call "the files" that contains more history than the average museum.

- **YE OLDE ANTIQUE SHOPPE:** Besides the teakettles and Confederate relics, many antique shops also have diaries, photos, and first-edition books by Black authors that are often overlooked by white collectors.
- **ANCESTORS AND ELDERS:** Your deceased grandmother's attic is a museum. The stories your great-uncle has told too many times are part of an oral tradition. Your family's Bibles, diaries, and old letters are historical documents.
- **WHITE LIES:** Whenever you encounter a weirdly specific anti-Black law, rumors of a place where Black people aren't allowed, an account of a "race riot," or any story about Black people that seems kinda semi-racist, there's probably some whitewashed history hiding somewhere in there.

ENDNOTES

Introduction

1. W. E. B. Du Bois, *The Souls of Black Folk* (First Avenue classics) (Minneapolis: First Avenue Editions, 2016).
2. Carter G. Woodson, *The Mis-Education of the Negro* (Washington, D.C.: Associated Publishers, 1933), p. 1.

Chapter 1: Earth, Wind, and America

1. Lerone Bennett, *Before the Mayflower: A History of Black America*, 4th ed. (Eastford, CT: Martino Fine Books, 1969).
2. Stanford E. Lehmberg, *The Reformation Parliament, 1529–1536* (Cambridge: Cambridge University Press, 1970).
3. UVA, *First Charter of Virginia* (Ipswich, MA: Great Neck Publishing, 2017).
4. John Smith, *The generall historie of Virginia, New-England, and the Summer Isles* (March of America facsimile series) (Ann Arbor, MI: University Microfilms, 1966).
5. *The Complete Works of John Smith (1580–1631)*, ed. Philip L. Barbour (Chapel Hill: The University of North Carolina Press, 1983), vol. 1, p. 53.
6. Helen C. Rountree, *Pocahontas, Powhatan, Opechancanough: Three Indian Lives Changed by Jamestown* (Charlottesville: University of Virginia Press, 2005), p. 113.
7. Paula Neely, "Jamestown Colonists Resorted to Cannibalism," *National Geographic*, 2013, www.nationalgeographic.com/science/article/130501 -jamestown-cannibalism-archeology-science; Joseph Stromberg, "Starving Settlers in Jamestown Colony Resorted to Cannibalism," *Smithsonian Magazine*, April 30, 2013, www.smithsonianmag.com/history/starving-settlers -in-jamestown-colony-resorted-to-cannibalism-46000815/.
8. Warren M. Billings, ed., *The Old Dominion in the Seventeenth Century: A Documentary History of Virginia, 1606–1700*, revised ed. (Chapel Hill: University of North Carolina Press, 2007), pp. 270–74; from Ralph Hamor, *A True Discourse of the Present Estate of Virginia, and the Success of the Affaires There till the 18 of June 1614* (London, 1615), pp. 61–68.
9. John Rolfe, *The Thomas Jefferson Papers Series 8*, Virginia Records Manuscripts, 1606–1737; Susan Myra Kingsbury, ed., *Records of the Virginia Company, 1606–1626*, vol. 3, pp. 241–42, 243–45, 247–48.

Chapter 2: The Church Fight That Started Slavery

1. Callixtus II, *Pope Callixtus II: Concerning Spain* (Vatican, 1123).

2. P. E. Russell, *Prince Henry "the Navigator": A Life* (New Haven, CT: Yale University Press, 2000), p. 84.

3. Joaquim Romero Magahães, "Africans, Indians, and Slavery in Portugal," *Portuguese Studies* 13 (1997): 143–51, www.jstor.org/stable/41105067.

4. Alastair Corston de Custance Maxwell Saunders, *A Social History of Black Slaves and Freedmen in Portugal, 1441–1555* (Cambridge: Cambridge University Press, 1982), pp. 19–21.

5. Christopher Columbus, *First Voyage to America: From the Log of the "Santa Maria"* (Mineola, NY: Dover Publications, 1991), p. 87.

6. Felipe Fernández-Arnesto, *Amerigo: The Man Who Gave His Name to America* (New York: Random House, 2008), p. 52.

7. Robert M. Poole, "What Became of the Taíno?," *Smithsonian Magazine*, October 2011.

Supplement: Before "Before"

1. Ricardo E. Alegría, *Juan Garrido, el Conquistador Negro en las Antillas, Florida, México y California, c. 1503–1540* (San Juan, PR: Centro de Estudios Avanzados de Puerto Rico y El Caribe, 1990), pp. 6, 127–38.

2. Ibid.

3. Douglas T. Peck, *Ponce de León and the Discovery of Florida: The Man, the Myth and the Truth* (St. Paul, MN: Pogo Press, 1993), p. 23.

4. Robert H. Fuson, *Juan Ponce de León and the Discovery of Puerto Rico and Florida* (Blacksburg, VA: McDonald & Woodward Publishing, 2000), pp. 121–39.

5. Michael Grunwald, *The Swamp: The Everglades, Florida and the Politics of Paradise* (New York: Simon & Schuster, 2007), pp. 25–26.

6. Kurt Johansson and Karin Solveig Bjornson, *Genocide and Gross Human Rights Violations: In Comparative Perspective* (Piscataway, NJ: Transaction Publishers, 1999), p. 202.

7. Dora Beale Polk, *The Island of California: A History of the Myth* (Lincoln: University of Nebraska Press, 1995), p. 22.

8. Matthew Restall, "The African Experience in Early Spanish America," *The Americas* 57, issue 2 (October 2000): 171–205.

9. Gillian Brockell, "Before 1619, There Was 1526: The Mystery of the First Enslaved Africans in What Became the United States," *Washington Post*, September 7, 2019, https://www.washingtonpost.com/history/2019/09/07/before-there-was-mystery-first-enslaved-africans-what-became-us/.

10. Dennis Herrick, *Esteban: The African Slave Who Explored America* (Albuquerque: University of New Mexico Press, 2018), p. 11.

11. Álvar Núñez Cabeza de Vaca, trans. and annotated by Martin Favata and José Fernández, *The Account: Álvar Núñez Cabeza de Vaca's "Relación"* (Recovering the U.S. Hispanic Literary Heritage) (Houston: Arte Publico Press, 1993), p. 18.

12. Ibid.

13. Herrick, *Esteban*, p. 77.

14. Ibid., pp. 84–85.

15. "The Viceroy's Letter to the King, April 17, 1540," in Richard Flint and Shirley Cushing Flint, eds., trans., and annotated, *Documents of the Coronado Expedition, 1539–1542* (Albuquerque: University of New Mexico Press, 2012), p. 240.

16. Lhoussain Simour, "(De)slaving History: Mostafa al-Azemmouri, the Sixteenth -Century Moroccan Captive in the Tale of Conquest," *European Review of History* 20, issue 3 (June 2013): 345–65, http://dx.doi.org/10.1080/13507486 .2012.745830.

17. Joe Sando, *Pueblo Nations: Eight Centuries of Pueblo Indian History* (Santa Fe, NM: Clear Light Publishing, 1992), p. 86.

Chapter 3: The World, Recentered

1. Virginia Company of London, "'Instructions to George Yeardley' by the Virginia Company of London (November 18, 1618)," *Encyclopedia Virginia*, https:// encyclopediavirginia.org/entries/instructions-to-george-yeardley-by-the -virginia-company-of-london-november-18-1618/.

2. Laura Croghan Kamoie, "The Negroes to Serve Forever: The Evolution of Black's Life and Labor in Seventeenth-Century Virginia" (M.A. dissertation, College of William & Mary, 1994), https://dx.doi.org/doi:10.21220/ s2-erp9-a557, p. 26.

3. General Assembly, "'Negro Womens Children to Serve According to the Condition of the Mother' (1662)," *Encyclopedia Virginia*, https:// encyclopediavirginia.org/entries/negro-womens-children-to-serve-according -to-the-condition-of-the-mother-1662.

4. U.S. Census Bureau, "Colonial and Pre-Federal Statistics," www2.census.gov/ prod2/statcomp/documents/CT1970p2-13.pdf, p. 1172.

5. David Armitage, "John Locke, Carolina, and the 'Two Treatises of Government,'" *Political Theory* 32, no. 5 (2004), www.jstor.org/stable/4148117.

6. Jeffrey R. Young, "Ideology and Death on a Savannah River Rice Plantation, 1833–1867: Paternalism Amidst 'a Good Supply of Disease and Pain,'" *Journal of Southern History* 59, no. 4 (1993): 673–706, doi: 10.2307/2210538.

7. Peter A. Coclanis, "Rice," *South Carolina Enclyclopedia* (June 20, 2016), www.scencyclopedia.org/sce/entries/rice/.

8. Judith Ann Carney, *Black Rice: The African Origins of Rice Cultivation in the Americas* (Cambridge, MA: Harvard University Press, 2001), p. 84.

9. Debora Gray White, *Ar'n't I a Woman? Female Slaves in the Plantation South* (New York: W. W. Norton, 1999), pp. 64–65.

10. Alexander Moore, *Nairne's Muskhogean Journals: The 1708 Expedition to the Mississippi River* (Jackson: University of Mississippi Press, 1988).

11. Carney, *Black Rice*, p. 107.

12. Robert Francis Withers Allston, *The South Carolina Rice Plantation as Revealed in the Papers of Robert F. W. Allston* (Columbia: University of South Carolina Press, 2004), pp. 316, 326.

13. Peter Wood, *Black Majority* (New York: Knopf Doubleday Publishing Group, 2012), p. 94.
14. Gary S. Dunbar, "Colonial Carolina Cowpens," *Agricultural History* 35, no. 3 (1961): 127–28, www.jstor.org/stable/3740623.
15. Julian Mason, "The Etymology of 'Buckaroo,'" *American Speech* 35, no. 1 (February 1960): 51–55.
16. Dunbar, "Colonial Carolina Cowpens."
17. Young, "Ideology and Death on a Savannah River Rice Plantation."
18. Philip D. Morgan, "Work and Culture: The Task System and the World of Lowcountry Blacks, 1700 to 1880," *William and Mary Quarterly* 39, no. 4 (1982): 564–99, doi: 10.2307/1919004.
19. Robert M. Weir, *Colonial South Carolina: A History* (Millwood, NY: KTO Press, 1983).
20. "Slaves Imported into Charleston, S.C., by Origin, 1706 to 1775," "Colonial and Pre-Federal Statistics," U.S. Census Bureau, p. 1173, www2.census.gov/prod2/statcomp/documents/CT1970p2-13.pdf.
21. Weir, *Colonial South Carolina*, p. 175.
22. Joshua Coffin, *An Account of Some of the Principal Slave Insurrections, and Others, Which Have Occurred, or Been Attempted, in the United States and Elsewhere, During the Last Two Centuries. With Various Remarks* (New York: American Anti-slavery Society, 1860), www.loc.gov/item/10032268/.
23. Ibid.
24. William Rawlin, "No. 329. An Act for the Governing of Negroes (10 July 1688)," in *The Laws of Barbados Collected in One Volume by William Rawlin, of the Middle-Temple, London, Esquire, and Now Clerk of the Assembly of the Said Island*, University of Michigan Library, Early English Books Online Text Creation Partnership, https://quod.lib.umich.edu/e/eebo2/A30866.0001.001/1:8.281?rgn=div2;view=fulltext.

Box: Ana Nzinga: The King of Queens

1. Beth Austin, "1619: Virginia's First Africans," Hampton History Museum, December 2018, https://hampton.gov/DocumentCenter/View/24075/1619-Virginias-First-Africans?bidId=.
2. Iyabode Omolara Akewo Daniel, "How Did We Get Here? A Historical Profile of the African Woman," *Gender & Behaviour* 14, no. 3 (2016): 7693–710.
3. "Njinga Mbandi: Queen of Ndongo and Matamba," UNESCO Digital Library, https://unesdoc.unesco.org/ark:/48223/pf0000230103.

Supplement: The Unenslaving of Jemmy

1. Russell Menard, "Slave Demography in the Lowcountry, 1670–1740: From Frontier Society to Plantation Regime," *South Carolina Historical Magazine* 101, no. 3 (July 2000): 190–213.

2. Mark Smith, *Stono: Documenting and Interpreting a Southern Slave Revolt* (Columbia: University of South Carolina Press, 2005), p. 63.

Box: How White People Were Invented

1. W. E. B. Du Bois, *The Souls of Black Folk* (First Avenue Classics) (Minneapolis: First Avenue Editions, 2016), p. 24.
2. Gregory Jay, "Who Invented White People? A Talk on the Occasion of Martin Luther King Day," https://web.archive.org/web/20070502063801/http://www .uwm.edu/~gjay/Whiteness/Whitenesstalk.html.
3. William Waller Hening, ed., *The Statutes at Large; Being a Collection of All the Laws of Virginia from the First Session of the Legislature, in the Year 1619* (Philadelphia: R. & W. & G. Bartow, 1823), vol. 3, pp. 447–63.
4. James Madison, *The Debates in the Federal Convention of 1787, which framed the Constitution of the United States of America, reported by James Madison, a delegate from the state of Virginia*, eds. Gaillard Hund and James Brown Scott (Oxford: Oxford University Press, 1920).
5. "Debate in Virginia Ratifying Convention, Article 1, Section 8, Clause 12," http://press-pubs.uchicago.edu/founders/documents/a1_8_12s27.html.
6. *Reports of the proceedings and debates of the convention of 1821, assembled for the purpose of amending the constitution of the state of New York: containing all the official documents, relating to the subject, and other valuable matter. By Nathaniel H. Carter and William L. Stone, reporters; and Marcus T. C. Gould, stenographer*, New York (State) Constitutional Convention, Carter, Nathaniel Hazeltine, 1795–1849, Stone, William L. (William Leete), 1792–1844.
7. Ibid.
8. Roger Brooke Taney and Supreme Court of the United States, "U.S. Reports: *Dred Scott v. Sandford*, 60 U.S. (19 How.) 393 (1856)," Library of Congress, www.loc.gov/item/usrep060393a/.

Chapter 4: Survival and Resistance: The Black American Revolution

1. George van Cleve, "'Somerset's Case' and Its Antecedents in Imperial Perspective," *Law and History Review* 24, no. 3 (2006), www.jstor.org/ stable/27641404.
2. Ruth Holmes Whitehead, *Black Loyalists: Southern Settlers of Nova Scotia's First Free Black Communities* (Halifax, NS: Nimbus Publishing, 2014), p. 115.
3. Gerald Horne, *The Counter-Revolution of 1776: Slave Resistance and the Origin of the United States of America* (New York: MJF Books, 2018), p. 211.
4. Jack Newlon, Rob Spooner, and Alicia Spooner, "Continental Army," U-S -History.com, www.u-s-history.com/pages/h3996.html.
5. *By his Execellency the Right Honourable John Earl of Dunmore, his Majesty's Lieutenant and Governour-General of the Colony and Dominion of Virginia, and Vice-admiral of the same. A proclamation Declaring martial law and to cause the same to be*, Norfolk, Virginia, 1775.

6. Catherine Reef, *African Americans in the Military* (New York: Facts on File, 2010), p. 229.

7. Graham Russell Hodges, *Slavery, Freedom and Culture Among Early American Workers* (Armonk, NY: M. E. Sharpe, 1998), p. 45.

8. Ray Raphael, *Founding Myths: Stories That Hide Our Patriotic Past* (New York: New Press, 2004), p. 185.

9. "The Philipsburg Proclamation," archived from the original on November 17, 2007, www.blackloyalist.com/canadiandigitalcollection/story/revolution/philipsburg.htm.

10. Peter Kolchin, *American Slavery: 1619–1877* (New York: Hill & Wang, 1994), p. 73.

11. Boston King, "Memoirs of the Life of Boston King, a Black Preacher," *Methodist Magazine* (March 1798, April 1798).

12. Raphael, *Founding Myths*, p. 188.

13. George Washington Williams, *History of the Negro Race in America*, 2 vols. (New York: Bergman Publishers, 1968), p. 384.

14. W. E. B. Du Bois, *The Gift of Black Folk: The Negroes in the Making of America* (New York: AMS Press, 1971), p. 82.

15. W. E. B. Du Bois, *The Souls of Black Folk* (First Avenue classics) (Minneapolis: First Avenue Editions, 2016), 82.

Supplement: Fear of a Black Nation

1. Alfred W. Crosby, *The Columbian Exchange: Biological and Cultural Consequences of 1492*, 30th anniversary ed. (Westport, CT: Greenwood, 2003), p. 194.

2. Ibid.

3. Adelaide C. Hill, "Revolution in Haiti, 1791 to 1820," *Présence Africaine*, Nouvelle série, no. 20 (juin-juillet 1958): 5–24.

4. Douglas Kierdof, "Getting to Know the Know-Nothings," *Boston Globe*, January 10, 2016.

5. Carolyn E. Fick, *The Making of Haiti: The Saint Domingue Revolution from Below* (Knoxville: University of Tennessee Press, 1990), p. 93.

6. Nick Nesbitt, *Universal Emancipation: The Haitian Revolution and the Radical Enlightenment* (Charlottesville: University of Virginia Press, 2008), pp. 202–3.

7. James Perry, *Arrogant Armies: Great Military Disasters and the Men Behind Them* (Edison, NJ: Castle Books, 2005), p. 83.

8. Joan Dayan, *Haiti, History and the Gods* (Berkeley and Los Angeles: University of California Press, 1998), p. 5.

Chapter 5: Drapetomaniacs: Get Free or Die Trying

1. William H. Holcombe, "Yellow Fever Made Contagious by Fear—Its Moral Treatment," *Clinical Reporter*, no. 11 (November 1888): 321.

2. Samuel A. Cartwright, "Report on the Diseases and Physical Peculiarities of the Negro Race," *New Orleans Medical and Surgical Journal* (May 1851): 691–715.

3. Samantha Smalls, *Behind Workhouse Walls: The Public Regulation of Slavery in*

Charleston, 1730–1850 (Durham, NC: Duke University Press, 2015), https://hdl
.handle.net/10161/11394.

4. Anonymous, "Recollections of Slavery by a Runaway Slave," *The Emancipator*,
   August 23, 1838.

5. Ronald H. Bayer, *The Columbia Documentary History of Race and Ethnicity in
   America* (New York: Columbia University Press, 2004), p. 60; "Burned at the
   Stake (1681)," Celebrate Boston, www.celebrateboston.com/crime/puritan
   -burned-at-stake-maria.htm.

6. Eugene Frazier, *A History of James Island Slave Descendants and Plantation
   Owners: The Bloodline* (Charleston, SC: History Press, 2010), p. 88.

7. Octavia V. Rogers Albert, *The House of Bondage; or, Charlotte Brooks and
   Other Slaves*, The Black Heritage Library Collection (Freeport, NY: Books for
   Libraries Press, 1972).

8. Daniel O. Sayers, *A Desolate Place for a Defiant People: The Archaeology of
   Maroons, Indigenous Americans, and Enslaved Laborers in the Great Dismal
   Swamp* (Gainesville: University Press of Florida, 2014), p. 24, www.jstor.org/
   stable/j.ctvx073z9.

9. Timothy James Lockley, *Maroon Communities in South Carolina: A
   Documentary Record* (Columbia: University of South Carolina Press, 1998),
   p. 98.

10. Arna Alexander Bontemps, *The Punished Self: Surviving Slavery in the Colonial
    South* (Ithaca, NY: Cornell University Press, 2008), p. 98.

11. "Chatham County Superior Court Minutes," *Chatham Gazette*, October 19, 1786.

12. William Spivey, "Partus Sequitur Ventrem—The Rule That Perpetrated Slavery
    and Legalized Rape," *Dialogue and Discourse*, Medium, October 5, 2019,
    https://medium.com/discourse/partus-sequitur-ventrem-the-rule-that
    -perpetrated-slavery-and-legalized-rape-e3c423692bc2.

13. Georgia Writers Project, *Drums and Shadows: Survival Studies Among the
    Georgia Coastal Negroes* (Athens: University of Georgia Press, 1986),
    pp. 150–51.

14. Michael Coard, "Anniversary of Historic, Courageous 'Igbo Landing,'"
    Philadelphia Tribune, May 4, 2020.

15. Mark Reinhardt, *Who Speaks for Margaret Garner? The True Story That Inspired
    Toni Morrison's "Beloved"* (Minneapolis: University of Minnesota Press, 2010),
    p. 642.

16. J. Brent Morris, "'The Celebrated Bandit Joe': Uncovering Forest Joe's
    Lowcountry Maroon Campaign of 1821–23," speech, January 6, 2012, Chicago
    Marriott Downtown.

17. Lockley, *Maroon Communities in South Carolina*, p. 95.

18. "Acts and Resolutions of the General Assembly," 1822, no. 46; verbatim copy
    to the Senate, 1822, no. 65, South Carolina archives.

19. Southern Patriot, *Charleston City Gazette*, November 2, 1822.

20. Lockley, *Maroon Communities in South Carolina*, p. 97.

21. Ibid., p. 114.

22. Gary Potter, "The History of Policing in the United States, Part 1," June 25, 2013, EKU Online, https://plsonline.eku.edu/insidelook/history-policing-united-states-part-1; Olivia B. Waxman, "The History of Police in America and the First Force," *Time*, March 6, 2017, 38.

23. South Carolina Historical Society, Pineville Police Association Minutes, October 2, 1823.

24. Lockley, *Maroon Communities in South Carolina*, pp. 110–11.

25. Olivia B. Waxman, "How the U.S. Got Its Police Force," *Time*, May 18, 2017, https://time.com/4779112/police-history-origins/.

26. Lockley, *Maroon Communities in South Carolina*, p. 109.

Supplement: To Kill Whites

1. Daniel Rasmussen, *American Uprising: The Untold Story of America's Largest Slave Revolt*, 1st ed. (New York: Harper, 2011), p. 32.

2. Ibid.

3. Peter Linebaugh and Marcus Rediker, *The Many-Headed Hydra: Sailors, Slaves, Commoners, and the Hidden History of the Revolutionary Atlantic* (New York: Verso, 2000).

4. Louisiana St. Charles Parish, Original Acts, Book 41, 1811, #2, pp. 17–20.

5. Simon Schama, *Citizens: A Chronicle of the French Revolution*, 1st ed. (New York: Knopf, 1989).

6. *Original Acts*, Act 17, 20 February 1811, Book 1810–1811.

Chapter 6: The Negro, Spiritual

1. "There Is a Balm in Gilead," traditional African American spiritual.

2. Steve Crowder, "Black Folk Medicine in Southern Appalachia" (M.A. thesis, East Tennessee State University, 2001), https://dc.etsu.edu/etd/149.

3. Fisk University Jubilee Quartet, John Wesley Work, Alfred Garfield King, Noah Walker Ryder, and J. A Myers, "I Couldn't Hear Nobody Pray" (1909), audio: www.loc.gov/item/jukebox-128142/.

4. UVA, *First Charter of Virginia* (Ipswich, MA: Great Neck Publishing, 2017), http://RE5QY4SB7X.search.serialssolutions.com/?V=1.0&L=RE5QY4SB7X&S=JCs&C=TC0001897342&T=marc.

5. William Henry Whitmore, *The Colonial Laws of Massachusetts: Reprinted from the Edition of 1672 with the Supplements Through 1686: Containing Also a Bibliographical Preface and Introduction Treating of All the Printed Laws from 1649 to 1686: Together with the Body of Liberties of 1641, and the Records of the Court of Assistants, 1641–1644* (Boston: Rockwell and Churchill, city printers, 1890), p. 53.

6. Leviticus 25:42–46 (King James Version).

7. Octavia V. Rogers Albert, *The House of Bondage* (New York: Cosimo Classics, 2005), p. 66. Originally published by Oxford University Press in 1890.

8. Charles Ball, *Slavery in the United States. A Narrative of the Life and*

Adventures of Charles Ball, a Black Man, Who Lived Forty Years in Maryland, South Carolina and Georgia, as a Slave Under Various Masters, and Was One Year in the Navy with Commodore Barney, During the Late War, electronic ed. (Chapel Hill: University of North Carolina Press, 1999).

9. Sylviane A. Diouf, "Muslims in America, A Forgotten History," Al-Jazeera, February 10, 2021.

10. *Drums and Shadows*, Georgia Writers' Project (Works Progress Administration, 1940), p. 211.

11. "'An act declaring that baptisme of slaves doth not exempt them from bondage' (1667)," *Encyclopedia Virginia*, https://encyclopediavirginia.org/entries/an-act-declaring-that-baptisme-of-slaves-doth-not-exempt-them-from-bondage-1667/.

12. Charles Colcock Jones, *The Religious Instruction of the Negroes in the United States* (Savannah, GA: Thomas Purse Publisher, 1842), p. 103.

13. Michel Martin, "Slave Bible from the 1800s Omitted Key Passages That Could Incite Rebellion," *All Things Considered*, NPR, December 9, 2018, www.npr.org/2018/12/09/674995075/slave-bible-from-the-1800s-omitted-key-passages-that-could-incite-rebellion.

14. W. E. B. Du Bois, *Black Folk Then and Now* (The Oxford W. E. B. Du Bois) (New York: Oxford University Press, 2007), p. 142.

15. Eugene Frazier, *A History of James Island Slave Descendants and Plantation Owners: The Bloodline* (Charleston, SC: History Press, 2010), p. 144.

16. Steven Mintz, "Historical Context: The Constitution and Slavery," Gilder Lehrman Institute of American History, www.gilderlehrman.org/history-resources/teaching-resource/historical-context-constitution-and-slavery#:~:text=Of%20the%2055%20delegates%20to,members%20of%20anti%2Dslavery%20societies.

17. Richard Allen, *A Narrative of the Proceedings of the Black People During the Late Awful Calamity in Philadelphia, in the Year 1793: And a Refutation of Some Censures, Thrown upon Them in Some Late Publications* (Philadelphia: Printed for the authors, by William W. Woodward, at Franklin's Head, no. 41, Chestnut Street, 1794), https://archive.org/details/2559020R.nlm.nih.gov/mode/2up.

18. William Goodell, *The American Slave Code in Theory and Practice*, pt. 2 (New York: American & Foreign Anti-Slavery Society, 1853), https://archive.org/details/americanslavecod00lcgood/mode/2up.

19. Thomas Jefferson, *Notes on the State of Virginia*, 1st hot-pressed ed. (Philadelphia: R. T. Rawle, publisher, John Thompson, printer, 1801), p. 144.

20. Frederick Douglass, *The Life and Times of Frederick Douglass: From 1817–1882* (London: Christian Age Office, 1882), p. 50.

21. David Walker, *David Walker's Appeal to the Coloured Citizens of the World* (N.p.: Ravenio Books, 2000), pp. 37, 73.

22. William Still, "Trial of the Emancipators of Col. J.H. Wheeler's Slaves, Jane Johnson and her Two Little Boys," in *The Underground Railroad* (Philadelphia: Porter & Coates, 1872), pp. 94–95.

23. Robert L. Harris Jr., "Charleston's Free Afro-American Elite: The Brown

Fellowship Society and the Humane Brotherhood," *South Carolina Historical Magazine* 82, no. 4 (1981): 93.

24. "Row over Statue to Bermudian's Slave," Bernews, January 3, 2011, http://bernews.com/2011/01/row-over-statue-to-bermudians-slave/.

25. Will of James S. Bradley, Old Salem County Courthouse Records, 1851–1888.

26. Ibid.

Food Stop: The Top-Secret Recipe to Aunt Phyllis's Fried Chicken

1. John F. Mariani, *The Encyclopedia of American Food and Drink* (New York: Lebhar-Friedman, 1999), pp. 305–6.

2. Josie Dunlap, "American Fried Chicken Has Its Origins in Slavery," *The Economist*, June 2, 2021, www.economist.com/1843/2021/07/02/american -fried-chicken-has-its-origins-in-slavery.

Box: Onesimus Saves the World

1. Kathryn S. Koo, "Strangers in the House of God: Cotton Mather, Onesimus, and an Experiment in Christian Slaveholding," *Proceedings of the American Antiquarian Society* 117 (2007): 143–75.

2. Ibid., p. 148.

3. Arthur Boylston, "The Origins of Inoculation," *Journal of the Royal Society of Medicine* 105, no. 7 (2012): 309–13, doi: 10.1258/jrsm.2012.12k044.

4. Koo, "Strangers in the House of God," p. 143.

5. Ted Widmer, "How an African Slave Helped Boston Fight Smallpox," *Boston Globe*, October 12, 2014, www.bostonglobe.com/ideas/2014/10/17/how -african-slave-helped-boston-fight-smallpox/XFhsMMvTGCeV62YP0XhhZl/ story.html%C2%A0.

Chapter 7: The Black Emancipation Proclamation: A Poem

1. David W. Blight, "Lecture 2—Southern Society: Slavery, King Cotton, and Antebellum America's 'Peculiar' Region," Yale Open Courses (Yale University, 2021), https://oyc.yale.edu/history/hist-119/lecture-2.

2. Murray N. Rothbard, *The Mystery of Banking* (Auburn, AL: Ludwig von Mises Institute, 2008), p. 219.

3. Benjamin F. Hunt, "The Argument of Benj. Faneuil Hunt in the case of the arrest of the Person claiming to be a British Seaman, under the 3d section of the State Act of Dec. 1822, in relation to Negroes, &c before the Hon. Judge Johnson, Circuit Judge of the United States, for the 6th Circuit" (Charleston, 1823), in *Slavery, Race, and the American Legal System 1700–1872*, ed. Paul Finkelman (New York, 1988), vol. 2, pp. 2–3.

4. Abraham Lincoln, "A Letter from the President," *Daily National Intelligencer*, August 23, 1862.

5. Editorial, "Mr. Lincoln and Negro Equality," *New York Times*, December 28, 1860, www.nytimes.com/1860/12/28/archives/mr-lincoln-and-negro-equality.html.

6. W. E. B. Du Bois, *Black Reconstruction: An Essay Toward a History of the Part Which Black Folk Played in the Attempt to Reconstruct Democracy in America, 1860–1880*, 1st ed. (New York: Russel & Russel, 1935), p. 49.

7. Stephanie Gilbert, "The Gist of Freedom," Blogtalk Radio, www.blogtalkradio .com/thegistoffreedom/2013/01/11/rescues-boycotts-literature-black -abolitionists-chp-45.

8. "The Ordeal of Shadrach Minkins," Massachusetts Historical Society, 2018, www.longroadtojustice.org/topics/slavery/shadrach-minkins.php.

9. Unknown, "Editorial," *The Commonwealth* (Frankfort, KY), October 24, 1859.

10. Unknown, "An Underground Railway Story: How a Threatened Uprising of Slaves Was Forestalled by the Civil War," *Minneapolis Journal*, reprinted from *Denver Post*, July 4, 1901.

11. Taborian Reporter, "The Founder and Father of the International Order of Twelve, Knights and Daughters of Tabor, which Convened in Grand Session in the City Last Week—An Interesting Career," *The Freeman*, July 31, 1897.

12. Unknown, *Denver Post*, July 4, 1801.

13. Ibid.

14. J. T. Mabry, "A Week Among the Secret Societies of Iowa," *The Bystander* (Des Moines, IA), July 24, 1903.

15. Henry Louis Gates Jr., "Which Slave Sailed Himself to Freedom?," PBS, www.pbs.org/wnet/african-americans-many-rivers-to-cross/history/which -slave-sailed-himself-to-freedom/.

16. "Mr. Lincoln and Negro Equality."

17. Barbara Jeanne Fields and Ira Berlin, *The Destruction of Slavery* (Cambridge: Cambridge University Press, 1985), pp. 123–25.

18. Abraham Lincoln, "Abraham Lincoln Papers: Series 2. General Correspondence. 1858 to 1864: Abraham Lincoln to Horace Greeley, Friday (Clipping from Aug. 23, 1862, *Daily National Intelligencer*, Washington, D.C.)," www.loc.gov/item/ mal4233400/.

19. Robert L. Hayman, *The Smart Culture: Society, Intelligence, and Law* (New York: NYU Press, 2000), p. 60.

20. William A. Gladstone, *United States Colored Troops, 1863–1867* (Gettysburg, PA: Thomas Publications, 1996), p. 120.

21. Denise M. Watson, "Who Was Civil War Spy Mary Louvestre? New Research Reveals a More Complete, Complex Life Story," *Virginian-Pilot*, February 21, 2021.

22. Fred Bateman and Thomas Joseph Weiss, *A Deplorable Scarcity: The Failure of Industrialization in the Slave Economy* (Chapel Hill: University of North Carolina Press, 1981), pp. 4, 42.

23. Ta-Nehisi Coates, "What Cotton Hath Wrought," *The Atlantic*, July 30, 2010, www.theatlantic.com/personal/archive/2010/07/what-cotton-hath -wrought/60666/.

24. Stanley Turkel, *Heroes of the American Reconstruction: Profiles of Sixteen Educators, Politicians and Activists* (Jefferson, NC: McFarland, 2009), p. 136.

25. *Georgetown* (SC) *Semi Weekly Times*, November 9, 1895.

Supplement: The Lost Cause, Explained

1. "Explain Like I'm a Racist 5-Year-Old," The Root, www.theroot.com/c/explain -like-im-a-racist-5-year-old.
2. "Confederate States of America—Declaration of the Immediate Causes Which Induce and Justify the Secession of South Carolina from the Federal Union," Lillian Goldman Law Library, Yale Law School, https://avalon.law.yale.edu/19th_ century/csa_scarsec.asp.
3. Ibid.
4. Leroy Stafford Boyd, "The Original Kappa Alpha," *Banta's Greek Exchange* VIII, no. 4 (September 1919): 3.
5. "Samuel Zenas Ammen—Kappa Alpha Order," www.kappaalphaorder.org/ka /history/ammen/.
6. Taulby Edmonson, "The Campus Confederate Legacy We're Not Talking About," *Chronicle of Higher Education*, July 8, 2020.
7. Ibid.
8. Annie Cooper Burton, *The Ku Klux Klan* (Los Angeles: W. T. Potter, 1916), p. 9.
9. Karen L. Cox, *Dixie's Daughters: The United Daughters of the Confederacy and the Preservation of Confederate Culture* (Gainesville: University Press of Florida, 2003), p. 2.
10. Emily Guskin, Scott Clement, and Joe Heim, "Americans Show Spotty Knowledge About the History of Slavery but Acknowledge Its Enduring Effects," *Washington Post*, August 28, 2019, www.washingtonpost.com /education/2019/08/28/americans-show-spotty-knowledge-about-history -slavery-acknowledge-its-enduring-effects/.
11. Cameron Easley, "As Trump Defends Confederate Flag, Democratic Voters Increasingly Say It's Racist," Morning Consult, July 22, 2020, https:// morningconsult.com/2020/07/22/conferederate-flag-racism-southern-pride -polling/.
12. "Whose Heritage? Public Symbols of the Confederacy," Southern Poverty Law Center, 2016, www.splcenter.org/sites/default/files/whose-heritage-report -third-edition.pdf, p. 10.
13. Debra McKinney, "Stone Mountain: A Monumental Dilemma," *Intelligence Report*, 2018 Spring Issue (February 10, 2018), 24.
14. Jess Engebretson, "How the Birthplace of the Modern Ku Klux Klan Became the Site of America's Largest Confederate Monument," KQED, July 21, 2015, www.kqed.org/lowdown/19119/stone-mountains-hidden-history -americas-biggest-confederate-memorial-and-birthplace-of-the-modern -ku-klux-klan.
15. McKinney, "Stone Mountain."
16. Jas. B. Ramsey, "Address to the Daughters of the Confederacy," *Minutes of the Annual Convention of the United Daughters of the Confederacy, North Carolina Division*, vol. III, 1910–1913 (Raleigh, NC: Capital Printing), p. 17.
17. David Blight, *Race and Reunion: The Civil War in American Memory* (Cambridge, MA: Harvard University Press, 2001), pp. 272–73.

18. Mildred Lewis Rutherford, *A Measuring Rod to Test Text Books, and Reference Books in Schools, Colleges and Libraries* (Athens, GA: United Confederate Veterans, 1920), pp. 5–6.

19. Greg Huffman, "Twisted Sources: How Confederate Propaganda Ended Up in the South's Schoolbooks," *Facing South*, April 10, 2019, www.facingsouth.org/2019/04/twisted-sources-how-confederate-propaganda-ended-souths-schoolbooks.

20. Rex Springston, "Happy Slaves? The Peculiar Story of Three Virginia School Textbooks," *Richmond Times-Dispatch*, April 14, 2018.

21. Kathryn Tucker Windham, *Exploring Alabama* (Huntsville, AL: Strode Publishers, 1970).

Chapter 8: Construction

1. W. E. B. Du Bois, *Black Reconstruction: An Essay Toward a History of the Part Which Black Folk Played in the Attempt to Reconstruct Democracy in America, 1860–1880*, 1st ed. (New York: Russel & Russel, 1935), p. 137.

2. Eugene Frazier, *A History of James Island Slave Descendants and Plantation Owners: The Bloodline* (Charleston, SC: History Press, 2010), p. 132; Douglas Bostick, Monica Beck, and Susan Kammeraad Campbell, *Proposed Restoration and Interpretation McLeod Plantation* (James Island, SC: Sea Island Historical Society, 2000), p. 5.

3. Charles F. Kovacik and Robert E. Mason, "Changes in the South Carolina Sea Island Cotton Industry," *Southeastern Geographer* 25, no. 2 (1985), www.jstor.org/stable/44370777.

4. Frazier, *A History of James Island Slave Descendants and Plantation Owners*, p. 133.

5. Bostick, *Proposed Restoration & Interpretation McLeod Plantation*, p. 60.

6. Ibid., p. 102.

7. *Congressional Globe*, March 16, 1863, Series No. 98, Published by John C. Rives, Washington, D.C., p. 1553.

8. *Statutes at Large, Treaties, and Proclamations of the United States of America*, vol. 13 (Boston, 1866), pp. 507–9.

9. Ira Berlin, Thavolia Glymph, and Steven F. Miller, *The Wartime Genesis of Free Labor: The Lower South* (Cambridge: Cambridge University Press, 1991), pp. 331–38.

10. *Statutes at Large, Treaties, and Proclamations of the United States of America*, vol. 13 (Boston, 1866), pp. 507–9.

11. Special Field Orders No. 15, *Official Records of the American Civil War*, Series I—Military Operations, Volume XLVII, Part II, pp. 60–62.

12. National Archives, 1860 Census, South Carolina Schedule, NARA microfilm series M653, Roll 1232.

13. Douglas W. Bostick, *A Brief History of James Island: Jewel of the Sea Islands* (Charleston, SC: History Press, 2008), p. 112.

14. Du Bois, *Black Reconstruction*, p. 117.
15. Travis Dorman, "Andrew Johnson, the Impeached President Who Wanted a 'White Man's Government,'" *Knoxville News Sentinel*, July 30, 2020, www.knoxnews.com/story/news/local/tennessee/2020/07/30/andrew-johnson-impeached-president-tennessee-history/5450438002/.
16. Steven Hahn, Steven F. Miller, Susun E. O'Donovan, John C. Rodrigue, and Leslie E. Rowland, eds., *Freedom: A Documentary History of Emancipation, 1861–1867*, Series 3, vol. 1, *Land and Labor, 1865* (Cambridge: Cambridge University Press, 1982), p. 350.
17. Bostick, *A Brief History of James Island*, p. 7.
18. Dwight L. Dumond, "An Empire of Hate," *Negro Digest*, vol. XV, no. 12 (October 1966): 6.
19. Frazier, *A History of James Island Slave Descendants and Plantation Owners*, pp. 149–50.
20. Du Bois, *Black Reconstruction*, p. 117.
21. Khalilah Brown-Dean, Zoltan Hajnal, Christina Rivers, and Ismail White, *50 Years of the Voting Rights Act: The State of Race in Politics* (Joint Center for Political and Economic Studies, 2015), pp. 9–11.
22. "African American Members of Congress," United States House of Representatives, https://history.house.gov/Exhibitions-and-Publications/BAIC/Historical-Data/Black-American-Representatives-and-Senators-by-Congress/.
23. Ron Chernow, *Grant* (New York: Penguin Press, 2017), pp. 574–75.
24. Charles Snyder, "Reports of Conditions and Operations July 1865–Dec. 1866," Records of the Assistant Commissioner for the State of South Carolina, Bureau of Refugees, Freedmen and Abandoned Lands, 1865–1870, National Archives Microfilm Publication M869, Roll 34.
25. Herbert Shapiro, "The Ku Klux Klan During Reconstruction: The South Carolina Episode," *Journal of Negro History* (January 1964): 49.
26. "Miscellaneous Reports and Lists Relating to Murders and Outrages Mar. 1867–Nov. 1868," Records of the Assistant Commissioner for the State of Louisiana, Bureau of Refugees, Freedmen and Abandoned Lands, 1865–1869, National Archives Microfilm Publication M1027, Roll 34.
27. Eric Foner, *Reconstruction: America's Unfinished Revolution, 1863–1877* (New York: Harper, 2011).
28. *Acts of the General Assembly of the State of South Carolina Passed at the Sessions of 1864–65* (Columbia, SC, 1865), pp. 291–304.
29. Ibid.
30. D. T. Corbin, Letter to Governor D. H. Chamberlain, October 9, 1876, *Miscellaneous Documents, 30th Congress, 1st Session–48th Congress, 2d Session and Special Session*, Volume 6, Part 3, p. 323.
31. Jerry L. West, *The Bloody South Carolina Election of 1876: Wade Hampton III, the Red Shirt Campaign for Governor and the End of Reconstruction* (Jefferson, NC: McFarland, 2010), p. 127.
32. Bostick, *A Brief History of James Island*, p. 23.

Chapter 9: Something Else

1. Charles B. Dew, "Tightening the Noose," *New York Times*, May 21, 2000, https://archive.nytimes.com/www.nytimes.com/books/00/05/21/reviews/000521.21dewlt.html.

2. Francis Butler Simkins, *Pitchfork Ben Tillman, South Carolinian*, 1st paperback ed. (Baton Rouge: LSU Press, 1944), p. 83, quoting Tillman inauguration speech on December 4, 1890.

3. Stephen Kantrowitz, *Ben Tillman and the Reconstruction of White Supremacy* (Chapel Hill: University of North Carolina Press, 2000), p. 132.

4. W. T. Groce, "John B. Gordon (1832–1904)," *New Georgia Encyclopedia*, www.georgiaencyclopedia.org/articles/government-politics/john-b-gordon-1832-1904.

5. David Holthouse, "Activists Confront Hate in Selma, Ala," *Intelligence Report* (Winter 2008), www.splcenter.org/fighting-hate/intelligence-report/2008/activists-confront-hate-selma-ala.

6. Neil R. McMillen, *Dark Journey: Black Mississippians in the Age of Jim Crow* (Urbana and Chicago: University of Illinois Press, 1990), p. 43.

7. Phillip Dray, *At the Hands of Persons Unknown: The Lynching of Black America* (New York: Random House, 2002), pp. 13–15.

8. Ibid., p. 15.

9. Leon Litwak, *Trouble in Mind: Black Southerners in the Age of Jim Crow* (New York: Vintage, 1999), p. 281.

10. "The Shame of America," History Matters, http://historymatters.gmu.edu/d/6786/.

11. "Was Made a Living Torch," *Boston Post*, May 30, 1901.

12. "Undesirables Are Driven Out of Byhalia Following Lynching," *Oxford Eagle*, December 3, 1914.

13. "Memphis Mob," *The Appeal*, March 26, 1892.

14. Ida B. Wells, *Crusade for Justice: The Autobiography of Ida B. Wells* (Chicago: University of Chicago Press, 1970), pp. 51–52.

15. Ibid.

16. Ibid., p. 53.

17. Ibid., p. 48.

18. Ida B. Wells, *Southern Horrors: Lynch Law in All Its Phases* (New York: New York Age, 1892), pp. 3–5.

19. Ida B. Wells-Barnett, "Booker T. Washington and His Critics," National Humanities Center, https://nationalhumanitiescenter.org/ows/seminars/progressive/bookertweb/wellsbookertwashingtoncritics.pdf.

20. Ibid.

21. "The Race Problem," *New York Voice*, October 23, 1890.

22. "The Race Problem: Miss Willard on the Political Puzzle of the South," *New York Voice*, reprinted for the Frances Willard House Museum, "Truth-Telling: Frances Willard and Ida B. Wells," https://scalar.usc.edu/works/willard-and-wells/1893-wctu-anti-lynching-resolution?path=timeline.

23. "The 1894 WTCU Convention," Frances Willard House Museum, https:// scalar.usc.edu/works/willard-and-wells/presidents-address-1894-wctu -convention?path=timeline.

24. Wells, *Crusade for Justice*, p. 326.

25. Ibid., p. 318.

Food Stop: The Difference Between Soul Food and Southern Cuisine

1. Becky Bullingsley, *A Culinary History of Myrtle Beach and the Grand Strand: Fish, Grits, Oyster Roasts and Boiled Peanuts* (Charleston, SC: American Palate, 2013).

2. William Parker Cutler, Julia Perkins Cutler, Ephraim Cutler Dawes, and Peter Force, *Life, Journal, and Correspondence of Manasseh Cutler*, vol. 2 (Cincinnati: R. Clarke & Co., 1888), pp. 71–72.

Chapter 10: Whites Gone Wild: Uncle Rob Explains "Separate but Equal"

1. "H. R. 40, Naturalization Bill, March 4, 1790," 2021, www.visitthecapitol.gov /exhibitions/artifact/h-r-40-naturalization-bill-march-4-1790.

2. U.S. Census Bureau, "The 1870 Census: Vol. I. The Statistics of the Population of the United States," www2.census.gov/library/publications/decennial/1870 /population/1870a-07.pdf, p. 34.

3. "The Battle of Liberty Place | 64 Parishes," @64parishes, 2021, https://64parishes.org/entry/the-battle-of-liberty-place.

4. Steve Luxemberg, "The Forgotten Northern Origins of Jim Crow," *Time*, February 12, 2019, https://time.com/5527029/jim-crow-plessy-history/.

5. "U.S. Senate: Landmark Legislation: Civil Rights Act of 1875," www.senate.gov /artandhistory/history/common/generic/CivilRightsAct1875.htm.

6. *Civil Rights Cases*, 109 U.S. 3 (1883).

7. Paul Kinny, "Defeat but Not Ignominy: The New Orleans Afro-Creoles Behind *Plessy v. Ferguson*," *Undergraduate Research* 1, issue 1 (Winter 2021): 64–99.

8. H. W. Brands, *American Colossus: The Triumph of Capitalism, 1865–1900* (New York: Random House, 2010), pp. 463–64.

9. *Plessy v. Ferguson*, 163 U.S. 537 (1886).

10. Louisiana Constitutional Convention, *Official journal of the proceedings of the Constitutional convention of the state of Louisiana: held in New Orleans, Tuesday, February 8, 1898. And calendar.* (New Orleans: Printed by H. J. Hearsey, 1898), p. 10.

11. *Plessy v. Ferguson*.

12. Louisiana Constitutional Convention (1898), 37.

13. Khalilah Brown-Dean, Zoltan Hajnal, Christina Rivers, and Ismail White, *50 Years of the Voting Rights Act: The State of Race in Politics* (Joint Center for Political and Economic Studies, 2015), https://jointcenter.org/wp-content /uploads/2019/11/VRA-report-3.5.15-1130-amupdated.pdf, p. 9.

14. Louis R. Harlan, ed., *The Booker T. Washington Papers*, vol. 3 (Urbana: University of Illinois Press, 1974), pp. 583–87.

15. Ibid.

16. Glen Jeansonne, *The Life of Herbert Hoover: Fighting Quaker, 1928–1933* (New York: Palgrave Macmillan, 2012), p. 306.

17. Dewey W. Grantham, "Dinner at the White House: Theodore Roosevelt, Booker T. Washington, and the South," *Tennessee Historical Quarterly* 17, no. 2 (1958): 112–30, www.jstor.org/stable/42621372.

18. Clarence Lusane, *The Black History of the White House* (San Francisco: City Lights Publishers, 2013), p. 254.

19. Emmett J. Scott and Lyman Beecher Stowe, *Booker T. Washington: Builder of a Civilization* (New York: Doubleday, Page & Company, 1916), p. 116.

20. W. E. B. Du Bois, *Darkwater: Voices from Within the Veil*, reprinted in *The W. E. B. Dubois Collection* (Blackmore Dennett, 1970), p. 1267.

Supplement: Funny AF

1. Douglas Gilbert, *American Vaudeville: Its Life and Times* (Mineola, NY: Dover Publications, 1963), p. 153.

2. Frederick Douglass, "The Hutchinson Family.—Hunkerism," *North Star*, October 27, 1848.

3. Richard Henry Little, "Vaudeville," *Buffalo Enquirer*, June 1, 1901.

4. Joe Laurie Jr., *Vaudeville: From the Honky Tonks to the Palace* (New York: Henry Holt, 1953), p. 192.

5. Eddie Tafoya, *The Legacy of the Wisecrack: Stand-Up Comedy as the Great American Literary Form* (Boca Raton, FL: BrownWalker Press, 2011), p. 111.

6. Robert A. Stebbins, *The Laugh-Makers: Stand-up Comedy as Art, Business and Life-Style* (Montreal: McGill-Queen's UP, 1990), pp. 7–8.

7. Lester A. Walton, "Dramatics and Athletics," *New York Age*, November 30, 1916.

8. Laurie, *Vaudeville*, p. 192.

Chapter 11: So Devilish a Fire: The Black Women Who Started the Civil Rights Movement

1. Mary Church Terrell, "Purity and the Negro," Iowa State University, Archives of Women's Political Communication, January 1, 1905, https://awpc.cattcenter .iastate.edu/2019/12/10/purity-and-the-negro-1905/.

2. Joan Quigley, *Just Another Southern Town: Mary Church Terrell and the Struggle for Racial Justice in the Nation's Capital* (Oxford: Oxford University Press, 2016).

3. W. E. B. Du Bois, *The Gift of Black Folk: The Negroes in the Making of America* (Boston: Stratford Company, 1924), p. 272.

4. Edward White, "A Girl Full of Smartness," *Paris Review*, June 2, 2017, www .theparisreview.org/blog/2017/06/02/a-girl-full-of-smartness/.

5. Ibid.
6. Tom Huddleston Jr., "Mary Ellen Pleasant, One of the First Black Self-Made Millionaires, Used an Ingenious Trick to Build Her Fortune," CNBC, www.cnbc.com/2020/02/14/how-mary-ellen-pleasant-became-one-of-the-first-black-millionaires.html.
7. Mary Ellen Pleasant Financial Correspondence and Notes, MS-R102, Special Collections and Archives, UC Irvine Libraries, Irvine, CA.
8. Du Bois, *The Gift of Black Folk*, p. 272.
9. Henry Hampton and Steven Freyer, *Voices of Freedom: An Oral History of the Civil Rights Movement, 1950–1980* (New York: Bantam, 1991), p. 58.
10. Jeremy Gray, "The Execution of Jeremiah Reeves: Alabama Teen's Death Sentence Helped Drive Civil Rights Movement," *Birmingham News*, February 4, 2015, www.al.com/news/2015/02/the_execution_of_jeremiah_reev.html.
11. Leaflet, "Don't Ride the Bus, Come to a Mass Meeting on 5 December," Martin Luther King and the Global Struggle for Freedom, https://web.archive.org/web/20150402155441/http://mlk-kpp01.stanford.edu/index.php/encyclopedia/documentsentry/leaflet_dont_ride_the_bus_come_to_a_mass_meeting_on_5_december/.
12. "Eleanor Roosevelt and Civil Rights," National Park Service, https://web.archive.org/web/20070104113920/http://www.nps.gov/archive/elro/teach-er-vk/lesson-plans/notes-er-and-civil-rights.htm.
13. "The Extraordinary Life of Mary McLeod Bethune," National World War II Museum, July 20, 2020, www.nationalww2museum.org/war/articles/mary-mcleod-bethune.
14. Executive Order 8802, June 25, 1941, General Records of the United States Government; Record Group 11; National Archives.
15. Audrey Thomas McCluskey and Elaine M. Smith, eds., *Mary McLeod Bethune: Building a Better World; Essays and Selected Documents* (Bloomington: Indiana University Press, 2001), p. 240.
16. Todd Moyle, *Freedom Flyers: The Tuskegee Airmen of World War II* (New York: Oxford University Press, 2010), p. 94.
17. Ulysses Lee, *United States Army in World War II: Special Studies; The Employment of Negro Troops* (Washington, D.C.: Center for Military History, United States Army, 2000), p. 63.

Supplement: Sister Rosetta Tharpe

1. Janice Kaplan, "Sister Rosetta Tharpe: The Forgotten Mother of Rock-and-Roll," Daily Beast, September 11, 2016, www.thedailybeast.com/sister-rosetta-tharpe-the-forgotten-mother-of-rock-and-roll.
2. Chris Long, "Rosetta Tharpe's Mind-Blowing Station Show," BBC News, May 7, 2014, www.bbc.com/news/uk-england-manchester-27256401.
3. Pop Matters Staff, "Sister Rosetta Tharpe Got Rock Rolling Long Before Elvis," PopMatters, February 26, 2007, www.popmatters.com/sister-rosetta-tharpe-got-rock-rolling-long-before-elvis-2495821302.html.

Chapter 12: The Race War III: The Conspiracy Theory That Was True

1. "The Hoover Legacy: 40 Years After," Federal Bureau of Investigation, www.fbi
   .gov/news/stories/copy_of_the-hoover-legacy-40-years-after.
2. Curt Gentry, *J. Edgar Hoover: The Man and the Secrets* (New York: W. W.
   Norton & Company), p. 68.
3. Kenneth O'Reilly, "The Jim Crow Policies of Woodrow Wilson," *Journal of
   Blacks in Higher Education*, no. 17 (1997), https://doi.org/10.2307/2963252,
   http://www.jstor.org/stable/2963252.
4. Woodrow Wilson, *A History of the American People*, 5 vols. (New York: Harper
   & Brothers, 1903), p. 58.
5. Diane Roberts, "Thomas Dixon Jr.: The Great-Granddaddy of American White
   Nationalism," *Washington Post*, January 21, 2019, www.washingtonpost.com
   /outlook/2019/01/21/thomas-dixon-jr-great-grandaddy-american-white-
   nationalism/.
6. Claudia Kolker, "A Painful Present as Historians Confront a Nation's Bloody
   Past," *Los Angeles Times*, February 22, 2000, www.hartford-hwp.com
   /archives/45a/316.html.
7. Mark E. Benbow, "Birth of a Quotation: Woodrow Wilson and 'Like Writing
   History with Lightning,'" *Journal of the Gilded Age and Progressive Era* 9, no. 4
   (2010), www.jstor.org/stable/20799409.
8. Athan G. Theoharis and John Stuart Cox, *The Boss: J. Edgar Hoover and the
   Great American Inquisition* (Philadelphia: Temple University Press, 1988), p. 109.
9. Chad L. Williams, *Torchbearers of Democracy: African American Soldiers in the
   World War I Era* (Chapel Hill: University of North Carolina Press, 2010), p. 3.
10. Ibid., pp. 31–32.
11. Archibald Coody, *The Race Question from the White Chief: A Story of the Life
    and Times of James K. Vardaman* (Vicksburg, MI: Mississippi Printing Co., 1944).
12. "For Action on Race Riot Peril," *New York Times*, October 5, 1919.
13. "Lynchings: By State and Race, 1882–1968," Archives at Tuskegee Institute,
    http://archive.tuskegee.edu/repository/wp-content/uploads/2020/11/
    Lynchings-Stats-Year-Dates-Causes.pdf.
14. Thelma B. Yarborough, "Contemporary Journalistic Treatment of a Lynching:
    Ell Parsons in 1917–Memphis Tennessee," *Griot* (Houston), vol. 7, issue 2 (Fall
    1988): 10.
15. "Soldier in Uniform Is Beaten in Georgia Town," *Chicago Defender*, April 5, 1919.
16. "Soldier Lynched," *Chicago Defender*, May 10, 1919.
17. "Race Trouble at Macon," *Columbus* (GA) *Dispatch*, June 8, 1919.
18. "For Action on Race Riot Peril," *New York Times*, October 5, 1919, https://
    timesmachine.nytimes.com/timesmachine/1919/10/05/106999010
    .html?pageNumber=112.
19. Kenneth R. Durham Jr., "The Longview Race Riot of 1919," *East Texas Historical
    Journal* 18, issue 2 (1980).
20. Cameron McWhirter, *Red Summer: The Summer of 1919 and the Awakening of
    Black America* (New York: Henry Holt, 2011), p. 152.

21. Walter C. Rucker and James N. Upton, *Encyclopedia of American Race Riots*, vol. 2 (Westport, CT: Greenwood, 2007).

22. Michel duCille, "Black Moses, Red Scare," *Washington Post*, February 12, 1997, www.washingtonpost.com/archive/1997/02/12/black-moses-red-scare /8a6aff0a-6f38-4b50-8c45-77ba7eb5d714/.

23. Ibid.

24. Michael Burns, "Trove of Papers Reveals a Rosa Parks Who Did Much More Than Sit Down," *Washington Post*, February 3, 2015, www.washingtonpost .com/local/artifacts-show-a-rosa-parks-steeped-in-freedom-struggle-from -childhood/2015/02/02/90ee01f4-a7de-11e4-a7c2-03d37af98440_story .html.

25. Jeanne Theoharris, "How History Got the Rosa Parks Story Wrong," *Washington Post*, December 1, 2015, www.washingtonpost.com/ posteverything/wp/2015/12/01/how-history-got-the-rosa-parks-story-wrong/.

26. Helen Shores Lee, Barbara Shores, and Denise George, *The Gentle Giant of Dynamite Hill: The Untold Story of Arthur Shores and His Family's Fight for Civil Rights* (Grand Rapids, MI: Zondervan, 2012).

27. Henry Hampton and Steve Fayer, *Voices of Freedom: An Oral History of the Civil Rights Movement from the 1950s Through the 1980s* (New York: Random House, 2011), p. 136.

28. Wayne Greenshaw, "Black Politicians Make Great Gains in State Election," *Alabama Journal*, November 4, 1970.

29. M. S. Handler, "Malcolm X Pleased by Whites' Attitude on Trip to Mecca," *New York Times*, May 8, 1964.

30. "The Monumental Plot," *Time*, February 26, 1965, http://content.time.com /time/subscriber/article/0,33009,833472-1,00.html.

31. "Fred Hampton," National Archives, August 25, 2016.

32. Jeffrey Haas, *The Assassination of Fred Hampton: How the FBI and the Chicago Police Murdered a Black Panther* (Chicago: Lawrence Hill Books /Chicago Review Press, 2010).

33. Rod Bush, *We Are Not What We Seem: Black Nationalism and Class Struggle in the American Century* (New York: NYU Press, 2000), p. 216.

34. *Iberia Hampton, et al. v. Plaintiffs-Appellants, v. Edward V. Hanrahan, et al., Defendants-Appellees* (Nos. 77–1968, 77–1210, and 77–1370).

35. Haas, *The Assassination of Fred Hampton*.

36. Amy Goodman, "From COINTELPRO to Snowden, the FBI Burglars Speak Out After 43 Years of Silence (Part 2)," *Democracy Now!*, January 8, 2014, www .democracynow.org/blog/2014/1/8/from_cointelpro_to_snowden_the_fbi.

37. J. Patrick Brown et al., *Activists Under Surveillance: The FBI Files* (Cambridge, MA: MIT Press, 2019).

38. Richard Belzer and David Wayne, *Dead Wrong: Straight Facts on the Country's Most Controversial Cover-ups* (New York: Skyhorse, 2012).

39. J. Edgar Hoover, "The FBI Sets Goals for COINTELPRO," *HERB: Resources for Teachers*, City University of New York.

40. Ward Churchill and Jim Vander Wall, *The COINTELPRO Papers: Documents*

from the FBI's Secret Wars Against Dissent in the United States (Boston: South End Press, 2002), p. 193.

41. Gary May, *The Informant: The FBI, the Ku Klux Klan, and the Murder of Viola Liuzzo* (New Haven, CT: Yale University Press, 2005), p. 37.

42. Michael T. Kaufman, "Gary T. Rowe Jr., 64, Who Informed on Klan in Civil Rights Killing, Is Dead," *New York Times*, October 4, 1998, www.nytimes .com/1998/10/04/us/gary-t-rowe-jr-64-who-informed-on-klan-in-civil-rights -killing-is-dead.html.

43. Howell Raines, "Rounding Up the 16th Street Suspects," *New York Times*, July 13, 1997.

44. Betty Medsger, *The Burglary: The Discovery of J. Edgar Hoover's Secret FBI* (New York: Alfred A. Knopf, 2014), p. 241.

Chapter 13: Thug Life: The Other Civil Rights Movement

1. Essie Harris, *Testimony Taken by the Joint Committee to Inquire into the State of Affairs in the Late Insurrectionary States, North Carolina* (Washington, D.C.: Government Printing Office, July 1, 1872), pp. 88–90.

2. J. Scott and L. P. Poland, *Report of the Joint Select Committee to Inquire into the Condition of Affairs in the Late Insurrectionary States, Made to the Two Houses of Congress February 19, 1872: Testimony, North Carolina* (Washington, D.C.: Government Printing Office, 1872).

3. William Ivy Hair, *Carnival of Fury: Robert Charles and the New Orleans Race Riot of 1900* (Baton Rouge: LSU Press, 2008), p. 14.

4. Gary Krist, *Empire of Sin: A Story of Sex, Jazz, Murder, and the Battle for Modern New Orleans* (New York: Crown, 2015), p. 104.

5. Ida B. Wells, *Mob Rule in New Orleans: Robert Charles and His Fight to Death, the Story of His Life, Burning Human Beings Alive, Other Lynching Statistics* (Good Press, 2019), p. 87. Originally published in 1900.

6. Donna M. Lucey, "The 'Fighting Editor' of the *Richmond Planet*," *Humanities* 31, no. 4 (July/August 2010), www.neh.gov/article/fighting-editor-richmond -planet.

7. Ibid.

8. Ibid.

9. Timothy B. Tyson, "Robert F. Williams, 'Black Power,' and the Roots of the African American Freedom Struggle," *Journal of American History* 85, no. 2 (September 1998): 547.

10. Ibid., p. 546.

11. Robert F. Williams Wanted Poster, https://upload.wikimedia.org/wikipedia /commons/a/ac/Hooverwarrantforwilliams.jpg.

12. Tyson, "Robert F. Williams," p. 570.

13. Bailey Williams, "A Half-Century Ago in Jonesboro, Armed Black Men Fought Back," *Daily Advertiser*, June 7, 2020, www.theadvertiser.com/story/news /local/louisiana/2020/06/07/civil-rights-history-deacons-defense-fought-kkk -louisiana/3164717001/.

14. Ibid.
15. *Black Identity Extremists Likely Motivated to Target Law Enforcement Officers*, Federal Bureau of Intelligence, August 3, 2017.

Supplement: All-the-Way Free

1. Joseph Williams, "Charleston Work House and 'Sugar House,'" *Discovering Our Past: College of Charleston Histories*, https://discovering.cofc.edu/items/show/31.
2. Edward Ayers, *Vengeance and Justice: Crime and Punishment in the Nineteenth-Century American South* (Oxford: Oxford University Press, 1984), p. 76.
3. U.S. Congress, *Senate Executive Document No. 2, 39th Congress, 1st Session* (Washington, D.C.: Government Printing Office, 1865), pp. 93–94.
4. "Texas Black Codes," University of Houston, Digital History, www.digitalhistory.uh.edu/disp_textbook.cfm?smtid=3&psid=3681.
5. Ellen Terrell, "The Convict Leasing System: Slavery in Its Worst Aspects," Library of Congress, June 17, 2021, https://blogs.loc.gov/inside_adams/2021/06/convict-leasing-system/.
6. Ayers, *Vengeance and Justice*, p. 196.
7. Robert Perkinson, *Texas Tough: The Rise of America's Prison Empire* (New York: Henry Holt, 2010), p. 105.
8. Ayers, *Vengeance and Justice*, pp. 200–201.
9. Bureau of Justice Statistics, *State and Federal Prisoners, 1925–85* (Washington, D.C.: Department of Justice, 1986), p. 2, https://perma.cc/6F2E-U9WL.
10. U.S. Census Bureau, "QuickFacts: South Carolina," www.census.gov/quickfacts/SC; "Profile of Inmates in Institutional Count," South Carolina Department of Corrections, June 30, 2022, www.doc.sc.gov/research/InmatePopulationStats/ASOF-FY20_Institutional_Count_Profile.pdf.
11. "Frequently Asked Questions," South Carolina Department of Corrections, www.doc.sc.gov/faqs.html.
12. "Table 1.23B–Illicit Drug Use in Lifetime: Among People Aged 12 or Older; by Age Group and Demographic Characteristics, Percentages, 2019 and 2020," Center for Behavioral Health Statistics and Quality, National Survey on Drug Use and Health, 2019 and Quarters 1 and 4, 2020, www.samhsa.gov/data/sites/default/files/reports/rpt35323/NSDUHDetailedTabs2020/NSDUHDetailedTabs2020/NSDUHDetTabsSect1pe2020.htm.
13. Ashley Nellis, "The Color of Justice: Racial and Ethnic Disparity in State Prisons," The Sentencing Project, October 13, 2021, p. 6.

Chapter 14: The Great White Heist

1. "Statistics: Slaves and Slaveholdings," Gilder Lehrman Institute of American History, www.gilderlehrman.org/history-resources/teaching-resource/statistics-slaves-and-slaveholdings.
2. Kriston McIntosh, Emily Moss, Ryan Nunn, and Jay Shambaugh, "Examining the

Black-White Wealth Gap," Brookings Institution, www.brookings.edu/blog/up
-front/2020/02/27/examining-the-black-white-wealth-gap/.

3. Leon Jones, "Desegregation and Social Reform Since 1954," *Journal of Negro Education* 43, no. 2 (1974): 155–71, https://doi.org/10.2307/2966817.

4. Rebekah Dobrasko, "Equalization Schools: South Carolina's History of Unequal Education," Lowcountry Digital History Initiative, College of Charleston, https://ldhi.library.cofc.edu/exhibits/show/equalization-schools/about-the-author.

5. Andre Perry, Jonathan Rothwell, and David Harshbarger, "The Devaluation of Black Assets in Black Neighborhoods: The Case of Residential Property," Metropolitan Policy Program at Brookings, November 2018, p. 2.

6. Daphne Kenyon, Bethany Paquin, and Semida Munteanu, "Public Schools and the Property Tax: A Comparison of Education Funding Models in Three U.S. States," *Land Lines*, April 2022, p. 33.

7. *23 Billion*, Edbuild, March 2019, https://edbuild.org/content/23-billion/full -report.pdf.

8. John Harrington and Grant Suneson, "What Were the 13 Most Expensive Wars in U.S. History?," *USA Today*, June 13, 2019.

9. Muhammad Khalid Anser, Zahid Yousaf, Abdelmohsen A. Nassani, et al., "Dynamic Linkages Between Poverty, Inequality, Crime, and Social Expenditures in a Panel of 16 Countries: Two-Step GMM Estimates," *Economic Structures* 9, no. 43 (2020), https://doi.org/10.1186/s40008-020-00220-6.

10. Martin Luther King Jr., "I Have a Dream," August 28, 1963, Lincoln Memorial, Washington, D.C., Transcript, The Avalon Project, Lillian Goldman Law Library, Yale Law School, https://avalon.law.yale.edu/20th_century/mlk01.asp.

11. Kate Ellis and Stephen Smith, "Shackled Legacy," APM Reports, September 4, 2017, www.apmreports.org/episode/2017/09/04/shackled-legacy; Tracy Scott Forson, "Enslaved Labor Built These Universities. Now They're Starting to Repay the Debt," *USA Today*, February 12, 2020, www.usatoday.com /story/news/education/2020/02/12/colleges-slavery-offering-atonement -reparations/2612821001/.

12. Stacy M. Brown, "The Major Role the Catholic Church Played in Slavery," *Amsterdam News*, September 18, 2018, https://amsterdamnews.com /news/2018/09/18/major-role-catholic-church-played-slavery/.

13. Brad Greenwood, Rachel Hardeman, Laura Huang, and Aaron Sojourner, "Physician–Patient Racial Concordance and Disparities in Birthing Mortality for Newborns," *Proceedings of the National Academy of Sciences of the United States of America* 117, no. 35 (September 1, 2020), www.pnas.org/doi/10.1073 /pnas.1913405117.

14. Delvin Davis and Joshua M. Frank, "Under the Hood: Auto Loan Interest Rate Hikes Inflate Consumer Costs and Loan Losses," Center for Responsible Lending, April 19, 2011, www.responsiblelending.org/other-consumer-loans /auto-financing/research-analysis/Under-the-Hood-Auto-Dealer-Rate -Markups-Executive-Summary.pdf.

15. Julia Angwin, Jeff Larson, Lauren Kirchner, and Surya Mattu, "Minority Neighborhoods Pay Higher Car Insurance Premiums Than White Areas with the

Same Risk," ProPublica, April 5, 2017, www.propublica.org/article/minority -neighborhoods-higher-car-insurance-premiums-white-areas-same-risk.

16. Kelly M. Bower, Roland J. Thorpe Jr., Charles Rohde, and Darrell J. Gaskin, "The Intersection of Neighborhood Racial Segregation, Poverty, and Urbanicity and Its Impact on Food Store Availability in the United States," *Preventive Medicine* 58 (January 2014): 33–39, doi: 10.1016/j.ypmed.2013.10.010.

17. Zoë Roller, *Closing the Water Access Gap in the United States: A National Action Plan*, Dig Deep Right to Water Project, U.S. Water Alliance, 2019, https://static1.squarespace.com/static/5e80f1a64ed7dc3408525fb9/t/6092d dcc499e1b6a6a07ba3a/1620237782228/Dig-Deep_Closing-the-Water -Access-Gap-in-the-United-States_DIGITAL_compressed.pdf.

18. Michael Harriot, "White Water Welfare: Jackson, Baltimore and the Other Racial Wealth Gap," *The Grio*, September 8, 2022, https://thegrio .com/2022/09/08/white-water-welfare-jackson-baltimore-and-the-other -racial-wealth-gap/.

Supplement: The Black Women Who Won Reparations

1. Thomas Franklin Waters, Sarah Goodhue, and John Wise, *Ipswich in the Massachusetts Bay Colony* (Ipswich Historical Society, 1917).

2. Emily Blanck, *Tyrannicide: Forging an American Law of Slavery in Revolutionary South Carolina and Massachusetts* (Athens: University of Georgia Press, 2014), p. 10.

3. "Massachusetts Constitution," https://malegislature.gov/laws/constitution.

4. Ben Railton, "How Two Massachusetts Slaves Won Their Freedom—and Then Abolished Slavery," *Washington Post*, July 3, 2017, www.washingtonpost.com/ news/made-by-history/wp/2017/07/03/how-two-massachusetts-slaves-won -their-freedom-and-then-abolished-slavery/.

5. Belinda Royall, *Belinda's Petition to the Massachusetts General Court, February 14, 1783*, original manuscript, Massachusetts Archives, http:// web.archive.org/web/20060712134132/http:/www.medfordhistorical.org /belinda.php.

6. Belinda Sutton's 1783 Petition, Royall House & Slave Quarters, https:// royallhouse.org/wp-content/uploads/2013/11/Belindas_Petition.pdf.

Chapter 15: The Race of Politics: Uncle Rob Explains the Two-Party System

1. United States Senate, "African American Senators," www.senate.gov/ pagelayout/history/h_multi_sections_and_teasers/Photo_Exhibit_African _American_Senators.htm.

2. "GOP Holds Edge in Leaned Party Affiliations Among Whites, Fare Worse Among Other Groups," Pew Research Center, June 6, 2020, www .pewresearch.org/politics/2020/06/02/democratic-edge-in-party -identification-narrows-slightly/.

3. Phillip Bump, "When Did Black Americans Start Voting So Heavily Democratic?," *Washington Post*, July 7, 2015, www.washingtonpost.com/news/the-fix/wp/2015/07/07/when-did-black-americans-start-voting-so-heavily-democratic/.

4. Democratic National Convention, *Proceedings of the National Democratic Convention: Held in . . . Baltimore, on the 5th of May, 1840. Embracing Resolutions, Expressive of the Sentiments of the Democratic Party of the Union: and an Address, in Support of the Principles and Measures of the Present National Administration* (Printed at the office of the Republican, 1840), https://books.google.com/books?id=O8IxAQAAMAAJ.

5. "Rankin, Jeannette," History, Art & Archives, United States House of Representatives, https://history.house.gov/People/Listing/R/RANKIN,-Jeannette-(R000055)/.

6. Neil R. McMillen, *Dark Journey: Black Mississippians in the Age of Jim Crow* (Urbana: University of Illinois Press, 1990), p. 36.

7. Ibid.

8. William Edward Burghardt Du Bois, "Another Open Letter to Woodrow Wilson," *The Crisis*, September 1913.

9. "H.R. 7152. Civil Rights Act of 1964. Adoption of a Resolution (H. Res. 789) Providing for House Approval of the Bill as Amended by the Senate," www.govtrack.us/congress/votes/88-1964/h182.

10. David Caplovitz and Norman M. Bradburn, "Social Class and Psychological Adjustment: A Portrait of the Communities in the 'Happiness Study.' A Preliminary Report" (Chicago: National Opinion Research Center, 1964).

11. Associated Press, "Miller Says Foes Soft on Crime," *San Antonio Express*, October 10, 1964.

12. H. R. Haldeman, *A Conversation with H. R. Haldeman*, *Vital History Cassettes no 1 for Mar 75* (New York: Encyclopedia Americana/CBS News Audio Resource Library, 1975), sound recording, on side B of 1 sound cassette (22 min., 57 sec.): analog., 03751 Grolier.

13. Alexander P. Lamis, *The Two-Party South* (New York: Oxford University Press, 1988), p. 26.

14. Peniel E. Joseph, "From Ronald Reagan in Philadelphia, Miss., to Donald Trump in Tulsa, a Pattern of Racially Divisive Politics," *Washington Post*, June 19, 2019, www.washingtonpost.com/nation/2020/06/19/ronald-reagan-philadelphia-miss-donald-trump-tulsa-pattern-racially-divisive-politics/.

15. "How Groups Voted in 2020," Roper Center for Public Opinion Research, https://ropercenter.cornell.edu/how-groups-voted-2020.

16. Daniel Victor, "What, Congressman Steve King Asks, Have Nonwhites Done for Civilization?," *New York Times*, July 18, 2016, www.nytimes.com/2016/07/19/us/politics/steve-king-nonwhite-subgroups.html.

17. "Biographical Directory of Article III Federal Judges, 1789-Present," Federal Judiciary Center, www.fjc.gov/history/judges, accessed October 1, 2021.

18. "Racially Disproportionate Drug Arrests," Human Rights Watch, www.hrw.org/reports/2000/usa/Rcedrg00-05.htm#P332_70258.

Box: The End of the Multiracial Coalition

1. "Chairman F.M. Simmons Issues a Patriotic and Able Address, Summing Up the Issues, and Appealing Eloquently to the White Voters to Redeem the State," *Raleigh News and Observer*, November 3, 1898.
2. Richard Wormser, *The Rise and Fall of Jim Crow* (New York: Macmillan, 2004), pp. 85–86.
3. Alexander Manly, "Vile and Villainous," UNC Libraries, https://exhibits.lib.unc.edu/items/show/2172.

Chapter 16: Homework

1. Louis Harris and Associates poll, October 1966, data provided by Roper Opinion on Public Research.
2. Survey Research Center, University of Michigan, June 28–August 31, 1969.
3. Roper Center for Public Opinion Research, "Public Opinion on Civil Rights," Civil Rights Movement Veterans, www.crmvet.org/docs/60s_crm_public-opinion.pdf.
4. Bureau of Labor Statistics, BLS Data Finder, www.bls.gov/bls/data_finder.htm.
5. Elizabeth Hinton, Julily Hohler Hausman, and Vesla M. Weaver, "Did Blacks Really Endorse the 1994 Crime Bill?," *New York Times*, April 13, 2016.

INDEX

Page numbers in italics refer to illustrations.

Abernathy, Ralph, 272
abolitionism, 81, 92, 95, 111, 139, 143–44, 162, 164–73, 239, 263–64, 357
Acoli, Sundiata, 303
Acuña, Manuel Méndez de, 24
Adams, John, 350–51
Adams, John Quincy, 357–58
Aeterni regis, 33
African Methodist Episcopal Church, 140
Agriculture, U.S. Department of (USDA), 271, 273, 379
Aiken, D. Wyatt, 202
Alabama National Guard, 360–61
Alegría, Ricardo, 43
Alexander VI, Pope, 35
Ali, Muhammad, 304
Allen, Richard, 139–40
Allston, Robert, 62
all-the-way free, 325, 332
Alton, Suzanne, 89
American Citizens' Equal Rights Association (ACERA), 241
American Descendants of Slavery (ADOS), 343–44
American History (Muzzey), 182
American Missionary Association, 198, 199
American Revolution. *See* Revolutionary War
Ammen, Samuel Zenas, 177–78
Anderson, C. Alfred "Chief," 280
Andry, Gilbert, 123, 125–26
Andry, Manuel, 120–28
Anglican Church, 136
Anti-Federalists, 356–57
anti-immigrant sentiments, 289–90, 364
Apalachee, 48, 49, 50
Appomattox Court House, 194
Argall, Samuel, 21–22, 25
armed resistance, 310–21. *See also* slave rebellions
Armstrong, Samuel, 245
Arnold, Henry "Hap," 279
Ashanti Kingdom, 9, 111, 119, 125
Ashley, John, 350–51

Atlanta Compromise, 246
Atlanta Constitution, 213–14
Atlanta Federal Penitentiary, 292–93
Atlanta University, 213
Atwater, Lee, 362–63
Aurelia S. Browder, et al. v. W. A. Gayle, et al., 276
Autobiography of Malcolm X, The, 3
Ayllón, Lucas Vásquez de, 47–48, 58, 377

"Back to Africa" movement, 221, 291–92
Baker, Ella, 268–70
Baker, Frank, 168
Balagoon, Kuwasi, 303
Ball, Charles, 135
barbecue (BBQ), 230
Barca, Hannibal, 96
Barracoon (Hurston), 272–73
Barrett, William, 216–19
Barry, Marion, 269
Barton, Clara, 171*n*
Bas du Fleuve, 107
Battle of Liberty Place, 237–38, 240
Battle of New Orleans, 126–27
Bell, Thomas, 264–66
Beloved (Morrison), 113
Bennett, Thomas, 115
Bernier, François, 74
Berry, Chuck, 283, 285
Berry, Lee, 303
Bethune, Mary McLeod, 277–81
Bethune-Cookman University, 277
Bett and Brom v. Ashley, 351
Bevel, James, 272
Beyoncé, 94, 220, 363
Bill of Rights, 75, 100
Bird, Joan, 303
Birmingham, Alabama, 295–97, 306
Birth of a Nation, The (movie), 288
biscuits, 226, 231, 232
Black, Hugo, 277*n*
Black American Revolution, 78–87, 163–73
"Black-and-Tan" faction, 359–60
Black Brigade, 83, 85

Black Codes, 201–2, 203–4, 236, 327
Black Emancipation Proclamation, 157–59
Blackface, 256–57
Black faith and churches, 130–48, 152–54
Black Guard, 317
Black Identity Extremists (BIE), 319–20
Black Liberation Front, 299, 299n
Black Loyalists, 84–85, 86, 139, 140, 166
Black Majority (Wood), 62
Black Panthers, 298–304, 319, 379–80
Black Pioneers, 85, 189
Black Power, 298, 306
Black Reconstruction in America (Du Bois), 159–60, 162–63, 188, 198
Blackstone Rangers, 302
Bleeding Kansas, 161–62, 163
blood aunt, 228–29
Blucke, Stephen, 85
Blumenbach, Friedrich, 74
Bond, Julian, 269
books, recommended, 386–87
Booth, John Wilkes, 194
Border Ruffians, 162
Boukman, Dutty, 90
Bowe, Walter Augustus, 299
Bowser, Yvette Lee, 159
Boyd, Leroy Stafford, 177–78
Boylston, Zabdiel, 156
Boynton, Amelia, 270–73
Boynton v. Virginia, 272, 293
Bradley, Ervin, 145–46
Bradley, James S., 2, 145–46
Braun, Carol Moseley, 354–55
Brazil, 36–37, 38
Bréda, François-Dominique, 92–94
Brenston, Jackie, 285
Briggs, Harry and Eliza, 337
Briggs v. Elliott, 337
British Women's Temperance Association, 222
Brooks, Charlotte, 137
Browder, Aurelia, 274
Brown, Bob, 301
Brown, Henry Billings, 243
Brown, James, 119–20, 121, 124, 127
Brown, John, 164–65, 263
Brown, Michael, Jr., 309–10
Brown, Morris, 145
Brown v. Board of Education of Topeka, 180, 337
Bruce, John Edward, 4
Bruce George Washington Carver Boynton v. Virginia, 272
Brunet, Jean Baptiste, 96
Bryan, Andrew, 141
Buffalo Soldiers, 291
Bull, William, 72
Bureau of Engraving and Printing, 314

Bureau of Investigation (BOI), 288–89, 292–93. See also Federal Bureau of Investigation
Burglary, The (Medsger), 306–7
Bush, George H. W., 362–63, 366, 378–79
Bush, George W., 379
Butler, Benjamin, 168–69
Buttonwood Agreement, 100
Bwa Kayiman, 89–90

Cabeza de Vaca, Álvar Núñez, 48–50
Cain, Richard, 199–200
Calhoun, John C., 161
California Gold Rush, 264
Callixtus, Pope, 28
Calloway, Cab, 285
Calusa Indians, 44–45
Camp Turel, 93
Capitol insurrection of 2021, 326
Cardozo, Francis Lewis, 199
Carlos I of Spain, 44, 51
Carmichael, Stokely, 269, 272, 297–98, 301, 305–6
Carter, Jimmy, 361, 362
Cartwright, Samuel Adolphus, 104–5
Carver, George Washington, 271
Cary, John B., 168–69
Casa da Guiné, 32, 37–38, 39
Casa de Contratación, 37–38
Case, Charles, 254–58
Catholic Church and slavery, 15, 27–39, 134–35, 137
Cattle, Benjamin, 65
Catts, Sidney J., 290
Chamberlain, Daniel, 204–5
Chaney, James, 297
Charles, Robert, 312–14
Charles II of England, 58–59
Charleston, South Carolina, 63, 71, 84–86, 106, 144–45, 189, 193–94, 326
Charleston Emanuel AME Church, 144, 145, 199
Charleston Light Dragoons, 190
Charlottesville Unite the Right Rally, 381
Chernow, Ron, 201
Chesapeake and Ohio Railway, 218
Cheyney University, 140
Chicago Defender, 290, 291
chicken, 230
  fried, 149–51
chicken bog, 64, 64n, 370–72
chicken perlo, 371–72
Christianity
  Black faith and churches, 130–48, 152–54
  slave trade and, 27–39
Church, Louisa Ayres, 260

Church, Robert Reed, 260
Church of God in Christ (COGIC), 284
CIA (Central Intelligence Agency), 304
Cicero, 14, 24
City Bank of New York (Citibank), 101
Civilian Pilot Training Program (CPTP), 279
Civil Rights Act of 1875, 239–40
Civil Rights Act of 1964, 344, 355, 361–62, 365–66, 378
Civil Rights Cases, 239–40, 242
civil rights movement, 293–98, 309–21, 378
  Black women's contributions to, 259–82
Civil War, 160, 194, 358
  Lost Cause explained, 174–87
  slavery and, 166–85
Claiborne, William, 125, 126
Clansman, The (movie), 288
Clapton, Eric, 284
Clare, Robert, 273–74
Clark, Jim, 271
Clark, Mark, 302
Clark Atlanta University, 198
Cleveland, James, 228
Clinton, Bill, 378–79
Clinton, Henry, 85
Clinton, Hillary, 304
Clotilda (schooner), 273
Clyburn, Dormetia, 78–79
Clyburn, Eric, 78–79
Clyburn, Marvell, 13, 78–79, 146
Clyburn, Reginald, 78–79, 146
Coatesville Call to Arms, 316–17
Code noir, 58
COINTELPRO, 305–7, 319
Coker, Simon, 211–12
Colfax massacre, 203
Collier, Robert, 303
Collins, Addie Mae, 297
Columbus, Christopher, 4–5, 33–38, 40, 88–89
Colvin, Claudette, 273–76
Combahee Ferry Raid, 171
Comité des Citoyens (Citizens' Committee), 241–43
Compromise of 1877, 205–6, 212, 212n, 239, 359
Confederate flag, 176 78, 182–84
Confederate States of America (Confederacy), 166–87, 190–91
  Lost Cause explained, 174–87
Confiscation Act of 1861, 168, 170
Confiscation Act of 1862, 170
Congressional Black Caucus, 380
Congress of Racial Equality (CORE), 269, 272, 293–96
Connor, Bull, 295, 306

conquistadores, 35–51
conspiracy theories, 161, 287–308
Constitution, U.S., 74–75, 192, 235–36, 357
Constitutional Convention of 1787, 139
Continental Army, 82, 84
Continental Congress, 82, 84
Cook, Tom, 306
Cooper, Anna Julia, 261
Corlie, John, 83
Cornelius, Titus, 83, 85
Corps d'Afrique, 171
Corps of Colonial Marines, 107
Cortés, Hernándo, 45–46, 51
COVID-19 pandemic, 343
Cox, Benjamin Elton, 296
Cox, Karen L., 179
Cranford, Alfred, 214
Crescent City White League, 237–38
Crisis, The, 225, 279
Critical Race Theory, 114, 381
Crusader, The, 240, 242
Crusades, 28, 31
Cuba, 34, 38, 45, 46, 101, 318
Cuney, Norris Wright, 359
Cushing, William, 351

Dallas County Voters League (DCVL), 271–72
Daniels, Christopher, 319–20
Daughters of Tabor, 166
Davis, Angela, 113
Davis, Jefferson, 169–70, 180
Dawson, William "Hardtime," 189–90, 194, 197
Dawson, William McCloud, 191
Declaration of Independence, 59, 82, 103
Democratic Party, 182–83, 354–56, 360–69
Democratic-Republican Party, 357–58
Desdunes, Rodolphe, 240–41
desegregation, 262–63, 271–72, 360–61
  Brown v. Board of Education, 180, 337
  Freedom Riders, 269, 272, 293–98, 305–6, 318
  Montgomery bus boycotts, 270, 273–76
Deslondes, Charles, 120–28
Dessalines, Jean-Jacques, 97–98
Dickson, Moses, 165–66
"Didn't It Rain" (song), 284
District of Columbia v. John R. Thompson Co., 263
Dixon, Thomas J., 178, 288
Douglass, Frederick, 143, 165, 223, 239, 256, 261, 261n
drapetomania (drapetomaniacs), 104–18
Drayton, John, 65
Drayton, Thomas and Ann, 59–61, 62

Dred Scott v. Sandford, 76
Du Bois, W. E. B., 9, 223, 315, 355, 360
  Black Reconstruction in America, 159–60,
    162–63, 188, 198
  The Gift of Black Folk, 87, 259
  on literacy, 141
  on lynching, 213
  National Negro Conference of 1909,
    224–25
  Pleasant and, 266
  The Souls of Black Folk, 3–4, 247–50
  Talented Tenth, 247–48
  "The Souls of White Folk," 74, 76–77
  Washington rivalry with, 9, 247–51, *248*
  Wells and, 223, 224–25
due process, 206, 213, 227
Duke, David, 364
Dylan, Bob, 221

Earth, Wind & Fire, 2, 11–13, *23*
Eastern Orthodox Church, 27–28
Edmund Pettus Bridge, 272
education, 4, 140–41, 180, 197–98, 199, 276,
  336–39, 340, 379
Edwards, James Malcolm, 319
Eisenhower, Dwight, 360
Elaine massacre, 290
election of 1824, 357
election of 1860, 162, 163
election of 1868, 202
election of 1876, 204, 205
election of 1912, 360
election of 1948, 360, 365
election of 1964, 361, 365–66
election of 1968, 362
election of 1972, 362
election of 1980, 363
election of 2020, 363
election of 2022, 364
Elfrith, Daniel, 25
Elizabeth I, 15
Ellington, Duke, 285, 340
Elliott, Roderick W., 337
Emancipation Proclamation, 100, 171, 173,
  192
Enforcement Act of 1870, 236, 236n
Enforcement Act of 1871, 236–37
Epps, Lonnie, 303
Erikson, Leif, 51
Espionage Act of 1917, 288–89
Esteban de Dorantes (Mustafa Azemmouri),
  47–51
Ethiopian Regiment, 83–84
Evers, Medgar, 315
Executive Order 8802, 278, 281

Fair Employment Practice Committee, 278
Fair Housing Act of 1968, 340
falsetto, 12
Fatal Glass of Beer, The (movie), 258
Fatiman, Cecile, 90
Federal Bureau of Investigation (FBI),
  292–93, 299–300, 302, 304–7, 319–20
Federal Council of Negro Affairs, 278
Federalists, 356–57
Felton, Rebecca L., 373
Ferdinand II of Aragon, 33, 38
Ferguson, D'Brickashaw, 245
Ferguson, John, 242
Fields, W. C., 258
Fifteenth Amendment, 199, 212, 235, 239,
  358
First African Baptist Church of Savannah,
  138, 140
Fisk University, 198, 218
Fitzgerald, Ella, 340
flag, Confederate, 176–78, 182–84
folk cures, 130–32
Foner, Eric, 203
Ford, George, 114–17
Forest Joe, 113–18
Fort, Jeff, 302
Fort Monroe, 168
Fort Mose, 71–72, 107
Fort Sumter, 167, 173
Fort Wagner, 171n
"forty acres and a mule," 190–96
Fossett, Joseph, 141
Fossett, Peter, 141
Foster, William, 273
Fourteenth Amendment, 199, 234, 239, 242,
  265, 335–36
Fourteenth of September Monument
  Association, 238
Franklin, Benjamin, 5, 83, 156, 326, 350
Franklin, James, 156
Franklin, William, 83
Fraternity (magazine), 222
Frazier, Eugene, 138
Frazier, Garrison, 193
Frazier, Joe, 304
Free African Society (FAS), 139–40
Freedmen's Bureau, 192–93, 195–98, 197,
  201, 202, 203–4, 266–67
freedmen's schools, 197–98, 199
Freedom Rides, 269, 272, 293–98, 305–6, 318
Freeman, Elizabeth "Mum Bett," 351, 353
Free People of Color, 91
French and Indian War, 80
French Revolution, 91–92
fried chicken, 149–51
Fugitive Slave Act of 1850, 143, 164, 264

Fundamental Constitutions of Carolina, 58–59
Fusion Coalition, 373–74

Gaillard, Thomas, 118
Gaines, Archibald K., 112
Garfield Park riot of 1919, 291
Garner, Margaret, 112–13
Garrido, Juan, 43–47, 51
Garvey, Marcus, 291–93, 316
Gates, Horatio, 82
General Order No. 9, 195–96
General Order No. 11, 168
generational-based reparations, 344
George, David, 140
George Washington University, 287–88
Georgia State Industrial College, 271
German Coast uprising of 1811, 119–28
G.I. Bill, 338–39
Gibbs, Ida, 261
Gift of Black Folk, The (Du Bois), 87, 259
Gingrich, Newt, 366
Glory (movie), 171
Glover, Quinn, 296
Goldberg, Reuben, 201
Goldwater, Barry, 361–62, 365–66
Gonçalves, Antão, 30–31, 38–39
Goodman, Andrew, 297
Goodwin, Lorinda, 134–35
Gordon, George W., 212
Gordon, John Brown, 212
grands blancs, 91, 92, 93
Grant, Ulysses S., 202, 239
Gray, Fred, 276
grease, 231–32
Great Depression, 277, 339–40, 343
Great Dismal Swamp, 107–9
Great Famine of 1315–1317, 54
Great White Heist, 334–46
Greeley, Horace, 169
Green, Cecelia Simmons, 106
Green, Shields, 165
Grimball Plantation, 106
Gullah-Geechee, 9, 64–65, 72, 173, 370, 371

Haiti, 34, 88–89, 88–102
Haitian National Bank, 100–101
Haitian Revolution, 88–100, 120, 343
Haldeman, H. R., 362
Hall, Shad, 136
Hamilton, Alexander, 100, 347, 356
Hampton, Fred, 300–303, 306
Hampton, Wade, 125, 204–5
Hampton Normal and Agricultural Institute, 245
Hampton University, 171

Hanrahan, Ed, 306
Harlem Radicalism, 315–16
Harpers Ferry raid, 164–65, 266
Harriot, Dorothy, 1–2, 3–4, 6–7, 13, 65, 229, 375–76, 377
Harriot, James, Jr., 11–14, 64
Harriot, James "Buck," 2–3, 209–11, 226
Harriot, Jannie, 322–25
Harriot, Marvell, 1–3, 130–32, 147–48, 209–11, 226
Harriot, Michael, 146
Harriot, Phyllis, 149
Harriot, Robert, 233–34, 251–52, 323, 325, 355–56, 364–65
Harriot McGee, Comelita, 229, 375–77
Harriot Molden, Seandra, 375–77
Harris, Essie, 311–12
Harris, Joel Chandler, 213–14
Harris, Richard, 303
Harrison, Benjamin, 261
Harrison, Hubert, 315–16
Hartsville Junior High School, 8
Hassan, Ali Bey, 303
Hawkins, Lydell, 329–31
Hayes, Rutherford B., 205–6, 212n, 239
Haynes, George, 290
Hemings, James, 141, 231
Hemmings, John, 141
Henderson, Stephen, 119
Henry, Patrick, 75, 84
Henry the Navigator, 28–39, 46
Henry VII of England, 34
Henry VIII of England, 15
Herbold, Hilary, 338–39
Hispaniola, 38, 43, 47, 48, 88–89
Holden, William Woods, 202–3
Holy Ghost, 131–33, 135, 146, 325
Home Owners' Loan Corporation (HOLC), 339–40
Hoover, Herbert, 365
Hoover, J. Edgar, 292–93, 299–300, 305–7, 308
Horton, Willie, 366
Hose, Sam, 213–14
House, Callie Guy, 266–68
Howard, Oliver, 197–98
Howard University, 198, 198n, 278, 379
Howard University Law School, 262–63, 271
Hulett, John, 298
Humphreys, Richard, 140
Hunter, David, 168–70, 173
Hurston, Zora Neale, 4, 272–73

IDGAF gene, 219–20
Igbo rebellion, 111–12
incarceration. *See* mass incarceration

Incidents in the Life of a Slave Girl (Jacobs), 111
Indian Citizenship Act of 1924, 235
Institute for Colored Youth, 140
Intolerable Acts of 1774, 80
Isabella I of Castile, 33–35, 37–38
Islam, 132–38, 155, 298–300

Jackson, Andrew, 126–27, 357–58
Jackson, Jesse, 380
Jackson, Lee, 272
Jackson, Thomas "Stonewall," 177, 180
Jacobs, Harriet, 110–11
Jacobs, John, 110
James I of England, 15, 19–23
James Island, 106, 189–90, 189n, 190, 196, 198
James Island (Frazier), 138
Jamestown, 14–25, 56–58, 66, 133–34
Japanese American internment camps, 342
Jay, Gregory, 74
Jefferson, Thomas, 5, 99, 141, 143, 231, 347, 356
Jemmy and Stono Rebellion, 70–73, 137
Jim Crow laws, 179, 181, 183, 205–6, 213, 218, 242, 244–45, 251, 270, 271, 277n, 359, 365
John I of Portugal (John of Aviz), 28–29
John II of Portugal, 34, 35
Johnny ("Speed"), 287–89, 292, 303
Johnson, Andrew, 99, 194–96
Johnson, Carrie, 317
Johnson, Jane, 144, 161
Johnson, Lyndon B., 272, 361–62
Johnson, R. O., 147–48
Johnson v. McAdoo, 267
Jones, Absalom, 139–40
Jones, Gabriel, 81
Joseph, Eddie, 303
juice, 230–31

Kaaba, 135
Kaepernick, Colin, 366
Kansas, 161–62, 163, 173
Kappa Alpha Order, 177–78, 183
Katara, Abayama, 303
Katznelson, Ira, 338
Kemp, Barrett G., 306
Kennedy, John F., 296, 360–61
Kennedy, Robert, 295
Kenner, Harry, 121, 127
Kent, Benjamin, 350–51
Kerner, William, 119
Killen, Edgar Ray, 363
Kiluanji of Ndongo, 68
King, Boston, 85–86
King, Martin Luther, Jr., 9, 345

armed resistance and, 315
Baker and SCLC, 268–69
Boynton and, 272
FBI and Hoover, 306
"Letter from a Birmingham Jail," 295
Montgomery bus boycotts and, 276
Poor People's Campaign, 380
Shuttlesworth and, 295
King James Bible, 136–37
Kinshasa, Kwando, 303
Kirk-Holden War, 202–3
Kite, Elijah, 112–13
Knight, Gladys, 231
Knight, Marie, 285
Knights of Liberty, 165–66
Knights of the White Camellia, 202, 203, 237
Kongo people, 42, 43, 64
Kook and German Coast uprising of 1811, 119–28
Kruttschnitt, Ernest, 243
Ku Klux Klan (KKK), 178–82, 188, 202–3, 212–13, 236–37, 271, 288, 289–90, 293, 294–95, 306, 311–12, 317, 318–19, 354, 363, 365
Kwanzaa, 329–32

La Florida, 44–45, 48
Lambe, Joshua, 106
lateens, 29–30
Laurie, Joe, Jr., 258
Laveau, Marie, 264
Lawry's seasoned salt, 229
Laws of Burgos, 38
Leclerc, Charles, 96–97
Lee, Archy, 265
Lee, Robert E., 177, 180, 185, 194, 277n
Lee, William, 81–82
"Letter from a Birmingham Jail" (King), 295
Leviticus, 134
Lewis, Cudjo, 273
Lewis, John, 269, 272, 297
Library of Congress, 287–88
Lily-White movement, 359–60
Lincoln, Abraham, 5
    assassination of, 194
    Civil War and slavery, 167, 168–69, 171, 173, 180
    election of 1860, 162, 163
    Reconstruction and, 191–92, 193
Linnaeus, Carl, 74
literacy, 141n, 142–43, 145
literacy tests, 243–44, 270–71, 374
Little, Wilbur, 290
Little Rock Central High School, 360–61
Liuzzo, Viola, 297
Livingston, Peter, 76

Locke, John, 58–59, 75
Logan, Rayford, 278
Longview, Lemuel, 291
"Lost Cause," 174–87
Lost Colony of Roanoke, 15
Louisiana, 236–38, 240–44. *See also* New Orleans
  Andry's Rebellion of 1811, 119–28
Louisville and Nashville Railroad, 241–42
Louverture, Toussaint, 93, 94–97
Louvestre, Mary, 172
Lowndes County Freedom Organization, 315
Lowndes County Freedom Party (LCFP), 297–98
Loyal League, 311
Lumpkin, Annie, 296
lynchings, 202, 211–27, 261–62, 290–91, 314–17, 373–74

Mack, Daniel, 290
Madison, James, 74–75
Magnolia Plantation, 59–61, 62, 65
Malcolm X, 3, 220, 298–300, 301, 316
Mallory, Shepard, 168
Malone, Bliss Anne, 296
Mandinka people, 42, 54, 63, 135
Manly, Alexander, 373
Manuel I of Portugal, 36
manumission, 140, 145, 145*n*
maroons, 108–10, 113, 114, 117, 344
Marshall, Thurgood, 272
Martinet, Louis, 240–41
Mason, George, 75
Massachusetts Bay Colony, 106
Massachusetts Constitution, 350–51
Massachusetts 54th Regiment, 171, 171*n*
Massachusetts 55th Regiment, 194
mass incarceration, 325–29, 333, 367, 379, 380
Mather, Cotton, 155–56
Matoaka, 21–22, 25
Matthews, Morris, 59
Maxwell Field, 279
Mayflower, 5
McCauley, Rosa, 293
McDonald, Susie, 274–75
McDowell, Calvin, 216–18
McEnery, John, 237–38
McGhee, Brownie, 283
McKeithan, John, 318–19
McLeod, William Wallace, 189–90, 196–97
McLeod Plantation, 189–90, 194, 196–98
McNair, Carol Denise, 297
McNeil, Earlene, 370
Meaher, Timothy, 272–73

Mechanics Institute, 201–2
Mechanics Savings Bank, 314
medical disorder, 106
Medsger, Betty, 306–7
Memphis Free Speech, 218–20, 226
Memphis lynchings of 1892, 216–19
Memphis Scimitar, 219, 250–51
Mendoza y Pacheco, Antonio de, 51
Menefie, George, 57
Mercator, Gerardus, 37
Metro-Goldwyn-Mayer (MGM), 258
Miller, William E., 362, 365–66
Millholland, John, 224
Minkins, Shadrach, 164, 172
minstrel shows, 255–57
Mis-Education of the Negro, The (Woodson), 4
Missionary Society for the Conversion of Negro Slaves, 136–37
Mississippi Freedom Democratic Party, 269–70
Mississippi State Penitentiary, 295
Missouri, 161–62, 165, 353
Missouri Compromise, 163
Mitchell, John, Jr., 314–15, 359–60
Mob Rule in New Orleans (Wells), 313–14
Mohomet, Hester, 136
Monitor, USS, 172
Monroe Doctrine, 99
Montgomery bus boycotts, 268, 270, 273–76, 293
Montgomery Improvement Association (MIA), 276
Moore, Aida White, 138, 198
Moore, Richard Earl, 303
Moors, 28, 31, 39, 40
Mora, August T., 312–13
Morgan, John Tyler, 212
Morgan v. Virginia, 293
Morris, Robert, 164
Morrison, Toni, 113
Moss, Thomas, 216–18, 261
"Motherless Children Sees a Hard Time" (song), 190
Muhammad, Bilal, 136
Murray, John, 4th Earl of Dunmore, 82–83
Musa I, 54–55
Muzzey, David. S., 182

Nairne, Thomas, 61–63
Napoleon Bonaparte, 93, 96
Narváez, Pánfilo de, 48–49
National Association for the Advancement of Colored People (NAACP), 214–16, 225–26, 262, 268, 270, 271–72, 274, 276, 300, 317–18
National Association of Colored Women, 262

National Ex-Slave Mutual Relief, Bounty and Pension Association (MRB&PA), 266–68
National Negro Conference of 1909, 224–25
National Rifle Association, 317
National Youth Administration, 278
Nation of Islam, 298–300
Naturalization Act of 1790, 75
Negro Act of 1740, 73
Negro Seaman Act of 1822, 161–62
Negro World, 291–92
New Deal, 339–40
New Negro movement, 289, 316
New Orleans, 107, 201, 236–38, 240–44
    Andry's Rebellion of 1811, 119–28
    Battle of Liberty Place, 237–38, 240
    massacre of 1866, 236
    riots of 1900, 312–14
Newport, Christopher, 17–21
Newton, Huey, 303, 319, 320
"New World," 37, 40
New York Age, 258
New York City, 100–101, 225, 291, 299, 303
New York Stock Exchange, 100
New York Tribune, 169
Nicholas V, Pope, 31
"Niggers in the White House" (poem), 250–51
Nixon, E. D., 276
Nixon, Richard, 328, 362, 366
Northwestern University Law School, 353
nullification, 163, 358
Nullification Crisis, 163
Nzinga of Ndongo and Matamba, 68–69

Obama, Barack, 161, 379–80
Oberlin College, 260–61
Oceti Sakowin, 8
Odinga, Baba, 303
okofokum, 120
Om, Shaba, 303
Omar, Najee, 159
Omnibus Railroad Company, 265
O'Neal, William, 302, 305–6, 306
Onesimus, 155–56
online resources, 387–88
Onward, USS, 167
Order of Twelve Knights, 166
origin story of African people in America, 41–51
origin story of America, 14–25
Ovington, Mary White, 225
Owens, Candace, 354
Oxford University, 299

Page, Jimmy, 284
Paine, Thomas, 89

Parks, Rosa, 270, 275–76, 293
partus sequitur ventrem, 110
Patriots, 83–84, 103, 166
Payne Reformed Methodist Union Episcopal Church, 198
Peake, Mary, 170–71
Pembina, USS, 191
penitentiary, 326
Penn, Davidson B., 237–38
Pennsylvania Anti-Slavery Society, 143
People's Grocery lynchings of 1892, 216–19
Perry, Albert E., 317
Pest in the Land, A (Alton), 89
petits blancs, 91
Pettus, Edmund, 212
Philadelphia Negro, The, 213
Philadelphia Society for Alleviating the Miseries of Public Prisons, 326
Phillips, Dewey, 285
Piggly Wiggly, 149–50
Pilgrims, 5, 14, 134
Pinchback, P. B. S., 240–41
Pineville Police Association, 118
Plane, Helen, 180
Planter, CSS, 166–67
Pleasant, Mary Ellen, 263–66
Pleasant v. North Beach & Mission Railroad Company, 265
Plessy, Homer, 242
Plessy v. Ferguson, 242–44
police brutality, 309–10, 312–15, 319–20
politics and race, 354–69
Pollard, Edward, 178n
Ponce de León, Juan, 43–45, 46–47, 51
Pooler, Robin, 375–77
Poor People's Campaign, 380
Porter, Dorothy B., 4
Portugal and slave trade, 28–39, 68–69
Powell, Curtis, 303
Powhatans, 16–21, 247
Pratt, Geronimo, 303
Presley, Elvis, 285
prison system. *See* mass incarceration
Proclamation of Amnesty and Reconstruction, 191–92
Proud Boys, 237
Public Law 18, 279
Puerto Rican Young Lords, 301
Puerto Rico, 38, 44, 46

Quakers, 83, 139–40
Quamana and German Coast uprising of 1811, 119–28

"race riots," 202, 316
race wars, 287–308

Racial Integrity Act of Virginia of 1924, 76
Racial Justice Act, 380
Radical Republicans, 162, 191–92, 199
"Rainbow Coalition," 301
Raines, John C., 296–97, 304–5
Randolph, Asa Philip, 278, 281, 316
Randolph, Benjamin, 200, 202
Ratcliffe, John, 20–21
Reagan, Ronald, 1–2, 362–63, 366, 378–79
recipes, 229–30
Reconquista, 28, 29
Reconstruction, 159–60, 188–208, 227
redlining, 339–41, 378, 380
Redoshi, 273
Red Record, The (Wells), 223
Red Summer of 1919, 290–92, 316
Reed, Jo, 215
Reed, Mary, 317–18
Reese, Jeanetta, 275
Reeves, Jeremiah, 274
Reinitz, Janet, 296–97
reparations, 334–53, 380
Republican Party, 162, 354–69
resources, 386–88
Revel, Hiram Rhodes, 200
Revere, Paul, 5
Revolutionary War, 80–87, 139, 141, 163–64, 166
Rhode Island's First Regiment, 84
rice cultivation, 60–65, 80
Richardson, James Burchill, 117
Richmond Planet, 314
Rights of Man, The (Paine), 89
Rio de Janeiro, 36–37
Roanoke Island Freedmen's Colony, 170–71
Robertson, Carole, 297
Robinson, Jo Ann Gibson, 274–77
Rochambeau, Donatien-Marie-Joseph de Vimeur, comte de, 96–97
Rochelle, Fred, 215
"Rocket 88" (song), 284
Rolfe, John, 21–22, 24–25
Rolling Stones, the, 284
Roman Empire, 27–28
Roosevelt, Eleanor, 277–78, 280–81
Roosevelt, Franklin, 277–78, 338, 360
Roosevelt, Theodore, 247, 250–51
Rosenwald Fund, 280
Rosewood massacre of 1923, 342
Rowe, Gary, 306
Royal African Company, 59
Royall, Isaac, 352
Rush, Benjamin, 84
Rust College, 218
Rustin, Bayard, 316

Saint-Domingue, 89–99, 102
Salem, Peter, 81–82
San Juan Bautista, 24–25
San Maló, Juan, 122, 127
San Miguel de Gualdape revolt, 47
Sawyer, Samuel, 110–11
Saxton, Rufus, 194, 195
Schomburg, Arturo, 4, 340
Schwerner, Michael, 297, 363
Scorsese, Martin, 294*n*
Scottsboro Boys, 268
Seabrook Plantation, 198
Sea Island cotton, 189–90
Seale, Bobby, 303–4
seasonings, 229
Second Amendment, 75
Sedgwick, Thomas, 351
segregation, 183, 238–45, 260, 262–63, 271–72, 336–38
    in the armed forces, 279, 281, 360
    Freedom Riders, 269, 272, 293–98, 305–6, 318
    Montgomery bus boycotts, 270, 273–76
    political parties and, 354–55, 360–61, 365
    railroad cars, 238–39, 240–44
    Selma to Montgomery marches, 272, 297–98
Semmes, Thomas, 244
"separate but equal," 233, 245, 251–52, 253, 337
Separate Car Act of 1890, 240–42
Servicemen's Readjustment Act of 1944, 338
"settin' up," 233–34
"settlers," 8–9, 14, 26, 52
Shake Weight, 104
Shakur, Lumumba, 303
Shakur, Tupac, 113, 277*n*
Shaw, Robert, 171*n*
Shaw University, 269
Sherman, William Tecumseh, 193–94
Shuttlesworth, Fred, 294–95
Sierra Leone, 60, 61, 86, 124, 135
Silver Bluff Baptist Church, 140
Singleton, William Henry, 170
16th Street Baptist Church bombing, 295, 297, 306
slave codes, 65, 73, 141
slave rebellions, 164–65
    German Coast uprising of 1811, 119–28
    Haitian Revolution, 88–102
    Igbo rebellion, 111–12
    Stono Rebellion of 1739, 71–73, 137, 164, 189
    Vesey's Rebellion, 144–45, 161, 164, 173
slavery, 8
    Black American Revolution and, 163–73
    Black faith and, 133–38, 140–45

Christianity and Catholic Church and, 27–39
Civil War and, 160, 166–85
Constitution and, 235–36
drapetomaniacs, 104–18
foods and, 228–29
origin story of African people in America, 41–51
origin story of America, 14–15, 17, 24–25, 56–65
political parties and, 356–58
Portugal and slave trade, 28–39, 68–69
Reconstruction and, 159–60, 188–207
reparations and, 334–36
Revolutionary War and, 81–87
Spain and slave trade, 33–39, 41–51
unenslaving of Jemmy, 70–73
Slew, Betty, 349
Slew, Jenny, 349–51
smallpox, 85–86, 155–56
Smalls, Robert, 166–68, 173, 199
Smith, Al, 365
Smith, James, 264
Smith, John, 17–21
Smith, Mary Louise, 275
Smith, Melvin Cotton, 302–3
Smith, Washington, 273
smiting, 131
Social Security Administration (SSA), 339
Somerset, James, 81
Somerset v. Stewart, 81
Sons of Liberty, 79–80
soul food, 228–32
Souls of Black Folk, The (Du Bois), 3–4, 247–50
"Souls of White Folk, The" (Du Bois), 74, 76–77
South Carolina
  during American Revolution, 84–87
  education and reparations, 336–38
  during Reconstruction, 188–93, 196–200, 203–5, 211–12
  slavery in, 46–47, 56–65, 70–73, 80, 105, 106, 109–10, 113, 114–15, 117, 161–62, 175–76
South Carolina Exposition and Protest (Calhoun), 161
South Carolina Land Commission, 199–200
South Carolina State Arsenal, 145
South Carolina State College, 337–38
Southern Christian Leadership Conference (SCLC), 268–69, 272
Southern cuisine, 228–32
Southern Democrats, 182–83, 267, 356, 360–61
"Southern heritage," 177, 182–83
Southern Homestead Act of 1866, 266
Southern Horrors (Wells), 221–22, 225

Southern Poverty Law Center (SPLC), 179
Southern Strategy, 362–63, 366
Spain and slave trade, 33–39, 41–51
Spann, Otis, 283–84
Special Field Orders No. 15, 193–94
spirituals, 2, 5, 137–38, 152, 190
Springsteen, Bruce, 285
Stanton, Edwin, 193
State of Louisiana v. Homer Adolph Plessy, 242
states' rights, 175–76, 179, 183, 186, 356, 358*n*, 363
States' Rights Democratic Party (Dixiecrats), 182–83, 360, 365
Stebbins, Robert, 257
Stewart, Charles, 81
Stewart, Pinckney Benton, 200
Stewart, Will, 216–18
Still, William, 143–44
Stone Mountain Memorial, 180
Stono Inlet, 167
Stono Rebellion of 1739, 71–73, 137, 164, 189
"Strange Things Happening Every Day" (song), 285
Student Nonviolent Coordinating Committee (SNCC), 269–70, 272, 293, 297, 298
Sullivan, Fred and Jane, 215
Summerton, South Carolina, 336–38
Sutton, Belinda, 352
Swann, Thomas, 106
Sweetwater Sabre Club, 211

Tabor, Michael, 303
Taft, William Howard, 247, 360
Taíno, the, 38, 43–44, 66, 89, 98, 230
Talented Tenth, 247–48
Taylor, Moses, 101
Tennessee Coal, Iron and Railroad Company (TCI), 327–28
Ten Percent Plan, 191–92
Terrell, Mary Church, 260–63
Terrell, Robert, 261
Terry, Sonny, 283
Tharpe, Rosetta, 283–86
Tharpe, Thomas, 284–85
That's the Way of the World (album), 12–13
Thirteenth Amendment, 192, 325, 327
"This Train" (song), 285
Thompson, William, 177
"thugs," 103, 114, 163, 309–10
Thurmond, Strom, 362, 365
Till, Emmett, 310, 363
Tillman, Benjamin "Pitchfork Ben," 211–12, 250
Timonius, Emanuel, 155
Tourgée, Albion, 241

Townsend, James, 168
Treasurer (schooner), 24–25
Treaty of Ghent, 126
Treaty of Tordesillas, 35
Trépagnier, François, 121, 124, 126
Tristão, Nuno, 30–31, 38–39
Truman, Harry, 360
Trump, Donald J., 364, 380–82
Truth, Sojourner, 250, 274
Tsenacommacah, 16–21
Tubman, Harriet, 48–49, 165, 169, 171, 173
Turner, Nat, 141
Tuskegee Airmen, 279–81
Tuskegee Experiment, 342
Tuskegee Institute, 271
Tuskegee Normal School, 245
Tuskegee University, 245, 290
Twain, Mark, 257

Underground Railroad, 48–49, 86, 107, 112, 140–41, 143, 164, 165, 166, 169, 171, 264, 265
Union Leagues, 358–59
United Daughters of the Confederacy (UDC), 178–82, 183
United Front Against Fascism, 301
United Negro College Fund, 277
United States Colored Troops (USCT), 171
Universal Basic Income, 380
Universal Negro Improvement Association (UNIA), 291–92
University of Alabama, 183, 360–61
utensils, 232

"vagrancy" laws, 327
Vandross, Luther, 235
Vardaman, James K., 212, 250, 289
Vesey, Denmark, 144–45, 161, 164, 173
Vespucci, Amerigo, 37–38
Virginia, CSS, 172
Virginia Charter, 16, 58, 134
Virginia Company, 15–25, 43, 56–58
voter registration, 199–200, 244, 297–98, 359
voting rights, 192, 202–5, 221, 236, 238–39, 243–44, 270–71, 297–98, 355–56, 358–59
Voting Rights Act of 1965, 272, 355, 368, 378

Wabash, USS, 191
Wade-Davis Bill, 191–92
Wahunsenacah, 16–22, 26, 49n
Wakanda, 54–55
Walker, Annie, 215–16
Walker, David, 143, 215–16
Walker, Maggie Lena, 359
Walker's Appeal to the Colored Citizens of the World, 143

Wallace, George, 272
Walters, Richard Martin Lloyd, 326
Walton, Lester, 258
War of 1812, 107, 126–27
War Powers Act of 1866, 195
Washington, Booker T., 9, 220–21, 225, 245–51
  Du Bois rivalry with, 9, 247–51, *248*
Washington, George, 5, 81–82, 84, 100
Waters, Muddy, 284
"welfare queens," 366
Wells, Ida B., 218–26, 261, 262, 313–14, 345
Wesley, Cynthia, 297
West, Kanye, 358
When Affirmative Action Was White (Katznelson), 338
Whipple, John, 349–50
White, Pappy, 198
White, Ralph, 303
white gravy, 230–31
White Knights, 202, 363
White League, 202, 237–38
White Lion, 24–25, 41, 68, 87, 168, 173
whiteness, 3, 9, 74–77
white people, invention of, 74–77
Whitesides, Phebe, 353
white supremacy, 9, 58–59, 68, 74–77, 93, 97, 99, 179, 180–81, 183–84, 201, 204–5, 235–38, 244, 287–88, 356, 364, 374, 381
White v. Clements, 204
Wilberforce University, 140, 261
Willard, Frances, 221–24
Williams, George W., 86–87
Williams, Robert F., 317–18
Willis, Cornelia Grinnell, 111
Wilson, Darren, 309–10
Wilson, Woodrow, 288, 360
Winfrey, Oprah, 220
Womanpower Unlimited, 295–96
Woman's Christian Temperance Union, 221–24
Wood, Henrietta, 353
Wood, Peter, 62
Wood, Ray, 299
Woodson, Carter G., 4, 5
Woolley, Celia Parker, 224
Works Progress Administration (WPA), 339
World War I, 288–89
Wright, Jeremiah, 379

Yeardley, George, 24, 25
Young, Samuel, 76
Young Negroes Cooperative-League, 268
Young Patriots, 302

Zuni people, 51